TEXAS PRE-LICENSE
Real Estate Finance

Texas Pre-License

Real Estate Finance

Introduction

This course provides an introduction to real estate finance. From qualifying the borrower and qualifying the property in the underwriting process to various types of financing, closing the sale, the Community Reinvestment Act and more, we discuss the monetary systems that control the market, delve into supply and demand, cover housing agencies, and discuss the government influence on real estate.

Most real estate is purchased with borrowed money. The methods of real estate finance are many and varied. Making real estate loans carries a certain amount of risk for lenders; for this reason, lenders must have a firm grasp of a borrower's financial qualifications. Lenders consider a borrower's income, credit, debt, source of funds, and net worth. However, no analysis, no matter how thorough, of a borrower's creditworthiness, can be enough to ensure that a loan is completely free of risk.

You will learn the methods used by lenders to qualify loan applicants and how lenders qualify the property to be mortgaged. This involves a thorough and accurate property valuation, using the sales comparison or cost approach for residential property and a cap rate or discounted cash flow analysis for investment property. These methods of valuation will be discussed in depth so that you will feel confident and familiar with them when you meet them in the real world.

The basics of the financing and the sale process are discussed over two lessons. You will learn how title (abstract ownership rights to the property) is transferred to the buyer with a deed. The earnest money contract will also be discussed: terms of the contract, contingencies, and earnest money deposits.

In another lesson, the focus turns to closing. You will learn the customary costs involved in a real estate transaction, how certain items are prorated between the buyer and the seller and the requirements set forth by the Real Estate Settlement Procedures Act (RESPA).

This course also covers foreclosure. We consider what happens when a borrower is in default of the mortgage contract and how lenders may help borrowers prevent foreclosure through forbearance, moratoriums, and recasting. Also discussed is how, when these techniques fail, the property is foreclosed and sold at auction and how the creditors are repaid.

No real estate finance course would be complete without discussing the types of mortgages available. We have two lessons that will detail the elements of conventional loans, both conforming and nonconforming; adjustable rate; graduated payment; growth equity; and reverse annuity mortgages, to name a few. The advantages and disadvantages of each type of financing are emphasized so that you may better understand the decision-making process inherent in real estate finance.

Two specific types of financing, FHA-insured and VA-guaranteed loans, are reserved for separate lessons. FHA loans are insured by the government and perceived as less risky by lenders. They are available to all natural and naturalized U.S. citizens, but they carry a monthly insurance premium that cannot be canceled. VA loans are guaranteed in part by the government, but are available only to veterans, active servicemen, and certain National Guard members and special reservists.

The final lesson deals with a topic important to real estate investment: Internal Revenue Code (IRC) Section 1031 exchanges (a k a 1031s). Buying and selling real estate investments can be a tax-heavy business. By "exchanging" their investments under the continuity of investment principle, investors can receive more financing and improve their portfolios.

At the end of each lesson, you will be required to complete a quiz for that lesson before moving on to the next lesson. The course ends with a real-world practice lesson that brings together the concepts and material discussed throughout the entire course.

This module addresses the following topics:

- Explain the basic concepts of real estate finance, describing them in detail
- Explain how interest rates affect the real estate market
- Distinguish between the principal instruments of financing-the promissory note, the mortgage, and the deed of trust-and explain how they are used
- Explain how mortgages are structured and that mortgages create a lien, identifying the difference between a secured note and an unsecured loan
- Explain the function of a discount point, when it is offered, and when it should be bought
- Discuss the operations of the secondary market for loans
- Calculate the monthly payments for a fully amortized, fixed-rate loan
- Distinguish between the tax deductions and tax credits associated with real estate ownership, and calculate each.
- Explain the use of and legal requirements placed on escrow accounts

- State who lends money to the purchasers of real estate, identifying them with 100 percent accuracy

- Distinguish between lien theory and title theory and know which theory Texas uses

- Explain what an assumption loan is and provide an example

- Explain how the forces of supply and demand in the real estate market affect and are affected by the primary lending market, identifying them in case studies

- Explain the economic theory of inflation, and define how this theory can influence the real estate market

- Demonstrate how the government influences real estate finance through agencies such as the Federal Reserve (the Fed) and the Department of Housing and Urban Development (HUD), and be able to cite examples.

- Identify the four main roles of the Federal Reserve

- Describe the primary provisions of the Community Reinvestment Act

- Describe the structure and the mission of the Texas Department of Housing and Community Affairs

- Demonstrate how the government can influence the real estate market through taxation policy, distinguishing between tax exemptions, tax deductions, and tax credits

- List the financial qualifications for obtaining mortgage loans, identifying the most important financial qualification

- Calculate a lender's qualifying income ratios

- List the five elements of a credit report, and explain how FICO scores affect a consumer's borrowing ability

- Explain the provisions of the federal legislation that affect real estate lending, and distinguish between those of the Fair Credit Reporting Act (FCRA), the Equal Credit Opportunity Act (ECOA), and the Truth in Lending Act

- Recall that when purchasers of real estate are ready to make a purchase, they are required to have cash in hand, identifying some common sources of funds

- List the classification of types of debts, identifying each in a case study

- Explain how a borrower's debts are used in determining whether she or he qualifies for a mortgage loan, listing two forms of qualifying ratio

- Define net worth and demonstrate how it is used in the determination of whether someone is qualified for a mortgage for a business property

- List the eight steps to completing an appraisal in the correct order

- Explain the principal appraisal methods and distinguish between Sales Comparison Approach and Cost Approach

- Explain the most common approach to valuing income-producing property-the cap rate analysis

- List the elements of a pro forma projection, in order, and describe its uses in discounted cash flow analyses

- Utilize spreadsheet and investment software to calculate net present values and internal rates of return

- Explain how taxes and depreciation are an important element of decision-making in real estate, identifying the procedure for calculating depreciation

- Distinguish between a mortgage broker and a loan officer, identifying each in a case study

- Explain the loan application process, defining prequalification, online applications, and floating rates

- Distinguish between constructive and actual notice and explain the buyer's obligations under the principle of caveat emptor

- List the lender's requirements for qualifying the title and explain how, through a title search, a title insurance company verifies that a mortgagee will have the first lien

- List the types of insurance policies, identifying characteristics of each

- Explain the purpose of surveys, and name the three main types

- Distinguish between the purpose and content of an earnest money contract and the earnest money deposit

- Explain the requirements for and the logic behind establishing escrow accounts

- Explain what a deed is and list the types of interest it can convey

- Explain the exceptions and reservations that can be placed on a title, providing specific examples

- Distinguish between a deed and a title, identifying each in a case study

- List the pre-closing requirements, distinguishing between seller's concerns and buyer's concerns

- List the required documents that the buyer and seller are each responsible for providing

- Distinguish between face-to-face and escrow closings, and cite who presides over each

- Name the proper form for reporting transactions to the IRS, and list the various parties who can be responsible for filing the form

- List the official responsibilities of the licensee, and utilize the closing checklist

- Explain the function of the Real Estate Settlement Procedures Act (RESPA), listing the procedures and disclosures that must happen during closing, in compliance with the Act

- List the basic conventions that determine how expenses are allocated in a typical real-estate transaction, and provide an example of each

- Name the two categories of nonrecurring closing costs, and list the costs associated with each.

- Distinguish between credits and debits, and demonstrate the procedure for calculating them

- Explain the process of prorating expenses, and provide examples of prepaid and accrued items

- Demonstrate the formula for calculating prorated expenses

- Outline the general guidelines for the HUD-1 Settlement Statement Form, and properly fill it in

- Complete the settlement charges section of the HUD-1

- Complete the borrower's transaction section of the HUD-1

- Complete the seller's transaction section of the HUD-1

- Demonstrate an understanding of closing transactions by completing a closing activity

- Explain the reasons for default, and define tax liens, insurance and maintenance, delinquency, moratoriums, forbearance, and recasting.

- Compare the different procedures that follow a default, identifying the various elements of foreclosure

- Explain what leads to a property being considered in distress, and compare the difference between liquidating and holding a distressed property

- Explain what is meant by a conventional loan, and distinguish between conforming and nonconforming loans

- List the current Fannie Mae and Freddie Mac conforming loan limits

- Explain private mortgage insurance (PMI) and state when it is required, when it is advisable, and when it is cancelable

- Detail Fannie Mae underwriting guidelines for loans

- Detail Freddie Mac underwriting guidelines for loans

- Discuss the function of Fannie Mae's Desktop Underwriter and Freddie Mac's Loan Prospector electronic underwriting programs

- List the requirements for a borrower's financial qualifications in a conforming loan, with 100 percent accuracy

- Define adjustable rate mortgages (ARMs) and compare these to float-to-fixed rate loans.

- Explain the 80-10-10 piggyback loan, and identify the appeal of this loan to a borrower

- Distinguish between graduated payment mortgage (GPM) and growth equity mortgage (GEM), listing the benefits of each

- Explain a balloon mortgage, and distinguish between a Fannie Mae balloon mortgage and a Freddie Mac balloon mortgage

- Identify the characteristics of a wraparound mortgage, and compare this to a purchase-money mortgage

- Explain the concepts of reverse annuity mortgages, blanket mortgages, and open-end mortgages, providing examples of each

- Explain the provisions of construction mortgages and the concept of draws

- Explain why a sale-leaseback is beneficial to the purchasing party

- Distinguish between permanent buy down and temporary buy down, listing the two advantages and two disadvantages of temporary buy downs

- Name additional loan payment plans

- Identify who may qualify for FHA loans, listing the benefits and limits

- Outline the qualification process, listing the six CAIVRS applicant categories

- Discuss the most important FHA programs, especially Section 203(b)

- Explain the mortgage insurance premium (MIP) and list the conditions borrowers must meet to be eligible for a refund on their mortgage insurance

- Explain FHA underwriting requirements, such as down-payment and closing-cost requirements, comparing the advantages and disadvantages of FHA loans

- Complete the FHA qualifying worksheet

- Distinguish between the FHA's mortgage insurance premium (MIP) and PMI, identifying each in a case study

- Explain the purpose and benefits of a VA loan, outlining what a VA loan can be used for

- List the types of loans available to qualified borrowers, and explain each

- Explain the underwriting requirements, and define the role of a VA appraiser

- State the current amount of a veteran's maximum entitlement and calculate remaining entitlement

- Explain the relationship between remaining entitlement and restored entitlement

- State who is eligible for the VA program and describe the documents required to prove one's eligibility

- Identify the necessary documentation for obtaining a VA loan

- Determine whether or not a veteran meets the VA debt service ratio requirement to receive a guaranteed loan in a practice activity

- Identify the purpose of the Equal Credit Opportunity Act, and list the restrictions placed on the lender as mandated in the Act

- Explain the Truth in Lending Act, and distinguish between the two principal regulations, Regulation M and Regulation Z

- Explain RESPA and identify the purposes of the various sections

- Explain the enforcement of RESPA against violators of the Act, and state the procedure for filing a complaint

- Distinguish between Titles I–VII of the Financial Services Modernization Act, detailing each with 100% accuracy

- Explain Computerized Loan Origination (CLO), identifying the new "final" rule of the CLO as issued by HUD

- Explain automated underwriting systems, distinguishing between Freddie Mac's Loan Prospector and Fannie Mae's Desktop Underwriter

- Explain the development of automatic underwriting on the Internet

- Discuss the concept of true value in investment in real estate

- Define capital gains and discuss the consequences of taxes on real property and how taxes may affect decisions, especially for investment or business property.

- Explain the purpose of Internal Revenue Code (IRC) Section 1031

- Define *like kind* and discuss what property qualifies for a like-kind exchange

- Distinguish between realized and recognized gain and explain how it is important to the tax laws

- Calculate an investor's adjusted basis in a property, and identify the relationship to boot

- Explain how boot is calculated
- Describe the different ways of doing 1031 exchanges, such as a simultaneous exchange and a delayed exchange
- Identify the role of the qualified intermediary (QI) as a safe harbor in the delayed exchange
- Explain the delayed (Starker) exchange format—the 45/180-day time limits and the rules for replacement property identification
- Explain the reverse exchange format, detailing the exchange accommodation titleholder (EAT), title parking, and describing allowable arrangements between the exchanger and the EAT.
- Explain how an investor can leverage saved capital from tax-deferred exchanges, citing examples
- Explain the tax benefits of installment sales
- Identify the differences among the various types of contracts
- Know the three elements of a contract
- Identify the five components of a legally enforceable contract
- Discern between valid, void, voidable, and unenforceable contracts
- Explain the different types of contract performance
- Apply the laws, doctrines, and statutes that govern real estate contracts, including the Uniform Commercial Code and the Statute of Limitations
- Distinguish the differences among the different types of real estate contracts
- Recall the important elements of leases and listing agreements
- Recognize and complete the forms promulgated by TREC
- Explain the key differences between contracts for deed and other real estate contracts
- Demonstrate the ability to apply what you have learned in this course to situations that you will likely encounter in your career, through analyses of case studies, real world situations, critical thinking questions, and other activities

Key Terms

Abstract of Title
A compressed history of the title of a property, prepared by an abstracter, including all actions that have affected the title (such as conveyances) and all current encumbrances affecting the title.

Acceleration Clause
A clause included in the loan document (such as the mortgage or the deed of trust) that makes the entire amount of the loan due immediately upon the default of the borrower.

Accrued Item
An expense that the buyer will pay after closing that must be divided between the buyer and the seller, such as the interest on an assumed mortgage or real estate taxes.

Actual Notice
In contrast with constructive notice, it is notice of a party's interest that is given expressly.

Adjustable Rate Mortgage (ARM)
A loan whose interest rate varies over specified adjustment periods with some independent market interest rate, such as Treasury Securities.

Ad Valorem Taxes
Property taxes based on the value of the property being taxed.

Amortization
The gradual reduction, through repayment, of the principal of a loan over time. A loan that is so paid down is said to be amortized; the time that it takes for the principal to be reduced to zero is known as the amortization period or loan term.

Annual Percentage Rate (APR)
The ratio of the total finance charge for a loan (including interest, discount points and loan fees) to the total loan amount, expressed as a yearly rate.

Appraisal
An estimation of a property's worth, performed by a licensed real estate appraiser and used for determining sale prices and maximum loan amounts.

Appreciation
An increase in the value of a property over time.

Assumption
Purchasing a property and taking with it the obligation of repaying an existing mortgage on that property.

Banker's Year
A year used in some real estate calculations containing 12 months of 30 days each.

Basis
The cost to a taxpayer of obtaining title to and maintaining (through capital improvements) a property. Used to calculate capital gains taxes.

Blanket Mortgage
Any mortgage that has more than one property as collateral for the loan amount.

Boot
In a 1031 exchange, any amount an investor receives for the sale of his or her property that is not subsequently used to purchase a replacement property and is therefore taxed normally. If the amount is in cash it is cash boot; if in the reduction of mortgage debt, mortgage boot.

Buydown
A reduction in a mortgage's interest rate, paid for either with discount points (permanent buydown) or with an escrow fund (temporary buydown).

Calendar Year
The actual year, when used in real estate calculations, containing months of their normal duration and years of 365 or 366 days, as opposed to a banker's year.

Capital Gains
The difference between the sale price of a property and the seller's adjusted basis in that property, if the adjusted basis is greater. Capital gains are taxed at a lower rate than income tax on regular income.

Capitalization Rate
The ratio of net operating income (NOI) to present value, used to estimate the value of a commercial property, given its income. Also known as the cap rate.

Certificate of Reasonable Value (CRV)
A property appraisal conducted by a VA-approved appraiser, used to determine a limit on the maximum amount of a VA loan.

Closing
The final step in the home-buying process, when the actual title to the property being purchased transfers from the seller to the buyer, and fees and prorated items are paid out of the escrow fund held by the closing entity.

Conforming Loan
A loan that conforms to the conventional loan underwriting guidelines set forth by Fannie Mae and Freddie Mac.

Construction Mortgage
A type of open-end mortgage used for the construction of new property-funds for construction are disbursed in draws as the construction proceeds, and the entire mortgage amount is due when the construction is complete.

Constructive Notice
Legal situation created when a party's interest in a property is properly recorded in the public record. If a party properly records its interest in a property, other parties are considered to have received constructive notice of that interest, whether they have searched those records or not.

Conventional Loan
A loan that is neither federally insured (like an FHA loan) nor federally guaranteed (like a VA loan).

Debt Service Ratio
The ratio of a consumer's total housing expense and long-term debt payments to his or her gross monthly income. Also known as the back-end ratio.

Deed
The legal written document that conveys the intangible ownership rights (title) of a property to another party.

Deed of Trust
A legal document used as security for a promissory note, which conveys temporary, but not full, title to a third party in a transaction, where it is held until either (a) the loan is paid off and the title is conveyed to the borrower or (b) the loan is foreclosed and the title is conveyed to the lender.

Deficiency Judgment
A legal judgment against a borrower to repay the remaining mortgage debt when the foreclosure and sale of the property was not itself enough to repay the debt.

Delayed Exchange
An exchange of property under Internal Revenue Code (IRC) Section 1031 for the sake of tax deferral, where the exchanger sells the relinquished property no more than 45 days before identifying, and 180 days before acquiring a replacement property or properties.

Demand
An economic term denoting the willingness and ability of buyers in a given market to purchase property.

Department of Housing and Urban Development (HUD)
Cabinet-level agency responsible for increasing homeownership and access to affordable housing, promoting fair housing practices, and supporting community development.

Discounted Cash Flow (DCF) Analysis
A method of valuing real estate by discounting predicted future cash flows to a net present value.

Discount Point
A percentage of the loan amount that a lender charges to lower the interest rate. One point equals one percent of the loan amount.

Discount Rate
1. The interest rate charged by the Federal Reserve to its member banks when it lends them money.
2. The rate at which future cash flows are discounted to a net present value in a discounted cash flow analysis.

Distressed Property
A property that is in poor condition either physically or financially.

Earnest Money Contract
A contract in which the buyer agrees to purchase (and seller agrees to sell) a seller's property for a specified amount and puts down a deposit of earnest money to demonstrate that her or his offer is in good faith.

Encumbrance
Any restriction, encroachment, claim, or lien on a property (such as a mortgage) that affects its value or use.

Entitlement
The amount of a loan that the Department of Veterans Affairs will guarantee for an eligible veteran.

Equal Credit Opportunity Act (ECOA)
Title VII of the Consumer Credit Protection Act, protecting consumers against unfair and discriminatory lending.

Equation
A mathematical formula with two terms on either side of an equals sign.

Escrow Closing
A closing conducted with the help of a disinterested third party (the escrow agent) who holds funds and documents until they are required to be disbursed to the parties in the transaction.

Fannie Mae
The Federal National Mortgage Association (FNMA), the most important buyer on the secondary mortgage market, which sets loan underwriting guidelines for conforming loans.

Federal Funds Rate
The interest rate at which banks lend money to one another at the Federal Reserve.

Federal Housing Administration (FHA)
Part of the Department of Housing and Urban Development that works to help increase homeownership and contribute to building healthy neighborhoods and communities. As part of this goal, the FHA loan program insures loans to qualified applicants, reducing the required down payment and other qualifying factors.

Federally Related
A term used to describe the types of real estate transactions that fall under the scope of RESPA, including most conventional, VA, and FHA loans.

Federal Open Market Committee (FOMC)
A committee formed by the Federal Reserve's Board of Governors and five other members who are the presidents of regional Federal Reserve banks, in charge of the open-market operations of the Federal Reserve, such as buying and selling government securities. Also, FOMC has influence over interest rates.

Federal Reserve (the Fed)
The central bank of the United States, responsible for determining its monetary policy, supervising, and regulating financial institutions and maintaining the financial stability of the market.

FICO® Scores
Scores on a 300–850 scale issued by a credit reporting agency that are used as indicators of a consumer's creditworthiness. High scores indicate low risk, and low scores indicate high risk.

Fixed Operating Expenses
Operating expenses that do not vary with the occupancy rate of a property.

Float-to-Fixed Rate Loans
A type of ARM loan that converts to a fixed-rate loan after a period specified in the note. See Hybrid ARM.

Forbearance
A lender's choice to not foreclose, even though he or she has the legal right to do so. This is usually accompanied with a payment moratorium or a recasting of the loan terms.

Fraction
A number expressed as a relation between a part and a whole, such as 1/5. Fractions may also be expressed as decimals (0.2), percentages (20%), and ratios (1:5).

Freddie Mac
The Federal Home Loan Mortgage Corporation (FHLMC), an important buyer on the secondary mortgage market and issuer of mortgage-backed securities.

Funding Fee
A fee charged by the Department of Veterans Affairs for guaranteeing loans to offset the cost of the VA guarantee program.

Graduated Payment Mortgage (GPM)
A type of mortgage with determinate monthly payment increases at determinate intervals usually at the beginning of the loan term, then leveling out to a fixed payment amount. It is set to fully amortize and has negative amortization in the early reduced-payment years.

Growth Equity Mortgage (GEM)
A mortgage that has periodically increasing principal payments with a fixed interest rate. In a GEM, unlike in a GPM, there is no chance of negative amortization.

Homestead
A residence owned and occupied as the principal home of a family or a single individual.

Housing Expense Ratio
The ratio of a borrower's PITI payments (Principal + Interest + Taxes + Insurance) to her or his gross income; used to qualify applicants for loans. Also known as the front-end ratio.

HUD-1 Settlement Statement
A statement that both the buyer and seller receive at closing, detailing the costs allocated to each. It is required by RESPA.

Hybrid ARM

A type of mortgage that has elements of both a fixed-rate loan and an adjustable rate mortgage (ARM). The float-to-fixed rate loan begins as an ARM and converts to a fixed-rate loan after a certain period. The fixed-to-float rate ARM, like the VA hybrid, starts with a certain period of fixed rates and then converts to an ARM.

Inflation

A general increase in prices over time. That is, more dollars chasing the same amount of goods and services.

Installment Sale

Any sale that involves payment in installments extending into another tax year.

Interest

The charge a borrower pays for the use of money.

Interest Rate Reduction Refinancing Loan (IRRRL)

A type of refinancing loan guaranteed by the VA for eligible people that must include a rate reduction and may not include an increased principal balance, except for fees financed into the loan.

Internal Rate of Return (IRR)

The discount rate that reduces all cash inflows and outflows from an investment to zero.

Jumbo Loan

Any conventional loan that is in excess of the loan limits set by Fannie Mae and Freddie Mac. All jumbo loans are, by definition, nonconforming; the reverse, however, is not true.

Lien

A claim that one person has on another's property as security for a debt. A mortgage or money owed to a contractor, for instance, sometimes creates a lien on a borrower's property.

Lien Theory State

A state that interprets the mortgage as creating a lien on the mortgaged property, while the borrower retains the title (ownership rights). The mortgage lender's lien is removed once all loan payments have been completed by the borrower. Texas is a lien theory state.

Like Kind Property

Property that is considered to be of the same nature or character by the Internal Revenue Code (IRC), which may be involved in a tax-deferred exchange.

Loan-to-Value (LTV) Ratio
The ratio of a loan amount to the value of the property that the loan is taken out against.

Market Equilibrium
The point at which the supply and demand curves cross. It is the point at which the quantity supplied is equal to the quantity demanded or the point at which the quantity offered for sale is equal to the quantity sought for purchase. Generally, markets tend to gravitate to the point of equilibrium.

Modified Internal Rate of Return (MIRR)
The internal rate of return of an investment (see IRR) when both the finance rate and the reinvestment rate are considered.

Moratorium
A period of time during which the lender suspends a borrower's principal and/or interest payments to help a borrower in financial difficulty avoid foreclosure. Moratoriums are often accompanied by a recasting of the loan terms.

Mortgage
A legal document that creates a lien on a property as security for a loan. Sometimes the term refers to both the mortgage document and the promissory note.

Mortgage-Backed Securities (MBS)
Securities issued by the owner of a pool of mortgages that pay their holders a percentage of the interest payments on the mortgages. Please note: These are often held in a "pool" but do not have to be.

Mortgage Credit Certificate (MCC)
Certificate issued by a state or federal authority allowing the recipient a mortgage interest tax credit.

Mortgage Insurance Premium (MIP)
A percentage of the loan amount that the Federal Housing Administration charges at the closing of a loan and annually in exchange for insuring the loan.

Net Present Value (NPV)
The value of an investment property (or any source of cash flows) when its future cash flows have been discounted (e.g., with the rate of an alternative investment or the interest or inflation rate) to a present value.

Nonconforming Loan
Any conventional loan that does not conform to the guidelines set forth by either Fannie Mae or Freddie Mac and, therefore, will not be purchased by those companies.

Note: Also known as a promissory note; it is a written promise to pay back a loan, stating the conditions under which this promise is to be met.

Open-End Mortgage
A mortgage that allows the borrower to receive future disbursements on top of the original loan amount.

Order of Operations
A mathematical convention that states that the arithmetical operations are to be performed first inside parentheses, and then in the following order: exponentiation, multiplication, division, and addition or subtraction.

Origination Fee
A charge, usually a percentage of the loan amount, that a lender charges for underwriting or "originating" the loan.

PITI
Principal + Interest + Taxes + Insurance, also known as the housing expense.

Power of Sale Clause
A clause in the loan document (e.g., mortgage, deed of trust, or note) that allows the lender to foreclose in the event of borrower default without the lender having to take judicial action.

Prepaid Item
An expense that the seller has paid before closing that must be divided between the buyer and seller at closing.

Prepayment Clause
A clause in the loan document (e.g., mortgage, deed of trust, or note) that describes the amount of the principal balance that the borrower may pay within a certain time period. The most common clause generally indicates that the borrower has the right to repay the loan in whole or in part at any time.

Price-to-Earnings (P/E) Ratio
The dividends that a share in a company returns to investors per dollar of stock purchased.

Private Mortgage Insurance (PMI)
An amount charged by a private company to a borrower, in the form of an up-front or monthly premium, to insure the lender against loss in the event of borrower default.

Promissory Note
A legal document wherein the borrower acknowledges his or her debt to a lender and agrees to repay it.

Real Estate Investment Trust (REIT)
A registered company that owns and operates commercial real estate. There are three types of REITs: equity, mortgage, and hybrid.

Real Estate Settlement Procedures Act (RESPA)
A federal act outlining the procedures and disclosures that are necessary at the closing of a real estate transaction.

Recaptured Depreciation
A portion of a seller's capital gains that is the difference between the property's original purchase price and the seller's adjusted basis in that property.

Recasting
A change in the loan terms, often after a moratorium, in a way that allows a borrower to pay off the loan amount and accrued interest and penalties. This can be accomplished by extending the term of the loan or by allowing for a balloon payment.

Redemption
A borrower's recovery of a property after it has been taken by a lender. Before the property has been foreclosed and sold at auction, a borrower has the equitable right of redemption to recover the property by paying the mortgage amount, accrued interest, and penalties. Some states allow the borrower to redeem the property after foreclosure, during a statutory redemption period.

Refinancing
The process of paying off an extant loan by taking out a new loan, for example, to receive a better interest rate.

Required Net Yield
The amount of income (yield) that a secondary market purchaser (such as Freddie Mac) requires to buy a note and/or issue mortgage-backed securities.

Reserve Requirement
A percentage of a bank's total funds that the Federal Reserve requires the bank to keep, in cash, in its account at the regional Federal Reserve Bank.

Reverse Annuity Mortgage
A loan based on the equity a borrower already has in her or his home, paid in monthly installments, and due when the home is sold.

Sale-Leaseback
An arrangement where the owner of an investment property sells it and immediately leases it back.

Secured Loan
A loan (note) that places a lien or title against a property as security for that loan.

Special Assessment
A tax on a property for a specific improvement that benefits it (such as street repair or lighting), which, unlike an ad valorem tax, is not calculated on the basis of the property's value but rather as a portion of the cost of the improvement.

Subject to Clause
A clause in the earnest money contract (and in the deed) in which the seller states that title is to be transferred subject to certain existing liens and encumbrances.

Sum
The result of adding two or more numbers. To express indefinite sums, we use a special notation involving the Greek letter sigma (Σ).

Supply
An economic term denoting the willingness and ability of sellers in a given market to sell their property.

Tax Credit
A dollar-for-dollar reduction in a taxpayer's tax liability, granted by the government.

Tax Deduction
A cost or expense that reduces the amount of a taxpayer's taxable income, such as the interest payment on a mortgage loan. It may or may not be a dollar-for-dollar reduction, as the tax credit is.

Tax Exemption
A reduction in the appraised value of taxable property.

Temporary Buydown
A temporary reduction in the interest rate of a mortgage, paid for through the establishment of an escrow fund.

Title
All the rights that ownership of real property entails.

Title Insurance
An insurance policy that covers the holder in the event of loss due to an uncovering of some fault in the title (such as forgery or poorly filed records).

Title Theory State
A state in which the title to the property is given to the lender as security for the loan, while granting the borrower the right to possession of the property. Texas is NOT a title theory state.

Total Debt Service Ratio
The ratio of a borrower's housing expense (PITI) and long-term debts to his or her gross income; used to qualify applicants for loans.

Truth in Lending Act (TILA)
Title I of the Consumer Credit Protection Act (CCPA), requiring that lenders disclose certain facts about loans they offer to consumers.

Underwriting
The process of approving or denying a loan application on the basis of an evaluation of the property to be mortgaged and the applicant's creditworthiness. The process, if it results in approval, involves the underwriter's selecting an appropriate interest rate and loan term.

Unsecured Loan
Any loan that does not place a lien or title against a property as security for the loan but is secured only by the borrower's promise to repay the debt.

Uniform Standards of Professional Appraisal Practice (USPAP)
A set of appraisal standards developed by the Appraisal Standards Board, now widely used by most state appraisal regulatory agencies.

Vacancy R
The ratio of the amount of unrented space in a commercial building to the amount of total space.

Variable Operating Expenses
Expenses that vary with the occupancy rate of a property.

Veterans Affairs, Department of (VA)
The government agency in charge of providing benefits to U.S. veterans and their dependants. As part of this mission, the VA guarantees portions of mortgages given to veterans that require no down payments and have limited purchaser closing costs.

Wraparound Mortgage

An arrangement in which a subordinate mortgage is created on a home that already has a mortgage at a lesser rate. The payments on the higher-rate subordinate mortgage are used to pay off the existing mortgage, and the holder of the subordinate mortgage receives the difference as a profit.

Table of Contents

LESSON 1: INTRODUCTION TO REAL ESTATE FINANCE
Lesson Topics:

- Mortgages
- Primary Mortgage Market
- The Secondary Market
- Amortization
- Discount Points
- Promissory Notes
- Secured vs. Unsecured notes
- Default
- Lien Theory and Title Theory
- Assumption
- Case Study: Monthly Payment
- Summary

LESSON 2: THE EFFECT OF THE MARKET AND THE GOVERNMENT ON REAL ESTATE FINANCE
Lesson Topics:

- Introduction
- Supply and Demand of Housing
- Inflation
- The Federal Reserve
- Taxes
- The Department of Housing and Urban Development
- Texas Department of Housing and Community Affairs
- Real Estate Investment Trusts
- Activity: Critical Thinking
- Case Study
- Summary

LESSON 3: FINANCIAL QUALIFICATIONS
Lesson Topics:

- Introduction
- Underwriting Guidelines and Process
- Income
- Credit
- Source of Funds
- Debts
- Net Worth
- Case Study: Borrower Qualification
- Summary

LESSON 4: PROPERTY VALUATION
Lesson Topics:

- Introduction
- Eight Steps of the Appraisal Process
- Appraisal Methods
- Cap Rate Analysis
- Discounted Cash Flow Analysis
- Pro Forma
- Taxes and Depreciation
- Activity: Critical Thinking
- Case Study: Net Present Value
- Summary

LESSON 5: THE FINANCING PROCESS
Lesson Topics:

- Introduction
- Mortgage Brokers
- Loan Officers
- Application
- Title

- Survey
- Earnest Money Contract
- Escrow Accounts
- Deed
- Closing
- Activity: Fill In the Blank
- Summary

LESSON 6: REAL ESTATE CLOSINGS
Lesson Topics:

- Introduction
- Pre-Closing Requirements
- Closing Procedures
- Required Documents
- Reporting Transactions to the IRS
- The Licensee's Role
- Real Estate Settlement Procedures Act (RESPA)
- Summary

LESSON 7: CLOSING EXPENSES
Lesson Topics:

- Introduction
- Allocating Expenses
- Nonrecurring Closing Costs
- Credits and Debits
- Prorating Expenses
- Summary

LESSON 8: THE HUD-1 SETTLEMENT STATEMENT
Lesson Topics:

- Introduction
- General Guidelines for the hud-1 Settlement Statement Form
- Settlement Charges

- Borrower's Transaction
- Seller's Transaction
- Activity: Closing
- Summary

LESSON 9: FORECLOSURE
Lesson Topics:

- Introduction
- Default
- Foreclosure
- Properties in Distress
- Activity: Fill In the Blanks
- Case Study: Forbearance
- Summary

LESSON 10: CONVENTIONAL LOANS
Lesson Topics:

- Introduction
- Conforming Loan Limits
- Private Mortgage Insurance
- Fannie Mae Underwriting Guidelines
- Freddie Mac Underwriting Guidelines
- Activity: Underwriting
- Case Study: Conventional Loan
- Summary

LESSON 11: ALTERNATIVE FINANCIAL INSTRUMENTS
Lesson Topics:

- Introduction
- Adjustable Rate Mortgage
- 80-10-10 Piggyback Loans
- Graduated Payment Mortgages
- Growth Equity Mortgages

- Balloon Mortgages
- Wraparound Mortgages
- Reverse Annuity Mortgages
- Blanket Mortgages
- Open End Mortgages
- Sale-Leaseback
- Permanent Buydowns
- Temporary Buydowns
- Additional Loan Payment Plans
- Summary

LESSON 12: FHA LOANS
Lesson Topics:

- Introduction
- Qualifications
- FHA Programs
- Mortgage Insurance Premium
- FHA Underwriting Requirements
- Advantages and Disadvantages
- Practice
- Case study: FHA loan vs. Conventional loan
- Summary

LESSON 13: VA LOANS
Lesson Topics:

- Department of Veterans Affairs
- Underwriting Requirements
- Entitlement
- Eligibility
- Documentation
- Activity: Fill In the Blanks
- Case Study: VA Loan
- Practice

- Summary

LESSON 14: FEDERAL AND STATE LAWS AND REGULATIONS
Lesson Topics:

- Equal Credit Opportunity Act
- Truth in Lending Act
- Real Estate Settlement Procedures Act
- Financial Services Modernization Act
- Summary

LESSON 15: CONVENTIONAL LOANS
Lesson Topics:

- Computerized Loan Origination (CLO)
- Automated Underwriting Systems
- Automatic Underwriting On the Internet
- Investment in Real Estate
- Summary

LESSON 16: 1031 EXCHANGES
Lesson Topics:

- Introduction
- Like Kind Property
- Capital Gains
- Simultaneous Exchanges
- Delayed Exchanges
- Qualified Intermediaries
- Three-Party Trades
- Reverse Exchanges
- Installment Sales
- Activity: Exchanging Numbers
- Case Study: Delayed Exchange
- Summary

LESSON 17: CONTRACTS
Lesson Topics:

- Introduction
- Types of Contracts
- Implied Contracts
- Express Contracts
- Bilateral Contracts
- Unilateral Contracts
- Executed Contracts
- Executory Contracts
- Valid Contracts
- Void Contracts
- Voidable Contracts
- Unenforceable Contracts
- Legally Valid Contracts Overview
- Mutual Assent
- Legally Competent Parties
- Consideration
- Lawful Objective
- Adherence to Statute of Frauds
- Contract Performance Overview
- Performance of a Contract
- Non-Performance of a Contract
- Contracts Overview
- Legal Forms
- Sales Contracts
- Listing Agreements
- Option Agreements
- Contract-For-Deed Agreements
- Leases
- Insight into Contracts, Purchase Agreements, and Sales Agreements
- The Statute of Limitations
- The Uniform Commercial Code
- Promulgated Contract Forms
- Contracts for Deed

- Activity
- Contracts, Purchase Agreements, and Sales Agreements Field Applications
- Summary

LESSON 18: REAL ESTATE PRACTICE
Lesson Topics:

- Introduction
- Critical Thinking Questions
- Case Studies
- Summary

Lesson 1:
INTRODUCTION TO REAL ESTATE FINANCE

This lesson focuses on the following topics:

- Mortgages
- Primary Mortgage Market
- The Secondary Market
- Amortization
- Discount Points
- Promissory Notes
- Secured vs. Unsecured notes
- Default
- Lien Theory and Title Theory
- Assumption
- Case Study: Monthly Payment
- Summary

By the end of this lesson, you should be able to:

- Explain the basic concepts of real estate finance, describing them in detail
- Explain how interest rates affect the real estate market
- Distinguish between the principal instruments of financing-the promissory note, the mortgage, and the deed of trust-and explain how they are used
- Explain how mortgages are structured and that mortgages create a lien, identifying the difference between a secured note and an unsecured loan
- Explain the function of a discount point, when it is offered, and when it should be bought
- Discuss the operations of the secondary market for loans
- Calculate the monthly payments for a fully amortized, fixed-rate loan
- Distinguish between the tax deductions and tax credits associated with real estate ownership, and calculate each
- Explain the use of and legal requirements placed on escrow accounts
- State who lends money to the purchasers of real estate, identifying them with 100 percent accuracy
- Distinguish between lien theory and title theory and know which theory Texas uses

- Explain what an assumption loan is and provide an example

Mortgages

Real estate is expensive. Most individuals don't have the money necessary to pay for a house in full. The real estate system in the United States is based on loans.

A borrower receives funds to purchase real property in exchange for signing a promissory note. In a promissory note (sometimes referred to simply as a *note*), the borrower acknowledges her or his debt and promises to repay the holder of the note. The note states the term of the loan, the interest rate, and the conditions of repayment. All notes are either secured or unsecured. A secured note has a mortgage or deed of trust as security for the loan.

A mortgage is a document that creates a lien, a claim that the mortgage holder has on the property. A deed of trust is a document that actually conveys temporary, but not full, title to the property to a trustee, who holds the title until the debt has been cleared. A secured note will make reference to the document, a mortgage, or a deed of trust that secures it. Unsecured loans, by contrast, have only the borrower's promise that the debt will be repaid.

Most notes contain an acceleration clause, which makes the entire loan amount due immediately upon default. Default occurs when the borrower violates any of the terms of the loan agreement, which is most often in the form of delinquent payments. The acceleration clause is important legally, because the lender would otherwise have to sue for each late payment as it became due.

The mortgage market has a two-tiered structure. At the first level is the primary market, where lenders underwrite loans to borrowers seeking to purchase real property. The secondary market is where the notes themselves are bought and sold. The secondary market helps to stabilize the primary market by replenishing the funds primary lenders have lent out. The entire system is driven by interest rates.

Interest Rates

Interest is the rent paid on money. Interest rates are determined by the market-the individual lenders-but are influenced by the Federal Reserve System's open-market activities and its primary lending discount rate (the interest rate the Fed charges to other banks). They are also limited by usury laws, which prohibit lenders from charging excessive interest on a loan.

Interest rates are inversely correlated with property values. That is, rising interest rates cause falling property values, and falling rates cause rising values. This is because most real estate is purchased with borrowed money: A borrower must pay more money to a lender during periods of high interest rates and thus is willing to spend less on the property itself.

Primary Mortgage Market

Most home purchase loans are made by one of these types of primary lenders:

- Savings and loan associations
- Commercial banks
- Savings banks
- Mortgage bankers
- Credit unions
- Private lenders

Savings and Loan Associations

Savings and loan associations (S&Ls), otherwise known as thrift lenders, were originally established by the government for the purpose of offering long-term, single-family home loans. For a long time S&Ls dominated the home loan market, but in the 1980s, deregulation led to a savings and loan crisis. Today, S&Ls are much like commercial banks and offer a wide variety of financial services. However, S&Ls are chartered by the government and must meet the qualified thrift lender (QTL) test to retain that charter and receive benefits from the Federal Home Loan Bank System. At least 70 percent of an S&Ls assets must be housing-related (for example, home mortgages, home equity loans and mortgage-backed securities) for it to meet the QTL test. The Financial Institutions Reform, Recovery and Enforcement Act (FIRREA) is responsible for regulating, supervising, and insuring savings and loans.

Commercial Banks

Commercial banks are the largest source of investment funds in the United States. They offer demand, time, and savings deposits. Commercial banks are called *commercial* because they originally specialized in short-term capital loans for business and construction. While commercial banks have continued to emphasize commercial loans, they also have diversified their lending with a substantial increase in consumer loans and residential mortgages. Most of the mortgages created by commercial banks are sold to buyers on the secondary market.

Credit Unions

Credit unions are more recent and less common than commercial banks, although they offer most of the same services. They are financial institutions that are controlled by their members, usually all of a certain group (for example, teachers, union members or the employees of a certain military base). In recent years, many credit unions have specialized in home equity loans. A home equity loan is a mortgage on the borrower's equity in the home he or she already owns. These are generally short-term loans.

Mortgage Bankers

Mortgage bankers (also known as mortgage companies) are not depository institutions. They function more in the role of intermediaries rather than a source of lending capital. Mortgage banks control the greatest share of the primary lending market. They manage capital, not from personal deposits, but from large investors such as insurance companies and retirement funds. Mortgage companies also will borrow money from commercial banks to finance loans. All of these loans are then sold on the secondary market, because mortgage companies do not hold loans in portfolio. Some mortgage companies operate entirely from the proceeds of secondary-market sales, selling their loans to insurance companies and retirement funds, as well as to buyers such as Fannie Mae and Freddie Mac (discussed later in the course).

Private Lenders

Real estate limited partnerships, real estate investment trusts, and other types of private investment groups put a great deal of money into real estate, but they do not offer loans to individual home buyers. From the home buyer's point of view, the most important type of private lender is the home seller. Sellers sometimes provide all the financing for the purchase of their homes, and it's fairly common for a seller to supplement the financing the buyer obtains from an institutional lender. Sellers are an especially important source of financing when institutional loans are difficult to obtain, particularly in times of high interest rates.

The Secondary Market

The secondary market is where real estate loans are bought and sold. A lender is willing to advance funds to a borrower in exchange for periodic interest payments for the use of those funds; and, for the same reason, an investor is willing to purchase a promissory note from a lender. These notes sell at present values. The idea is to give the note a relative worth, based on alternative investment opportunities open to the purchaser. If the investor could earn seven percent annual returns in the stock market, the net present value of the note is the value of the future cash flows from interest, discounted at a rate of seven percent.

Level of risk is important as well. Investments with high risk and low returns are of little interest to investors. To ensure that the level of risk associated with loans in the secondary market does not run too high, the largest buyers in the secondary market have established guidelines to which loans must conform if they are to be traded in the secondary market.

These conforming guidelines have a further benefit to the secondary market, in that they make loans easy to value and compare. These guidelines are established by three government-sponsored agencies that are the chief operators in the secondary market: the Federal National Mortgage Association (FNMA or Fannie Mae), the Federal Home Loan Mortgage Company (FHLMC or Freddie Mac), and the Government National Mortgage Association (GNMA or Ginnie Mae).

Secondary Market Agencies

Fannie Mae

Originally created by the government to provide a secondary market for FHA-insured loans (discussed in a later lesson), Fannie Mae is now a privately owned purchaser of FHA, VA, and conventional loans. Mortgages are purchased on an administered price system. That is, the required yields (the money each loan returns per unit of present value) are set daily. Lenders can check these requirements and place an order to sell by phone.

In addition to the purchase and sale of loans, Fannie Mae issues what are known as mortgaged-backed securities. These are investment instruments similar to stocks, which pay returns to their holders. They differ from stocks in that they have as collateral a pool of mortgages that the issuing institution (in this case, Fannie Mae) owns. Fannie Mae does not necessarily own or sell the securities; a lender brings a mortgage package to Fannie Mae, and Fannie Mae exchanges the guaranteed securities with the lender for the mortgages.

These securities are attractive to investors for two reasons: First, they cost less than purchasing an entire loan and are more easily liquidated; and second, they are guaranteed. That is, the holder of the security receives the full payment from it, whether or not the borrowers of the mortgages held as collateral pay their loans in full. For this guarantee, investors take slightly lower profits from the mortgages than if they held them themselves, through the payment of a guarantee fee.

More About: For more information, visit Fannie Mae online: http://www.fanniemae.com.

Freddie Mac

Freddie Mac was created to provide a secondary market for conventional loans during the savings and loan crisis of the 1980s. The success of the secondary market in ameliorating the losses in the primary market illustrates an important dynamic. Lenders are willing to lend large sums of money that are deposited in their institutions to borrowers because they receive cash flows from interest. However, until they receive this interest, they are lacking in funds to lend. By selling the loans on the secondary market, lenders receive the present value of those interest cash flows, which they can immediately lend to other borrowers, continuing the process. In addition, the primary market is stabilized by the mortgage-backed securities - liquid assets - that are issued by secondary market purchasers.

Freddie Mac's secondary market activities are, in part, what bailed out the S&Ls. Securities sold by Freddie Mac are known as participation certificates (or PCs), but they work in the same way as Fannie Mae's mortgage-backed securities (MBSs). Freddie Mac buys VA, FHA, conventional, and adjustable rate loans that meet its underwriting criteria.

More About: For more information, visit Freddie Mac online: http://www.freddiemac.com.

Ginnie Mae

Unlike Fannie Mae and Freddie Mac, Ginnie Mae is wholly owned by the government. Its activities are under the direct supervision of the Department of Housing and Urban Development Ginnie Mae plays an important role in the primary market, by offering loans to housing projects of interest to HUD's purposes, but not easily financed through private loans. However, Ginnie Mae's role in the secondary market, as the largest issuer of mortgage-backed securities, and the only issuer of government guaranteed mortgage-backed securities, is of greater importance. The government guarantee allows the type of special assistance and residential mortgage loans that Ginnie Mae deals with to rival other securities in the secondary market.

More About: For more information, visit Ginnie Mae online: http://www.ginniemae.gov.

Secondary Market Activities

The secondary market agencies have two main activities: buying loans and issuing mortgage-backed securities.

Buying Loans

A real estate loan is essentially an investment just like stocks and bonds. The lender (whether a lending institution or private party) is the investor. The lender commits its funds to the purchase or construction of a home, expecting a return in the form of interest payments. And just like other investments, real estate loans can be bought and sold.

Many factors determine the value of a loan; especially important is the degree of risk associated with the loan. A lender may sell mortgage loans directly to another lender in a different part of the country or to one of the secondary market agencies. The agency may, in turn, use those mortgages to create mortgage-backed securities.

Issuing Mortgage-Backed Securities

Securities (e.g., stocks and bonds) are investment instruments. Mortgage-backed securities are simply investment instruments that have mortgages as collateral. A secondary market agency creates mortgage-backed securities by buying a large number of mortgage loans, pooling them together, and pledging the pool as collateral for the securities. The securities are sold to investors, who receive a return on their investment in the form of periodic payments (usually monthly) from the agency. Mortgage-backed securities can be easily traded.

The secondary market agency obtains the funds to make payments to the investors from the borrowers' repayment of the mortgage loans that back the securities. Often the securities involve a guaranty so that the investor will receive the full monthly payment from the secondary market agency, whether or not payment has been collected from all of the borrowers.

The Development of the Secondary Mortgage Market

We have discussed how the secondary mortgage market has affected the mortgage market as a whole, and now we will briefly detail the development of the secondary mortgage market. Today, the secondary mortgage market is one of the largest, most liquid debt market segments in the world, with its outstanding debt totaling about $4.4 trillion. The secondary mortgage market reached its zenith with a century's worth of milestones-some assisted through government support, others representing the utter determination of competitive business professionals.

A century ago, mortgage business was not known in the market, and buying a home meant borrowing from a friend, relative, or local businessperson. In larger communities, savings and loan organizations (known as building and loans at that time) were the major source of mortgage financing. By 1999, about 5,800 of these institutions held about half a billion dollars in mortgage loans.

State-chartered banks and saving banks also made home loans on a smaller scale. During the same time, independent mortgage companies emerged, and their numbers reached about 200. Throughout the latter half of the 19th century, mortgage companies acted as conciliators between East Coast investors and frontier farmers who needed financing. Rather than purchase loans, most of these mortgages were production loans funds, which bought equipment and supplies, not a property itself.

In 1914, these mortgage companies formed a professional organization called the Farm Mortgage Bankers Association. The organization changed its name in 1923 and is now known as the Mortgage Bankers Association of America (MBA of America), which reflects its focus on residential mortgage lending. While discussing the industry's milestones, we should also keep in mind that the structure of mortgage loans was developed during this time. Primarily, mortgage loans were five-year, interest-only, 50 percent loan-to-value ratio instruments with the principal due at the end of the loan.

Principal on a mortgage loan was rarely repaid as most borrowers simply refinanced at the end of five years. But this arrangement turned out to be catastrophic after the Great Crash in October 1929. Today, the hardships of the Great Depression (the economic depression of the '30s) seem abstract, but in the darkest days, one-third of the country's labor force was unemployed. Between1931 and 1935, there were 250,000 foreclosures per year, and by 1935, 20 percent of all homes were owned by lenders. Today's mortgage lenders and borrowers learned from the tough lessons in the first half of the century, and a new system of financing developed.

The Federal Home Loan Bank Act of 1932 extended $125 million in credit to savings and loan institutions and created the Federal Home Loan Bank System with 12 regional banks. In1933, the Home Owners Loan Act gave savings and loans the ability to be chartered by the federal government, and the thrifts were given essential lending authority to offer emergency relief for homeowners who could refinance their home loan for 20 years. The terms of these new loans were revolutionary: The first fixed-rated, amortized loan was created. For the first time, borrowers received amortized loans with rates as low as 5 percent with an 80 percent LTV. By 1936, one in every 10 homeowners received financing through this law. In the first two years of its enactment, one million loans totaling $3 billion were made. The amortized, fixed-rate loan is now the industry standard.

In that same year, the Banking Act of 1933 helped the nation recover some financial confidence by creating the Federal Deposit Insurance Corporation. The Glass-Steagall Act-a law that defied repeal until 1999-redefined the way banks did business. One year later, the National Housing Act of 1934 created the Federal Housing Administration (FHA) and its government-backed insurance program, regulating loan requirements and allowing lenders to increase liquidity by selling pools of loans to investors, such as life insurance companies.

The Federal Mortgage Association, or "Fannie Mae," was one of the last pieces of Depression-era legislation enacted by the federal government. Back then, it was owned and run entirely by the federal government. In 1938, Fannie Mae purchased its first FHA-insured loans from lenders, securing the nation's first government-sponsored secondary market. In spite of the government support, the Great Depression still confounded the lending industry. In the 10-year period between the initial stock market crash in October 1929 and the tail end of the Great Depression in 1939, half of all banks and thrifts went out of business. However, the less numerous mortgage companies fared a little better, and many non-portfolio lenders found their niche in government loan originations and servicing. After WWII, there were few available homes still in good condition. The demand for housing, however, was at an all-time high. The federal government remedied the short supply of suitable housing by passing the National Housing Act in 1949.

Throughout the 1950s and 1960s, at least 50 percent of origination market share was held by the thrift industry. In 1965, the Department of Housing and Urban Development (HUD) was elevated to Cabinet-level status. HUD's mission was "a decent, safe and sanitary home and suitable living environment for every American." Both the FHA and Fannie Mae became agencies within HUD, until Fannie Mae's reorganization in 1968. Fannie Mae was split, and the "new" Fannie Mae became a private corporation, while another entity, Ginnie Mae, remained an organization within HUD. The privatization of Fannie Mae affected the secondary market. In 1965, the Government Sponsored Enterprises (GSEs) purchased $757 million in government mortgage loans; in just five years, that figure grew to slightly more than $5 billion.

Mortgage banking saw revolutionary changes during the 1970s. Adjustable-rate mortgages were introduced in this decade, launching the public's acceptance of shared interest-rate risk. Most importantly, the secondary market expanded, unleashing unprecedented capital into mortgage markets. The Emergency Home Finance Act of 1970 not only created Freddie Mac, but also authorized Fannie Mae to purchase conventional mortgages. Concurrent with the modern GSE structure, in 1970 Ginnie Mae issued the first mortgage-backed securities. Freddie Mac followed suit in 1971, and by 1975, lenders began to issue their own private mortgage-backed bonds.

Along with the increase of capital made possible by securitization, mortgage lending's major players changed dramatically during the 1980s. At the beginning of the decade, thrifts held 50 percent of origination's market share; mortgage companies and commercial banks equally shared the remaining half. Nine years later, the thrift agencies fell on hard times, and the origination market was divided equally among the remaining secure thrifts and the better-off mortgage companies and commercial banks.

Competition in the "mortgage company" industry reached an all-time high with the addition of new members, such as Sears, General Electric, and General Motors. Large commercial banks such as Citicorp and Chase Manhattan made major moves into home finance, as did more than half of the nation's 20,000 credit unions. New origination records were set in 1986 and 1987, before another October stock market crash brought the 1980s economic boom to a close.

In the late '80s and into the early '90s the nation experienced another slump. In 1991, the Federal Reserve lowered interest rates, and by late 1993, interest for fixed-rate mortgages dropped below 7 percent. Americans had not seen rates that low in 20 years, and in 1993 alone, mortgage lenders funded $1.1 trillion. It was in this same year that mortgage companies accounted for more than half of originations and Countrywide Home became the nation's largest mortgage lender.

Two and a half years later, the Federal Reserve again dropped rates. Fixed rate mortgages fell below seven percent and created another refinance boom that lasted through early spring of 1999. Again, origination records were set. Two economic booms of this caliber in one decade is quite remarkable, but perhaps even more remarkable is the advent and affect of electronic commerce and the industry's massive consolidation efforts. Today, the top 25 firms are responsible for more than half of all originations, and more than $4.1 billion in originations were conducted online during1998.

Nearly a decade into the 21st century, our industry continues to be a dynamic, vibrant, and growth-oriented sector. As lenders compete to provide personalized service to clients and customers, product diversification delivers a wealth of opportunities and advantages to both borrowers and lenders. Innovative technologies, mergers, acquisitions, and business line diversification all seek to provide a more complete, one-stop-shopping experience for potential buyers. The changes which occurred in 2007 and 2008 will have a big effect on the market for years to come.

Amortization

A loan will usually be paid off in portions over time or amortized. The word amortization is a Latin term that means "killing off." If the note is to be amortized, there will be equal monthly payments that contribute to both principal and interest until the entire loan is paid. The payments will be credited first to the interest when due, with any remainder credited to the principal.

If the payment being made is not sufficient to cover the interest due for any payment period, the unpaid interest is added to the principal balance. This is known as negative amortization or deferred interest.

Payments on amortized loans are calculated by using mortgage constant factors. These factors are the original principal balance on the loan, the annual or monthly interest rate, and the loan term.

Calculating Monthly Payments

Let P be the initial loan principal, i be the annual interest rate, J be the monthly interest rate (i/12), and n be the number of payments over the term of the loan (loan term in years × 12 months). Then, the fixed payment that will amortize the loan over that term can be calculated using the following formula:

Monthly Payment = $(P \times J) \div (1 - (1 + J)^{-n})$

For example, suppose the loan amount is $130,000, the term is 30 years and the interest rate is 8 percent. Then,

P = $130,000
i = 0.08
J = i/12 = 0.08/12 = 0.0067
n = 30 x 12 = 360

So the monthly payment M will be:

$$M = (\$130,000 \times 0.0067) \div (1 - (1 + 0.0067)^{-360})$$
$$= \$871 \div (1 - (1.0067)^{-360})$$
$$= \$871 \div (1 - (0.0904))$$
$$= \$871 \div 0.9096$$
$$= \$957.56$$

This, of course, is only an estimate, based on our approximation of the monthly interest payment as 0.67 percent. The actual payment would be $953.89, but the $4 difference isn't too important to the job of the real estate professional. The point of calculating monthly payments is, as we shall see in later lessons, to prequalify clients for loans, given a lender's qualifying ratios. To this purpose, a licensee can use the above formula in a pinch (it is important to understand, at least, the relationship between the principal, interest rate and monthly payment), or the licensee can use a scientific calculator or a mortgage calculator.

More About: The student can find an online mortgage calculator at: http://ray.met.fsu.edu/~bret/amortize.html.

Principal and Interest Payments

The monthly payment calculated in the previous section is actually just a part of the payment a borrower will make each month over the course of the loan. Those payments are the principal and interest payments; they don't include, for example, taxes, mortgage insurance, or hazard insurance. Nonetheless, the principal and interest figure is useful to have.

It can also be useful to know how much of any particular monthly payment is going toward the principal balance and how much is going toward interest. For instance, interest payments on a mortgage are often tax deductible. It can be important for a future financial plan to know what deduction one is to receive.

Interest on loans that do not negatively amortize is simple interest. For any payment period t, the interest payment equals the principal at period t − 1 times the periodic interest rate. So, if the loan balance last month was $8,000, and the monthly interest rate is 0.7 percent, then the interest due this month is $8,000 × 0.007 = $56. Whatever amount of the monthly payment is in excess of $56 goes toward reducing the principal. If the monthly payment is $300, then $8,000 −

($300 − $56) = $7,756 is this month's principal balance, which will be used to calculate next month's interest payment, and so on.

Loans that negatively amortize, however, have compounded interest. This is, in essence, paying interest on interest that went unpaid. For example, suppose Borrower B has a loan whose monthly interest rate is not fixed. The principal balance on the loan last month was $86,000, the monthly payment is $700, and this month's interest rate is 0.9 percent. The interest due this month is $86,000 × 0.009 = $774. Because this amount is in excess of the monthly payment, B's interest payment for the month is all $700 of the monthly payment, and his principal payment is $0. This isn't the end of the story. The unpaid $74 in interest is compounded to the principal, so that this month's principal balance, which is used to calculate next month's interest, is $86,074. As you can see, negative amortization can quickly become a serious problem.

We've shown how to calculate interest from the previous period's balance. Suppose, however, that we wanted to know the interest payment for an arbitrary payment period, for which we don't know the previous period's balance. Would we have to go back to the last period where we did know the balance and do all the calculations from there? Not exactly. While it would be difficult to crank out the interest payment mathematically, there are other ways of getting this information. An amortization schedule is a chart that shows the principal and interest payments for each month from the first to the last month of the loan term. Some financial spreadsheet programs and many online sites will provide amortization schedules, given the principal, interest rate and loan term.

Mortgage Interest Tax Deduction
For most homebuyers who are purchasing or improving their homes, the interest payment on a mortgage is tax deductible. However, interest on mortgages in excess of $1 million is not deductible. For example, if you purchase a home for $1.5 million, the interest on the first $1 million is tax deductible, but then the interest on the remaining $ 500,000 of the price of the house is not tax deductible.

Taxes and Insurance
In addition to principal and interest payments, the monthly amounts that a borrower pays to a lender also include taxes and insurance. Even though tax and insurance payments go to third parties (government bodies and insurance companies), the lender has an interest in their collection. Tax liens, which are created when a property owner fails to pay his or her property taxes, take precedence over the lender's mortgage lien. Therefore, if a borrower defaults on her or his loan *and* fails to pay taxes, the government has the right to recover damages first, which may limit the lender's ability to recover all of his or her losses. Similarly, if an uninsured house is destroyed, there is no longer any collateral to secure the loan.

An uninsured house is a problem because, in most cases, the loan for the mortgage is secured by the actual house that the mortgage covers. The house is used as collateral for the loan so that if the buyer defaults on the mortgage payments, the lender may foreclose on the house, sell it, and use the proceeds from the sale of the house to cover the money that had been loaned. But if the house is uninsured and is destroyed, there will not be a house or insurance money to replace the house. In this case the lender has nothing, unless the homeowner decides to continue making payments on a house that no longer exists.

Escrow Accounts

Lenders hold tax and insurance payments in escrow accounts. These are accounts held by disinterested third parties, from which money is paid as it becomes due. For example, when annual taxes are due, the sum of all the monthly payments toward taxes held in the escrow account is put toward the taxes owed on the property. Usually escrow accounts are set up at closing and contain several months of payments, which the borrower has prepaid. The escrow account can contain a cushion, an amount above the required payment amount, and some lenders will even use interest-bearing escrow accounts.

The Real Estate Settlement Procedures Act (RESPA), which will be discussed more thoroughly in the *Closing* lesson of this module, sets limits on the amount of money a lender is allowed to keep in an escrow account. It is important to note that the establishment of escrow accounts, cushions, and interest paid on these accounts are not required by law but are all options available to the lender.

RESPA limits the amount a lender is allowed to keep in an escrow account to 14 months of payments (that is, one year of payments plus a maximum cushion of one-sixth of that amount).

Suppose that a borrower has the following tax and insurance liabilities for the home: $1,500 tax payment in July, $850 tax payment in December, and a $350 hazard insurance payment in February. If the escrow account is established in January, how much money can the lender require to be in it?

To solve this problem, first we must determine the monthly escrow payment. This is one-twelfth of the total annual liabilities or (1/12) × ($1,500 + $850 + $350) = $225. Then we perform a hypothetical calculation to find what the monthly balances of the account would be if the initial balance of the escrow account were zero:

Month	Escrow Payment	Liabilities	Escrow Balance
January			$0
February	$225	$350	-$125
March	$225	$0	$100
April	$225	$0	$325
May	$225	$0	$550
June	$225	$0	$775
July	$225	$1,500	-$500
August	$225	$0	-$275
September	$225	$0	-$50
October	$225	$0	$175
November	$225	$0	$400
December	$225	$850	-$225
January	$225	$0	$0

Because the escrow account balance drops to its lowest at -$500, the initial balance must be at least $500 to keep the payments and liabilities balanced. However, the lender is allowed to keep one-sixth of the annual payments in addition to this minimum balance. Thus, the maximum allowable escrow requirement is:

$$\$500 + ((1/6) \times (\$350 + \$1{,}500 + \$850)) = \$950$$

RESPA also sets certain restrictions on the repayment of monies owed to, or by, the borrower. If the escrow account contains an amount in excess of the allowable limit, but less than $50, the lender may either return the money to the borrower or apply it to future payments, reducing the monthly escrow payment amount. If the amount owed the borrower is in excess of $50, the lender has 30 days to return the funds to the borrower. On the other hand, if the borrower owes the lender less than one month's escrow payment, the lender may request that the funds be paid within 30 days. Otherwise, the lender must spread the repayment over a 12-month period, thereby increasing the monthly escrow payment.

Taxes

There are a number of taxing authorities that tax any one property. Taxes come from the state, county, and city levels; from grade schools and community colleges; and from certain districts in which the property is located. For example, a property may be subject to taxes from a municipal utility district (MUD), which is a district set up by a subdivision to repay bonds that were issued to build water and sewer facilities.

Taxes that are calculated as a percentage of the appraised value of a property are called ad valorem taxes. These taxes create a lien on the property that holds priority over all other liens, including the lender's lien. This is the principal reason for the lenders' collection of taxes through the escrow method, so that they can ensure that taxes are paid and that their first lien position is not jeopardized.

In addition to ad valorem taxes, real estate taxes can also come in the form of special assessments. A special assessment is a tax that is used to pay for an improvement-such as sidewalks, street repavement, or streetlamps-that benefits the assessed property. For example, if the government were to repave a few streets in a residential neighborhood, every property in that neighborhood might receive a special assessment because better streets improve their value.

Special assessments, unlike ad valorem taxes, are not calculated on the basis of the value of the property assessed. Instead, they are calculated by the cost of the project and then distributed to the assessed properties. They are not usually distributed evenly, but rather in proportion to either the benefit each property will receive or to the property's size, in terms of front footage.

In determining a likely monthly payment, lenders typically estimate a new property's annual taxes to be between 2.5 percent and 2.75 percent. For existing properties, the lender will obtain the tax certificates from previous years to estimate the taxes in coming years.

Real estate taxes are deductible expenses. However, it is not always the case that all funds paid into an escrow account for the repayment of taxes are deductible. Only the actual sum that is paid in taxes out of the account is deductible. Some expenses paid to the government are not deductible. These include fees for specific services and benefits, such as a trash collection fee or money paid for the construction of a sidewalk. Special assessments, in general, are not tax deductible.

Mortgage Interest Tax Credit
The federal government provides certain first-time homebuyers with the opportunity to receive a tax credit for 20 percent of their mortgage interest payments if their gross annual income is less than $30,000 and for 10 percent if their income is greater than $30,000. To receive this credit, the homebuyer must obtain a mortgage credit certificate (MCC) before he or she obtains the mortgage loan. In using the credit, the taxpayer may still use the remaining 80 percent (or 90 percent) of the interest payment as a tax deduction. Any unused portion of the tax credit may be "carried forward" to the next tax year for up to three years.

The mortgage interest tax credit is important to the underwriting process because it reduces the long-term debt service of the borrower, allowing her or him to qualify for a higher monthly payment.

Mortgage Credit Certificate
Not everyone is eligible for the mortgage interest tax credit. Those seeking the credit must obtain a mortgage credit certificate (MCC). These certificates are

available only for first-time homebuyers, but that does not necessarily mean only those people buying a home for the first time. According to the law, a first-time homebuyer is anyone who has not had equity in a principal residence in the previous two years. Therefore, it is possible for one taxpayer to receive more than one MCC. The tax credit may be used only for the purchase of an owner-occupied one-to-four family principal residence.

Taxpayers applying for an MCC also must meet an income qualification, because the program is designed to encourage low- and moderate-income families to purchase homes. The income qualifications vary from state to state and county to county, and even within counties, as targeted and untargeted areas for the program.

In addition, the amount of the tax credit is subject to certain limits. If the MCC allows the taxpayer a credit in excess of 20 percent of his or her mortgage interest, the credit is limited to a maximum of $2,000. Furthermore, the credit may not exceed the taxpayer's regular tax liability, less other credits.

If a taxpayer sells a principal residence for which she or he used the tax credit benefit before possessing the home for more than nine years, some or all of the credit may have to be repaid.

Insurance

Property owners also may have to pay for a number of types of insurance to get a loan, the most common of which is hazard insurance. Hazard insurance, also called homeowners insurance, protects owners against losses from fire or severe weather (such as hail). The insurance rate will be dependent on the material from which the house was constructed; for example, insurance will be lower for masonry and brick homes than it is for frame and stucco ones.

If the owner lives on a floodplain or near a fault line, the lender also may require that the owner have flood or earthquake insurance policies. Flood insurance can be purchased only from the National Flood Insurance Program (NFIP). To receive this insurance, the property must be located in a floodplain and in a community that participates in the NFIP.

More About: To find out more about this insurance, visit the NFIP Web site: http://www.fema.gov/hazard/flood/info.shtm.

Some loans have insurance as well. The types of mortgage insurance available and required will be discussed in the coming lessons as they become relevant.

Prepayment

A borrower can lessen the term of his or her loan by making principal payments before they are due. This saves money because, provided that the monthly payments are enough to cover the interest on the loan, any prepayment goes directly toward reducing the principal balance. For this reason, some notes carry prepayment penalties to help lenders recover lost interest. Lenders also have recourse to prepayment and lock-in clauses. A prepayment clause limits the amount of the principal that can be paid annually; a lock-in clause, on the other hand, requires that the payments be no more or less than as established in the note. Notes can have all three: a lock-in clause, a prepayment clause, and penalties.

Discount Points

Discount points are percentages of the loan amount that the lender charges to lower the lending rate. One discount point is equal to one percent of the loan. Lenders will offer these points when the net present value of the future cash flows from interest is less than the value of the discount (see the section on valuation, below). Lenders also are motivated by the greater security discounts offer: If the interest is paid up front (in the form of a discount), it cannot be lost through borrower default.

A borrower who takes out a loan must determine the opportunity cost for the discount and compare it with the interest savings over time. This involves estimating how many years the borrower plans to keep the loan. For example, suppose a borrower can reduce his monthly payment by $11 by paying one discount point of $1,200. In order to see any savings, the borrower would have to keep the loan for $1,200 ÷ $11/mo. = 109 months. If the borrower plans to prepay any loan amount, the number of months would be increased. A borrower should buy a discount only if he or she plans to keep the loan long enough to save money.

Because discount points lower the interest rate, they are treated as prepaid interest for tax purposes and are partly deductible. They are not, however, fully deductible in the year of payment unless ALL of the following apply:

- The taxpayer's principal residence secures the loan on which the points were paid, and the loan is used to buy or build that residence.

- The points paid were customary in the area.

- The points weren't paid in lieu of other customary fees.

- The taxpayer's cash investment in the property at closing is at least as much as the amount of the points.

- The points were determined as a percentage of the loan amount.

- The amount of the points is stated on the settlement statement as a discount.

If these conditions are not met, the borrower must spread the deduction over the life of the loan. However, if the borrower accelerates payment, reducing the loan's life, she or he can deduct the remaining point balance in the year that the mortgage is repaid completely.

Promissory Notes

The promissory note is the common document for all loans, not just the ones commonly referred to as mortgages. It is an agreement between the obligor, maker, or payor (borrower) and the obligee or payee (lender), and it is the written agreement of the borrower's personal promise to repay the lender. In the note, the borrower acknowledges the debt, and the agreement provides for all of the terms of repayment.

The promissory note begins with an acknowledgment of the borrower's debt to the lender and the borrower's promise to repay the debt, either to the lender named in the note or to anyone who later holds the note.

The note is a negotiable instrument that can be sold to another investor or lender. It specifies the amount of the debt, the rate of interest and date on which interest charges are to begin, and the amount and terms of repayment. It is the complete contract or agreement of the loan terms between the borrower and the lender.

Secured vs. Unsecured notes

Promissory notes can be secured or unsecured. A *secured note* refers to a mortgage that pledges rights (a lien or title, depending on state law) against a property as security for the debt. An *unsecured note* has no collateral pledged for the loan and is a promise backed only by the signature of the borrower. This is often referred to as a *signature loan*. The note will, when applicable, refer to the mortgage or deed of trust that is security for it.

A mortgage is a document that creates a lien, a claim that the mortgage holder has on the property. A deed of trust is a document that actually conveys title to the property to a trustee, who holds the title until the debt has been cleared. If it is secured by a mortgage or deed of trust in favor of the lender, that document also will refer to the note for which it is security. Without mention of security, the note is an unsecured loan. Either type of note will provide for the signature of the borrower, who is required to sign the note to agree he or she owes the money. It is not required for the lender to sign the note, as notes are transferable.

What most people commonly refer to as a mortgage loan actually includes two documents: a mortgage and a promissory note. The mortgage is a document in which the borrower, known as the mortgagor, gives a lien against or title to her or his real estate as collateral for the loan to the lender, also known as the mortgagee. Whether it gives a lien against the property or actually transfers the title until the loan is repaid depends on state law. In Texas, a lien theory state, the borrower retains the title. The mortgage document makes reference to the promissory note that it secures.

Default

Usually included in a promissory note is an acceleration clause. It gives the lender the right upon any default by the borrower to make the entire balance plus accrued interest immediately due and payable. This clause is important because it gives the lender the right to foreclose on the property if the entire loan balance is not then paid. Without this clause, the lender would have to sue for each individual late payment. The acceleration clause allows the lender to make the remaining balance due and payable immediately after the borrower is declared in default and given required notice. The lender can then sue to foreclose on the whole amount.

Although nonpayment is the most common form of default, there are other reasons that could cause default and the execution of the acceleration clause. The borrower's failure to comply with any terms of the loan agreement, such as the requirement to pay taxes or insurance or failure to maintain the condition of the property also could be considered a default.

Lien Theory and Title Theory

States are divided into two classes, depending on their legal treatment of mortgages: lien theory states and title theory states.

Lien Theory
A lien, in legal terms, is a type of encumbrance. An encumbrance is any right or ownership share (called an interest) that someone who doesn't own the property, such as a lender, holds. Liens are encumbrances created by debts, such as a mortgage loan or unpaid taxes. In a lien theory state such as Texas, borrowers retain the legal rights of ownership in a property, and lenders have what are called equitable rights in the property, which are certain rights that are superseded by the borrower's legal ownership rights. Thus the borrower retains ownership of, and title to, the property, even in default, until the property is foreclosed. In states that have statutory periods of redemption, the borrower may retain these rights even after foreclosure. Texas is a lien theory state.

Title Theory

In a title theory state, the mortgage document conveys legal title to the property to the lender. The lender retains the legal rights, and the borrower retains certain equitable rights to the property. Lenders are still bound to uphold the statutory period of redemption, if applicable.

Assumption

Sometimes it is to a borrower's advantage to assume an existing loan rather than to take out a new loan for a property. For example, the interest rate or other terms of the note may be more favorable than the current market dictates. When the purchaser assumes a loan, he or she becomes personally responsible for repayment, along with the original borrower and any previous assumers.

Most assumable mortgages have a clause that requires the prior written consent of the lender in order for an assumption to occur; other mortgages have a due-on-sale clause. This clause provides that any transfer of the collateral property's ownership is subject to the lender's discretion and, if the lender chooses not to approve such a transfer, the entire loan balance becomes due immediately. This forces the seller to bring a request to the lender for the assumption, which in turn allows the lender to negotiate new terms with the assumer or to deny the assumption.

A buyer can also purchase the property *subject to any encumbrances*, as an alternative to assuming the loan. Here, the buyer would not be personally responsible for the repayment of the loan, and the lender could not sue her or him in the event of default. The drawback to purchasing a property with a lien on it and not also assuming the responsibility of repaying the debt is that the property could be foreclosed through no fault of the owner and may even come as a complete surprise.

Case Study: Monthly Payment

Suppose a borrower takes out a mortgage with the following specifics:

Sale price: $50,000	Annual Tax Liability: $1,500
Down Payment: 10%	Annual Insurance: $300
Annual Interest Rate: 7.5%	Mortgage Interest Credit: 10%
Loan Term: 30 years	

How much is the borrower's monthly payment for the first year?

First, we must calculate the monthly principal and interest payment. The original principal balance will be:

$50,000 Principal − 0.10($50,000) Down Payment = $45,000

And the monthly interest rate (J) will be:

0.075 Interest Rate ÷ 12 Months = 0.00625

With these figures we can calculate the monthly payment, M:

$M = (P \times J) \div (1 - (1 + J)^{-n})$
$M = (\$45,000 \times 0.00625) \div (1 - (1 + 0.00625)^{-360})$
$M = \$314.65$

Now we must calculate the escrowed taxes and insurance.

His total tax and insurance liabilities are:

$300 Insurance + $1,500 Tax = $1,800

The monthly escrow payment is one-twelfth of this, or $150. Therefore, the borrower's total monthly payment is:

$314.65 Principal and Interest + $150 Tax and Insurance Escrow = $464.65

Summary

Most real estate is bought with borrowed money. The instruments of real estate finance are the promissory note, the mortgage and the deed of trust. In a promissory note, the borrower acknowledges his or her debt and agrees to repay it. These notes are often secured by a mortgage, which creates a lien on the property that the loan is used to purchase, or a deed of trust, which conveys the property's temporary, not full, title to a third party until the debt has been repaid. Most notes have an acceleration clause, providing that the entire loan amount becomes due immediately in the event of default.

The real estate market is driven by interest rates. Interest is the rent paid on money. When lots of money is available, interest rates are low; when little money is available, interest rates are high. Low interest rates cause rising property values and high rates cause falling values. Institutions such as commercial banks, credit unions, and mortgage bankers lend money to both individuals and companies for real estate purchases in exchange for the profit they make from interest. These institutions replenish their funds by selling the mortgage loans on the secondary market.

The largest buyers on the secondary market are two private companies, the Federal National Mortgage Association (FNMA or Fannie Mae) and the Federal Home Loan Mortgage Company (FHLMC or Freddie Mac), and one government company, the Government National Mortgage Association (GNMA or Ginnie Mae). Some loans purchased by these companies are pooled to provide collateral for securities they issue, known as mortgage-backed securities (MBSs).

Real estate loans are paid off slowly over time, or amortized. The basis of the monthly payment is the principal and interest payment, which can be calculated mathematically, or with a financial calculator. An amortization schedule is a chart that shows the payments for the term of the loan and what amount goes toward principal and toward interest. Mortgage interest payments are tax-deductible and, for buyers who have a mortgage credit certificate (MCC), provide borrowers with a tax credit.

Not all loans have fixed monthly payments throughout the term of the loan, and sometimes payments are not enough to cover the interest charge. In such cases negative amortization (an increase in the loan balance) occurs. Borrowers may also desire to pay off their loans early. Some notes restrict prepayment-through the use of prepayment penalties, prepayment clauses and lock-in clauses-in order to protect the lender's investment (that is, his or her profit from interest).

The taxes and insurance due are collected in a monthly payment by the lender in an escrow account. The escrow then disburses the payments when they become due. The Real Estate Settlement Procedures Act (RESPA) provides certain restrictions on these accounts. Taxes paid on real estate are tax-deductible.

A discount point is one percent of the loan amount. Lenders charge discounts to lower the interest rate. Before deciding whether to buy discount points, the borrower must determine the savings by considering how long she or he plans to keep the property and whether he or she plans to prepay a portion of the loan. Discount points, like mortgage interest, are deductible over the life of the loan.

States can be categorized by their treatment of ownership rights as they pertain to lender/borrower relationships. In lien theory states, the borrower retains the rights of ownership and the lender has certain equitable rights. In title theory states, the reverse is true: The lender holds the title and ownership rights to the property, whereas the borrower has an equitable interest in the property.

Assumption is when the purchaser of a property assumes responsibility for the repayment of an existing loan. Lenders limit assumptions by requiring approval of all assumptions or by adding a due-on-sale clause to the note.

A buyer may also buy a property and not assume the existing loan. In such a case, the buyer is said to purchase the property subject to any encumbrances and is not responsible for the existing loan's repayment.

This concludes lesson one.

Return to your online course player to take the Lesson Quiz.

Lesson 2:
THE EFFECT OF THE MARKET AND THE GOVERNMENT ON REAL ESTATE FINANCE

This lesson focuses on the following topics:

- Introduction
- Supply and Demand of Housing
- Inflation
- The Federal Reserve
- Taxes
- The Department of Housing and Urban Development
- Texas Department of Housing and Community Affairs
- Real Estate Investment Trusts
- Activity: Critical Thinking
- Case Study
- Summary

By the end of this lesson, you should be able to:

- Explain how the forces of supply and demand in the real estate market affect, and are affected, by the primary lending market, identifying them in case studies
- Explain the economic theory of inflation, and define how this theory can influence the real estate market
- Demonstrate how the government influences real estate finance through agencies such as the Federal Reserve (the Fed) and the Department of Housing and Urban Development (HUD), and be able to cite examples
- Identify the four main roles of the Federal Reserve
- Describe the primary provisions of the Community Reinvestment Act
- Describe the structure and the mission of the Texas Department of Housing and Community Affairs
- Demonstrate how the government can influence the real estate market through taxation policy, distinguishing between tax exemptions, tax deductions, and tax credits
- Define real estate investment trusts (REITs), identifying three types and describing them in detail

Introduction

Real estate finance is constantly in a state of flux, and there are several factors that cause this. First among them is the real estate market: the supply of and demand for real property. The real estate market affects, and is affected by, the primary lending market, the basic subject of this course. This primary market is in turn affected by the secondary lending market.

In addition to market influences, the government plays a large role in shaping real estate financing. Two particular government agencies, the Federal Reserve, which is in charge of the nation's monetary policy, and the Department of Housing and Urban Development, which is responsible for the nation's housing policy, have the most significant roles.

For anyone interested in real estate finance, it is imperative to understand the economic indicators and market characteristics of the residential real estate market. Some such indicators:

- Supply and demand of housing
- Mortgage rates
- Other indicators influencing the market
- The monetary system

Supply and Demand of Housing

Supply and demand are the basic forces that control markets. A market is a theoretical construct that isolates the selling and purchasing of any one particular commodity from the economy as a whole. For instance, the sale of residential property constitutes a specific real estate market, and the sale of loan products by lenders constitutes another. For real estate finance, more than for any other type of real estate studies, it is necessary to know the basic workings of the market and, most especially, the impact of supply and demand on it.

Demand

The demand for real estate is affected by several factors. Price is the clearest example. When real estate costs more, fewer people are willing to buy. The price of a particular piece of real estate is influenced by many things. Some examples:

- An increase in construction costs
- An increase in the cost of financing
- An increase in property taxes

Additionally, the price of purchasing real estate can be affected by the prices of other commodities. For instance, if the cost of leasing an apartment is low, the cost of purchasing a house might decrease to attract more buyers.

The second factor affecting real estate demand is personal income. If the average salary goes down, or the unemployment rate goes up, the demand for certain types of housing is likely to decrease.

Finally, a buyer's expectations of the future state of himself or herself, and of the economy as a whole, will affect the demand for real estate. If buyers expect that their income will decrease in the near future; if they expect that the price of housing will decrease in the near future; or, if they expect that the price of housing will decrease at the time they expect to sell their house, then they may be less likely to buy.

The market demand for a commodity is often represented graphically by economists. In the graph below, the demand curve for real estate is shown. As price increases (vertically), the quantity of real estate buyers are willing to purchase (horizontally) decreases; as price decreases, the quantity increases. Each point on the curve represents a possible state of the current market: for example, at an average price of $100,000, buyers in this market are willing to purchase 15,000 properties.

Demand Curve

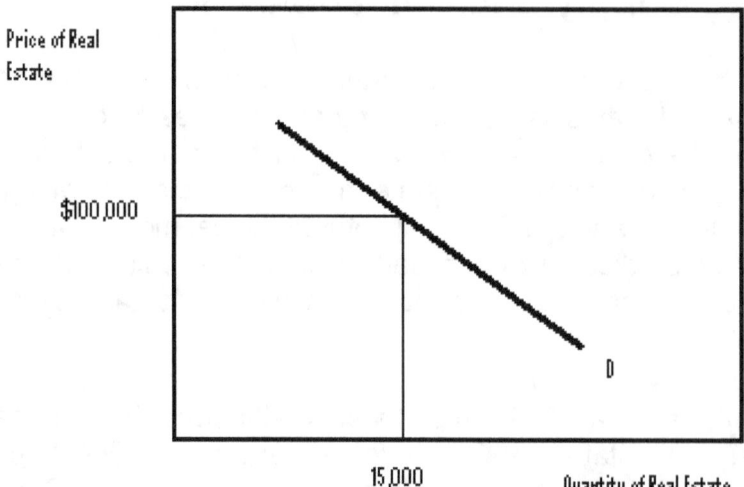

THE DEMAND CURVE FOR REAL ESTATE

Supply
Supply is an economic term meaning the willingness and ability of sellers in a given market to sell their property. Several factors affect supply. First among these is the selling price: As the price of housing increases, owners become

more willing to sell. Similarly, as the price of a loan increases-that is, as the interest rate goes up-lenders become more willing to lend (but buyers become less willing to take loans because of the higher interest rate).

To some extent, price does not play as important a role in real estate as it does in other types of commodities. For example, apartment complex managers are not more willing to rent when the price of apartments increases than when it decreases because to not rent is to not receive income-although they may be more desirous to offer long-term leases.

The supply of real estate also is affected by the cost of its production. If construction costs go down, it is cheaper to build houses, apartments, and office buildings, so more appear on the market. If, on the other hand, the cost of construction goes up, the greater expense to builders makes new housing scarcer. An increase or decrease in the price of raw land has a similar effect. However, because real estate is a long-lasting commodity, there is usually an existing supply of houses that have already been built on the market.

Finally, expectations affect supply as much as demand. If sellers expect the price of real estate to go up in the near future, they will be less likely to sell right now; and if sellers expect the price to go down soon, they will be more likely to sell now. The case is similar for lenders as the interest rate is expected to increase or decrease. However, lenders are much like apartment managers. They cannot afford to not receive interest for any significant period of time.

As with demand, supply may be represented graphically as a function of price. As you can see, supply increases when price increases and supply decreases when price decreases. On this supply curve we can see that, at an average price of $100,000, the sellers are willing and able to supply 25,000 properties in this particular market.

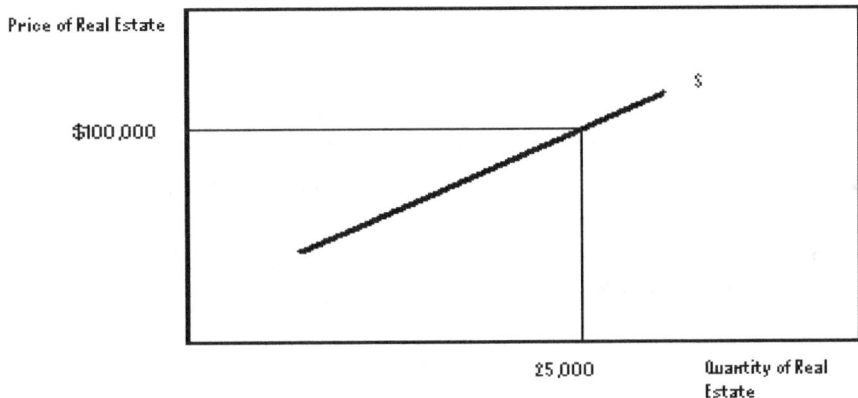

SUPPLY CURVE FOR REAL ESTATE

Supply And Demand

The two forces of supply and demand together help to determine the actual price and quantity of real estate on the market. The law of supply and demand states that the forces of supply and demand push the market price of any commodity to one particular point, the market equilibrium. This equilibrium is the point at which the supply and demand curves cross.

The graph below combines our supply curve S with our demand curve D to determine the market equilibrium. In this case, the equilibrium is a price of $95,000, at which buyers are willing to buy 20,000 properties. This means that if the average market price exceeds $95,000, sellers will have properties that they are unable to sell; and if the market price falls below $95,000, there will be more people who want houses than there are houses to be purchased.

Supply and Demand

MARKET EQUILIBRIUM OF SUPPLY AND DEMAND

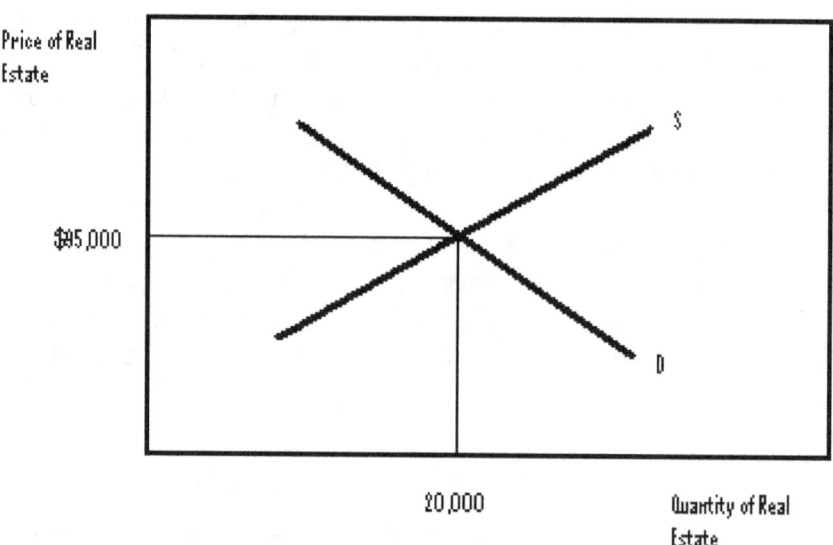

The supply curve and the demand curve for any particular commodity are independent of each other; however, they are not independent of the curves for other commodities. For instance, because most real estate is purchased with borrowed money, the supply of loans affects the demand for real estate. The supply of loans is in turn affected by the supply of money and the interest rate. This will be important to know when we come to discuss the Federal Reserve's monetary policies and their effect on the real estate market.

In short, one very important factor affecting the supply and demand of housing is the supply of money. In general:

- The higher the supply of money available to finance real estate ventures, the higher the demand for housing.

- When the demand for housing becomes higher than the supply, property price increases.

- The lower the supply of money available to finance real estate ventures, the lower the demand for housing.

- When the supply becomes higher than the demand, property price decreases.

This, in effect, is the real estate cycle, which repeats itself according to the conditions of supply and demand. Therefore, any person associated with the buying and/or selling of real estate should know the current economic cycle.

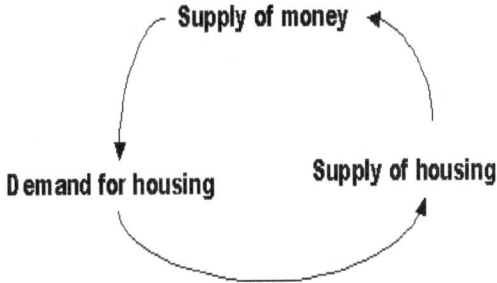

Mortgage Rates

Mortgage rates reflect the cost to a homebuyer of borrowing money for the purchase or refinance of a home. Mortgage rates are generally the interest rate that a lender would charge to lend money to a borrower.

The chart below shows the values for the 30-year fixed rate mortgage (FRM) and the one-year adjustable rate mortgage (ARM).

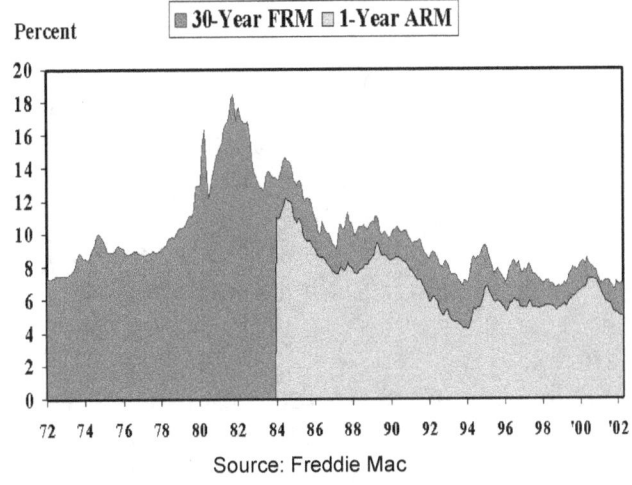

Source: Freddie Mac

Other Indicators Influencing the Market

The ability for people to afford a home drives demand. A Housing Affordability Index greater than 100 means that the median-income family could qualify for more than the median-priced home with an 80 percent loan. If the Housing Affordability Index is below 100, then the same median income cannot qualify to buy the median-priced home, which is normally the case during times of inflation and high interest rates.

Characteristics of the population, the social attitudes prevalent at the time, and the legal and tax structure of the economy also shape real estate expenditure.

Inflation

Inflation is a general rise in prices; it results in a decrease of the dollar's purchasing power. That is, because of inflation, what $1 could buy back in 1900 now takes many, many more dollars today. Inflation is a normal part of the operation of a free market and there are many indexes used today to measure it, such as the Consumer Price Index (CPI) and the Producer Price Indexes (PPI). It is important for those involved in real estate finance to be able to accurately predict rising or falling inflation, especially if it occurs at a quicker than average rate.

It is important to note that Inflation is very much influenced by some governmental actions such as increasing the money supply. For example, if the money supply only increases when added goods and services are produced, then inflation stays down.

Inflation Predictors

Economists, market analysts, and investors are highly concerned with predicting inflation. Unfortunately, it is one of the most difficult aspects of the economy to predict accurately, and there are several indicators, all of which are imperfect, that can be considered.

P*

One reliable predictor of inflation is known as P*. It is published by the Federal Reserve Board (the Fed) and is equal to the quotient of long-run aggregate demand and the Fed's estimate of potential domestic output. Thus, P* is the projected price level that should exist, given the accuracy of the variables. If P* is greater than the current price level P, inflation is expected; if P* = P, no inflation is expected; and if P* is less than P, deflation is expected.

The Exchange Rate

The exchange rate is the amount of a foreign currency that a dollar can buy. For example, if $1 can buy 11 Mexican pesos, then the exchange rate is 11 pesos on the dollar. When one currency buys less foreign currency than before, it is said to be depreciating. Depreciation of the dollar is a good indicator of a high inflation risk.

GDP
Strong economic growth can also indicate future inflation. Growth, measured by the gross domestic product or GDP, is often accompanied by an increase in aggregate demand. Greater demand leads to rising prices, that is, to inflation. One-year GDP growth is a more reliable predictor of inflation in the United States than it is in many other countries and can be monitored to an investor's benefit.

Unemployment
Falling unemployment often accompanies economic growth as well. When more people have jobs, there is more disposable income in circulation, thus greater demand and higher prices. Economists use a function called the Phillips curve, which states that high unemployment is correlated with deflationary pressures, and low unemployment with inflationary pressures. The point along the curve at which there is no pressure for either inflation or deflation is known as the NAIRU or non-accelerating inflation rate of unemployment.

The Effect of Inflation on Real Estate Investments
Real estate is recognized by most investors as a good hedge against inflation. That is, real estate investments are less likely than many other investments to suffer the ills of rising inflation. But it is not immune to such ills. During periods of high inflation, investors may rush to real estate to hedge against inflation and end up causing higher real estate prices through excessive demand.

An asset manager can benefit from accurate inflation prediction. For example, lower vacancy rates are to be expected during periods of high inflation.

In certain situations, inflation can be a predictor of a property's future value.

Inflation and Interest
High inflation also can be damaging to the real estate market. When inflation is low, interest rates are usually low as well. The opposite is also true: High inflation and high interest rates go hand-in-hand. Investors may desire to purchase real estate to hedge against high inflation, only to be deterred by the interest rates necessary to make a purchase. This can, however, be an advantage if the current owner holds an assumable loan at a rate lower than the market rate. An investor may be enticed to buy the property at a level much higher than market value in order to assume the favorable loan and hedge against inflation.

The Federal Reserve

In 1913, the Federal Reserve Act created the Federal Reserve, which acts as the central bank of the United States. The purpose of the bank is fourfold:

- Conduct the monetary policy of the United States
- Supervise and regulate financial institutions for the protection of the consumer
- Maintain the financial system's stability
- Provide services to the government, to financial institutions and to the public

More About: To visit the Federal Reserve's Web site, go to http://www.federalreserve.gov.

Organization

The Federal Reserve System (the Fed) is composed of 12 member banks across the United States, each serving a different geographical area. Visit the link below to see the system's districts and the locations of each of the Fed's banks. The president nominates seven people to serve on the Board of Governors for 14-year terms, and the Senate confirms the president's nominations. Additionally, the president appoints a chairman and vice chairman of the board from the seven nominees. The current Fed chairman is Ben Bernanke.

More About: To see the Federal Reserve Districts, go to www.federalreserve.gov/generalinfo/faq/faqfrbanks.htm#3.

The job of the Board of Governors is to set the discount rate and the reserve requirement for member banks (see below). Additionally, the board forms a proper part of the 12-member Federal Open Market Committee (FOMC). The remaining five members of the FOMC are appointed from the 12 Federal Reserve banks. The FOMC is in charge of the Fed's open-market operations, such as the purchase and sale of government securities.

Any bank may become a member of the Federal Reserve System, and all national banks are required to become members. By becoming a member of the system, a bank has the benefit of borrowing money from the Fed. In exchange for this benefit, member banks must abide by the Fed's regulations and requirements.

The Fed's Supervisory Role

The Fed's purpose is to implement and enforce the Federal Reserve Act (Federal Regulations, Title 12, Chapter II). The regulations that comprise this act are as follows:

A. Extensions of Credit by Federal Reserve Banks

B. Equal Credit Opportunity Act

C. Home Mortgage Disclosure Act

D. Reserve Requirements of Depository Institutions

E. Electronic Funds Transfers

F. Limitations on Interbank Liabilities

G. Disclosure and Reporting of CRA-Related Agreements

H. Membership of State Banking Institutions in the Federal Reserve System

I. Issue and Cancellation of Federal Reserve Bank Capital Stock

J. Collection of Checks and Other Items by Federal Reserve Banks and Funds Transfers through Fedwire

K. International Banking Operations

L. Management Official Interlocks

M. Consumer Leasing (comprises Truth-in-Lending Act with Regulation Z)

N. Relations with Foreign Banks and Bankers

O. Loans to Executive Officers, Directors, and Principal Shareholders of Member Banks

P. Privacy of Consumer Financial Information

Q. Prohibition against Payment of Interest on Demand Deposits

S. Reimbursement to Financial Institutions for Providing Financial Records; Recordkeeping Requirements for Certain Financial Records

T. Credit by Brokers and Dealers

U. Credit by Banks and Persons Other Than Brokers or Dealers for the Purpose of Purchasing or Carrying Margin Stocks

V. Fair Credit Reporting Act

W. Transactions between Member Banks and Their Affiliates

X. Borrowers and Securities Credit

Y. Bank Holding Companies and Change in Bank Control

Z. Truth-in-Lending Act

AA. Unfair or Deceptive Acts or Practices

BB. Community Reinvestment

CC. Availability of Funds and Collection of Checks

DD. Truth in Savings

EE. Netting Eligibility for Financial Institutions

Only five of these regulations-B, the Equal Credit Opportunity Act; C, the Home Mortgage Disclosure Act; V, the Fair Credit Reporting Act; and M and Z, the Truth-in-Lending Act-are of concern to our purpose in this module, and because these regulations involve the disclosure and fairness policies of lenders rather than the market, they will be discussed at their proper places in later lessons.

Monetary Policy and the Money Supply

The Fed has at its disposal three tools for implementing its monetary policy by influencing the money supply: the discount rate, the reserve requirement, and its open-market operations.

The Discount Rate

The discount rate is the interest rate at which the Fed lends money to its member banks. When a member bank in sound financial condition requires a short-term loan, the Fed will advance it the funds at what is known as the primary credit rate, the most important of the Fed's discount rates and the one often referred to as the discount rate. This rate is typically set slightly above the short-term market interest rate.

The Fed can influence the market by raising or lowering the discount rate. When the discount is raised, banks that must borrow money end up paying more for it. This makes financial institutions less willing to lend, as it costs them more money. In terms of the economic forces discussed above, a higher discount rate lowers the supply of loans by increasing the cost lenders pay to issue them. The shift in the supply curve may be represented graphically:

Decrease in Supply

SHIFT IN THE SUPPLY CURVE FOR LOANS

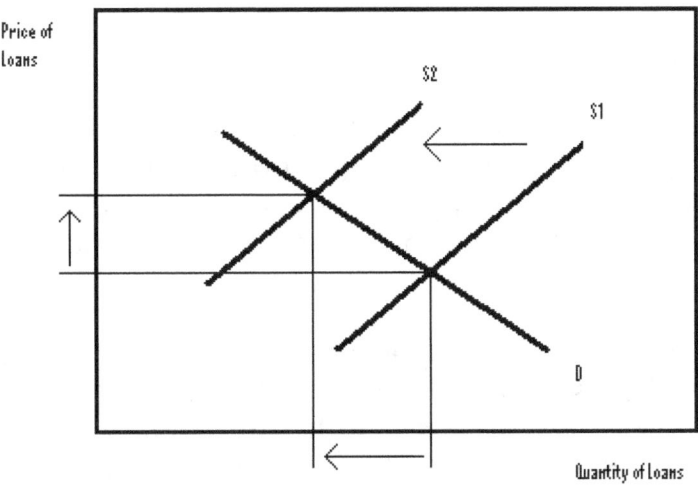

As you can see, when the supply curve decreases (that is, moves to the left from S1 to S2), the equilibrium moves up and to the left, meaning an increase in the price of loans and a decrease in the quantity of loans demanded. The increase in the price of loans is reflected in the higher rate that lenders charge borrowers because of the discount.

What affect does this have on the sale of real estate? We may once again turn to our supply and demand curves. The greater the cost of loans makes the purchase of real estate less attractive to buyers, thereby shifting the demand curve, as we may see below:

Decrease in Demand

A SHIFT IN THE DEMAND CURVE FOR REAL ESTATE

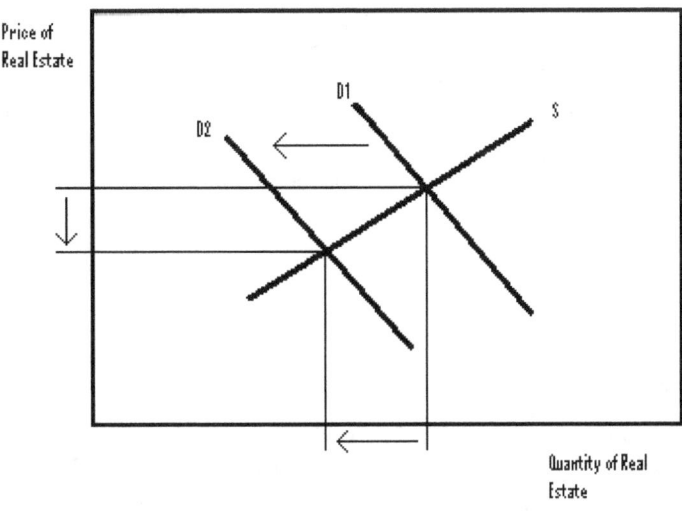

As you can see, a decrease in demand (D1 to D2) leads to a decrease in both the price of real estate and the number of properties sold. It is amazing to think that something so small as the Fed raising or lowering the discount rate a quarter of a point can dramatically affect the number of houses sold.

The Reserve Requirement
The reserve requirement is another method the Fed has of influencing the market. The Fed has the authority to require all depository institutions (not just member banks) to keep a certain percentage of their funds in the regional Reserve bank. Currently, the Fed may require an institution to reserve at most 0 percent of its first $2 million, 3 percent of the first $25 million after that and 10 percent of all other funds.

The adjustment of the reserve requirement has a similar effect on the economy as the adjustment of the discount rate, except it more directly affects the supply of loans. When the reserve requirement is high, banks literally have less money to lend. This shifts the demand curve for real estate, causing prices to drop and sales to fall off.

Similarly, when the requirement is low, banks have more money to lend, causing the demand for real estate to increase, raising prices and increasing the number of sales, as illustrated in the graph below:

Increase in Demand

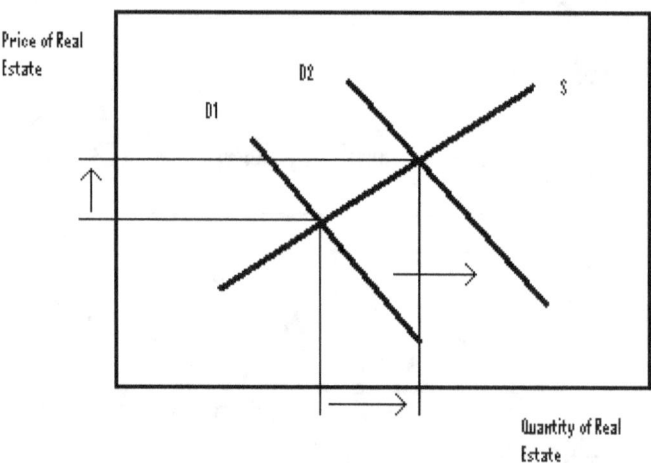

AN INCREASE IN THE DEMAND FOR REAL ESTATE

Open Market Operations
As stated previously, it is the Federal Open Market Committee (FOMC) that is in charge of the Fed's principal tool-its open-market operations. These operations consist of buying government securities, either from the U.S. Treasury or from

other federal agencies, and selling them. A security is a debt instrument, such as a mortgage loan, that is held as evidence of a debt to be repaid with interest. The U.S. Treasury sells securities when it needs to acquire funds to finance government activities or to repay other securities. Most of the Fed's securities holdings are issued by the U.S. Treasury: About half of them are Treasury bills (T-bills), and the other half are Treasury notes and bonds.

The Fed typically has one of two goals in mind when buying and selling securities: either to reach a targeted amount of reserve balances held at the Reserve or to reach a targeted federal funds rate. In connection with the reserve requirement, it was mentioned that banks have accounts with the Fed in which they keep their required reserves. These banks may also keep more than the required amount in their accounts. Excesses of the required reserves may be lent out to banks, usually for just one night, whose reserves may not meet the requirement. The lending rate between banks at the Federal Reserve is known as the federal funds rate.

The specific ways the Fed goes about reaching its goals through open market operations can be complex. For our purposes, it suffices to observe that when the Fed buys securities from the securities market, it increases the money supply by putting more money into the hands of consumers, and when the Fed sells securities, it decreases the money supply by collecting more money in exchange for the debt instruments.

Taxes

The government also influences the market by imposing taxes on consumers. Taxes raise the price of goods, and, therefore decrease the quantity consumers are willing to buy. The government may also increase the quantity demanded of a good or service by granting tax incentives. The same is true for supply. Taxes on builders or lenders will decrease the amount of real estate or loans that are available, and tax incentives will increase this amount.

Tax incentives include tax exemptions, tax deductions, and tax credits. A tax exemption is a dollar-by-dollar reduction in the appraisal value of a property. For example, if a property owner has a $15,000 exemption and that owner's property is appraised at $100,000, then she or he will pay ad valorem taxes as though the house were appraised at $85,000. Tax exemptions vary by state both in amount and qualifications, but some of the most common include the following:

Homestead exemption
A property that is occupied by its owner as a permanent residence is considered a homestead. Most states provide some sort of homestead exemption, either to a husband and wife or to a single person. For instance, the exemption in Florida,

as of this writing was $25,000, and in Texas it was $15,000 for school taxes, which may be supplemented by exemptions from other taxing authorities.

Disability exemption
People with disabilities may receive a property tax exemption in certain states. This exemption is sometimes augmented for those whose disability is related to military service.

Senior citizen exemption
Additionally, several states provide exemptions for senior citizens. Each state determines for itself the age at which a person is to be considered a senior citizen. Usually it is somewhere between 63 and 66. Texas offers a $10,000 senior citizen exemption in addition to the homestead exemption for residents who are 65 or older on January 1.

Tax incentives also include deductions and credits. Tax deductions are reductions in a taxpayer's taxable income, which in turn lower the amount of that taxpayer's tax liabilities (that is, his or her taxes owed). Tax credits, on the other hand, are immediate, dollar-for-dollar reductions in a taxpayer's tax liabilities. For example, if a taxpayer owes $100 in taxes and claims a $25 tax credit for the same tax year, then she or he owes only $75 in taxes.

Common tax-deductible expenses associated with real estate purchase and ownership include mortgage interest, real estate taxes, discount points paid at closing, and loan origination fees. In addition, married couples who sell their principal residences are exempt from the capital gains tax up to $500,000, and homeowners who are single are exempt up to $250,000 (Both are examples of a tax-free gain on the sale of a house).

Consider the following example: A taxpayer and homeowner sells her principal residence, realizing $40,000 in capital gains. If she makes $38,000 a year and paid $1,000 in mortgage interest in the year of sale, what is her taxable income?

To solve this problem we simply subtract the taxpayer's exemptions from her income:

$38,000 Gross Income
+$40,000 Capital Gains Income
−$40,000 Capital Gains Exemption
−$1,000 Mortgage Interest Exemption
$37,000 Taxable Income

The Department of Housing and Urban Development

The Department of Housing and Urban Development (HUD) is a government agency whose mission is "to increase homeownership, support community development, and increase access to affordable housing free from discrimination." HUD was created in 1937 by the U.S. Housing Act and became part of the president's Cabinet in 1965. The secretary of Housing and Urban Development is in charge of implementing HUD's policies.

HUD has many duties, one of which is the enforcement of the Fair Housing Act (Title VIII of the Civil Rights Act of 1968) and the Real Estate Settlement Procedures Act (RESPA). To this purpose, HUD has a staff of administrative law judges to oversee cases it prosecutes involving violations of these acts. HUD has the authority to seek damages and levy fines, the limits to which are set by Congress. It keeps a limited denial of participation (LDP) list of parties that have been suspended, disqualified, or otherwise excluded from HUD programs.

HUD also plays a role in real estate through the Federal Housing Administration (FHA) and the Government National Mortgage Association (GNMA or Ginnie Mae).

Community Reinvestment Act

Closely related to HUD in function is another governmental program, the Community Reinvestment Act (CRA). The CRA was enacted by the Congress in 1977 with the goal of encouraging depository institutions to help improve the communities in which they operate, including low- and moderate-income neighborhoods by making loans to meet the credit needs to grow healthy communities.

The CRA requires that each government-insured depository institution act in good faith to meet the credit needs of its entire community. The good faith of the institutions covered under the CRA is evaluated periodically by federal agencies responsible for regulating financial institutions. The CRA requires that lenders submit an annual statement including public comments about their attempts to help low-income communities. An institution's past performance of helping its community is taken into account in considering an institution's application for new banks, including mergers and acquisitions.

Some lending institutions limit the number of loans or the loan-to-value ratio in certain areas of a community or city. This is *redlining*. If an institution practices redlining because of an individual or group's membership in a protected class, then it violates both the federal Fair Housing Act and the Community Reinvestment Act.

The Federal Housing Administration

The FHA is the part of HUD that is charged with increasing homeownership and contributing to building healthy neighborhoods and communities. As part of this mission, the FHA insures private loans made to consumers. Many of the FHA's loan programs are targeted at promoting homeownership among traditionally disadvantaged classes, such as low- and moderate-income families and American Indians. The FHA will be discussed in more detail when we discuss the underwriting requirements for FHA-insured mortgages.

The Government National Mortgage Association

Another important duty of HUD is to supervise the Government National Mortgage Association (GNMA or Ginnie Mae). This agency issues loans for certain HUD programs and also issues government-guaranteed Mortgage-Backed Securities (MBSs) in the secondary mortgage market.

HUD also plays a role in other areas of the secondary market by overseeing the government sponsored enterprises: Fannie Mae and Freddie Mac. The secondary market and its effect on the primary real estate lending market will be discussed in greater depth in the next lesson.

Housing Finance Agencies

There are also state Housing Finance Agencies (HFAs), which are state-chartered entities that have the goal of "increasing housing opportunities for lower-income and underserved people through the financing, development, and preservation of affordable housing." They operate in every state, the District of Columbia, Puerto Rico, and the U.S. Virgin Islands. In Texas, the department that serves as an HFA is the Texas Department of Housing and Community Affairs.

Although they are different from state to state, they do have some commonalities. Most HFAs are independent and operate under the direction of a board of directors appointed by each state's governor. The state HFAs also coordinate and consolidate their power through the National Council of State Housing Agencies (NCSHA), which they created in 1974 to better lobby the federal government. NCSHA members comprise not only the HFAs, but also more than 350 nonprofit and for-profit organizations.

Although state HFAs have their own state-run programs, they rely heavily on three federally authorized programs administered by NCSHA:

- Mortgage Revenue Bonds (MRB)

- The Low Income Housing Credit

- The HOME Investment Partnerships Program (HOME)

NCSHA also participates in Section 8 contract administration and restructuring, and federal housing assistance programs, including homeless assistance and the Community Development Block Grant program.

Texas Department of Housing and Community Affairs

The Texas Department of Housing and Community Affairs (TDHCA) states as its mission:

> *To help Texans achieve an improved quality of life through the development of better communities*

This means that TDHCA is concerned with housing and community development issues such as economic development, infrastructure for rural communities, and energy assistance. Manufactured housing is also a large part of TDHCA's purview. TDHCA not only provides a regulatory environment that protects the health, safety, and welfare of the occupants of manufactured housing, but the department also provides titling, licensing, and inspection.

TDHCA fulfills its mission by providing services such as low-interest mortgage financing, emergency food or shelter, rental subsidy, energy assistance, weatherization, economic development, and the provision of basic public infrastructure for small rural communities.

More About: The Texas Department of Housing and Community Affairs (TDHCA) Web site is http://www.tdhca.state.tx.us/index.htm

Real Estate Investment Trusts

A real estate investment trust (REIT) is a registered company that owns and operates commercial real estate. (Typically, these companies must meet special federal rules to get a pass-through tax status.) Investors can take advantage of the benefits of owning real estate, such as hedging against inflation, by buying and selling REITs. Deciding which REITs to purchase works much the same way as deciding how to maximize one's own cash flows. The investor must evaluate the market and examine the benefits and risks each company takes in its investments.

There are three types of REITs: equity REITs, mortgage REITs, and hybrid REITs, which are hybrids of the first two. Equity REITs hold income-producing properties, whereas mortgage REITs extend credit to the owners of real estate.

Benefits

Actual ownership of real estate has several drawbacks from an investment standpoint resulting from its physical immobility and the sizeable investment required for its purchase. An investor who puts a significant amount of money into an office building, for example, cannot liquidate the asset quickly without likely incurring a loss; moreover, she or he stands to lose a lot should a disaster befall that investment. Holding REITs eliminates some of the drawbacks to holding real estate. Because most REITs are traded on the stock market, they are easily liquidated, and because they have many diverse holdings, the investor whose portfolio includes REITs is not subject to the risk of having his or her money tied up in just a few properties.

The Price-to-Earnings Ratio

A common method of predicting the price of a stock is the *price-to-earnings ratio* (P/E). However, this method is less widely used as a predictor of the price of real estate investment trusts.

The P/E tells an investor how much dividend he or she will receive per dollar of stock purchased. For example, if a REIT is selling at $144 a share and its expected dividend for the next fiscal year is $12 per share, then the P/E is $144/$12 = 12. As of this writing, P/Es at or below 16 are generally considered to be low ratios; those above 16 are high. Low ratios indicate solid earnings in the near future, but usually belong to companies that are more established and less likely to expand in the long run. High P/E stocks are usually found in rapidly expanding sectors and may be indicative of fast growth and higher future yields. These latter are, of course, riskier in general.

Activity: Critical Thinking

Instructions: In the following activity, consider a question and select the better of two answer choices. Answers are provided in the end.

Question1
An increase in supply (that is, a shift in the supply curve to the right) has which of the following effects?

- When supply increases, both the market equilibrium price and the amount of goods that people are willing to buy at the equilibrium price increase.

- When supply increases, the market equilibrium price decreases and the amount of goods that people are willing to buy at the equilibrium price increases.

Answer

This is best seen, perhaps, with an example. Suppose that it is a particularly hot summer but there is only one lemonade stand on the block. Supply is relatively low, and people are willing to pay more than usual to buy lemonade. Now suppose that four more lemonade stands open up on the block. Supply is increased: Lemonade is easier to find and easier to obtain, so prices drop and more people drink it. Considered graphically, when the supply curve shifts to the right, the equilibrium point moves down and to the right. Movement down indicates a decrease in price; movement to the left indicates an increase in quantity.

Question2

If the Fed wanted to increase the federal funds rate (the rate at which banks lend money to one another at the Reserve), which of the following might it do on the open market?

- Sell U.S. Treasury Securities. By selling securities, the Fed makes less money available for lending, because investors' money is tied up in the securities. This increases market interest rates across the board, including the federal funds rate.

- Buy U.S. Treasury Securities. By buying securities, the Fed increases the money available for lending. This increases the demand for consumer loans, drawing money out of each bank's reserve account at the Fed. This in turn creates a greater demand for overnight loans at the Fed and causes an increase in the federal funds rate.

Answer

When the Fed wants to increase the federal funds rate or the reserve ratio, it will sell securities. This causes money to run in a shorter supply, interest rates to go up (including the federal funds rate) and bank reserves to increase.

Question3

If the property tax rate were lower than the income tax rate, which would be more beneficial to taxpayers: a $10,000 tax exemption for their property or a $10,000 tax deduction for their income?

- The $10,000 deduction. Because income is taxed at a greater rate, deducting $10,000 from their taxable income would allow taxpayers to save more than exempting the same amount from property taxes.

- The $10,000 exemption. Because the lower property tax rate would be applied to the exemption, taxpayers would be able to keep a greater amount.

Answer
Deductions and exemptions are applied before taxes are assessed. A taxpayer would want to exclude from taxes whatever asset-income or property-that was taxed at the higher rate. In this case, that's income.

Question4
If periods of high inflation increase the demand for real estate, why do property prices remain relatively stable during such times?

- During periods of high inflation, the demand for real estate increases, but the price of real estate is kept from going up by the increase in supply that goes along with it. Because real estate is so easy to construct, builders react quickly to the increase in demand and build more houses and other property; this keeps demand from exceeding supply and causing a price increase.

- During periods of high inflation, the demand for real estate increases, but this increase is mitigated by the increase in interest rates that comes along with rising inflation. Higher interest rates increase the cost of purchasing property, thereby deterring many buyers.

Answer
Inflation and interest rates are positively correlated, meaning that an increase in one is accompanied by an increase in the other and a decrease in one by a decrease in the other. Higher interest rates mean a higher cost for borrowing money. Because most real estate is purchased with borrowed money, this lessens the demand for real property. It takes a while for builders to respond to an increase in demand in real estate. In addition, since inflation is a general rise in prices, any new property constructed during a period of high inflation would cost more to build, and, therefore cost more to buy on the market.

Question5
Which of the following is a reason that an investor might consider adding real estate investment trusts (REITs) to her portfolio?

- The investor doesn't have much current capital but expects to receive a large loan for investment in REITs. She hopes to see a significant economic payoff for the greater risk of investing in REITs rather than in real property directly and hopes to receive an annual depreciation reduction for the REIT's holdings.

- The investor doesn't want the added risk of a single, large real property investment but desires the diversity of a REIT. She knows that these securities still act as a hedge against inflation and that she can liquidate a REIT quickly and easily when she sees a new investment opportunity.

Answer

REITs have many of the benefits of real estate, such as an ability to hedge against inflation, without many of the drawbacks, such as high risk and illiquidity. These are all reasons why an investor might consider adding REITs to her portfolio. REITs, like stocks, are governed by the Securities Act of 1933 and cannot be purchased with borrowed money.

Case Study

An investor is considering adding real estate investment trusts (REITs) to her portfolio. What market factors should she consider before buying?

Interest Rates

Do interest rates affect the prices of REITs in the same way that they affect the prices of, for example, residential real estate?

Interest rates affect REITs differently. When interest rates rise, the residential mortgage market contracts: Consumers are less willing to purchase real estate because of the greater cost of financing. This, however, increases the occupancy rate of apartment complexes and other rental real estate. Because REITs are companies that own commercial property, an increase in the occupancy rate means an increase in returns, and, therefore, greater dividends for REIT-holders.

This increase in the dividends of REITs subsequently decreases the price-to-earnings ratio. Remember that low P/Es indicate solid and stable earnings. However, a rise in interest rates often accompanies a fall in the prices of the P/E's of REITs. This is because REITs compete with stocks, bonds, other securities, and bank CDs. When interest rates rise, the interest returns on certain investment tools that pay interest-such as bonds and CDs-increase. This causes investors to sell their other holdings and purchase these investments.

Type of REIT

Of course, the holdings of each REIT differ. A REIT that principally holds apartment complexes or mortgages might receive higher returns during a period of gradually increasing interest rates. A REIT that principally holds malls and shopping centers might receive higher returns during a period of gradual inflation when a lot of money is being spent on retail goods. Hybrid REITs might be more versatile investments, but they often have less opportunity of seeing large returns. An investor should always be careful to take into consideration his or her expectations for the market before making any particular investment.

Summary

Supply and demand are the basic forces that control markets. A market is a theoretical construct that isolates the selling and purchasing of any one particular commodity from the economy as a whole. Demand is the willingness and ability of buyers to purchase a commodity, and supply is the willingness and ability of sellers to provide it. Demand is determined by factors such as price, income, and borrowers' expectations; supply is determined by price, production costs, and sellers' expectations.

Economists represent supply and demand graphically as functions of price. The point where the two curves cross is called the market equilibrium: It is the point at which the quantity offered for sale is equal to the quantity sought for purchase. Generally, markets tend to gravitate toward the point of equilibrium. Both the supply and demand curves for real estate are affected by the supply of finance, which itself is influenced by the secondary lending market.

Inflation is a general rise in prices; it results in a decrease in the purchasing power of the dollar. That is, because of inflation, what a dollar could buy in 1900 requires many more dollars to buy today. Inflation is a normal part of the operation of a free market, and there are many indexes used today to measure it, such as the Consumer Price Index and the Producer Price Indexes. It is important for those involved in real estate finance to be able to accurately predict rising or falling inflation, especially if it occurs at a quicker than average rate.

Because real estate investment does not suffer from inflation as strongly as certain other investments, it is considered a *hedge* against inflation. During periods of high inflation, investors will seek to purchase real estate. However, high inflation is correlated with high interest rates, thus preventing a run on the market and inflation of real estate prices.

In addition to factors such as supply, demand, and inflation, the market is affected by factors outside itself, such as government influence. The Federal Reserve is the most important player in the U.S. economy. It is our central bank and it is in charge of conducting the nation's monetary policy. To achieve this goal, it has three tools at its disposal: the discount rate, the reserve requirement, and its open market operations.

The discount rate is the interest rate that the Fed charges member banks to borrow money. When the discount rate is higher, less money is borrowed, and banks have fewer funds. The reserve requirement is the amount that the Fed requires financial institutions to keep in accounts at the regional Reserve. The higher the requirement, the fewer funds banks have to lend out. The Fed's open-market operations consist of buying and selling U.S. securities. These operations are typically directed at reaching a targeted amount of reserve balances or a targeted federal funds rate. The federal funds rate is the interest rate banks charge other banks to borrow the money that they have on reserve at Federal Reserve.

Another way the government influences the real estate market is through taxes. The government's tax policy for real estate is based around incentives for buyers and sellers of principal residences. These incentives come in the form of exemptions, which are reductions in the appraised value of taxable property, deductions, which are reductions in the taxable income of a taxpayer, and credits, which are dollar-for-dollar reductions in the amount of taxes owed.

There is one specific government agency that is in charge of the nation's housing policy: the Department of Housing and Urban Development (HUD). HUD's mission is "to increase homeownership, support community development, and increase access to affordable housing free from discrimination." Its duties include the enforcement of the Fair Housing Act and the Real Estate Settlement Procedures Act (RESPA). In addition, part of HUD, the Federal Housing Administration (FHA) insures loans to consumers. HUD also oversees the Government National Mortgage Association (GNMA or Ginnie Mae).

The real estate market is not limited to property, mortgages, and mortgage-backed securities. In addition, investors may purchase shares of real estate investment trusts (REITs). These are publicly traded companies that own and operate commercial real estate. The benefit to owning REITs is that they do not require a large capital investment and they are relatively liquid, in that they may easily be converted to cash. These trusts may be valued by their price-to-earnings ratios (P/E), which is the return they yield annually per dollar invested.

This concludes Lesson two.

Return to your online course player to take the Lesson Quiz.

Lesson 3:
FINANCIAL QUALIFICATIONS

This lesson focuses on the following topics:

- Introduction
- Underwriting Guidelines and Process
- Income
- Credit
- Source of Funds
- Debts
- Net Worth
- Case Study: Borrower Qualification
- Summary

By the end of this lesson, you should be able to:

- List the financial qualifications for obtaining mortgage loans, identifying the most important financial qualification
- Calculate a lender's qualifying income ratios
- List the five elements of a credit report, and explain how FICO scores affect a consumer's borrowing ability
- Explain the provisions of the federal legislation that affect real estate lending, and distinguish between those of the Fair Credit Reporting Act (FCRA), the Equal Credit Opportunity Act (ECOA), and the Truth in Lending Act
- Recall that when purchasers of real estate are ready to make a purchase, they are required to have cash in hand, identifying some common sources of funds
- List the classification of types of debts, identifying each in a case study
- Explain how a borrower's debts are used in determining whether he or she qualifies for a mortgage loan, listing two forms of qualifying ratio
- Define net worth and demonstrate how it is used in the determination of whether someone is qualified for a mortgage for a business property

Introduction

Lenders take into account a variety of factors when determining whether to underwrite a loan for any particular borrower. These factors may be divided into two main categories: the financial qualifications of the loan applicant, which are the subject of this lesson, and the value of the property to be mortgaged, which is the subject of the next lesson. In order to determine the applicant's financial qualifications, an underwriter will typically look at five items: the applicant's income, credit, source of funds, debts, and net worth.

Underwriting Guidelines and Process

What factors do underwriters consider?

Underwriters approve or deny a mortgage loan application based on an evaluation of the following:

- Income and assets, which help determine the borrower's ability to pay a loan

- Credit, which shows the borrower's current credit use, shows how the borrower treated obligations in the past and helps determine the borrower's creditworthiness and willingness to repay a loan

- Property, which determines whether the property is adequate collateral for the loan

Underwriters base their decision on a combination or layering of these three factors.

How do layers of risk affect home ownership?

The presence of individual risk factors does not necessarily threaten a borrower's ability to maintain home ownership. However, when layers of risk-a number of interrelated high-risk characteristics-are present without sufficient offset, their cumulative effect dramatically increases the likelihood of default and foreclosure.

To help borrowers maintain long-term home ownership, underwriters work to understand borrowers' needs and to manage the present risks in their loans.

Income

The ultimate goal of researching an applicant's income is to determine whether that income is sufficient and reliable enough to repay the mortgage amount and the applicant's other recurring debts.

Sources of Income

In general, the underwriter looks for a two-year employment history, including a consistent working pattern that provides a good indication that the applicant's income will continue. All income reported by the applicant should be verified by the underwriter. Employers should be sent Verification of Employment forms, which request the length of the applicant's employment, gross salary, additional income (such as overtime, bonuses and royalties), and the likelihood of continued employment.

If the applicant's sole income is from commission, he or she should be requested to provide the previous two year's tax returns. If only part of the applicant's total income is from commission, two years of W-2 forms and a Verification of Employment form are typically proof enough of such income.

Additionally, an applicant's alimony or child support can be considered a source of income, provided that it has been court-ordered and that a history of payment can be verified. Of course, the length of time such an income can be expected to continue should be taken into consideration as well. A lender may not ask an applicant whether he or she receives alimony or child support, although the applicant may choose to reveal this knowledge to qualify for the loan. See the discussion of the Equal Credit Opportunity Act later in this lesson.

Net Operating Income

A loan applicant may also receive income from investment properties that she or he holds. Real estate investments come in many different forms, including malls, strip malls, offices, apartments, hotels, golf courses, ski lodges, residential rental property, and warehouses. Income from these investments is in the form of rent. The net operating income (NOI) can be calculated from the annual scheduled gross income as follows:

Scheduled Gross Income − Vacancies − Credit Losses = Effective Gross Income

Effective Gross Income − Operating Expenses = NOI

The NOI of each investment property held by the applicant should be considered as income for the purposes of the loan. Negative cash flows from properties running at a loss are to be counted as long-term debts (discussed in coming pages) by the underwriter.

Credit

Credit Reporting

Lenders and others offering lines of credit to consumers will evaluate the credit reports of those consumers. Credit reports are statements issued by one of the three credit reporting bureaus, Equifax, Experian, or Trans Union, that contain detailed information about a consumer's credit history. They are divided into five sections:

Personal Profile
The personal profile section of the report contains the personal and identifying information of the consumer. It lists his or her name, aliases, date of birth, current address, previous address(es), current employer, and previous employer(s).

Credit Summary
The credit summary includes all of the accounts a consumer has opened, their current status (open or closed), account balance, delinquencies, and the number of account inquiries. An account inquiry is the purchase of a credit report by a lender.

Public Records
The public records contained in a credit report include federal district bankruptcy records, state and county court records, tax liens (from unpaid taxes), and monetary judgments.

Credit Inquiries
This section contains the number of inquiries initiated, as well as the name(s) of the inquiring party or parties.

Account History
The report also contains information about the consumer's account history: all of the accounts the consumer has opened, the account number, status (open or closed), monthly payment, date opened, balance, terms, highest balance reached, limit, past-due amounts, and the payment status of the account.

In addition, lenders and consumers seeking a credit report can purchase a "credit score" which is calculated by the reporting bureau using the information from the credit report.

Residential Mortgage Credit Report
To meet the specific needs of residential mortgage lenders, credit reporting agencies have developed the residential mortgage credit report (RMCR), which contains all of the information necessary for underwriting a loan to sell on the secondary market. These reports not only contain information about a loan applicant's employment history and residence, but they also include the requisite verifications for underwriting.

In addition, the account history of the RMCR is significantly more detailed. These histories generally include detailed information about account activity in the past two years, including late payments, the date(s) on which an account was delinquent, the number of times each account has been past due, the duration of its past-due status (30-59, 60-89 or 90+ days), and the type and balance of each account.

FICO Scores and Credit Rating

The three credit bureaus also provide *credit scores*, otherwise known as FICO scores, to lending institutions. The credit bureaus all use software developed by Fair Isaac and Co. (hence the name FICO), but the scores of any one consumer can vary from bureau to bureau, if the credit reporting information of that consumer is not the same at the three different agencies. Lenders who receive all three scores will sometimes use them all, sometimes use the average and sometimes use the median score. A score from Equifax is called a BEACON® score, one from Experian is called an Experian/Fair Isaac Risk Model score, and one from TransUnion is called an EMPIRICA® score.

Credit scores are given on a scale of 300-850, with higher scores indicating lower risk. There is no one score below which a consumer is considered "bad" and above which he or she is considered "good." Lenders take into account a variety of information, such as the specifics of the loan being sought, when they evaluate the risk of a particular borrower.

The scores are calculated using only the information in a consumer's credit report. That is, they are not biased with regard to race, religion, national origin, gender, or familial status because the use of such information is prohibited by the Equal Credit Opportunity Act and because it has not been demonstrated to be a predictor of consumer credit risk. The FICO software assigns points to the different items of information in the credit report, which are weighted according to their effectiveness as credit risk predictors.

FICO scores will often influence the interest rate a lender is willing to offer a potential borrower. According to www.myfico.com, the rates lenders typically offer for certain FICO score ranges at the current time are as follows:

FICO Score	Interest Rate
720-850	5.465%
700-719	5.589%
675-699	6.124%
620-674	7.269%
560-619	8.590%
500-559	9.589%

Fair Credit Reporting Act

The Fair Credit Reporting Act (FCRA), passed in 1971 and since amended several times, was enacted to ensure the rights of consumers to have accurate, unbiased credit reporting. Under the act, a credit bureau must disclose all of the information in a consumer's report if the consumer requests the information. The Fair Credit Reporting Act (FCRA) requires each of the nationwide consumer reporting companies-Equifax, Experian, and Trans Union-to provide you with a free copy of your credit report, at your request, once every 12 months. Additional reports are available if the consumer (a) pays a fee charged by the reporting bureau or (b) meets the fee waiver requirements. A consumer does not have to pay a fee if any of the following occurs:

- The consumer is unemployed and intends to seek employment within 60 days.

- The consumer is on welfare.

- The consumer's report is inaccurate because of fraud.

- Someone has taken action against the consumer on the basis of a credit report, such as denying him or her credit.

If someone takes action against a consumer, the consumer must be told which bureau that person received the report from and must be given the name, address, and phone number of that bureau. All three reporting agencies have online access to the reports and scores. Fees for the reports range from $9 to $9.95 and, for the scores, $3.95 to $5. Packages also are available from each agency that include the scores and reports from the other agencies. It is recommended that a consumer seeking her or his report call each agency and determine whether that agency has a report on him or her to avoid paying for reports that don't exist.

The FCRA also requires that a consumer be able to dispute information that appears on the report and that proven inaccuracies must be removed. Consumers who believe their reports contain inaccurate information should notify both the reporting bureau and the source of the information (for example, the company claiming that a bill wasn't paid) in writing. Disputed information must be reinvestigated and removed if inaccurate.

The law also deals with time limits on negative information. In general, negative information may be reported for only seven years. However, information about bankruptcy proceedings may be reported for 10 years, and there is no time limit on reporting criminal convictions, applications to jobs with salaries greater than $75,000, and applications for credit lines or insurance greater than $150,000. Lawsuits and legal judgments may be reported after the seven-year limit until the statute of limitations runs out.

The Equal Credit Opportunity Act
Title VII of the Consumer Credit Protection Act (CCPA), passed in 1968, is known as the Equal Credit Opportunity Act (ECOA). The ECOA protects borrowers seeking credit from unfair and discriminatory practices by lenders. The law is applicable both to lenders and to real estate brokers who arrange financing.

The ECOA provides that when someone applies for a loan, the lender may not:

- Discourage the applicant from applying because she or he is of a certain race, nationality, age, marital status, or sex, or because he or she is on welfare

- Require that the applicant disclose her or his race, nationality, sex, or religion, although the lender may ask for voluntary disclosures of all but the applicant's religion

- Ask whether the applicant is widowed or divorced
  - The lender may, however, ask whether the applicant is married or unmarried-and if married, whether he or she is separated.
  - This is true in Texas and other community property states, but not in most states.

- Ask about the applicant's desire to have or raise children

- Ask whether the applicant receives child support or alimony, unless the payments are being used to qualify for the loan
  - A lender may, however, ask whether the applicant is required to make such payments.

When a lender considers a loan, he or she may not:

- Consider the race, nationality, age, marital status, or sex of the applicant

- Consider whether the applicant has a telephone number listed in his or her own name
  - The lender may, however, consider whether the applicant has a telephone at all.

- Consider the racial composition of the area in which the property to be mortgaged is located

- Consider the applicant's age, unless she or he is a minor, or he or she is over the age of 62 and the lender intends to favor the applicant for that reason

When evaluating an applicant's income, the lender may not:

- Refuse to consider the applicant's public assistance as though it were any other source of income

- Discount income on the basis of the applicant's sex or marital status

- Refuse to consider or discount income from retirement benefits, annuities, or pensions

- Refuse to consider alimony or child support, if there is a demonstrable history of payment

The lender must:

- Accept or deny an application within 30 days

- Tell an applicant who was denied a loan the reason he or she was denied

- Tell an applicant who is offered less favorable terms than she or he applied for the reason for the less favorable terms

The Federal Trade Commission (FTC) and the U.S. Department of Justice are in charge of enforcing the ECOA.

More About: For more information, visit the Trade Commission online at http://www.ftc.gov.

Truth in Lending Act

Title I of the CCPA is known as the Truth in Lending Act (sometimes TILA). The act is designed to help consumers compare the costs of credit from different lenders, the cost of buying with cash, and to protect consumers from unfair and inaccurate credit practices. The act has two principal regulations, referred to as Regulation M and Regulation Z. Regulation M applies to leased property and will, therefore, not be a concern of ours in this course.

Regulation Z applies to credit transactions where credit:

- Is extended to consumers

- Is offered on a regular basis (that is, Mr. A offering his friend Mr. B a loan would not fall under Regulation Z, but a car dealership that offered consumer financing on a regular basis would)

- Is either subject to a finance charge, such as an interest rate or financing fees, or is to be paid in four or more installments

- Is to be used for personal, family, or household purposes (that is, not for business, commercial, or agricultural purposes)

- Is a closed-end transaction (that is, any line of credit that is not open-end or revolving-see the section on Debt)

The regulation requires that certain disclosures be made to all consumers seeking credit. Lenders must disclose the following:

- The application fee for obtaining the loan

- The address of the property that is to be collateral for the loan

- The total sale price, including the down payment

- The amount financed, which is the sale price plus any other financed fees, less the down payment

- The loan's finance charge, which is the sum of the discounts, fees, and interest payments

- The total amount of the loan payments

- The annual percentage rate (APR), which is the ratio of the finance charge to the total amount of the loan payments

- Any prepayment penalties

- The charge for late payments

- Whether the loan is assumable or not

- If the loan is an adjustable rate mortgage (ARM; see the Alternative Financial Instruments lesson), what the highest interest rate possible is

- If the loan is an ARM, how the periodic interest rate is calculated and how monthly payments are derived from it

Additionally, lenders must provide ARM borrowers with a pamphlet titled "Consumer Handbook on Adjustable Rate Mortgages," or any other literature containing the same information.

Business Credit Report

It would make little sense for a lender who was considering a loan application from a business to obtain personal credit reports from a bureau like Equifax. The credit ratings of any one or several individuals in a company is not a good indicator whatsoever of the company's credit. For this reason, there are business credit reporting agencies. Although Equifax, Experian, and TransUnion all have business credit reporting services, they are not the largest providers of such reports. Companies such as Dun & Bradstreet and Business Credit USA offer these services.

Source of Funds

When a person is ready to purchase real estate, she or he will already have some cash in hand. This cash can come from a variety of sources. This section of the lesson will discuss some of the common sources of funds used to purchase real estate.

Liquidated Assets

An underwriter will often consider a borrower's assets when underwriting the loan application. If these are liquid assets, such as stocks or bonds, they may not need to be liquidated at closing; other non liquid assets, such as real estate and automobiles, must be liquidated if they are to be used to offset debt payments.

For example, if when taking out a new loan, a borrower does not want an existing mortgage to be included in his or her long term debt total-because the borrower intends to repay the mortgage with the sale of the property to which it is attached-the property must either be sold or have a contract to purchase when the lender underwrites the new loan. This is to ensure that the property will be sold and the mortgage on the existing property satisfied.

Gifts

A borrower who does not have sufficient funds for closing may use gift funds. A gift is cash that the borrower receives from a relative, fiancée, or domestic partner and that does not need to be repaid. Some gifts can come from charitable or nonprofit organizations. Gifts cannot come, however, from interested parties in the transaction, such as the seller, unless the party also is a relative of the borrower. Like other funds, the lender must verify the amount of the gift and that the donor can afford it. The lender does this by sending a gift form to the donor.

The gift form asks the donor to state the following:

- The amount of the gift
- His or her relationship to the borrower
- That the funds need not be repaid

Funds that come from the seller are known as concessions or seller contributions. Lenders will often allow, but limit, seller contributions. It is normal for the seller to pay certain closing costs and discount points of the buyer's.

Retirement Vehicles

A borrower may own one or more retirement vehicles, such as a 401(k) plan or an Individual Retirement Account (IRA), containing funds with which she or he may purchase real property under certain conditions. Funds in a retirement account such as a 401(k) may be used to purchase investment properties that are maintained within the account itself. Investment properties are properties such as rental homes, apartment complexes, and strip malls, at which the holder of the account does not live, visit, or vacation.

In addition, the Taxpayer Relief Act of 1997 provides that first-time homebuyers may withdraw up to $10,000 from their IRAs, at any time, penalty-free for the purchase of a principal residence. A first-time homebuyer, as defined by the act, is any individual who has had no equity in a principal residence in the previous two years. So, conceivably, an IRA holder can take advantage of this benefit more than once, but all of the withdrawals must add up to no more than $10,000 until the disbursement age is reached. An account holder's immediate family, grandchildren, and descendants may also use the withdrawn funds. All withdrawn funds must be used within 120 days of withdrawal to avoid the penalty.

If the loan applicant intends to purchase an investment property with his or her retirement account, or to use the penalty-free IRA withdrawal for the purchase of a principal residence, these funds should be considered by the underwriter in her or his decision.

Debts

The underwriter must use the information he or she has about the applicant's financial qualifications to determine whether that applicant can make the monthly mortgage payment and service all of her or his other debts over the term of the loan. One important component of this determination is the *qualifying ratio*, of which there are two: the housing-expense-to-income ratio and the total debt service ratio. It is helpful for real estate professionals to learn the use of these qualifying ratios for two reasons: first, because they will be able to prequalify their clients by determining the maximum monthly payment they can afford, and second, because they will be able to determine, from the monthly payment on a property, the amount of income necessary to qualify for the loan.

Types of Debt

Installment Debts
Installment debts are those debts that have determinate beginning and ending dates. A mortgage, a car loan, an improvement loan, and a student loan are all examples of installment debts. Generally, installment debts with more than six months of payments remaining are counted as long-term debts.

Revolving Debts
Revolving debts are those debts that have an open-ended line of credit with a minimum monthly payment. Credit cards, department store charge cards, and gas cards are all examples of revolving debts. Different lenders will treat revolving debts in different ways. For instance, a particularly lenient lender could consider only the minimum monthly payment as the payment of the debt. Other lenders, however, may take into account the full balance of the credit line and sometimes even impute additional debt to that line, up to the line's limit. Lenders must make sure they treat all applicants similarly to avoid violating the fair-housing laws.

Other Recurring Liabilities

An applicant may also have other recurring liabilities, such as alimony, child support, and legal judgments. Currently, Fannie Mae and Freddie Mac do not include child support in the long-term debt calculation.

Housing-Expense-To-Income Ratio

The housing expense is the PITI payment. PITI stands for Principal, Interest, Taxes, and Insurance. The housing expense ratio is fairly straightforward: It is the annual PITI payment divided by the borrower's annual income. This ratio is sometimes referred to as the front-end ratio.

Various lenders will set different maximum housing expense ratio limits, as will secondary mortgage traders such as Fannie Mae, and insuring bodies such as the Federal Housing Authority (FHA). To qualify for a loan, the borrower will have to have a ratio below the maximum limit set by his or her lender. For that loan to be conventional, the ratio will have to fall below the limit set by Fannie Mae, and for it to be insured by the FHA, it will have to fall below the FHA limit.

Example

Suppose that the applicant's annual income is $72,000. If monthly taxes and insurance are $200 and the housing expense ratio is 33 percent, what is the maximum loan amount that the applicant can afford? Assume a loan term of 30 years and an interest rate of 8 percent.

To solve this problem, first we must determine the maximum principal and interest payment the borrower can afford. We know:

Ratio = (Principal + Interest + Taxes + Insurance) ÷ Gross Monthly Income
33% = (Principal + Interest + $200) ÷ ($72,000/12)
0.33 = (Principal + Interest + $200) ÷ $6,000
$6,000 × 0.33 = Principal + Interest + $200
$1,980 = Principal + Interest + $200
Principal + Interest = $1,780

This will allow us to calculate the principal amount using our monthly PI equation:

$M = (P \times J) \div (1 - (1 + J)^{-n})$
$\$1,780 = 0.08P \div (1 - (1.08)^{-360})$
$0.08P = \$1,780 \times (1 - (1.08)^{-360})$
$P = (\$1,780 \times (1 - (1.08)^{-360})) \div 0.08$

Using a financial calculator, this gives us:

P = $242,584.62

Total Debt Service Ratio

The second important qualifying ratio used by lenders is the total debt service ratio, also called the back-end ratio. This is equal to:

(PITI + all long-term debts) ÷ Gross income

Typically, both an applicant's housing expense ratio and his or her total debt service ratio must fall below the maximum limits set by lenders for the applicant to qualify for the loan. However, there is a recent trend toward using only the debt service ratio, as there is some evidence that indicates there is no correlation between high housing expense ratios and default, when the debt service ratio is held constant.

Example

Suppose that the sale price of a property is $100,000, and the borrower puts 10 percent down. The loan amount will be $90,000 at 8 percent for 20 years. At this rate, the monthly principal and interest payment will be $752.80. If the lender estimates taxes at 2.5 percent of the sale price per year, monthly taxes should be:

($100,000 × 2.5%) ÷ 12 months = $208.33

In the particular area that the property is located, hazard insurance costs $1,800 a year, or $150 a month. Thus the homeowner's PITI payments are:

$752.80 + $208.33 + $150 = $1,111.13

Suppose the borrower's recurring liabilities are as follows:

Credit card minimum payment: $30
Car payment: $339
Car insurance: $75
Telephone and utilities: $230
Internet service: $25.95
Cable TV: $60
Total liabilities: $759.95

If the lender requires a total debt service ratio of no greater than 36 percent, what is the minimum gross income necessary for the borrower to qualify? We can use our formula to solve this problem:

(PITI + all long-term debts) ÷ gross income = total debt service ratio
($1,111.13 + $759.95) ÷ GI = 0.36
$1,871.08 ÷ GI = 0.36
0.36 × GI = $1,871.08
GI = $5,197.44

So, the borrower would need a gross income of at least $5,197.44 monthly.

Net Worth

A person's net worth is all of her or his assets minus all of his or her liabilities. Assets may include the following: accounts in banks, savings and loans, and credit unions; stocks and bonds; retirement funds; the net cash value of insurance policies; real estate; automobiles; personal possessions; business equipment; and business aircraft, among others.

Lenders will sometimes-especially for business loans-have a qualifying total-liabilities-to-net-worth ratio. This is usually about 400 percent. This may sound like a lot, but keep in mind that net worth is assets less liabilities. Suppose that a consumer only has one asset, a car valued at $50,000, and only one debt, $40,000 in car payments. Her total-liabilities-to-net-worth ratio will then be:

$$\$40,000 \div (\$50,000 - \$40,000) = 400\%$$

The 400 percent requirement essentially says that a business must not owe more than four-fifths of the value of all its assets.

Case Study: Borrower Qualification

Borrower X comes to a lender looking to qualify for a loan. She has a job as a consultant for a computer company and earns a gross salary of $70,000 a year. To prequalify the borrower, the lender is willing to consider the pay stubs she has brought with her; but he nonetheless fills out a Verification of Employment Form and sends it to her employer. In addition to her salaried work, Borrower X rents out a house to another couple for $450 per month. Although there is a two-year history for this rental income, the lender is willing to consider only 75 percent of it, in the event of vacancy.

The lender obtains a credit report and credit score for the borrower. Her credit status is favorable and she has a credit score of 676, which entitles her to an interest rate of 6.124 percent. She has one recurring liability, a credit card with a current balance of $750 and a minimum payment of $10. However, it is the lender's practice to impute an additional 10 percent of the balance on any revolving debts to a borrower's debt service.

To determine the maximum loan amount Borrower X qualifies for, the lender must first determine the maximum monthly payments she can afford based on his qualifying ratios: a housing expense ratio of 28 percent and a total debt service ratio of 36 percent. The borrower's gross monthly income is:

($70,000 Salary ÷ 12 Months) + (0.75 x $450 NOI) = $6,170.83

Then we can calculate the PITI payment for which she will qualify:

Calculation 1:
Housing Expense Ratio = PITI ÷ Gross Income
0.28 = PITI ÷ $6,170.83
PITI = $1,727.83

Calculation 2:
Debt Service Ratio = (PITI + Long Term Debts) ÷ Gross Income
0.36 = (PITI + $85) ÷ $6,170.83
PITI + $85 = $2,221.50
PITI = $2,136.50

The maximum allowable monthly PITI payment is the least of these two calculations: $1,727.83. To determine the maximum principal amount, the lender must estimate the taxes and insurance and subtract these from the maximum PITI payment. If the lender estimates a tax and insurance escrow payment of $200 per month, his financial calculator tells him that the principal amount will be $251,475.66 on a 30-year loan.

Summary

The underwriter considers two main factors in underwriting a loan: the condition and value of the property to be purchased and the financial qualifications of the borrower. A borrower's financial qualifications are his or her income, credit, net worth, source of funds, and debts.

In general, underwriters look for borrowers with an established two-year employment history. Those who make most of their money from commissions must be able to verify a sustained income for two years with past W-2 forms. Those who receive child support or alimony and choose to reveal this fact to qualify for the loan must also demonstrate a history of receiving regular payments. Underwriters will also try to verify that a source of income is likely to continue. They will consider a portion, adjusted for vacancy, of the net operating income (NOI) of all income-producing properties held by the borrower. Sometimes lenders will also consider rental income from the property to be purchased, if the properties, or portions of it, are to be rented.

Underwriters establish the creditworthiness of a borrower in part by obtaining a credit report from one of the three major credit reporting bureaus: Experian, Equifax, and TransUnion. These credit reports contain five sections: a personal profile, a credit summary, a summary of public records, a list of credit inquiries, and an account history of the consumer. Another widely used tool of the underwriter is the FICO credit score. These scores are based upon the information each credit bureau has on a consumer and made with proprietary software developed by Fair Isaac & Co. The scores are on a range of 300-850, with 300 being the lowest possible score.

Legislation exists to regulate the practices of lenders. Of particular interest to us are the Fair Credit Reporting Act (FCRA) and the Equal Credit Opportunity Act (ECOA). The FCRA deals with credit reports-what may and may not appear on them and how a consumer may dispute information. The act sets time limits for how long items can remain on credit reports (such as a bankruptcy) and guidelines for the disputation process. The ECOA protects borrowers from discrimination on the basis of race, nationality, sex, age, marital status, welfare status, desire to have or raise children, and receipt of child support or receipt of alimony payments. The act requires lenders to inform denied applicants of the reason(s) for which they were denied.

There are several types of debt. Installment debts are those that, like a car or mortgage payment, have a fixed beginning and ending date. Revolving debts, like credit cards or department store charge cards, have no fixed ending date, but require a periodic minimum payment, and often have a limit on the amount of debt that can accrue. Debts are included under the larger heading of recurring liabilities, which are obligations one has to pay periodically. Other recurring liabilities include alimony and child support payments.

Underwriters use certain percentages called qualifying ratios to qualify applicants for loans. The two most important qualifying ratios are the housing expense ratio and the total debt service ratio. The housing expense ratio, also known as the front-end ratio, is the ratio of a borrower's PITI payment to her or his gross monthly income. The total debt service ratio, or the back-end ratio, is the ratio of the sum of a borrower's PITI payment and his or her long-term debts to gross monthly income.

Underwriters may also consider the liabilities-to-net-worth ratio, especially for business loans. An entity's net worth is defined as its assets minus its liabilities. Thus, a liabilities-to-net-worth qualifying ratio of 400 percent requires that the entity should not owe more than four-fifths of the value of its assets.

This concludes lesson three.

Return to your online course player to take the Lesson Quiz.

Lesson 4:
PROPERTY VALUATION

This lesson focuses on the following topics:

- Introduction
- Eight Steps of the Appraisal Process
- Appraisal Methods
- Cap Rate Analysis
- Discounted Cash Flow Analysis
- Pro Forma
- Taxes and Depreciation
- Activity: Critical Thinking
- Case Study: Net Present Value
- Summary

By the end of this lesson, you should be able to:

- List the eight steps to completing an appraisal in the correct order
- Explain the principal appraisal methods and distinguish between Sales Comparison Approach and Cost Approach
- Explain the most common approach to valuing income-producing property-the cap rate analysis
- List the elements of a pro forma projection, in order, and describe its uses in discounted cash flow analyses
- Utilize spreadsheet and investment software to calculate net present values and internal rates of return
- Explain how taxes and depreciation are an important element of decision-making in real estate, identifying the procedure for calculating depreciation

Introduction

A borrower's financial qualifications and creditworthiness cannot be considered in and of themselves. A loan underwriter also must consider the value of the property that will act as security for the loan. No matter how creditworthy a borrower may be, it is always possible that the lender will have to foreclose. In such an event, the value of the collateral property is the only means of recovering the loan amount. This makes property valuation an important part of real estate finance.

For non-income-producing properties, value can be ascertained using a property valuation from an appraiser. For income-producing properties, the underwriter must be able to verify that the property will be able to consistently produce the cash flows necessary to amortize the loan over its term. To this end, the underwriter has the tools of the *cap rate* and *discounted cash flow* analyses at his or her disposal.

Eight Steps of the Appraisal Process

These are the eight steps to completing an appraisal:

- Stating the objective
- Listing the data needed
- Gathering and recording data
- Determining the highest and best use
- Estimating the land value
- Estimating value using applicable approaches to appraisal
- Reconciling the final value estimate
- Completing and presenting the value report

Various procedures comprise each of the eight steps, which an appraiser completes depending upon the particularities of a job.

Step 1: State the Objective
The first thing an appraiser does is state her or his task. The appraiser points out the purpose of the appraisal, the date, the property location, and any other aspects that make the specific appraisal project unique. When stating the objective, an appraiser performs all of the following tasks:

- Identifying the property with a complete legal description
- Establishing which property's rights are to be appraised: Usually this will be fee simple ownership, which is full ownership; however, it may be less than full ownership, such as tenant's leased occupation rights, right-of-way or an easement
- Stating the type of value the appraisal seeks to define, which is typically the market value; however, investment value, value in use or appraised value also determine property value in certain situations

- Determining the effective date of the valuation because value changes over time

- Clarifying any limitations-This protects the appraiser

Step 2: List Necessary Data and Their Sources

To complete this step, the appraiser must establish which approach or approaches (discussed in the coming pages) he or she expects to use in the appraisal. Once that is established, the appraiser then decides what information is needed and how to go about collecting it. It is imperative that the appraiser be familiar with common sources of data to complete this step smoothly.

Step 3: Gather, Record, and Verify Data

An appraiser must now actually collect, record, and verify the data that he or she needs to complete the appraisal. It is up to the appraiser to establish that the data are accurate and correct.

Usually, this step begins with gathering general information relating to geographic and economic characteristics of the area in which the property is located. The specifics of this step will vary according to the type of value and ownership right that the appraiser hopes to evaluate; however, every appraiser must collect a detailed physical description of the property. This is particularly important for the sales comparison approach to appraisal. Only with a complete physical account of all the comparables and the subject property can the appraiser properly compare the properties.

An adequate physical description is so important that many appraisers use a photo journal to record the condition of the property. This is so that all relevant parties can quickly resolve any problematic disputes that may arise after the appraiser completes the project. For example, if an appraiser estimates the value of a home and then someone damages it shortly following the appraisal, then the appraiser may have to prove that his or her estimate represents the home's market value at the time she or he completed the project. Photographs document the status of the property at the time of the appraisal, which not only protects the appraiser but also validates and professionalizes his or her report.

Step 4: Determine the Highest and Best Use

The value principle of the highest and best use states that there is one most profitable and efficient use of any given tract of land and that this best use should dictate a tract's development. An appraiser conducts a highest and best use study to establish the one most profitable, legal, and plausible use for the property, upon which the appraiser will place his or her final value estimate. The appraiser might discover that the current use does not constitute the highest and best use. Whether the appraiser's decision is in favor of or against the property's current use depends upon the information she or he gathers in Step 3. In essence, the appraiser takes the information gathered in Step 3 pertaining to governmental controls, economic status, and physical characteristics of the property and considers to what extent each of these attributes meets the marketplace's needs.

Step 5: Estimate the Land Value
An appraiser commonly evaluates the land parcel separate from any improvements upon it. Here, the appraiser locates similar parcels to adjust and then compare with the subject land parcel. An appraiser completes this in accordance with the sales comparison approach.

Step 6: Estimate Value with Applicable Approaches
The main subject of this lesson will be the methods of valuing real estate. While each method will be treated separately, it is important to remember that an appraiser should use all of the applicable methods of valuation at his or her disposal to determine a final value.

Step 7: Reconcile of the Final Value Estimate
When an appraiser uses more than one method, she or he has to combine the data from each of the approaches. We call this reconciliation. An appraiser does not simply average his or her various facts. Instead, the appraiser places the most weight on the data and approach that are most relevant to the subject property.

Step 8: Write and Present the Value Report
The Appraisal Standards Board (ASB) is responsible for establishing the rules for completing an appraisal and compiling its report. In addition, the ASB also enforces the Uniform Standards of Professional Appraisal Practice (USPAP), which outlines the ethical and professional standards of real estate appraisal. In this step, the appraiser completes his or her report in accordance with USPAP standards and presents it to the client. Written reports are the industry standard; however, the USPAP does allow oral reports. Generally, the appraiser presents her or his findings in the written format that the client requests.

Appraisal Methods

Appraisers
A professional real estate appraiser evaluates the worth of a property. Anybody may request an appraisal-an individual or a company-and it may be sought for any reason, such as determining a loan value or for insurance coverage. An appraiser submits his or her evaluation in the form of an appraisal report, for which the appraiser must conduct a thorough study of the property.

An appraiser will take on many roles as she or he prepares a report. He or she may wear the hat of broker, surveyor, economist, and possibly even accountant.

An appraiser should not engage in any activities, either expressly or implied, for which that appraiser does not possess education, license, or certification requisite.

Sales Comparison Approach

The sales comparison approach to appraisal uses two value principles: the principle of substitution and the principle of contribution. The value principle of substitution states that a person will pay only as much for a property as he or she must pay to acquire a comparable property. The principle of contribution states that an improvement to a home is worth only as much as it adds to the property's market value and does not always relate to the improvement's actual cost.

When an appraiser uses the sales comparison approach, he or she collects data from the previous sales of other properties with similar features-such as amenities, square footage, number of rooms, and location. The appraiser analyzes how much these comparable properties have sold for and accounts for the differences in the properties; then, from this study, the appraiser estimates the subject property's market value.

Appraisers rely heavily upon the sales comparison approach for appraising residential properties and vacant land. The appraiser adds or subtracts the contributing value of these differences, called adjustments, and takes the remainder as the subject property's value. This can be represented with the following equation:

Comparable Property Sale Price ± Adjustments = Subject Property Value

Exercise

Subject Property A has hardwood flooring and air conditioning. Comparable Property B has hardwood flooring but no air conditioning (valued at $2,500); it recently sold for $150,000. Comparable Property C does not have hardwood flooring (valued at $1,500) but has an air conditioner; it sold for $140,000. Comparable Property D has both hardwood flooring and air conditioning, but it is located in a different neighborhood; it sold for $160,000. Using the sales comparison approach, what range does the subject property's value fall into?

Answer

For the sales comparison approach, we can map out a chart to note any adjustments so that it is easier to see the differences:

Property	B	C	D
Sale price	$150,000	$140,000	$160,000
Location	0	0	-$10,000
Air Conditioner	0	+$2,500	0
Hardwood Flooring	+$1,500	0	0
Adjusted Value	$151,500	$142,500	$150,000

Therefore, the value of the subject property ranges from $142,500 to $151,500. Remember that any significant differences in value occur when the appraiser uses dissimilar properties.

Cost Approach

To estimate a property's current market value using the cost approach, the appraiser needs to estimate the cost of reconstructing the property with improvements. To obtain the real estate's value, this estimate is added to the value of the land, and then depreciation of the home since it was first built is subtracted from that total.

When the appraiser uses the cost approach, he or she:

- Establishes the improvement's reproduction cost

- Estimates the existing building's depreciation

- Establishes the value of a comparable land parcel

- Makes the appropriate adjustments to the comparable parcel

- Combines the figures from the previous steps into the cost approach formula

- States the value of the subject property

Once the appraiser has determined the necessary components required to use the cost approach, she or he plugs the information into following equation:

Cost of Reproduction − Depreciation Value + Land Value = Property Value

Exercise

The subject property is similar to another newly constructed property in size, amenities, and location. The newly constructed property cost $200,000 to build. Over the years, the subject property has depreciated 15 percent. The land that the subject property is situated on is valued at $50,000. What is the property value of the subject property, using the cost approach?

Answer

Step 1: Set up the equation
$200,000 − ($200,000 × 0.15) + $50,000 = Property Value

Step 2: Calculate
$200,000 - $30,000 + $50,000 = <u>$220,000</u>

CAP Rate Analysis

Capitalization rates, or cap rates, are the most widely used method of valuing income-producing real estate. The cap rate is equal to the net operating income (NOI) divided by the net present value of the property.

A cap rate valuation works like this: Suppose that the current fair-market value of a property is $90,000 and its NOI is $8,100, or 9 percent. Based on the current market trends, an investor then estimates the average cap rate that investors will desire in 10 years. This average rate is not tied directly to the NOI of the particular property being valued, but an investor can use information about comparable properties to estimate a rate. In this case, let us suppose our investor estimates a future cap rate of 8.5 percent. Finally, the investor estimates the NOI of his investment in 10 years at, let's say $9,000. The future value will be:

Future Value = Projected NOI ÷ Projected Average Cap Rate = $9,000÷8.5% = $105,882

The investor, therefore, expects to make a profit of $14,882 from his original purchase price. A projected decrease in cap rates makes profit likely under good management; this, however, does not mean that a property should be purchased merely because it has a low current cap rate. In many cases, high cap rates are good indicators of greater returns, although they bespeak a greater risk as well.

The cap rate analysis overlooks the deeper reasons behind NOI. If a property is converting its capital at a low rate instead of a high rate, there must be some cause-poor management, ill repair, or high vacancy from low demand, to name a few reasons. The discounted cash flow (DCF) analysis, however, is concerned with precisely those factors that lead to the production of income and is therefore gaining ground in the valuation of real property.

Discounted Cash Flow Analysis

A discounted cash flow (DCF) analysis can be used to evaluate the price of a property and the return of several alternatives. An owner's cash flow is the net income the owner receives, plus expenditures for non-cash charges, such as depreciation or a decrease in net working capital. A DCF analysis takes projected future cash flows and discounts them to a net present value. The DCF figures for several alternatives can then be compared to determine the best plan of action.

Net Present Value
The first method of DCF analysis compares the net present value (NPV) of alternatives. The NPV is calculated by subtracting the discounted present value of an investment alternative from the cost of implementing that alternative.

The formula for NPV is:

$$NPV = \sum_{i=0}^{n} [(\text{Cash Flow at } i) \div (1 + \text{Discount Rate})^{t(i)}]$$

Here, i is the date of each cash flow, t(i) is the time elapsed since the first cash flow and Discount Rate is the rate used to discount the cash flow, which can be any rate the investor wants to compare the investment with, such as the inflation rate, the market interest rate, or the rate of an alternative investment.

We can use Microsoft's Excel spreadsheet software to perform difficult NPV calculations. Excel uses a set of predefined formulas that are represented to the user as functions. The user specifies a range of values for the function, and Excel calculates the answer. Suppose that we have the following information entered into our spreadsheet about a particular investment we are considering, Property A, and the expected returns for the first four years of operations:

NOI: First Four Years

	A	B
1	First Year Operations	$8,500
2	Second Year Operations	$9,200
3	Third Year Operations	$9,500
4	Fourth Year Operations	$9,800
5	Net Present Value	

We want the program to calculate the NPV for our investment on the basis of our desired rate of return. The function is:

=NPV (rate, values)

If our desired rate of return is 10 percent, we enter the following into cell B5:

=NPV (0.1, B1:B4)

The program will return our NPV, $29,161. Essentially, this figure tells us that if we were to invest $29,161 at 10 percent per annum for four years, we would receive the same amount of money that we received through our first four years of operations.

Most investment calculations for real estate are based on a 10-year holding period, but for the sake of simplicity, let's suppose that we plan to sell Property A after four years. If the purchase price is $86,500 and we estimate an average of 3 percent appreciation per year, we expect to sell the property for:

$86,500 + $86,500 × 0.03 × 4 = $96,880

We can calculate the NPV by adding $96,880 to our fourth year operations figure in the spreadsheet. Our new NPV is $95,331.94. Suppose our alternative to investing in Property A is investing in the stock market at an expected rate of 5 percent. The NPV to receive the same amount of returns from the stock market at this rate is $112,412.27. The required stock purchase well exceeds the cost of buying Property A for $86,500, so Property A is the better alternative.

Internal Rate of Return

The internal rate of return (IRR) of an investment is the yield of the investment within itself-that is, when all of the cash inflows and outflows to the investment have been discounted to zero. The IRR can be used to make asset allocation decisions. Investors consider a decision to be a good one if the IRR is greater than the opportunity cost of the capital required to implement it.

IRR can be difficult to calculate. We have to use our formula for NPV and estimate rates. The formula, as above, is:

$$NPV = \sum_{i=0}^{n} [(\text{Cash Flow at } i) \div (1 + IRR)^{t(i)}]$$

Because the NPV is the discounted value of all the cash flows, and IRR is the rate of return independent of all cash flows, we have to find the value for IRR that makes NPV = 0. Unfortunately, there is no mathematical formula we can use to do this for us. We have to estimate a value for IRR and see how close our NPV is to 0, then use that knowledge to estimate a closer value, etc. Software is available that does this for us, and by far the most prevalent is Microsoft's Excel spreadsheet software, which is included with many people's personal computers. If you have Excel, you can use the formula:

=IRR (values, guess)

To calculate IRR, record the payments as negative values and the income as positive values in the order paid or received in a column. Suppose that the values you enter are in column B, cells 2 through 37, and your estimated IRR is 10 percent. You would write in cell B 38 the following formula:

=IRR (B2:B37, 0.1)

The software would then give you an IRR figure. Your estimated rate of return does not have to be too close to the original; if you do not enter a figure, Excel will use a 10 percent initial estimate and work from there.

To use the internal rate of return, simply compare it with the other investment opportunities available. If the interest rate for fixed-rate securities is 8 percent, the typical return on stock market portfolios is 9 percent and the IRR of a different investment opportunity is 8.5 percent, then stick with the 10 percent IRR. With the aid of software, this method is simple, but not foolproof.

Modified Internal Rate of Return

The internal rate of return can be inaccurate because it neglects to consider the actual rate at which cash flows from the investment will be reinvested. To compensate for this, some investors use the Modified IRR or MIRR, which calculates a rate of return on the basis of the finance rate (determined from the cost of the investment) and the rate the investor expects to receive on reinvestment. The formula for MIRR is too complex to consider here; but, as with the IRR, it can be calculated with Excel or other investment programs.

Pro Forma

DCF analyses are conducted through the use of pro forma projections. These are financial statements for the property, given certain assumptions or hypothetical situations. They can be done by hand or with a spreadsheet program like Excel; they can also be done with special DCF programs available on the market today. Typical pro formas have projections for the next 10 years' revenue and expenses.

The Elements of a Pro Forma Projection

Potential Gross Revenue

The potential gross revenue for a particular year is the sum of all of the rents for that year, less vacancy and concessions (such as a tenant's free rent period).

Suppose a real estate salesperson is composing a pro forma for an office building to show to an interested investor. The building has three offices: Office A, 600 square feet, currently under lease for four more years; Office B, 1,200 square feet, currently under lease for one more year; and Office C, 600 square feet, currently vacant. Suppose further that the rents for the three offices are $3.50, $3, and $3.50 per square foot per month, respectively. The real estate salesperson expects that there will be low demand in the next two years and that Office C will remain vacant for those years, even if the landlord offers three months' free rent. Furthermore, Office B will not have a new tenant until Year 3. The real estate salesperson also expects that the tenant currently leasing Office A will not renew in Year 5, and that the office will be vacant for half the year.

Potential Gross Revenue

	Year 1	Year 2	Year 3	Year 4	Year 5
Office A	$25,200	$25,200	$25,200	$25,200	$25,200
Office B	$43,200	$43,200	$43,200	$43,200	$43,200
Office C	$25,200	$25,200	$25,200	$25,200	$25,200
Vacancy	-$25,200	-$68,400	-$0	-$0	-$25,200
Concessions	-$0	-$0	-$6,300	-$0	-$0
TOTAL	$68,400	$25,200	$87,300	$93,600	$68,400

Note, for instance, that Year 1's rent for office A is calculated with the formula:

$$\text{Monthly Rate} \times \text{Square Footage} \times 12 \text{ months} = \$3.50 \times 600 \times 12 = \$25,200$$

Operating Expenses

Operating expenses are the costs of maintaining the investment—for example, paying the property manager, fixing the air conditioner, and cutting the grass. Some operating expenses are fixed, meaning they are costs incurred regardless of occupancy, and others are variable, meaning they vary depending upon occupancy.

Suppose the office building for which we are creating a pro forma has current operating expenses of $2 per square foot, which are expected to increase by 2 percent annually. Further suppose that 80 percent of the expenses are fixed and the others are variable. Therefore, the maximum current operating expense is $2 per square foot × 2,400 square feet = $4,800. However, only 80 percent of these costs are fixed: That is, the owner is paying 0.8 × $4,800 = $3,840 in fixed expenses and ($4,800 − $3,840) × 0.75 = $720 in variable expenses (because only 1,800/2,400 square feet = 75 percent of the building is occupied) for a total of $4,560. Of course, by the time the new owner takes over, the expenses will have risen by 2 percent.

The real estate salesperson adds the operating expenses to the pro forma projection as follows:

Operating Expenses

	Year 1	Year 2	Year 3	Year 4	Year 5
Maximum	$4,896	$4,994	$5,094	$5,196	$5,300
Fixed	$3,917	$3,995	$4,075	$4,157	$4,240
Vacancy	25%	75%	0%	0%	25%
Variable	$734	$250	$1,019	$1,039	$795
TOTAL	$4,651	$4,245	$5,094	$5,196	$5,035

Some sample calculations are given below.

Year 3 Maximum = Year 2 Maximum × 1.02 = $4,994 × 1.02 = $5,094

Year 2 Fixed Expenses = Year 2 Maximum × 0.8 = $4,994 × 0.8 = $3,995

Year 1 Variable = (Year 1 Maximum − Year 1 Fixed) × (1 − Vacancy)
                = ($4,896 − $3,917) × (1 − 0.25)
                = $734

An actual pro forma will generally be more specific, including the types of fixed and variable costs, such as landscaping, utilities, permits, zoning, and legal work.

Net Operating Income

The net operating income (NOI) figure is important to investors for several aspects of analysis, including cap rates and cash flows. NOI is the difference between the effective gross income (rent less vacancy) and total operating expenses.

Given the calculations we've made already, we can add NOI to our pro forma:

Net Operating Income

	Year 1	Year 2	Year 3	Year 4	Year 5
Income	$68,400	$25,200	$87,300	$93,600	$68,400
Expenses	-$4,651	-$4,245	-$5,094	-$5,196	-$5,035
NOI	$63,749	$20,955	$82,206	$88,404	$63,365

Total Pre-Tax Cash Flow

Several payments are not considered in the calculation of NOI, such as debt service and leasing commissions, which must be subtracted from the NOI to determine the total pre-tax cash flow of an income-producing property.

Loans for income-producing property are often based on a 75 percent loan-to-value (LTV) ratio, meaning that the investor pays 25 percent of the purchase price of the investment and borrows the rest of the funds. Suppose that the purchase price of the investment property we have been considering is $200,000 and the investor, if he decides to purchase it, will take out a 75 percent LTV loan for $150,000 over a term of 15 years at an annual rate of 7.5 percent. We can use an amortization calculator to determine the annual payments on the loan. In this case, annual payments will be $16,686.

Another recurring expense not included in the NOI is the commission of the real estate broker. Brokers often earn commission based on the rent received from tenants. If the commission rate is eight percent, we can calculate our pre-tax cash flow on the pro forma as follows:

Total Pre-Tax Cash Flow

	Year 1	Year 2	Year 3	Year 4	Year 5
Rent	$68,400	$25,200	$87,300	$93,600	$68,400
NOI	$63,749	$20,955	$82,206	$88,404	$63,365
Loan	-$16,686	-$16,686	-$16,686	-$16,686	-$16,686
Commission	-$5,472	-$2,016	-$6,984	-$7,488	-$5,472
Pre-Tax Cash Flow	$41,591	$2,253	$58,536	$64,230	$41,207

After-Tax Cash Flow

Many expenses can be deducted from the property owner's annual taxes, including the interest on the loan, improvements made to the property, any loan fees that are amortized over the course of the loan and the commissions paid to the broker(s).

More About: To determine the annual interest paid on a loan with fixed rate payments, we can use an amortization schedule, which can be calculated at several online sites, such as http://www.hsh.com.

For a $150,000 loan at 7.5 percent interest over 15 years, the schedule looks like this:

	Year 1	Year 2	Year 3	Year 4	Year 5
Interest	$11,059	$10,622	$10,152	$9,644	$9,098
Principal	$5,627	$6,064	$6,535	$7,042	$7,589
Total	$16,686	$16,686	$16,686	$16,686	$16,686
Balance	$144,373	$138,309	$131,774	$124,733	$117,144

So the final, after-tax cash flow for the property we are considering is:

After-Tax Cash Flow

	Year 1	Year 2	Year 3	Year 4	Year 5
NOI	$63,749	$20,955	$82,206	$88,404	$63,365
Interest	$11,059	$10,622	$10,152	$9,644	$9,098
Commission	$5,472	$2,016	$6,984	$7,488	$5,472
Taxable Income	$47,218	$8,317	$65,070	$71,272	$48,795
Taxes@27%	$12,749	$2,246	$17,569	$19,243	$13,175
Pre-Tax CF	$41,591	$2,253	$58,536	$64,230	$41,207
After-Tax Cash Flow	$28,842	$7	$40,994	$44,987	$28,032

Some sample calculations are given below:

Year 3 Taxable Income = Year 3 NOI − Year 3 Interest − Year 3 Commission
= $82,206 − $10,152 − $6,984
= $65,070

Year 3 Taxes = Year 3 Taxable Income × 0.27 = $65,070 × 0.27 = $17,569

Year 3 ATCF = Year 3 PTCF − Year 3 Taxes = $58,563 − $17,569 = $40,994

Using the Pro Forma Projection

Pro formas are used to determine the cash flows for alternative investments or asset management decisions. The discounted cash flow (DCF) analysis allows an investor or manager to compare several alternatives by discounting the cash flows of each to a net present value, which can then be compared.

Taxes and Depreciation

An important element of decision-making in real estate is taxes. Income from income-producing properties is taxed at normal income tax rates (that is, according to the rates of the property's owner), but income from long-term capital gains, such as the sale of a property held for more than one year, is taxed according to the capital gains rates.

The gain realized on the sale of real estate is based upon the investor's taxable basis in the property. The basis when an investor acquires a property is usually the price he or she paid for the property. This basis is adjusted for depreciation over the life of the asset. Depreciation is a decrease in the value of an asset that has a limited life. For example, land is not depreciable, because it is not considered to have a limited life, although the property built on that land is depreciable. Only property used in business or held for investment is depreciable.

The IRS publishes the depreciation rates for the various types of investments. Many assets can be depreciated using several methods of the taxpayer's choice, but investment property, both residential and commercial, must be depreciated using the straight-line method. This means that the rate of depreciation does not increase or decrease over the useful life of the property. Nonresidential property, for example, is considered to have a useful life of 39 years and depreciates at a constant rate of 2.564 percent annually. Suppose an investor purchases an office building for $80,000 in April 2004. What is her basis in March 2014? To determine the investor's basis, we must use the rates provided by the IRS, in the table below:

Depreciation Rates for Nonresidential Property

	Year 1	Years 2 up to 39	Year 40
January	2.461%	2.564%	0.107%
February	2.247%	2.564%	0.321%
March	2.033%	2.564%	0.535%
April	1.819%	2.564%	0.749%
May	1.605%	2.564%	0.963%
June	1.391%	2.564%	1.177%
July	1.177%	2.564%	1.391%
August	0.963%	2.564%	1.605%
September	0.749%	2.564%	1.819%
October	0.535%	2.564%	2.033%
November	0.321%	2.564%	2.247%
December	0.107%	2.564%	2.461%

Depreciation for the first year is 1.819% × $80,000 = $1,455.20, because the property was acquired in April. Depreciation for 2005-2013 is based upon the original value, not upon the depreciated value of the previous year, so we can just multiply the rates 2.564% annual rate x 9 years = 23.076%. Thus depreciation over that time is equal to 23.076% x $80,000 = $18,460.80. The property cannot be depreciated in the year of sale because it is no longer possessed by the investor when taxes are due.

$1,455.20 + $18,460.80 = $19,916

If the investor sells the property in March, her basis will be:

$80,000 − $19,916 = $60,084

Therefore, if she sells the building for $90,000, she has realized $90,000 − $60,084 = $29,916 in capital gains.

In addition to the tax on capital gains, there is a 50 percent tax on recaptured depreciation. The amount of depreciation recovered is equal to the original purchase price of the property less the adjusted basis at the time of sale if the property is sold for more than its original purchase price. If it sells for less, the recaptured depreciation is the final sale price less the adjusted basis at the time of sale. Properties sold at a loss recover no depreciation. If the investor's basis is $60,084 at the time of sale, the recaptured depreciation equals $80,000 − $60,084 = $19,916, so her total taxes are:

Capital Gains:	$29,926 × 0.36 tax rate	= $10,773.36
Recaptured depreciation:	$19,916 × 0.5 tax rate	= $9,958
Total:		= $20,731.36

Activity: Critical Thinking

Consider these questions and select the better of the two answer choices:

Question1
An appraiser needs to determine the value of a hospital building. Which of the following methods of appraisal is best suited to the task?

- The sales comparison approach. A hospital is typically a large building with many specific features and improvements. Its appraisal requires the use of a valuation technique that can account for these features individually with adjustments. An appraiser should have no trouble finding comparable properties in the vicinity. This is important because the value of a hospital is much more likely to fluctuate with the property market than with the costs of construction.

- The cost approach. Hospitals are specialized properties for which it is very difficult to find comparables. The cost approach allows the appraiser to determine a reasonable market value based upon intrinsic features of the property itself. It also allows for enough leeway to adjust for obsolete or ineffective design not in accordance with the hospital's highest and best use.

Answer
Hospitals are few compared with other sorts of real estate, and it is unlikely that an appraiser could find comparable properties to use the sales comparison approach. The cost approach allows the appraiser to consider the value of the special features of the property itself, by equating it with the construction costs less depreciation. Although the cost approach partly includes the sales comparison approach in the valuation of land, it should not be difficult to find comparable parcels of land nearby.

Question2
If a property's cap rate increases, its value _____.

- Increases. High cap rates mean high returns. An investor seeks to make a substantial return on his investment—that is, to increase the net operating income (NOI). Because NOI and the capitalization rate are positively correlated (an increase in one means an increase in the other), high cap rates are indicative of high returns. This makes properties with high or increasing cap rates hot commodities on the market.

- Decreases. Cap rates are inversely correlated with the property values of investment real estate. Increases in cap rates that are not associated with increases in a property's net operating income (NOI) indicate a reduction in that property's value. Investors look for properties with low current cap rates and look to decrease the cap rate of the properties they own.

Answer
Although it is true that an increase in the cap rate may indicate in increase in return, it also indicates a decrease in value. The formula for determining them is Capitalization Rate = NOI ÷ Value.

Question3
Which of the following is true of fixed expenses?

- They never change. Fixed expenses are rightly so-called: They are fixed and do not vary, as opposed to variable expenses. Variable expenses include all of the expenses involved in tenant upkeep, including repairs and services for tenants.

- They can change, but they are not affected by vacancy. By definition, fixed expenses are just those expenses that do not involve tenant upkeep. They include such things as grounds maintenance and the salary of the property manager. These expenses can increase over time, but they are called "fixed" because they are not affected by vacancy.

Answer
Fixed expenses are fixed with respect to vacancy, although they may vary with respect to other factors, such as the salaries of any full-time employees needed for the property, property tax rates, regular maintenance, waste disposal, property insurance, and mortgage payments.

Question4
A lender wants to charge discount points and simultaneously decrease the lending rate, not to increase her profit, but to make it more certain. How should she determine the amount of the discount to be charged?

- The lender should use a discounted cash flow (DCF) analysis. She can calculate the future cash flows from interest from both the current lending rate and the rate after the discount. The difference between these two cash flows is the cash flow the lender is giving up. This she discounts, using a DCF analysis, to a net present value (NPV). She should make sure that the amount of the discount charged on the loan is equal to the NPV of the cash flows she forgoes through the rate reduction.

- The lender should use a cap rate analysis. She can calculate the net operating income she receives from interest (the rent on money) from both the current lending rate and the rate after the discount. She can then use the capitalization rate from the loan before the discount to determine the value of the interest after the lending rate is reduced. The difference between these two values is the amount she forgoes by reducing the lending rate and should be the amount of the discount.

Answer
The discounted cash flow analysis is especially useful in this situation because the lender must balance two values: a present value (the value of the discount) and future values from the interest payment cash flows. She can balance these by discounting the future cash flows to a present value using her best alternative investment (that is, what she will invest the amount of the discount in). Cap rates may be useful for valuing income-producing properties, but they are not very useful with these types of cash flows. A cap rate analysis is based on the idea that a future investor desiring a certain NOI at a certain cap rate would be willing to pay an amount of future dollars that is a function of the two.

Question5
An appraiser needs to appraise a noncommercial, suburban, single-family home. What is the best approach to valuation in this case?

- The sales comparison approach. The value of a residential property is best discovered by considering the sale price of comparable properties in the vicinity. The difference between the costs of construction and the market value of a home may vary widely with supply, demand, and other current market factors.

- The cost approach. Because new houses are being constructed all the time, the true value of a home is best approximated by considering the cost of rebuilding it. When the cost approach is an available method, it is more accurate because there are so many factors affecting the sale of comparable properties, such as buyer and seller negotiations, that obscure the true value of a home.

Answers
The sales comparison approach is not only the most accurate method for appraising residential real estate, it is also the approach most heavily weighted by the real estate appraiser in such cases. However, this may not always be so. An appraisal performed for an insurance company might weight the cost approach more heavily, because it seeks to determine a value for repairing or rebuilding the property if it is damaged. It is not always true that new houses are being constructed, and even if they were, the cost approach fails to fully account for important market factors, such as supply and demand, in its calculation of a property's value. However, the cost approach might sometimes be more useful, such as when the appraisal is performed for an insurance company. An insurer wants to know the cost of repairing or rebuilding a property if it is damaged, and this is best shown by the cost approach.

Case Study: Net Present Value

Investor X wants to purchase a 15,000-square-foot, four-unit strip mall. She brings a pro forma for the property to Lender Y. Based upon the 10-year cash flows indicated below, if the lender is willing to lend 75 percent of the strip mall's NPV, what is the size of the loan Investor X can receive? Use Lender Y's interest rate for large investments, eight percent, as the discount rate.

Year	After-Tax Cash Flow	Year	After-Tax Cash Flow
1	$21,200	6	$24,900
2	$23,000	7	$25,500
3	$22,800	8	$26,600
4	$23,600	9	$27,000
5	$24,100	10	$27,800

To help you grasp the nature of NPV calculations, we will perform this one by hand. NPV works like this: Suppose the investment property brings in $21,200 after taxes in its first year. Then the future value (at one year) of that cash flow is $21,200, but its present value is less. This is because if the investor had invested his money at a rate of 8 percent interest, he would have needed a smaller amount of current dollars to have $21,200 in one year. In fact, he would have needed:

Current Dollars × (1 + 8%) = $21,200
Current Dollars = $21,200/(1 + 8%)
Current Dollars = $19,629.63

The amount of current dollars the investor needs to purchase a future cash flow is the NPV of that cash flow. Therefore, the NPV of this particular investment after one year is $19,629.63.

The NPV of the second year is a little different. We can't simply figure how many current dollars it would take at 8 percent to arrive at a future cash flow of $23,000 in two years. This is because the 8 percent return on our investment the first year has an 8 percent return itself the second year. Therefore, the present value for the second year is:

NPV = $23,000/(1.08 × 1.08) = $19,718.79

And so on for each successive year. The NPV of the entire investment is just the sum of each year's NPV for the first 10 years, or:

$$NPV = \sum_{i=0}^{n} [(Cash\ Flow\ at\ i) \div (1 + Discount\ Rate)^{t(i)}]$$

The figures are as follows:

Year	Cash Flow	$(1 + \text{Discount})^{\text{year}}$	NPV
1	$21,200	1.080000	$19,629.63
2	$23,000	1.166400	$19,718.79
3	$22,800	1.259712	$18,099.38
4	$23,600	1.360489	$17,346.70
5	$24,100	1.469328	$16,402.06
6	$24,900	1.586874	$15,691.23
7	$25,500	1.713824	$14,879.01
8	$26,600	1.850930	$14,371.15
9	$27,000	1.999005	$13,506.72
10	$27,800	2.158925	$12,876.78
Total: $162,521.45			

It's OK that each successive year's NPV after Year 2 is lower than the year before. With each passing year, a future cash value increases in present value. For example, the NPV of the cash flow in Year 6 is $15,691.23 today; but in Year 5, the cash flow in year 6 has an NPV of $23,055.56.

Based upon the NPV of the investment after 10 years, Lender Y is willing to lend 0.75 × $162,521.45 = $121,891.09. Of course, he must also approve the loan itself, by making sure that Investor X has sound credit, that the cash flows of the property will be able to amortize the loan, and so on.

Summary

A loan applicant's creditworthiness cannot be considered in and of itself: The condition and value of the property to be purchased must also be obtained if the lender is to make an informed decision. Appraisers are those whose job it is to value property. For noncommercial property, appraisers have two methods of valuation: the sales comparison approach and the cost approach.

The eight steps to completing an appraisal are: stating the objective, listing the data needed, gathering and recording data, determining the highest and best use, estimating the land value, estimating value using applicable approaches to appraisal, reconciling the final value estimate, and completing and presenting the value report.

A professional real estate appraiser evaluates the worth of a property. Anybody may request an appraisal-an individual or a company-and it may be sought for any reason, such as determining a loan value or for insurance coverage. An appraiser submits her or his evaluation in the form of an appraisal report, for which he or she must conduct a thorough study of the property.

In the sales comparison approach, the appraiser collects data on the sale prices of comparable properties in the vicinity of the property to be appraised (the subject property). According to the principle of substitution, a buyer will be willing to spend on the subject property just as much as she or he could pay to obtain a comparable property. To properly compare the sale prices the appraiser has collected, he or she adjusts the sales amount by the value of certain positive or negative aspects in which they differ from the subject property (such as location or improvements). In the sales comparison approach, improvements are valued only so far as they add to the market value of a property, in accordance with the principle of contribution. The appraiser can then estimate a value for the subject property using the adjusted sale prices of the comparable properties.

In the cost approach, the appraiser operates on the principle that a buyer will be willing to spend on the subject property just as much as he or she could pay to reconstruct that property from scratch. To calculate the value, then, the appraiser determines the cost of purchasing a comparable parcel of land (usually with the sales comparison approach applied to the raw land in the area), adds the price of reconstructing the subject property and subtracts the amount of depreciation.

For commercial properties, the sales comparison and cost approaches are not as reliable. The most widely used method of valuing income-producing property is the cap rate analysis. The cap rate is the quotient of a property's net operating income (NOI) to its current value. Thus, to estimate the current value of a property, the appraiser determines its likely future NOI. He or she divides this by the cap rate the appraiser believes a future investor will want to determine the future value of the property. The difference between the future value and the current value of the property is the investor's return on investment. Investors will be willing to pay for the subject property just as much as they could pay to receive the same return on investment from another investment.

Another method of valuation, which is gaining ground in the market today, is the discounted cash flow (DCF) analysis. These analyses use pro forma projections-future financial statements incorporating certain assumptions and hypotheses-to determine an alternative's cash flows. These cash flows are then discounted to an NPV using a complex equation that many software programs, such as Excel, can perform. The investor or manager then compares the difference between the discounted present value and the cost of several alternatives, to determine the best asset allocation strategy. This type of NPV analysis is closely related to the internal rate of return (IRR). This rate can be compared with other available rates, such as stock market returns or securities investments, to determine an asset allocation strategy. Some investors use the modified internal rate of return (MIRR) instead, considering it a more accurate assessment of value.

This concludes Lesson four.

Return to your online course player to take the Lesson Quiz.

Lesson 5:
THE FINANCING PROCESS

This lesson focuses on the following topics:

- Introduction
- Mortgage Brokers
- Loan Officers
- Application
- Title
- Survey
- Earnest Money Contract
- Escrow Accounts
- Deed
- Closing
- Activity: Fill In the Blank
- Summary

By the end of this lesson, you should be able to:

- Distinguish between a mortgage broker and a loan officer, identifying each in a case study
- Explain the loan application process, defining prequalification, online applications, and floating rates
- Distinguish between constructive and actual notice and explain the buyer's obligations under the principle of caveat emptor
- List the lender's requirements for qualifying the title and explain how, through a title search, a title insurance company verifies that a mortgagee will have the first lien
- List the types of insurance policies, identifying characteristics of each
- Explain the purpose of surveys and name the three main types
- Distinguish between the purpose and content of an earnest money contract and the earnest money deposit
- Explain the requirements for, and the logic behind, establishing escrow accounts
- Explain what a deed is and list the types of interest it can convey

- Explain the exceptions and reservations that can be placed on a title, providing specific examples
- Distinguish between a deed and a title, identifying each in a case study

Introduction

So far we have covered the basic concepts involved in real estate finance and the methods by which an underwriter qualifies borrowers and properties. The next two lessons seek to complete the picture. Before a borrower can be qualified, he or she must meet with a mortgage broker or loan officer and fill out an application. After approval, the lender still requires a title search, title insurance, a survey, and a deed to convey the title. It is at closing (discussed in the next lesson) where the appropriate funds and documents exchange hands and the financing process concludes.

Mortgage Brokers

A mortgage broker (not to be confused with a mortgage banker) is a licensed professional who originates mortgage loans that are financed by one of several lenders the broker works with. Since mortgage brokers deal exclusively with the residential home loan process, they are highly specialized and can be beneficial in several ways to potential buyers.

The majority of a mortgage broker's commissions come from the approval of loan applications, so it is in her or his best interest to find lenders with the lowest rates and the most relaxed underwriting standards. Each state's licensing laws will cover the requirements of mortgage brokers. In some states, including Texas, mortgage brokers must have a mortgage broker license.

Loan Officers

Loan officers are like mortgage brokers in that they facilitate the mortgage loan process and often receive a commission for their services. The difference is that loan officers are employed by one specific financial institution. They usually specialize in commercial or residential loans, contacting potential clients to persuade them to apply for a loan from their sponsoring institution. Since a loan officer works for one institution, she or he has no interest in finding the best loan on the market for a consumer; however, the loan officer should be able to find the best loan at his or her sponsoring institution. Those seeking real estate financing often are directed by their real estate broker to a specific loan officer with whom the broker has an arrangement.

Loan officers are typically required to have a four-year degree in finance or economics. Two subgroups of loan officers are loan counselors and loan collection officers. Loan counselors help those for whom traditional financing is not available by explaining financing alternatives and by helping with the loan application. Loan collection officers assist those with payments past due and, if a repayment plan cannot be worked out, initiate the foreclosure process.

Application

The loan process begins with the loan application. The borrower first meets with a mortgage broker or loan officer to fill out the application (an example is included in the supplementary materials of this course, as the Uniform Residential Loan Application, Fannie Mae Form 1003). After the application is filed, its information is checked. For example, the salary and employment information is checked against the Verification of Employment Form sent to the applicant's employer. The loan officer then will order an appraisal and send this package-the verified application and the appraisal-to the underwriter.

The underwriter's role has been discussed in the previous two lessons. He or she evaluates the applicant's creditworthiness and the value of the property to decide whether to approve the loan. After the application is approved, it is sent to the closing department of the financial institution, where the title is inspected and insured, the survey is ordered, and the deed is prepared. The rest of this lesson will discuss these finalizing processes. In the next lesson, we will cover closing, the final step in the real estate financing process.

Prequalification
When a borrower applies for a loan, she or he must have a sales contract for the property to be mortgaged. When the borrower doesn't yet have a sales contract, or doesn't know yet which property he or she plans to purchase, the lender will prequalify the borrower for the loan. Often, a broker will require a prospective buyer to be prequalified before showing properties. Prequalification can be relatively informal, involving only verbal information provided by the borrower, or as formal as a loan application, with a credit check and other documentation.

Online Applications
The Internet has made obtaining financing more accessible than ever. Many lenders now have Web sites where borrowers can apply for loans online.

Floating Rates
Interest rates that are not fixed but rather are tied to the market are said to float. The float rate is the interest rate at any particular moment. Borrowers are attracted to loans when the float rate is low. The idea is to lock in a low interest rate and save money throughout the term of the loan. Interest rates, however, are locked in when the loan is issued. This means that between the time of

application and closing, the rate could float up and leave the borrower with a higher interest rate than he or she would desire-after it is too late to get out of the loan.

For this reason, many lenders allow borrowers to pay a lock-in fee to lock in the float rate at the time of the loan's approval. A borrower using a mortgage broker should make sure to ask to see the lender's commitment letter stating that the rate has been locked, as it is the practice of some insidious brokers to keep the lock-in fee in the hopes that the float rate won't change-sometimes leaving borrowers high and dry if the rate does change.

Title

A mortgage lien guarantees repayment to the lender if the borrower does not make the required payments; it allows the lender to force the sale of a property to recoup any losses; the borrower uses the property as collateral and places it as security for a home equity loan. A mortgage allows the borrower to have full legal title to a property, but the lender has a lien (a legal claim against property for owed money) on the property and can foreclose the property if the borrower does not make mortgage payments. Mortgage lenders generally require a preferred lien, also known as a first mortgage lien, which means that (other than real estate taxes) no other major liens against the property can take priority over the mortgage lien. In some states, a deed of trust is used rather than a mortgage lien because the lender can sell or use the property only if loan terms are not met.

Since the lender has only the mortgaged property for collateral, in addition to a property appraisal, she or he should do his or her best to gather information pertaining to the background and title of the property. The lender should perform a title search, examine the abstract of title and chain of title, gather evidence of title, and inspect the property. This responsibility is based on the caveat emptor adage.

Caveat Emptor
The maxim caveat emptor, which means "let the buyer beware," applies to real estate transactions, where the responsibility of investigating the condition of the property belongs to the buyer. The seller needs only to disclose latent defects to the buyer; therefore, the buyer must either ask the seller about defects or inspect the property carefully to discover any obvious damages to the property. Once an individual has knowledge about a defect in a certain property, he or she is considered to have been given notice of this acquired information or interest, either through constructive notice or actual notice.

Constructive Notice
Constructive notice serves two interests; one pertaining to filers who have an interest in a property and one pertaining to buyers. If legal interest in a property

has been properly filed in the public record, that filing serves as legal notice to everyone of that party's interest, but if that party fails to properly file, then that party's interest in the property may be forfeited or very difficult to claim. For potential buyers, it is their responsibility to check the public record for any possible claims of interest to a piece of property. If some party's interest has been properly recorded and the buyer has failed to look in the public record for claims of interest, such as a lien, then the buyer may have problems when the interested party decides to claim her or his legal interest. Constructive notice basically means that if notice is anywhere in the public record, it is a legal claim regardless of whether it is communicated. A property owner also may give constructive notice of ownership by visibly occupying or making use of the property.

Actual Notice

After an individual has researched a property through public records and personal inspection, he or she now has direct knowledge of the property from information that the individual self-acquired. With that self-acquired information, the individual is expected to be able to infer, or at least ask about, subjects that may not be in the public record but are nonetheless legal interest in the property. For example, a buyer looks at a site and notices that there are two utility poles on the property. The buyer should be able to infer that the utility company has an easement right to install and service the utility poles-and if uncertain, should ask about it. Actual notice in the public record of the easement by the utility company is not required for its legal interest to be valid.

Priority

Disputes often arise concerning who recorded a deed first, who had constructive or actual notice or who took possession of a property first; therefore, it is important to note that taking possession of a parcel of land or property takes precedence over recording a deed. Priority, in this case, refers to the order of rights in relation to time. This means that if neither party has taken possession of the property, then whoever recorded the deed first has ownership rights.

Title History

Certain liens, such as real estate taxes and some inheritance and franchise taxes, do not need to be recorded at the office of the county clerk. However, as previously stated, documents that need to be recorded in the public record include deeds, judgment liens, and mechanics' liens, so that the history and background of a property is available for reference. Interested parties need to perform title searches, obtain abstracts of titles, and review the chain of title in order to trace the previous owners of the property as well as to identify any liens and encumbrances placed on the property. The history of a title reveals any information that a prospective buyer or property owner needs to know in order to successfully transfer the title of a property.

Title Search

When an individual performs a title search, he or she examines available public records to ensure that no clouds on the title exist; therefore, the property owner can legally transfer ownership of the property. The title search begins with the present owner and traces the lineage back to the original owner (or grantor), thereby examining each ownership to ensure that no encumbrances, forged documents, or gaps in ownership exist. Lawyers, qualified title searchers, or insurance companies usually perform title searches for prospective buyers or mortgagees.

Abstract of Title

An abstract of title is a condensed listing of a property's history and chronicles any transfers in ownership as well as any liabilities and encumbrances attached to the real estate. An abstracter prepares the document by performing a title search, which will return the title's history. From this information, the abstracter summarizes all events that previously affected the title as well as current liens and encumbrances and their status. The abstracter also will attach a document to the abstract of title that lists the records that she or he used or did not use to generate the abstract.

Chain of Title

A chain of title is similar to an abstract of title, except that a chain of title displays only the previous owners of the property, how the property became vested and where the record is located. An individual can search for past grantors and grantees by accessing the grantor-grantee indexes; these books display the names of all grantors and grantees according to year. A complete line of ownership can be established by performing a search of the grantor-grantee indexes. When there is a gap in the chain, a suit to quiet title must be called to establish ownership; this occurs when ownership cannot be established through an unbroken chain.

Title Plants

A title plant is a collection of title records that is privately owned and maintained, usually by a title insurance company.

Title Insurance

Title insurance protects a policyholder from any events that occurred before the issuance of the policy; this protects the policyholder against any losses that may arise from defects in the title (such as a forged title). If the insurance company deems the title insurable (based upon an examination of the public records), they agree to compensate the policyholder for any losses he or she may encounter from unidentified defects in the title (that existed prior to the policyholder's ownership). However, by agreeing to settle any claims for a policyholder, the insurance company has the right of subrogation, which allows the insurance company to assume the rights of the policyholder in order to reclaim any damages against those responsible for the claim.

Lenders require an extensive examination of public records before they issue a loan; therefore, lenders consider title insurance the ideal form of evidence of title because insurance companies thoroughly examine public records before issuing a policy to protect against any defects in the title. This process involves a title search performed by an abstracter, attorney, or company employee. Afterward, the company attorney issues an opinion regarding who she or he thinks has a legitimate claim to the property. Once the insurance company has discovered all pertinent public record information, it issues a title commitment, which ensures that the company will issue a policy.

Despite the precautions taken to ensure a valid property conveyance, mistakes can still occur. The following are some examples of title defects that might cause a borrower to lose his or her home and a lender to lose collateral:

- At some point in the title's history, the property was conveyed by one spouse without the consent or knowledge of the other. In some states, this would not be a defect if the conveying spouse owned the property himself or herself, but in a community property state such as Texas, this would be a defect.

- At some point in the title's history, a deed was executed by a minor, by someone psychologically incapable of executing a deed or by someone pretending to be the owner or forging the owner's signature. In all of these cases, ownership would revert to the person who held the property before the invalid deed was executed.

- An estate holder died and did not leave a will. Normally, ownership would pass to her or his heirs, but suppose that, unbeknownst to anyone involved, he or she had a missing or undisclosed heir. The government might sell the estate holder's property at auction, but when the missing heir turned up, that heir could claim it.

- A deed may have been executed by someone who seemed to have the owner's power of attorney but, because the documents granting them that power were invalid or expired, did not truly have the right to do so.

- A property may have a lien on it due to unpaid taxes. Since tax liens are not recorded, it would be difficult for a title search to uncover such information. If the taxes remained unpaid, the government would be able to foreclose on the property to recover its losses.

It is, however, very rare for any of these situations to occur. The importance of title insurance is the guarantee it gives to the lender. A title insurance company will not issue a policy if there is even a small chance it will have to pay for a title defect. Therefore, title companies perform thorough title searches, searches of the tax records, searches of legal records for judgments, and sometimes even informal property inspections to determine whether there are undisclosed easements.

Title Commitment

A title commitment is a promulgated form that offers to issue a title policy; it is a statement of the terms and conditions that the insurance company wishes to uphold and to offer the policyholder. The title commitment also illustrates the condition of the property at the time the commitment is made, lists only the current property owner and identifies only the mortgage loans that have not been removed.

Types of Policies

Insurance companies offer various types of policies to accommodate the different types of customers who need insurance. These are the most common types of insurance policies:

Mortgage Title Insurance

Policy that assures lenders that they have a first lien against the property. If there is an issue with the title, the policy will pay for any court costs required to defend the title against a lawsuit and will pay for any losses the policyholder suffers due to defective title.

Leasehold Title Insurance

Policy that assures lessees that they have a valid lease.

Owner's Policy of Title Insurance

Policy that insures the buyer, as opposed to the lender, against title defects.

Certificate of Sale Title Insurance

Policy that is issued during court sales and protects the buyer's interest in property sold by the court.

Standard title insurance policies can protect policyholders against the following:

- Fraud
- Forgery
- Abstract of title errors
- Incompetent grantors
- Foreclosure
- Unmarketable titles

Attorney's Opinion of Title

If a prospective borrower or buyer wants to use an attorney's opinion of title as evidence of title, the borrower must first hire an abstracter to prepare an abstract, which contains a summary of all of the events that have affected or currently affect the title, as well as a listing of records that he or she did and did not use. Abstracters do not give opinions concerning the condition of the title; therefore, abstracters should exercise proper care by accurately recording and conveying all information in order to avoid claims of negligence.

After the abstracter generates the abstract, the buyer's attorney inspects the document by evaluating all of the information on the abstract. The attorney then prepares an attorney's opinion of title that addresses the ownership condition of the property. Although the attorney's opinion of title and abstract are carefully produced, these reports do not guarantee against defects not found in the public records, nor can attorneys and abstracters promise that no errors occurred in the process.

Survey

Lenders often will require a survey before originating a loan. All loans sold on the secondary market require title insurance and an accurate survey. There are three main types of surveys: geodetic, cadastral, and topographic.

Earnest Money Contract

The earnest money contract is an important part of the home-buying process. Because real estate deals require time and energy, offers usually are not made or accepted without some sort of guarantee that the buyer has a genuine interest in purchasing the property. The seller does not want to lose valuable marketing time with an uninterested buyer.

In an earnest money contract, the buyer states an offering price-the price he or she is willing to pay for the property-and actually puts down a portion or all of the down payment as an earnest money deposit.

There are no limits on the amount of money that can be put down in the earnest money deposit. A buyer does not want to put down too little and risk having the seller believe that she or he is not serious, but neither does the buyer want to put down too much and risk having a large amount of money tied up in the event of legal difficulty. Buyers usually put down 1 percent to 1.5 percent of the sale price as an earnest money deposit. These deposits are not refundable unless so stated in the contract. The contracts usually allow for certain contingencies, or circumstances in which the deposit is to be refunded. Examples include the following:

- The buyer fails to receive financing.
- The seller changes his or her mind.

- The property is rezoned, damaged, or destroyed.
- The property fails to pass certain requisite inspections (which usually leads to the buyer failing to receive financing as well).

In addition to the earnest money deposit and the offer to purchase, the earnest money contract includes the following:

- A legal description of the property to be purchased
- The buyer's full down payment (including the earnest money deposit)
- The type and source of financing
- The relationship of the brokers involved to the parties of the contract
- Any requisite inspections
- The title insurance policy
- The survey
- The seller's disclosure

When the earnest money contract is ratified (signed) by both parties, it can be presented to the lender as a contract for sale, allowing the borrower to get qualified for a loan and receive the financing necessary for a purchase.

Escrow Accounts

Escrow accounts are accounts held by the lending institution to which the borrower pays monthly installments for property taxes, insurance, and special assessments. Lenders also disburse these sums as they become due from these accounts. When a LTV loan that is greater than 80 percent is made, these accounts are required on all loans, regardless of whether conventional, FHA, or VA.

Escrow accounts generally contain the following payments:

- Taxes
- Hazard insurance
- Private mortgage insurance
- One-time PMI premium

Deed

A deed is not the same thing as title. "Title" is the rights or ownership of real property; a "deed' is a legal written document that conveys rights or ownership. Title is intangible; a deed is tangible.

Depending on location and local regulations, the deed is prepared by a lawyer or settlement agent. If title is to be held by a trustee as security for the loan, a deed of trust is used; otherwise, the deed conveys title directly to the borrower, and a mortgage is used as security.

Only a deed that meets all state requirements and the requirements of a valid contract successfully conveys title. This act of title conveyance is called a grant. While there are slight differences in state statutes pertaining to valid conveyance, in general, states share many of the same criteria. A deed has the following components:

- Grantor

- Grantee

- Consideration

- Granting clause

- Habendum clause

- Limitations

- Legal description

- Exceptions and reservations

- Grantor's signature

- Acknowledgment

- Delivery and acceptance

The following sections discuss each of these components in detail.

Grantor
The grantor is the individual who is voluntarily conveying title to another. Because all parties to a contract must have contract capabilities, the grantor in a deed must be:

- 18 years of age or older

- Of sound mind

- Legally competent

- Of legal existence

As in all contracts, a grantor must be of the age of majority and of competent and sound mind. Generally, it is deemed that the grantor is of sound mind if she or he is capable of understanding the issues or actions covered in a contract.

It is important that the grantor's name be properly and consistently spelled throughout the deed. If a grantor's name changed since he or she acquired title, then any conveyance document should include both names. If two names are needed, it may appear as illustrated below:

"Ms. A, now known as Ms. B"

Marriage may further complicate the grantor section of a deed, as it may necessitate two grantors. If a grantor is married, then in many states his or her spouse needs to sign the deed as well. This is because, in some states, a person has title to her or his spouse's property. Consequently, both spouses must sign the deed to release marital rights.

Grantee
In a deed, the grantee is the person accepting the property; he or she is the purchaser. The grantee must be readily identifiable for a deed to properly transfer title. A deed that has as the grantee a fictitious person, a club or society that is not properly incorporated, or a company that does not exist is not enforceable.

Consideration
All contracts require some consideration-something of value that induces a party to join in a contract. Deeds also require consideration. While we think of consideration as a property's sale price, most deeds do not include the actual sale price. Instead, most deeds contain a minimal statement of consideration. If it is a common purchaser/seller deed, a statement such as, "For ten dollars and other good and valuable consideration," is used. If the property is a gift to a friend or relative, the consideration may be worded, "For natural love and affection." In both instances, those phrases are sufficient to meet the consideration requirement. Only when a corporation or trustee executes an instrument or when a court orders conveyance is a deed likely to contain the full consideration amount.

Granting Clause
A granting clause is a formal statement declaring that the grantor wishes to convey his or her current interest at that time. No deed may state that a grantor wishes to convey interest in the future. Deeds convey current interest at the time of deliverance only. Sometimes the granting clause is called words of conveyance.

The extent and wording of a granting clause depends upon the type of deed and the deed's exact objective. Depending upon the grantor's intent, any of these words or wordings may be used:

- "Grant"
- "Grant, sell, and convey"
- "Remise, release, and quitclaim"

Note: A quitclaim is a relinquishing of all, if any, current interest. Also, a quitclaim deed uses the wording "quit claim" rather than "grant, sell, and convey."

If there is more than one grantee, then the granting clause should clarify the type of interest passed to each. There are different types of ownership and interest in property. It is necessary that the granting clause address this. If the type of interest or use of the property under the deed needs further explanation, then the deed will include a habendum clause.

Habendum Clause
A habendum clause generally follows a granting clause as needed. When used, it will contain a phrase describing the extent of ownership. For example, a habendum clause commonly contains the phrase, "To have and to hold." A habendum clause clarifies the type and extent of interest conveyed by the granting clause. If the two are at odds, then the granting clause supersedes. The most common types of interest conveyed are fee simple, life estate, and easement.

Fee Simple Estate
Fee simple estate is the most general and most complete ownership one can hold. A fee simple estate means that the grantor is giving to the grantee full disposal of a property for the grantee's lifetime with the right to do with the property as the grantee sees fit and the right of inheritance for the grantee's heirs.

Life Estate
A life estate is more restrictive than fee simple ownership. A life estate limits ownership to the lifetime of the owner or some other party. While a fee simple estate includes inheritance rights for the grantee's heirs, a life estate does not.

Easement
An easement, or right-of-way, is the right to use a part of someone's property. It is not ownership in the most traditional or generic sense. For example, if a party wishes to use resources on someone's property or place wiring or pipes through someone's property, then he or she is likely to obtain a right-of-way.

Limitations

A deed should specifically state any limitations to ownership; however, it is common for deeds to state the absence of any such limitation as well. For example, if a grantor conveys a fee simple estate, then the deed may include a phrase similar to this:

"To Ms. X and to her heirs and assigns forever"

To convey a life estate, one type of limited title, a grantor may use the following phrase:

"To Ms. X for the duration of her natural life"

Legal Description

For a deed to adequately convey title, the property must be identified and distinguished from all other properties in the world. This is called legal description. Only legal land description methods, such as metes and bounds or rectangular survey description should be used. An address, district, or any other form of informal land description will not meet the legal description method.

Exceptions and Reservations

When there are no limitations on title, we say that the title is clear. Any type of limitation, such as an encumbrance or reservation that affects the title, must be stated. Common limitations include the following:

- Liens (such as a mortgage, mechanics lien or tax lien)
- Easements
- Taxes
- Restrictions

A lien is an outstanding debt or financial obligation on a property, such as a mortgage. An easement, as previously defined, is the right to use a part of someone's property. Taxes are payments to the local, state, or national jurisdictions governing a subject property. A restriction is a private, land-use control that limits property use and development. Most deed restrictions are developed by neighborhood associations or by a subdivision developer. For example, a common deed restriction in subdivisions states that homes may be used only for residential purposes.

A limitation or restriction is sometimes called a subject to clause (see the section on Assumption). This is because a deed without a clear title may convey ownership to a grantee with the phrase subject to. For example, a deed for a property with an outstanding first mortgage may convey title "subject to an existing first mortgage loan, which the grantee assumes and agrees to pay."

Grantor's Signature

All the grantors listed in a deed must sign the deed to convey title. If the person is unable to sign the deed for one reason or another, there are two ways in which a deed can meet the grantor's signature requirement:

- Signature by mark

- Signature by an attorney-in-fact

Signature by Mark

A grantor who cannot sign his or her literal name may sign a deed that adequately conveys title using a "mark." Most states allow one to sign a deed using a mark, providing two or more witnesses see the grantor's execution of the deed and sign the deed as witnesses. Generally, one of the witnesses will print the grantor's name on the deed and the grantor will mark the deed next to her or his printed name.

Signature by an Attorney-in-Fact

Most states permit an attorney-in-fact, one acting under power of attorney, to sign deeds on behalf of the grantor. An attorney-in-fact is an individual who, through specific written authority, may execute legal documents on behalf of a grantor.

Acknowledgment

Acknowledgment is a formal declaration that one is acting under one's own free will, signed before a public notary or authorized public officer. In essence, acknowledgment serves as proof before the public that a grantor is who he or she says he or she is and that the grantor is acting voluntarily and under her or his own volition.

Generally, valid deeds do not require acknowledgment; however, customarily deeds do contain it. Some states may require proof that the grantor's signature is genuine in order to record the deed in the public record, and others may not allow that use of a signature in court unless the genuineness of the signature can be validated.

Delivery and Acceptance

The grantee's signature is not required for valid conveyance. This is because his or her receipt of a deed is accomplished through "acceptance." Before a deed transfers title, it must be delivered by the grantor and either actual or implied acceptance by the grantee must occur. A grantor or the grantor's attorney may deliver the deed, or a third party (escrow agent) may deliver the deed. Regardless of the means of delivery, the delivery must occur during the lifetime of both the grantor and the grantee. Title cannot transfer to, or from, an individual post mortem.

Title passes when the deed is delivered. If an escrow agent or other third party delivers the deed, then the delivery date is the day the deed passed to the third party.

Closing

Closing is the final step in the financing process, when title actually transfers from seller to buyer and the property is paid for. In the next lesson, we will discuss the legal requirements at closing as set forth in the Real Estate Settlement Procedures Act (RESPA), the costs and fees that must be paid, and how these costs are allocated to the buyer and the seller.

Activity: Fill In the Blank

As you read the story of homebuyer Mr. X, choose the term from the word bank that best fits the blank according to what you have learned in the lesson. The Feedback section after this activity will tell you the correct answers.

Word Bank		
Acceptance	Exceptions and reservations	Prequalifies
Acknowledgement	Fee Simple	Priority
Actual	Grantee	Title
Caveat emptor	Granting	Title history
Consideration	Grantor	Title insurance
Constructive	Habendum	Title search
Deed	Mortgage broker	

Fill in the Blanks

Mr. X is looking to buy a home. He locates a property that interests him and employs the services of a (1) _____ to find him a competitive rate from one of several lenders. The lender whom X decides to use (2) _____ him for the loan until X obtains a sales contract. When X obtains the contract, a closing date is set, and the lender looks to qualify the property and its rights of ownership, or (3) _____.

The seller has informed X of a home equity loan she has taken out, thereby giving X (4) _____ notice of the lien. All other liens that are on public record give X (5) _____ notice, which she and the lender are obligated to review by the adage of (6) _____.

The lender seeks evidence that his lien will have first (7) _____, which he considers best achieved by obtaining (8) _____. An insurance company will perform a (9) _____, resulting in a (10) _____, a compressed version of which is the abstract of title.

After the lender is satisfied as to the title's condition, the sale proceeds as usual. When it is time for the seller to convey her title, her attorney draws up a document of conveyance known as a (11) _____. The process of transferring title is the granting process: It happens between the seller, known in the document as the (12) _____ , and the buyer, known as the (13) _____.

The deed contains a formal declaration of the grantor's intention to transfer her interest in the property in the (14) _____ clause. The (15) _____ clause clarifies the type of interest being conveyed. In this case, the seller transfers the full rights of ownership without limitation, otherwise called (16) _____ interest. However, the buyer purchases the property subject to the lien of the home equity lender, and this is indicated in the (17) _____ section.

Traditionally, the deed contains a nominal fee paid by the buyer for the transfer of interest. This fee, the (18) _____, is not always the actual amount of money the buyer gives to the seller. In this case, it is only $10, far short of the sale price. The deed also contains the grantor's signature and her statement that she is acting of her own free will, called (19) _____. When the deed is drawn up, interest is conveyed through the ceremony of (20) _____, when the deed is delivered to the grantee.

Feedback

1. A **mortgage broker** is a licensed real estate professional who specializes in obtaining finance for his or her clients. Mortgage brokers work with several lenders to find a competitive note rate and loan terms.

2. Before a borrower has obtained a sales contract, a lender will **prequalify** her or him for a loan. Many, if not all, of the factors considered in the borrower qualification process are considered in prequalification.

3. The rights that come with the ownership of land are called the owner's **title**.

4. **Actual notice** is any direct knowledge that a party has been given concerning the status of the title. For example, if the seller tells the buyer of a lien or encumbrance on the property, whether or not it is recorded, the buyer has received actual notice of that encumbrance.

5. **Constructive notice** is any publicly available knowledge that the buyer may access. This includes all liens and encumbrances that are matters of public record.

6. A buyer is obligated to investigate public records by the adage of **caveat emptor**, "let the buyer beware." The buyer should make every reasonable effort to protect his or her interests, lest through negligence lose them.

7. Creditors' claims on a property are satisfied in order of **priority**. A lender seeks to have a position of first priority so that in the event of foreclosure, the lender will have the best opportunity to recover damages.

8. The lender considers **title insurance** to be the best evidence of first priority, because the insurance company stands to lose money if it does not carefully and thoroughly examine the public documents and make sure the title is free and clear.

9. A **title search** is the act of examining the public records to uncover a title's history, including current liens and judgments against it. Title searches are performed by lenders, insurance companies, title insurance companies, or anyone else who has a vested interest in learning a title's history.

10. The **title history** reveals all of the information relevant to the transfer of title through a deed. This history is summarized in the abstract of title.

11 A **deed** is a tangible document-a valid, legally binding contract-that conveys title.

12. The **grantor** is the party in the deed that is relinquishing interest; in this case, the seller. Grantors must be of the age of majority, of sound mind, legally competent, and legally existent. For example, they cannot be dead.

13. The **grantee** is the party to whom the title is conveyed by the deed; in this case, the buyer, Mr. X.

14. The act of title conveyance is called granting. In a deed's **granting** clause, the grantor uses specific legal language to convey his or her interest in the property to the grantee.

15. It is the job of the **habendum clause** to clarify the interest conveyed in the granting clause. There are three common types of interest held: fee simple interest, leasehold interest, and easement.

16. In this case, the interest held is **fee simple**, the most complete type of interest, allowing the holder full disposal of the property without limitation.

17. In the **exceptions and reservations** section of the deed, the grantor states any liens, easements, tax obligations, or restrictions (such as a homeowner's association's requirement that the grass be kept a certain length) that affect the

title. In this case, the lien of the home equity creditor affects the title and must be stated.

18. The **consideration** is the thing of value that entices one party to enter the contract. In most seller/purchaser sales, the deed states something like "for ten dollars and other good and valuable consideration," rather than the actual sale price.

19. The grantor testifies to her or his free, uncoerced action in the **acknowledgement**, a customary clause in most contracts.

20. The buyer actually receives title through the process of **acceptance**. The deed is delivered by either the grantor or his or her attorney, and the grantor accepts it either actually or implicitly.

Case Study: Caveat Emptor

Buyer B wishes to learn about Seller A's property; therefore, she calls him and asks about the property's title. She wants to know if the title has a clean history, if it has any liens or encumbrances, if it has any clouds on the title, and if Seller A knew the past owners of the title. Seller A assures Buyer B that the title has had no defects since his acquisition of the title. Feeling reassured after talking to Seller A, Buyer B decides to purchase the property without title insurance. Seller A gives Buyer B a deed, which she records at the county clerk's office.

Three months later, Buyer A receives a foreclosure notice from the court calling for the sale of the property to repay all debts owed to lenders. Is Buyer B responsible for damages?

Yes
No
Possibly

Answer
Buyer B did not adhere to the caveat emptor adage, which warns the buyer to obtain all possible information regarding a purchase. She assumed that her interview with Seller A served as actual notice and did not actively pursue constructive notice by investigating the available public records. By failing to check the public record or to have a title company issue title insurance, Buyer B has made a costly error. Essentially, Buyer B should have performed a title search and had an abstracter generate an abstract of title for her, and she should have purchased title insurance. Therefore, due to her carelessness, she has to suffer the loss.

However, depending upon the specific circumstances of the situation, Seller A could have some liability. If we assume that Seller A did not deceive Buyer B, because he specifically told her that the title has had no defects since his acquisition of the title and because he was unaware of previous encumbrances, then Seller A would probably not be held liable for fraud. On the other hand, if a court determines that Seller A intentionally withheld information, then Seller A would probably be held liable for fraud. Therefore, the correct answer is possibly.

Summary

A mortgage broker (not to be confused with a mortgage banker) is a licensed professional who originates mortgage loans that are financed by one of several lenders the broker works with. Loan officers are like mortgage brokers in that they facilitate the mortgage loan process and often receive a commission for their services. The difference is that loan officers are employed by one specific financial institution. Two subgroups of loan officers are loan counselors and loan collection officers. Loan counselors help those for whom traditional financing is not available by explaining financing alternatives and helping with the loan application. Loan collection officers assist those with payments past due and, if a repayment plan cannot be worked out, initiate the foreclosure process.

The loan process begins with the loan application. The borrower first meets with a mortgage broker or loan officer to fill out the application. After the application is filed, its information is checked: For example, the salary and employment information is checked against the Verification of Employment Form sent to the applicant's employer. The loan officer will then order an appraisal and send this package-the verified application and the appraisal-to the underwriter. When the borrower doesn't yet have a sales contract or doesn't know yet which property she plans to purchase, the underwriter will pre-approve her for the loan. Otherwise, the underwriter uses the techniques discussed in the previous two lessons to qualify the borrower and the property.

A mortgage allows the borrower to have full legal title to a property, but the lender has a lien on the property and can foreclose the property if the borrower does not make mortgage payments. Mortgage lenders generally require a preferred lien, also known as a first mortgage lien, which means that (other than real estate taxes) no other major liens against the property can take priority over the mortgage lien.

Potential buyers are not liable for liens and encumbrances that are not filed on public record; however, if a buyer does not examine the available public documents, he or she can be held liable because she or he had constructive notice. Actual notice refers to any information or knowledge that an individual has pertaining to a property; therefore, if an individual has actual notice of a property's condition, that individual may not use lack of constructive notice (such as unrecorded deeds) to invalidate a claim.

An abstract of title is a compressed listing of a property's history and chronicles any transfers in ownership as well as any liabilities and encumbrances attached to the real estate. A chain of title is similar to an abstract of title, except that a chain of title displays only the previous owners of the property, how the property became vested and where the record is located. Title insurance protects a policyholder from any events that occurred before the issuance of the policy. This protects the policyholder against any losses that may arise from defects in the title. Lenders require an extensive examination of public records before issuing a loan; therefore, lenders consider title insurance the ideal form of evidence of title.

Additionally, lenders will often require a survey before originating a loan. All loans sold on the secondary market require title insurance and an accurate survey.

In the earnest money contract, the buyer pledges a certain amount of the down payment, the earnest money deposit, as a sign that his or her interest in purchasing the property is genuine. The contract sets forth the price the buyer is willing to pay for the property and other terms and conditions of the sale. When ratified by both the seller and the buyer, the contract allows the buyer to receive financing for the purchase.

A deed is not the same thing as title. Title is the rights or ownership of real property; a deed is a legal written document that conveys rights or ownership. Title is intangible, and a deed is tangible. Depending upon the location, the deed is prepared by a lawyer or the settlement agent. If title is to be held by a trustee as security for the loan, a deed of trust is used; otherwise, the deed conveys title directly to the borrower and a mortgage is used as security. Only a deed that meets all state requirements and the requirements of a valid contract successfully conveys title. This act of title conveyance is called a grant. While there are slight differences in state statutes pertaining to valid conveyance, in general, all states share many of the same criteria.

A valid deed has the following components: grantor, grantee, consideration, granting clause, habendum clause, limitations, legal description, exceptions and reservations, grantor's signature, acknowledgement, delivery, and acceptance.

When the earnest money contract has been ratified and the buyer has successfully received financing, title is transferred to the seller at a set date called the closing date. At that time, the costs and fees of the transaction are allocated to the seller and the buyer and paid.

This concludes lesson five.

Return to your online course player to take the Lesson Quiz.

Lesson 6:
REAL ESTATE CLOSINGS

This lesson focuses on the following topics:

- Introduction
- Pre-Closing Requirements
- Closing Procedures
- Required Documents
- Reporting Transactions to the IRS
- The Licensee's Role
- Real Estate Settlement Procedures Act (RESPA)
- Summary

By the end of this lesson, you should be able to:

- List the pre-closing requirements, distinguishing between seller's concerns and buyer's concerns
- List the required documents that the buyer and seller are each responsible for providing
- Distinguish between face-to-face and escrow closings, and cite who presides over each
- Name the proper form for reporting transactions to the IRS, and list the various parties who can be responsible for filing the form
- List the official responsibilities of the licensee, and utilize the closing checklist
- Explain the function of the Real Estate Settlement Procedures Act (RESPA), listing the procedures and disclosures that must happen during closing, in compliance with the Act

Introduction

Closing, or settlement, is the final step of the home-buying and commercial sale process, when actual title to the property being purchased is transferred from the seller to the buyer. Payments are made to cover various costs of the process, and prorated items are settled from the escrow account held by the closing entity.

In many states, a real estate licensee's official, legal responsibilities to the principals involved in a real estate transaction end with the signing of the sales contract. Even though a licensee may not have any legal obligation to provide services throughout the closing process (the final stage of the real estate transaction), it is not prudent simply to walk away from a transaction after the sales contract has been signed. Deals can and *do* fall apart during the closing process, and when a transaction fails to close, this can mean unsatisfied clients and no commission. Real estate professionals who understand closing procedures and regulations can stay involved right up to the end of a transaction, helping to ensure that their principals' transactions close appropriately.

Note: Most real estate licensees are not lawyers; so unless a real estate professional is also a licensed attorney, he or she does not have the authority to give legal advice and can face liability and punishment for the unauthorized practice of law. If the buyers and sellers with whom you work need legal advice, or if they ask you for legal advice, you should recommend that they consult real estate attorneys before signing any legally binding documents.

Pre-Closing Requirements

The closing process is the culmination of a real estate transaction, in which a buyer pays a seller to transfer the property's title to that buyer. This process will proceed more smoothly if both the buyer and the seller have made the appropriate preparations beforehand.

Sellers' Concerns

In most transactions, a seller is primarily concerned with getting as much as possible of her or his requested purchase price. Therefore, a seller should verify that a prospective buyer has the necessary funds or has obtained appropriate financing before agreeing to close a real estate transaction. To prevent any delays, a seller should also make certain that he or she has complied with all of the prospective buyer's requirements, such as making repairs to the property or having the property inspected for rodents and insects.

Though price is an important consideration for most sellers, each transaction will present its own unique issues that will be determined by a seller's specific goals and desires. Regardless of a transaction's distinctive features, sellers should be discouraged from becoming so focused on price that they neglect other significant concerns.

Buyers' Concerns

As we noted above, a seller will generally be quite concerned about a prospective buyer's ability to pay for the property. Before closing, then, a prospective buyer must do everything she or he can to demonstrate that he or she will be able to complete the transaction that has been negotiated with the seller. The specific things that a particular buyer must do to demonstrate this will vary from case to case, but licensees can be of great help by providing general guidance about financing and directing prospective buyers to financial professionals who can help them with funding and documentation.

Once a buyer has secured funding for the transaction, he or she is generally primarily concerned with getting a marketable title from a seller, that is, most buyers are focused on obtaining a title that is apparently complete and otherwise in proper order. This does not mean that it is *in fact* free of defects or other inaccuracies, only that it seems to cover the subject property in its entirety and to be otherwise complete.

A marketable title need not be perfect; it may have liens, encumbrances, or other defects as long as these are openly accepted by the buyer as part of the purchase contract. A marketable title is one that permits an owner to sell or transfer a property freely, and it is generally understood to be a title that prospective buyers can or should accept without objection. When a buyer accepts a marketable title, he or she can usually feel secure in the purchase because a marketable title is one that the buyer will not have to defend against other claimants.

A marketable title, then:

- Allows the recipient of the title to exercise ownership rights without having to defend those rights through litigation
- Shows that the property can be sold or mortgaged at fair market value by a practical and knowledgeable individual
- Does not have any defects that have not been openly accepted by the buyer
- Does not have any liens or encumbrances that have not been openly accepted by the buyer

Many real estate transactions *aim* at exchanging a marketable title for a property's purchase price, but it is not always easy to ensure that a title is actually marketable. A clear or marketable title can only be provided through the work of a seller's attorney or title insurance company.

Before closing, a buyer will want to do the following things to help ensure that she or he receives a marketable title:

- Ensure that the proper professionals (e.g., title abstracters or title insurance agents) examine all records and paperwork associated with the title, including public records, current and past leases, evidence of title, the deed, and any documents connected with liens or other encumbrances

- Make certain that the property survey is accurate, perhaps by asking an independent surveyor to examine it
- Conduct a final inspection (or walk-through) with a professional inspector to ensure that the property is as the seller has represented it to be

Pre-closing responsibilities regarding FHA-insured mortgages

When working with borrowers on transactions that rely on FHA-insured mortgages, lenders are required to give buyers the one-page *Notice to the Homebuyer* form. This form was created as part of the NAR® and HUD's joint Homebuyer Protection Initiative; it explains the difference between an appraisal and a home inspection and recommends that buyers obtain an inspection.

Closing Procedures

Let's assume that Broker A, Seller B, and Buyer C have arrived at an agreement about the sale of Seller B's condominium. The principals have settled on a price and taken all the necessary steps to ensure a smooth sale: they have hired professionals to research and insure the title; they have had the property professionally appraised and inspected; and the buyer has secured appropriate financing. It is now time to transfer the title from Seller B to Buyer C and sign all of the important documents associated with the sale.

The first step in closing the property is to make sure that all principals understand the terms and conditions of the purchase contract, as well as any addenda. One or both parties may wish to consult an attorney before signing the sale paperwork; licensees should encourage those who desire legal advice (or any other guidance that falls outside the licensee's field(s) of expertise) to enlist the help of a professional. Once the parties are sure they understand everything to which they are agreeing, there are a variety of ways the contract and the other essential paperwork associated with the closing process can be completed.

Face-to-Face Closing

Some closings are aptly described by the phrase "passing papers," a process in which the principals and their representatives meet face-to-face and exchange the documents required to close the sale.

Face-to-face closings can be held in a variety of locations, including a broker's office, the buyer's attorney's office, the seller's attorney's office, a title company office, the lending institution office, the offices of the county clerk or recorder, or at the escrow company. A face-to-face closing involves the principals to the transaction, but it frequently involves other individuals as well.
Example: Buyers and sellers may have their attorneys and brokers present, if they wish. In addition, representatives from lending institutions and the title insurance companies may attend closings.

Usually one person presides over the closing, such as a broker, the buyer's or seller's attorney, a representative from the lending institution or a title company representative. That person is responsible for calculating the settlement, that is, for calculating the division of expenses and funds between the buyer and the seller.

Escrow Closing

The term "escrow closing" describes a closing transaction in which a disinterested third party (often an escrow agent) presides over the closing. This third party has no personal interest in the transaction and does not represent either of the principals.

One of the parties selects a company or individual to serve as the escrow agent (or escrow holder); this might be the escrow department of a bank or other lending institution, an attorney, a title company, a trust company, or an escrow company. This disinterested third party generally acts according to escrow instructions that have been created by the principals involved in a transaction.

It is usually the case that this third party is entrusted with funds and many of the important documents that are involved in a real estate transaction; paperwork is often handled through this third party, and the other parties might not be present at the closing. If one or both of the principals is absent from the closing meeting, copies of the settlement statement should be mailed or delivered to the absent parties immediately after closing. In Texas, title companies normally handle closings.

Note: Some states have laws or regulations specifying which party (or parties) may choose the escrow agent. Otherwise, the parties negotiate to decide which party gets to choose or to select an escrow agent together.

In an escrow closing, the buyer and the seller first sign the sale contract, and then the broker gives the earnest money to the escrow agent to deposit in a trust account; this money is described as being held in escrow. Before the closing date, the buyer and seller must give the escrow agent all of the completed, legally valid documents that will be needed to complete the closing.

Required Documents

Diverse individuals have an interest in the outcome of any real estate transaction; these varied interests are reflected in the documentation that is required for a real estate sale. For example, the lender that is helping to finance the purchase has an interest in the property and will want assurance that its title is marketable, that the property's taxes and insurance are maintained and that the lender's mortgage lien will have priority over any other liens. Before closing, a lender may require the following items:

- A title insurance policy
- A fire and hazard insurance policy
- A survey
- A pest inspection certificate
- A reserve account for property taxes and insurance

These documents help lenders to identify and evaluate the property for which the loan is intended, and to determine whether the risks associated with that loan are ones they want to assume. Lenders may require other documents as well; the list above is only meant to convey a general idea of the kind of supporting paperwork that is likely to be required.

Beyond these documents, the buyer and seller will have to supply additional paperwork to complete the transaction. If the closing will be face-to-face, they can bring the documents with them. If an escrow agent is conducting the closing, the buyer and seller will need to give the documents to the escrow agent before the closing date.

The documents that the seller must supply include:

- Title evidence (legal documentation regarding the current condition of a property's title)
- The deed
- Hazard insurance policies
- Any affidavits of title or other documents needed to clear the title
- Any payoff statements or mortgage reduction certificates (documents issued by a mortgage lender that show the exact amount required to pay an existing loan)

The documents that the buyer must supply include:

- Evidence that he or she has secured a loan
- Property insurance policies
- The agreed-upon amount of cash (usually in the form of a cashier's check) needed to close on the property

- Any other documents required by the title company

The specific documents that are necessary in a given transaction will be determined by the particular features and requirements of that transaction. The documents listed here are only intended to give a general picture of the paperwork that is often involved in a typical real estate sale.

Reporting Transactions to the IRS

Form 1099-S

Licensees need to be aware that the sale of stock in cooperative housing corporations, as well as sales of land, condominium units, and permanent structures, including residential, commercial, and industrial buildings, must be reported to the Internal Revenue Service (IRS). Usually the closing agent or the mortgage lender will fill out the Form 1099-S for this type of transaction, but any licensees involved in the transaction could be held liable if the IRS is not properly notified.

Various parties can be designated as the person responsible for filing the 1099-S, including the transferor's attorney, the transferee's attorney, and the disbursing title or escrow company. The IRS provides extensive guidelines about who can be held responsible for filing this form, and in what circumstances.

More About: IRS instructions for Form 1099-S can be found online here: http://www.irs.gov/instructions/i1099s/ar02.html#d0e189.

We have provided a copy of IRS Form 1099-S, for educational purposes only. If you need this form for your own work, obtain one from the IRS to ensure that you have the most recent version of the form.

Foreign Investment in Real Property Tax Act

If a transaction is subject to the Foreign Investment in Real Property Tax Act of 1980 (FIRPTA), then the person who is buying or receiving property must determine whether the individual who is selling or transferring property is a citizen of the United States. If the seller is *not* a citizen, then the buyer (or his or her representative) must withhold 10 percent of the sale proceeds and send it to the IRS within 10 days of closing. A comprehensive purchase and sale agreement should include a paragraph that explains this act, to ensure that all parties are advised of their responsibilities in this regard.

There are exceptions to FIRPTA. One of the most common exceptions to FIRPTA releases a transferee (i.e., a purchaser or a buyer) from the obligation to withhold tax in cases in which the buyer purchases real estate for use as her or his home and the purchase price is not more than $300,000. Residential property transactions that meet these conditions are thus often exempt from FIRPTA's requirements. Licensees should encourage principals to consult with tax attorneys on this point, however, and should not advise people about whether FIRPTA applies to their transaction.

More About: IRS Publication 515, Withholding of Tax on Nonresident Aliens and Foreign Entities, can be found online here: http://www.irs.gov/publications/p515/index.html.

More About: Of special interest for our purposes is the section of Publication 515 that discusses U.S. real property interest; this section can be found online here: http://www.irs.gov/publications/p515/ar02.html#d0e5964.

You may also write to receive advice and information on FIRPTA from the IRS at:

> Director, Philadelphia Service Center
> P.O. Box 21086
> Drop Point N-423 FIRPTA Unit
> Philadelphia, PA 19114–0586

The Licensee's Role

As we noted earlier, a licensee's official responsibilities in the closing process vary from state to state. However, *all* licensees can do things that can help to make sure a transaction goes smoothly, regardless of what their state-mandated responsibilities may be.

Licensees can help to facilitate transactions in a variety of ways, including the following:

- When working with buyers, communicate with their lenders
    - Find out exactly which documents are required, and the date by which they must be submitted
- When working with sellers, make sure that they comply with all requirements imposed by the buyer and the lender
- Regardless of whether your client is a buyer or a seller, ensure that the client is meeting important deadlines
- Communicate with the other party's broker
- Stay involved!

Use the following checklist to keep track of all of the details in the closing process.

Closing Checklist

Name of Client:

Loan Information:	**Additional Information:**

Type _____
Amount _____
Down payment _____
Interest rate_____
Loan fee _____
Points _____

Processing

	Due Date	Completed
Trust account deposit	_____	_____
Loan application completed	_____	_____
Appraisal ordered	_____	_____
Credit report ordered	_____	_____
Income and funds verified	_____	_____
Loan approved	_____	_____
All parties notified of approval	_____	_____
Termite inspection completed	_____	_____
Other work completed	_____	_____
_____	_____	_____
_____	_____	_____
Buyer's hazard insurance	_____	_____
Loan documents signed	_____	_____
Arrange possession date	_____	_____
Loan funded	_____	_____
Loan funds disbursed	_____	_____
Keys to buyer	_____	_____
Remove sold sign and lock box	_____	_____
Other _____	_____	_____
Other _____	_____	_____
Other _____	_____	_____

Real Estate Settlement Procedures Act (RESPA)

The Real Estate Settlement Procedures Act (RESPA) was enacted in 1974 by the U.S. Department of Housing and Urban Development (HUD). RESPA is a consumer protection statute that aims to help educate consumers about closing and settlement services. One important goal of RESPA is to provide information that will teach consumers to be savvy judges of these services' proper cost, and thus eliminate referral fees and other questionable tacked-on fees that can unnecessarily increase the cost of closing and settlement services. RESPA is enforced by HUD's Office of RESPA and Interstate Land Sales.

RESPA applies to most loans that are secured by a mortgage lien placed on a one- to four-family residential property. These loans include most purchase loans, assumptions, and property improvement loans; they also generally include refinancing loans and equity lines of credit. The primary condition for a loan's falling under RESPA is that it be what is called a "federally related mortgage loan," defined broadly in RESPA as a loan that is directly or indirectly supported by federal regulation, insurance, guarantees, supplements, or assistance. This term also covers loans that the originating lender intends to sell to a federal program, such as Fannie Mae. This range of loans covers the majority of loans that are secured for home purchases.

RESPA stipulates certain procedures and disclosures that must happen during closing. First, within three days of receiving a loan application, the lender must provide the applicant with the following material:

- A booklet entitled "Settlement Costs and You," published by HUD, concerning settlement services

- A truth-in-lending statement, indicating the total credit costs and the annual percentage rate (APR) of the loan, which may differ from the initial rate a borrower will pay on the loan

- A good-faith estimate of settlement costs, detailing the expected costs of closing and indicating which settlement services are mandated by the lender

RESPA also requires that any time the closing agent refers a borrower to a firm with which the lender is affiliated; the lender must inform the borrower of the connection through an Affiliate Business Arrangement (AfBA) Disclosure stating the relationship and that the buyer need not use affiliated firms. For example, if the borrower is referred to an appraiser whose firm is owned by the owners of the lender's firm, the lender must inform the borrower.

In addition to the above requirements, RESPA also contains several prohibitions for transactions that involve federally related mortgage loans. These regulations apply to transactions involving the purchase of a one- to four-family home:

- No party (such as a seller, lender, or servicer) may give or accept a fee or anything else of value for the referral of a closing service.

- No party may charge a fee for a service that is not actually performed, nor may it split an earned fee with another party that has not performed or helped to perform the service for which the fee was charged.

- The seller may not require as a condition of sale that the borrower use a specific title insurance company.

RESPA also requires that both the borrower (i.e., the buyer) and the seller receive the HUD-1 Settlement Statement at closing. The HUD-1 Settlement Statement is a standardized form that shows all of the borrower's and seller's charges arising from the settlement of their real estate transaction. We will discuss this form in greater detail in Lesson Eight.

NOTE: Some states require that licensees give their clients an estimate of the expenses involved in closing the transaction at the time the purchase contract is signed. The HUD-1 Settlement Statement can be used to figure these estimates, as can the Good Faith Estimate form.

Some of RESPA's regulations-such as its disclosure requirements-apply only to lenders. However, RESPA includes sections that impose regulations which also apply to licensees. For example, one section of RESPA is specifically concerned with reducing the unnecessary and ethically dubious charges that can sometimes be associated with settlement and closing services. This part of RESPA explicitly "prohibits anyone from giving or accepting a fee, kickback, or anything of value in exchange for referrals of settlement service business involving a federally related mortgage loan." This means, for example, that licensees cannot accept payment of any sort for referring clients to a bank. Licensees who provide computerized loan origination services also need to comply with RESPA regulations.

Violations of RESPA regulations can lead to serious penalties for both licensees and lending institutions' employees. Fines of up to $10,000 can be assessed, as can prison terms of up to a year. Further details about penalties can be found in Section 8 of RESPA. We will talk more explicitly about the details of this act in Lesson 14.

More About: You can read more about RESPA on HUD's Web site at http://www.hud.gov/offices/hsg/sfh/res/respa_hm.cfm. Specific details about the requirements imposed by the RESPA statutes can be found here http://www.hud.gov/offices/hsg/sfh/res/respa_st.cfm.

Annual Percentage Rate
As stated above, RESPA requires lenders to disclose the annual percentage rate (APR) to borrowers in the truth-in-lending statement. The APR is *not* the same as

the interest rate: it is the ratio of the total cost of financing to the loan amount. The cost of financing includes interest paid, discount points, and loan fees but does not include other fees that would have to be paid regardless of financing (for example, title insurance or home inspection fees).

The APR is not simple to calculate, and it is not always calculated in the same way. Each lender decides which fees and charges go into the calculation. The following are usually, but not always, included in a lender's APR calculation (these fees will be discussed in detail at the end of this lesson):

- Application fee
- Discount points
- Document preparation fees (when paid for the lender's document preparation)
- Origination fee
- Private mortgage insurance (PMI) premiums
- Processing fee
- Underwriting fee

Several fees, however, are not typically included in the calculation of the annual percentage rate. These may include the following:

- Appraisal fee
- Attorneys' fees
- Credit report fee
- Home inspection fee
- Notary fees
- Pest inspection fee
- Recording fee
- Title insurance

The idea behind the APR is that the rate will more accurately represent the actual cost of the loan to the borrower. For example, suppose a lender is offering two options: a loan with one discount point at a certain interest rate and a loan with two discount points at a slightly lower rate. Which option is better? To determine this, a borrower can simply compare APRs. The loan with the lower APR costs the borrower less money over time; if the APRs are equal, both loans cost the borrower the same amount.

Summary

Licensees' responsibilities vary from state to state, and in many areas, their official legal responsibilities end with the signing of the purchase contract. However, when a licensee understands the closing process, he or she can stay involved in a transaction after the purchase contract is signed. Licensees who remain involved can use their professional expertise to ensure that their hard work culminates in a transaction that closes smoothly.

Before closing a real estate transaction, buyers and sellers should ensure that their interests in the transaction are secure. The buyer should hire professionals (e.g., title abstracters) to examine all relevant documentation related to the property; he or she should also hire an inspector to conduct a final inspection of the property. The seller should make sure that he or she has satisfied all of the buyer's requirements and that the buyer has obtained appropriate financing. Both parties must work to ensure that all of the preliminary conditions imposed on their transaction have been met; once they agree that this is the case, the licensee needs to work with the buyer and seller to ensure that they completely understand the purchase contract.

Though licensees are unlikely to be held legally responsible for these issues, they should still help to ensure that principals receive proper loan disclosures, and retain appropriate withholding for sales that fall under FIRPTA withholding requirements. Buyers with FHA-insured mortgages should receive the one-page *Notice to the Homebuyer* form. The Real Estate Settlement Procedures Act (RESPA) requires that borrowers who apply for federally related mortgage loans receive the following disclosures:

- A Special Information Booklet containing consumer information about real estate transactions and real estate settlement services.

- A Good Faith Estimate (GFE) of closing and settlement costs.

- A Mortgage Servicing Disclosure Statement.

Once the principals have judged all documentation and funding to be satisfactory and the licensee and other professionals overseeing the transaction believe everything is in order, the transaction can move toward closing. Closing can be conducted through a face-to-face meeting between the principals and their representatives; the closing process can also be overseen and conducted by an escrow agent. In all cases, the documents that the seller must supply include:

- Title evidence (legal documentation regarding the current condition of a property's title)

- The deed

- Hazard insurance policies
- Any affidavits of title or other documents needed to clear the title
- Any payoff statements or mortgage reduction certificates (documents issued by a mortgage lender that show the exact amount required to pay an existing loan)

The documents that the buyer must supply include:

- Evidence that he or she has secured a loan

- Property insurance policies

- The agreed-upon amount of cash (usually in the form of a cashier's check) needed to close on the property

- Any other documents required by the title company

The lender may also require additional documents before approving the loan for the transaction. The specific documents that are necessary in a given transaction will be determined by the particular features and requirements of that transaction. The documents listed here are only intended to give a general picture of the paperwork that is often involved in a typical real estate sale.

RESPA is a consumer protection statute that aims to help educate consumers about closing and settlement services. One important goal of RESPA is to provide information that will teach consumers to be savvy judges of these services' proper cost, and thus eliminate referral fees and other questionable tacked-on fees that can unnecessarily increase the cost of closing and settlement services. RESPA is enforced by HUD's Office of RESPA and Interstate Land Sales.

Although some of RESPA's regulations (such as its disclosure requirements) apply only to lending institutions, licensees need to be aware that the act also prohibits licensees from accepting fees, kickbacks, or any kind of payment in exchange for their referrals of settlement service business involving a federally related mortgage loan. Specific information about these prohibited payments can be found in the RESPA statutes.

This concludes Lesson six.

Return to your online course player to take the Lesson Quiz.

Lesson 7:
CLOSING EXPENSES

This lesson focuses on the following topics:

- Introduction
- Allocating Expenses
- Nonrecurring Closing Costs
- Credits and Debits
- Prorating Expenses
- Summary

By the end of this lesson, you should be able to:

- List the basic conventions that determine how expenses are allocated in a typical real-estate transaction, and provide an example of each
- Name the two categories of nonrecurring closing costs, and list the costs associated with each
- Distinguish between credits and debits, and demonstrate the procedure for calculating them
- Explain the process of prorating expenses, and provide examples of prepaid and accrued items
- Demonstrate the formula for calculating prorated expenses

Introduction

The closing statement (also called a "settlement statement") is a document that provides a detailed list of each party's expenses as well as how much she or he has already contributed to the transaction thus far. This statement also provides an accounting of the final amount that the buyer must bring to the closing. To complete a closing or settlement statement properly, one must know which principal is responsible for each transaction expense. A licensee must also have a clear understanding of credits and debits and should know how to prorate expenses that must be divided between the principals.

Allocating Expenses

There are a variety of expenses associated with any real estate transaction. For example, brokers' commissions must be paid and loans often come with significant fees. These expenses can be divided in various ways between the principals involved in the transaction; their legal responsibility varies from state to state, and many expenses can be negotiated between the principals. These variables mean that there is no single set of general guidelines that can teach a licensee how these expenses are divided between principals.

Nonetheless, there are conventions that often determine the way these expenses are allocated in a typical real estate transaction. The following table illustrates the general guidelines for allocating expenses:

ITEM	PAID BY
Brokers' Commissions	Either party or both, by agreement
Attorneys' Fees	Either party or both, by agreement
Title Expenses	Both parties responsible for different title expenses
Transfer Tax	Seller
Recording Expenses	Both parties responsible for different recording expenses
Loan Fees	Both parties responsible for different loan fees
Appraisal Fees	Either party or both, by agreement
Survey Fees	Both parties responsible for different survey fees
Tax and Insurance Reserves	Buyer

Brokers' Commissions
A seller usually pays the commission for any broker who has been hired to represent the seller. If a broker represents the buyer or if each party has a broker of his or her own, each party may pay some part of the total cost of commission(s).

Attorneys' Fees
If a buyer and a seller are paying their attorneys out of their own pockets, then the attorneys' fees are often omitted from the closing statement. However, if one or more attorneys' fees are to be deducted from the proceeds from the closing, then the party who hired the attorney as her or his representative will generally be debited for the attorney's fees.

Title Expenses
Generally, a seller is required to pay for the title search. However, if a buyer conducts another search of his or her own, then she or he usually pays for that additional research. The buyer also usually pays for title insurance policies.

Transfer Tax
Transfer taxes are usually a seller's responsibility.

Recording Expenses

A seller is generally responsible for recording expenses (i.e., filing fees and other similar costs) related to clearing defects from the property's title, such as recording satisfactions of liens, affidavits, and quitclaim deeds. A buyer is usually responsible for the recording expenses associated with the title transfer, such as the costs associated with publicly recording the deed that gives him or her title.

Loan Fees

A buyer is usually responsible for paying loan origination fees for a new loan, and for paying assumption fees if she or he assumes the seller's existing loan. If a seller is paying off a mortgage before its due date, he or she may be required to pay a prepayment fee.

Appraisal Fees

The party that ordered the appraisal usually pays the fees associated with that appraisal.

Survey Fees

A buyer usually pays property survey fees, especially if he or she obtains a new mortgage.

Tax and Insurance Reserves

A buyer is often required to open an escrow account to cover real estate taxes that are assessed during the time the transaction is taking place. In this case, he or she generally deposits at least enough in the account to pay for the taxes through the end of the month of closing. However, a seller is debited and a buyer is credited for any of the seller's unpaid taxes. A buyer often also pays at least the first year's premium on fire or hazard insurance at closing.

It is worth repeating that state laws may stipulate arrangements other than those described above, as may the regulations associated with certain types of financing. In addition, many transactions leave substantial leeway for the principals to negotiate about how expenses are allocated. In all of these cases, the final division of fees may look considerably different than the general example above. Purchase contracts should reflect all negotiated and stipulated agreements regarding the allocation of expenses.

Additional Transaction Fees

Certain kinds of financing can result in additional transaction costs. These expenses include the following:

- If a loan has private mortgage insurance, then a buyer generally pays for one year's premium, or before, the time of closing.

- If a loan is FHA-insured, a buyer is usually debited for the mortgage insurance premium unless it is financed with the loan.

- If a loan is a Veterans Affairs loan, the buyer is debited for a funding fee to the VA.

Nonrecurring Closing Costs

Let's take a moment to look at the costs according to who is responsible for them. Nonrecurring closing costs may be divided into two categories: those that are not associated with the lender, but rather with the home-purchase process, such as title and inspection fees, and those that are associated with the lender, such as the loan origination fee.

Nonrecurring Closing Costs Not Associated With the Lender

Closing/Escrow/Settlement Fee
A fee paid to the settlement agent or escrow holder.

Courier Fee
Deals with the costs associated with delivering documents to the buyer, seller, lender, title company, law firm, county recorder, and so on to facilitate the closing process.

Home Inspection Fee
Fee a home buyer must pay if he or she did not pay it at the time the home was inspected.

Homeowner's Association Transfer Fee
The fee charged by a homeowner's association for transferring all of their ownership documents to the new owner.

Home Warranty
Optional fee paid for an insurance policy covering items such as major appliances; not to be confused with a warranty provided by the builder of a new home that would cover the structure itself.

Legal or Document Preparation Fee
Fee paid to a lawyer or law firm for preparation of legal documents for transaction and lender-required forms. May also be paid to the lender for documents prepared in house.

Notary Fees
Fee for forms that must be attested to, or notarized.

Option Fee
A negotiated fee paid by the potential purchaser at the time of contracting for an option to terminate the contract for so many days, as spelled out in the earnest money contract.

Pest Inspection/Treatment
Fee for inspection or treatment and repairs of pest infestations, wood rot, and water damage (as a lender may require as a precondition of procuring the loan).

Recording Fees
Fee for recording legal documents with a local county recorder.

Title Insurance
Assurance to the potential homeowner that she or he is receiving clear title to the property being purchased-free of liens and encumbrances, as well as discrepancies in boundaries and area, if a survey was done.

Nonrecurring Closing Costs Associated With Lender
The following costs are collected only at closing and do not continue to be collected during the loan period (nonrecurring). The exact amount of each fee should appear on the HUD-1 Settlement Statement at closing.

Administration Fee
Additional fee sometimes charged by a lender to establish the loan.

Appraisal Review Fee
Fee sometimes charged by a lender for a second appraiser to review the original appraisal when findings are considered questionable.

Appraisal Fee
Fee paid to a licensed real estate appraiser, usually by the lender, to appraise the value of the property. The appraisal fee varies, depending upon the value of the home and the difficulty involved in justifying value. Appraisal fees on VA and FHA loans are higher than on conventional loans because they require the appraiser to inspect items not strictly associated with value (but such inspections are not for the borrower and should not be substituted for an independent inspection done for a borrower before purchase, if the borrower so chooses). This fee is usually negotiated directly with the lender, who orders the appraisal.

Assumption Fee
Fee charged by the lender for allowing the assumption of a loan by another party and forgiving the original borrower's obligation.

Credit Report Fee
Fee paid to a credit reporting service for reviewing the borrower's credit history.

Escrow Waiver Fee

Fee paid when an escrow account is not being established. Some states (including, Illinois, New York, Oregon, and the District of Columbia) have barred lenders from charging this fee, as it may violate the RESPA section disallowing parties from charging a fee for services that are not actually performed.

Flood Certification Fee

Fee for a service hired to determine whether a property is located in a federally designated flood zone.

Flood Monitoring

Fee paid to a service to maintain monitoring on whether flood remapping affects a property.

Loan Origination Fee

The loan origination fee is often referred to as *points.* On an FHA loan, the loan origination fee is one point. On a VA loan, the loan origination fee is determined at the discretion of the lender. Anything in addition to one point (on government loans) is called *discount points.* A point is equal to one percentage point of the loan amount. This amount is paid directly to the lender as a fee to set up the loan.

Mortgage Broker Fee

Broker processing fees. Sometimes there are several of these under different names since some brokers have other "fees" listed that are beyond the scope of this course, sometimes referred to as "junk fees" since the fee covers nothing but netting more money for the mortgage broker. Agents need to have their borrowers ask questions about this fee (or fees) to the broker directly since some of these are negotiable and can be reduced or eliminated.

Tax Service Fee

Fee for a service that checks to make sure property tax payments are made or have been made.

Underwriting Fee

Fee sometimes charged by lender if reselling the loan in the secondary market.

Wire Transfer Fee

Fee charged if funds are wire transferred at closing for a buyer or seller.

Warehousing Fee

Fee charged by lender as additional amount for establishing loan.

Credits and Debits

A closing statement provides a detailed accounting of each party's debits and credits. A credit is a positive balance or a positive amount. For our purposes, it is a figure entered in a party's favor when determining the overall costs associated with a transaction. On closing statements, credits reflect expenses that have been paid by a particular individual or expenses that are owed to that individual. Credits stand in contrast to debits.

A debit is a negative balance or a negative amount. For the purposes of our discussion, a debit is an amount due from or owed by a particular individual when determining the overall costs associated with a transaction. On closing statements, debits reflect charges made to the parties involved in the transaction.

The actual amount that a buyer is to pay at closing is calculated by subtracting the buyer's total credits (such as prepaid earnest money or the balance of a loan that the buyer will assume from the seller) from the buyer's total debits (such as the purchase price). The remaining total is the amount that the buyer must bring to the closing to complete the transaction.

To determine how much money a seller will receive from a transaction, we subtract the seller's total debits (such as the balance of a mortgage loan) from the seller's total credits (such as the purchase price). The remaining total is the amount that the seller will receive.

In most cases, when we are tallying up credits and debits, it will be clear which party is responsible for a given transaction expenses. However, some expenses cannot be allocated so easily. Many items that are prepaid or paid after a certain amount of time has passed, such as taxes, need to be divided proportionately between a buyer and a seller. The process of making this proportional division is called "proration."

Prorating Expenses

For our purposes, the proration process is a method of dividing accrued items and prepaid items between a seller and a buyer. Accrued items are costs that are owed by a seller (such as real estate taxes in a state where these are not prepaid), but which will ultimately be paid by a buyer after he or she receives title to a property. That is to say, these expenses have been (or are being) incurred at the time of sale, but need not be paid at the time the sale closes. In an effort to ensure that these expenses are handled fairly, the seller generally pays the buyer for these items through credits at closing. For example, a seller might credit a buyer for the proportion of annual real estate taxes that were charged during the part of the year that the seller occupied the property.

A prepaid item is an item that has been paid for ahead of time, generally by the seller. For example, a seller might have prepaid an insurance policy that is required by the local homeowner's association. A buyer must then generally "purchase" this item from the seller at the time of the sale, either with cash, credits or in some other way that the principals have negotiated.

The following table shows examples of prepaid items and accrued items.

PREPAID	ACCRUED
<ul><li>Fuel oil on hand</li><li>Insurance and tax reserves for the mortgage</li><li>Prepaid water charges and other utility bills</li><li>General real estate taxes in a state where these are prepaid</li></ul>	<ul><li>Interest on an existing mortgage assumed by the buyer</li><li>Unpaid water charges and other utility bills</li><li>Unpaid taxes</li><li>General real estate taxes in a state where these are *not* prepaid</li></ul>

Accrued items are generally debited to the seller and credited to the buyer, and prepaid items are credited to the seller and debited to the buyer.

Calculating Prorated Expenses

Federal and state laws, as well as the negotiated terms of a particular purchase agreement, may dictate whether certain expenses can be prorated or how they should be prorated. In Texas, prorations are calculated through the closing date. The following guidelines for calculating a prorated expense are provided for educational purposes and may not reflect the actual procedures that are required in a specific case. A prudent licensee will not make assumptions about prorated expenses. Instead, familiarize yourself with relevant state laws and check with local lenders to identify the procedures they generally follow when prorating property taxes, insurance, and interest.

When calculating prorated expenses, the first step is determining an annual charge for the item being prorated. This amount is then divided by 12 to calculate the monthly charge for the item. It may be necessary to go further and calculate a daily charge for the item. In this case, there are two methods commonly used to calculate daily charges:

A 360-day year

The 360-day year is known as the "banking year;" it is commonly used in banking and other financial calculations, and is divided into 12 months of 30 days each. To figure daily charges using a 360-day year, you can divide the yearly charge by 360 or divide the monthly charge by 30.

A 365-day year

The 365-day year is sometimes also called the "conventional calendar year," because its divisions reflect the actual months of the calendar that most of us use. To calculate the daily charge for an item using the conventional calendar year, divide the yearly charge by 365 (366 in a leap year).

The actual number of days or months in the period for which you are calculating the prorated expense is then multiplied by the monthly or daily charge (whichever is appropriate) to determine the accrued amount or prepaid amount for the item.

Before you begin calculating prorations, then, you will need to answer the following three questions:

- What kind of item is being prorated? Is the charge for the item assessed daily, monthly, annually, or according to some other schedule?
- Is this item accrued or prepaid?
- Which calculation method should be used?

Note: Throughout this section of the course, we will use the 360-day year. However, regulations in your area may require that you use the 365-day year. Also, in our calculations we will assume that the seller is responsible for expenses incurred on the closing date. However, state laws determine whether the seller is in fact legally responsible for charges incurred on this date; these laws vary and you should confirm the standard used in your state before finalizing your calculations.

Now let's look at some examples.

Prorating an Accrued Item

A sale is to be closed on the second of July. The property's water bill for the entire year has been estimated at $300. Assuming that the seller is responsible for expenses on the day of closing, the accrued period is six months (January through June) and two days (July first and second). This is the amount of time for which the seller should be held responsible for the property's water bills, because the seller occupied or was otherwise responsible for the property during this time. Let's calculate the monthly and daily prorated costs for the water bill, using a 360-day year:

Monthly charge: $300 ÷ 12 months = $25
Daily charge: $25 ÷ 30 days = $0.833

Now we will multiply the monthly and daily charge by the number of months and days in the period:

$25 × 6 months = $150

$$\$0.833 \times 2 \text{ days} = \$1.666$$

Finally, we add the two amounts together:

$$\$150 + \$1.666 = \$151.666$$

We can then round this figure to the second decimal place, giving us a total of $151.67. This is the amount that should be credited to the buyer and debited to the seller as we calculate the various settlement expenses associated with the transaction.

Prorating a Prepaid Item

When calculating prorated expenses for a prepaid item, it is first necessary to determine the period of time for which the expense has been prepaid. For example, let's assume that a seller lives in a state in which real estate taxes are prepaid. She or he has prepaid all real estate taxes for the year 2005, up to and including December 31; the total amount of prepaid taxes is $2,000. The sale's closing date is October 5, 2005. Using a 360-day year, we can calculate the number of prepaid months and days beyond the closing date as follows:

	Months	Days
Amount paid to Dec. 31	12	30 per month (in a 360-day year)
Closing date = Oct. 5	-10	-5
Prepaid period	2 months	25 days

As we noted above, the total paid was $2,000. Now that we know the number of prepaid months and days beyond the closing date, we can calculate the amount that will be credited to the seller and debited to the buyer using the following formulas:

$$\text{Total amount} \div 12 \text{ months} = \text{Monthly charge}$$
$$\$2,000 \div 12 \text{ months} = \$166.666$$

$$\text{Monthly charge} \div 30 \text{ days} = \text{Daily charge}$$
$$\$166.666 \div 30 \text{ days} = \$5.555$$

$$\text{Monthly charge} \times \text{Number of months in period} = \text{Monthly amount}$$
$$\$166.666 \times 2 \text{ months} = \$333.332$$
$$\text{Daily charge} \times \text{Number of days in period} = \text{Daily amount}$$
$$\$5.555 \times 25 \text{ days} = \$138.875$$

$$\text{Monthly amount} + \text{Daily amount} = \text{Total}$$
$$\$333.332 + \$138.875 = \$472.207$$

We can then round this figure to the second decimal place, giving us a total of $472.21. This is the total amount that the seller has prepaid beyond the closing date–that is, the seller has paid $472.21 in taxes for a period during which the buyer should be held responsible for these charges. This amount will be credited to the seller and debited to the buyer as we calculate the various settlement expenses associated with the transaction.

Additional Guidelines for Calculating Prorated Expenses

- In many states, the seller is held responsible for any expenses incurred on the closing date. However, some states specify that the buyer owns the property as of the closing date, and he or she is, therefore, held responsible for any expenses incurred on that date. In Texas, the seller is considered the owner through the date of closing.

- Estimates of utility charges and other similar expenses are often based on the most recent bill.

- Rents are usually prorated using a 365-day year, which reflects the actual amount of days for which rent is collected. The seller generally receives rents that are due as of the closing date, but again, you should check your state laws to be certain of the regulations in your state.

- Security deposits are usually transferred from the seller to the buyer; these funds are held in trust for tenants, and are not properly understood to be either the seller or the buyer's property.

- The way in which one is to calculate prorated real estate taxes varies from state to state. Check the rules for your state before finalizing any calculations.

- Expenses like water and utilities, mortgage interest, and real estate taxes are frequently prorated using the 360-day banking year. However, some areas require that the 365-day year be used. Familiarize yourself with local laws, and contact local lenders to determine the standards they use when calculating prorated expenses.

- Some special assessments are billed in installments (such as assessments for sewer improvements). When a transaction involves expenses of this sort, the buyer often assumes all future payments with interest. This amount is not generally prorated at closing.

Case Study: Proration
Seller S and Buyer B are in the process of closing a transaction. There are three items that must be prorated, or divided between the two parties: the prepaid hazard insurance policy, the accrued monthly interest on the loan that the buyer assumes, and the accrued real estate taxes for the year of the transaction.

Closing happens on September 23, 2004, and state law requires that prorations at closing be calculated through the day of closing, using a banker's year. The hazard insurance policy on the house has been prepaid by Seller S. It is a 10-year, $2,000 policy beginning on January 1, 2000. To calculate the daily rate, it is first necessary to determine the number of days in the policy. Since banker's years have 360 days each, the total number of days is:

$$360 \text{ days} \times 10 \text{ years} = 3,600$$

The cost of the policy is then divided by this number to determine the daily rate:

$$\$2,000 \div 3,600 = \$0.56/\text{day}$$

The final step is to determine the number of days Buyer B will have left on the policy and multiply this by the daily rate. The seller had the policy for three years, eight months and 23 days, or:

$$360 \times 3 + 30 \times 8 + 23 = 1,343 \text{ days}$$

Leaving the buyer with:

$$3,600 - 1,343 = 2,257 \text{ days}$$

And a charge of:

$$2,257 \times \$0.56 = \$1,263.92$$

The accrued items in the transaction are the monthly interest on the mortgage loan that the buyer will assume and the real estate taxes he will have to pay. Seller S's original mortgage on the property was for $46,000 over 30 years at an interest rate of 9 percent. Look over the amortization schedule for the year to determine September's interest.

Amortization Schedule

Mo.	Mo. Principal	Mo. Interest	Tot. Principal	Tot. Interest	Balance
Jan	$32.89	$337.24	$1,067.06	$12.627.75	$44,932.94
Feb	$33.13	$337.00	$1,100.19	$12,964.75	$44,899.81
Mar	$33.38	$336.75	$1,133.57	$13,301.50	$44,866.43
Apr	$33.63	$336.50	$1,167.20	$13,638.00	$44,832.80
May	$33.88	$336.25	$1,201.08	$13,974.25	$44,798.92
Jun	$34.14	$335.99	$1,235.22	$14,310.24	$44,764.78
Jul	$34.39	$335.74	$1,269.61	$14,645.98	$44,730.39
Aug	$34.65	$335.48	$1,304.26	$14,981.46	$44,695.74
Sep	$34.91	$335.22	$1,339.17	$15,316.68	$44,660.83
Oct	$35.17	$334.96	$1,374.34	$15,651.64	$44,625.66

| Nov | $35.44 | $334.69 | $1,409.78 | $15,986.33 | $44,590.22 |
| Dec | $35.70 | $334.43 | $1,445.48 | $16,320.76 | $44,554.52 |

The monthly interest for September is $335.22. The daily rate then is:

$$\$335.22 \div 30 = \$11.17$$

Seller S owes Buyer B for the first 23 days of September:

$$23 \times \$11.17 = \$256.91$$

The seller does not owe any money for the principal portion of the monthly payment because, in essence, the buyer is purchasing the equity the seller has in the home. However, since real estate taxes are usually paid for the previous year, the seller owes the buyer for the annual taxes through September 23. If the annual real estate taxes are $960, then the daily rate is:

$$\$960 \div 360 = \$2.67/\text{day}$$

Since Seller S owes taxes for the first 263 days, he will owe:

$$\$2.67 \times 263 = \$702.21$$

This leaves a total debit for the borrower of:

$$\$1,263.91 \text{ Prepaid Insurance} - \$256.91 \text{ Accrued Interest}$$
$$- \$702.21 \text{ Accrued Taxes} = \$304.80$$

Summary

There are a variety of expenses associated with any real estate transaction. For example, brokers' commissions must be paid and loans often come with significant fees. These expenses can be divided in various ways between the principals involved in the transaction; their legal responsibility varies from state to state, and many expenses can be negotiated between the principals. These variables mean that there is no single set of general guidelines that can teach a licensee how these expenses are divided between principals.

Dividing the various expenses associated with a transaction is essential in the preparation of a closing statement (also called a "settlement statement"). The details of this preparation process are the topic of our next lesson; for now, it is enough for us to know that a closing statement provides a detailed accounting of each party's debits and credits. A credit is a positive balance or a positive amount. For our purposes, it is a figure entered in a party's favor when determining the overall costs associated with a transaction. On closing statements, credits reflect expenses that have been paid by a particular individual or expenses that are owed to that individual. Credits stand in contrast to debits.

A debit is a negative balance or a negative amount. For the purposes of our discussion, it is an amount due from or owed by a particular individual when determining the overall costs associated with a transaction. On closing statements, debits reflect charges made to the parties involved in the transaction. A careful accounting of credits and debits will allow a licensee to determine exactly how much a buyer must pay to complete a transaction, as well as the amount that a seller will actually take away from a sale, which is rarely the same amount as the purchase price.

Some of the expenses associated with a real estate transaction, such as transaction fees, are clearly the responsibility of either the buyer or the seller. State laws and the negotiated terms of the purchase contract will offer further guidelines that help a licensee determine which party is properly held responsible for a given expense. Other expenses must be divided proportionally between the parties, so that the charges to each party properly reflect the amount of money she or he owes or has prepaid. We call these "prorated expenses," and the process by which we calculate them is called "proration."

For our purposes, the proration process is a method of dividing accrued items and prepaid items between a seller and a buyer. Accrued items are costs that are owed by a seller (such as real estate taxes), but which will ultimately be paid by a buyer after he or she receives title to a property. That is to say, these expenses have been (or are being) incurred, but need not be paid at the time the sale closes. In an effort to ensure that these expenses are handled fairly, the seller generally pays the buyer for these items through credits at closing. For example, a seller might credit a buyer for the proportion of annual real estate taxes that were charged during the part of the year that the seller occupied the property.

A prepaid item is an item that has been paid for ahead of time, generally by the seller. For example, a seller might have prepaid an insurance policy that is required by the local homeowner's association. A buyer must then generally "purchase" this item from the seller at the time of the sale, either with cash, credits, or in some other way that the principals have negotiated.

When calculating prorated expenses, the first step is determining a yearly charge for the item. That amount is then divided by 12 to calculate the monthly charge for the item. It may be necessary to go further and calculate a daily charge for the item. In this case, there are two methods commonly used to calculate daily charges: the 360-day banking year and the 365-day conventional calendar year; which one is appropriate in a particular case will depend on your state's laws and regulations in this regard. Once you have determined the daily or monthly charge for the item, you can multiply it by the number of days or months in the period for which the prorated expense is being calculated.

The next lesson will discuss preparing pre-settlement estimates of closing costs and settlement statements.

This concludes lesson seven.

Return to your online course player to take the Lesson Quiz.

Lesson 8:
THE HUD-1 SETTLEMENT STATEMENT

This lesson focuses on the following topics:

- Introduction
- General Guidelines for the hud-1 Settlement Statement Form
- Settlement Charges
- Borrower's Transaction
- Seller's Transaction
- Activity: Closing
- Summary

By the end of this lesson, you should be able to:

- Outline the general guidelines for the HUD-1 Settlement Statement Form and properly fill it in
- Complete the settlement charges section of the HUD-1
- Complete the borrower's transaction section of the HUD-1
- Complete the seller's transaction section of the HUD-1
- Demonstrate an understanding of closing transactions by completing a closing activity

Introduction

As we discussed in the previous lesson, the settlement statement (also called a "closing statement") is a detailed, comprehensive document that summarizes each party's debits and credits, as well as the funds that each party has contributed to the transaction thus far. This document is also often used to calculate the total amount that the buyer must bring to the settlement. There is no generally accepted format that all settlement statements must follow.

However, all transactions that fall under RESPA regulation are required to use the HUD-1 Settlement Statement form. This means that all transactions involving a federally related loan used to purchase a one- to four-family home must use the HUD-1 Settlement Statement form; this in turn means that nearly all residential purchase transactions will require this form. Therefore, the HUD-1 Settlement Statement is the most commonly used form for settlement statements, and all licensees who deal in residential property should be familiar with it.

Note: The HUD-1 Settlement Statement may also be used for transactions that are not covered by RESPA regulations-that is to say, there are no prohibitions against using it for sales that fall outside of RESPAs domain.

There are many details to consider when filling out a HUD-1 Settlement Statement. The settlement agent is responsible for this task; in some states, licensees may act as settlement agents. Regardless of who acts as a settlement agent, that individual must be careful and accurate. The material in this lesson will familiarize you with this common form and educate you about how to complete it properly.

General Guidelines for the HUD-1 Settlement Statement Form

In most states, the settlement agent completes the HUD-1 Settlement Statement. Current RESPA regulations do not define the term "settlement agent," but previous definitions suggest that we should understand this term to mean "the individual who is conducting or handling the settlement of the transaction." If the lender and the principals have not designated a particular individual as the settlement agent, then the lender is often considered to be the settlement agent.

However, licensees should familiarize themselves with the requirements imposed by the states in which they live. State laws may require that this form be completed by a particular party, or may stipulate that only certain individuals can serve as settlement agents. These sorts of details cannot be left to chance, and a prudent licensee will do everything that she or he can to ensure that all transactions go as smoothly as possible.

As we have already noted, the settlement statement provides a detailed accounting of the principals' debits and credits; this is true of the HUD-1 form as well. However, some of the settlement information may not be available until the last minute; there is no legal requirement that the form be fully completed before closing. The buyer may request to receive a copy of the HUD-1 Settlement Statement one day before closing, but even at this late stage, some important expenses or credits may remain unknown. In such cases, the settlement agent should complete the settlement statement to the best of his or her knowledge and ensure that all parties are aware that at least some of the costs given at that point are only estimates.

At closing, the settlement agent should ensure that both the buyer and the seller receive a copy of the settlement statement. Some sections of the form allow for the seller's information to be omitted from the buyer's copy of the statement, and vice versa, thus protecting each party's privacy (see, for example, Section J, which is discussed in detail later in this lesson). However, each principal should receive a copy of the form that has been adequately completed, so that each may use it to draw conclusions about his or her transaction. In addition, the settlement agent should retain a copy of the settlement form that includes any omitted information for both principals, to provide the fullest possible accounting of the closing transaction.

For escrow closings in which the buyer, the seller, or both principals are absent, the settlement statement should be mailed or delivered immediately after closing. In all types of closings, the buyer and the seller should carefully review the settlement statement with their attorneys and brokers to ensure that all of the information it contains is accurate.

The settlement statement must be completed in a clear and legible fashion, though it may be hand-written, typed, or completed on a computer. If any of the expenses mentioned on the form have been paid outside of the settlement, their respective lines should be marked "P.O.C.," indicating that they were paid outside of closing. Additional pages may be attached to the statement to include information required by local or state laws, or to make sure that the purchase contract's settlement provisions are thoroughly explained in the statement.

We will now examine the HUD-1 form in greater detail.

General Guidelines for Entering Basic Transaction Information on the HUD-1 Form

Let's assume that Seller A's property is located at 100 Olive Street, Smallville, Texas 78702; Seller A currently resides at this address. The home is listed with Pro Real Estate, which is located at 550 Congress Street, Smallville, Texas 78702. Buyer B (who lives at 325 W. Mary St., Smallville, Texas, 78702) and Seller A have agreed that Buyer B will purchase the house for $115,000, and that the transaction will be closed on July 10, 2005, at the Pro Real Estate office. Buyer B has obtained a new conventional loan through Your Bank, which is located at 100 Main Street, Smallville, Texas 78702, and Buyer B did not need to buy insurance for the loan because the loan-to-value ratio is less than 80 percent. The file number and loan number are not available at this point.

How would we enter this information into the blank HUD-1 Settlement Statement form?

A. U.S. DEPARTMENT OF HOUSING AND URBAN DEVELOPMENT SETTLEMENT STATEMENT				
B. TYPE OF LOAN	1. □ FHA	2. □ FmHA	6. File Number	7. Loan Number
3. □ CONV. UNINS.	4. □ VA	5. □ CONV. INS.	8. Mortgage Insurance Case No.	
C. NOTE: This form is furnished to give you a statement of actual settlement costs. Amounts paid to and by the settlement agent are shown. Items marked "(p.o.c.)" were paid outside the closing; they are shown here for informational purposes and are not included in the totals.				
D. NAME AND ADDRESS OF		E. NAME AND ADDRESS OF		F. NAME AND ADDRESS OF

BORROWER:	SELLER:	LENDER:
G. PROPERTY LOCATION:	H. SETTLEMENT AGENT:	
	PLACE OF SETTLEMENT:	I. SETTLEMENT DATE:

Section A. Do not enter any information here.

Section B. Check the appropriate loan type and then enter the specific loan information in spaces 6, 7, and 8.

Section C. No entry required.

Section D. Enter the full legal name of the borrower (buyer), along with his or her current mailing address and zip code. If there is more than buyer, enter complete information for all of them. Use an additional page if necessary.

Section E. Enter the full legal name of the seller, along with her or his current mailing address and zip code. If there is more than one seller, enter complete information for all of them. Use an additional page if necessary.

Section F. Enter the name, current mailing address, and zip code of the lender.

Section G. Enter the street address and zip code of the property. If no street address is available, you may enter a legal description instead, but the zip code must still be entered.

Section H. Enter the full legal name of the settlement agent, current mailing address, and zip code. Enter the address and zip code of the place of settlement.

Section I. Enter the date of settlement.

Now, recalling the information from our example, let's look at the completed form for this situation.

A. U.S. DEPARTMENT OF HOUSING AND URBAN DEVELOPMENT SETTLEMENT STATEMENT				
B. TYPE OF LOAN	1.☐ FHA	2. ☐ FmHA	6. File Number	7. Loan Number
3. **X** CONV. UNINS.	4. ☐VA	5. ☐ CONV. INS.	8. Mortgage Insurance Case No.	
C. NOTE: This form is furnished to give you a statement of actual settlement costs. Amounts paid to and by the settlement agent are shown. Items marked "(p.o.c.)" were paid outside the closing; they are shown here for informational purposes and are not included in the totals.				
D. NAME AND ADDRESS OF BORROWER: **Buyer B** **325 W. Mary St.** **Smallville, TX 78702**		E. NAME AND ADDRESS OF SELLER: **Seller A** **100 Olive St.** **Smallville, TX 78702**		F. NAME AND ADDRESS OF LENDER: **Your Bank** **100 Main St.** **Smallville, TX 78702**

G. PROPERTY LOCATION: **100 Olive St.** **Smallville, TX 78702**	H. SETTLEMENT AGENT: **Pro Real Estate**	
	PLACE OF SETTLEMENT: **550 Congress Street** **Smallville, TX 78702**	I. SETTLEMENT DATE: **July 10, 2005**

This, then, is the preliminary part of the HUD-1 Settlement Statement, which identifies the principals involved in the transaction as well as the property being transferred. This part of the form also specifies what kind of funding will be used in the sale and designates a settlement agent. We will now look in detail at the body of the HUD-1 form. The main part of this form is divided into three major sections:

- Summary of Borrower's Transaction (Section J)

- Summary of Seller's Transaction (Section K)

- Settlement Charges (Section L)

Although the Settlement Charges section (Section L) is the final section of the form, you will probably want to fill out this section *first* because the totals from this section are needed for calculations in the other sections of the form.

We have provided a copy of the HUD-1 Settlement Statement here, for educational purposes only. We will now discuss each of the HUD-1 form's three sections in greater detail.

Settlement Charges

As we noted earlier, the settlement charges section of the HUD-1 (Section L) is actually the final section of the form. However, information contained there is needed to complete the earlier sections, so we will treat this section of the form first. The first portion of the settlement charges section (Lines 700—704) deals with the brokers' commissions. Scroll over each line for an explanation of how that line should be completed.

L. SETTLEMENT CHARGES		
700. **TOTAL SALES/BROKER'S COMMISSION based on price** $ _____ @ __% = _____	PAID FROM BORROWER'S FUNDS AT SETTLEMENT	PAID FROM SELLER'S FUNDS AT SETTLEMENT
Division of Commission (line 700) as follows:		

701. $ to		
702. $ to		
703. Commission paid at Settlement		
704.		

Line 700: Enter the commission charged by the licensee. If the commission is a percentage of the purchase, enter the property's selling price, the percentage of the commission and the dollar amount of the total commission paid by the seller.

Lines 701 and 702: If the commission is being split between two or more licensees, or between a licensee and some other third party who is legally permitted to receive commissions, enter the respective dollar amounts that these parties will receive on these lines.

Line 703: Enter the amount of the sales commission to be paid at settlement. If the licensee is keeping part of the earnest money to pay for all, or part of, her or his commission, list *only* the commission being paid at settlement and note the amount of the earnest money deposit being kept by the broker on line 704 with a P.O.C. note.

Line 704: Enter any additional charges imposed by the licensee, as well as any commission being charged to the buyer that is to be paid out by the settlement agent.

Lines 800 through 811 detail the items payable in connection with the loan(s). Each loan fee and charge needs to be itemized. These lines of the form are fairly self-explanatory; the person completing the form simply needs to fill in the information requested, which should be readily available from the borrower or from the lender. Lines 808 through 811 should be used to note any additional loan charges. As we discussed in Lesson Two, most loan fees and charges will generally be charged to the buyer (i.e., the borrower), but make certain that the completed settlement form reflects any negotiated arrangements between the seller and the buyer with respect to loan charges.

	PAID FROM BORROWER'S FUNDS AT SETTLEMENT	PAID FROM SELLER'S FUNDS AT SETTLEMENT
800. **ITEMS PAYABLE IN CONNECTION WITH LOAN**		
801. Loan Origination Fee %		
802. Loan Discount %		
803. Appraisal Fee to		
804. Credit Report to		
805. Lender's Inspection Fee		

806. Mortgage Insurance Application Fee to		
807. Assumption Fee		
808.		
809.		
810.		
811.		

Lines 900 through 905 list items that the lender stipulates must be paid at closing (except for the reserves, which are listed on lines 1000 through 1008). Note, however, that these charges are not necessarily paid to the lender. Generally, the buyer is responsible for these expenses.

	Borrower's Funds	Seller's Funds
900. ITEMS REQUIRED BY LENDER TO BE PAID IN ADVANCE		
901. Interest from _____ to _____ @ $ ____/day		
902. Mortgage Insurance Premium for _____ months to		
903. Hazard Insurance Premium for _____ years to		
904. years to		
905.		

Line 900: Do not enter any information on this line.

Line 901: Enter any interest that is being collected at closing for part of a month or part of a payment period that occurs between settlement and the time of the first monthly payment. Include any per diem charges. Do not enter any amount on this line if interest will not be collected until the first monthly payment.

Line 902: Enter mortgage insurance premiums that are due at closing (not including any reserves collected by the lender, which will be recorded elsewhere). If the buyer is paying a lump sum mortgage insurance premium, record that total on this line with a note indicating that this premium covers the life of the loan.

Line 903: Enter hazard insurance premiums that are due at closing (again, not including any reserves collected by the lender, which will be recorded elsewhere).

Lines 904 and 905: Enter any additional items required by the lender (e.g., flood insurance). You should also use these lines to enter here any amounts paid at closing for other insurance not required by the lender. As with the other 900-series lines, do not include reserves in the figures you record here.

As we mentioned earlier, lines 1000 through 1008 detail the reserves that have been, or need to be, deposited with the lender.

Note: This section requires a different type of accounting than the rest of the settlement sheet. HUD offers the following guidance in this regard:

"After itemizing individual deposits in the 1000 series using single-item accounting, the servicer shall make an adjustment based on aggregate accounting. This adjustment equals the difference between the deposit required under aggregate accounting and the sum of the deposits required under single-item accounting. The computation steps for both accounting methods are set out in 3500.17(d). The adjustment will always be a negative number or zero (-0-). The settlement agent shall enter the aggregate adjustment amount on a final line in the 1000 series of the HUD-1 or HUD-1A statements.

During the phase-in period, as defined in 3500.17(b), an alternative procedure is available. If a servicer has not yet conducted the escrow account analysis to determine the aggregate accounting starting balance, the settlement agent may initially calculate the 1000 series deposits for the HUD-1 and HUD-1A settlement statement using single-item analysis with a one-month cushion (unless the mortgage loan documents indicate a smaller amount). In the escrow account analysis conducted within 45 days of settlement, the servicer shall adjust the escrow account to reflect the aggregate accounting balance."

These instructions are taken from HUD's instructions for completing the HUD-1 Settlement Statement (HUD RESPA Final Regulations, Appendix A), which can be found online at http://www.hud.gov:80/offices/hsg/sfh/res/resappa.cfm.

Sections 3500.17(b) and 3500.17(d), mentioned in these instructions, can be found in the HUD RESPA Final Regulations, Appendix B, which is online at http://www.hud.gov/offices/hsg/sfh/res/resappb.cfm.

	Borrower's Funds	Seller's Funds
1000. **RESERVES DEPOSITED WITH LENDER**		
1001. Hazard Insurance _____ months @ $ ____ per month		
1002. Mortgage insurance _____ months @ $ ___ per month		
1003. City property taxes ____ months @ $ ___ per month		
1004. County property taxes ____months @ ___$ per month		
1005. Annual assessments _____ months @ $___ per month		
1006. _____ Months @ $_____ per month		
1007. _____Months @ $_____ per month		
1008. Aggregate Adjustment ____months @ $___ per month		

Line 1000: This line requires no entry.

Lines 1001 through 1007: Enter amounts collected by the lender and held in escrow or trust for making future payments. Record these amounts as monthly payments of specific amounts, with a total in either the "borrower's funds" column or the "seller's funds" column. Lines 1006 and 1007 can be used to account for items other than those listed; for example, a lender might require reserves to cover flood insurance.

Line 1008: Enter the aggregate adjustment amount, per HUD's accounting instructions, outlined in the earlier note. Remember that HUD's instructions can be found in HUD RESPA Final Regulations, Appendix A, which is online at http://www.hud.gov:80/offices/hsg/sfh/res/resappa.cfm; further details can be found in Appendix B, which is online at http://www.hud.gov/offices/hsg/sfh/res/resappb.cfm.

Lines 1100 through 1113 list title charges and attorneys' fees associated with the transaction. Scroll over each line to see an explanation of how each line should be completed.

Note: In some transactions, a single individual or company performs more than one of the services listed on lines 1101 through 1106, for a single aggregate fee.

For example, an attorney might perform notary duties, execute a title examination and prepare documents. In cases like these, that individual's aggregate fee should be entered on line 1107 (if the individual is an attorney) or on line 1108 (for title companies). Under lines 1107 and 1108, space is provided in which you should give the line item number of each service performed by that individual or company. If you do this, you need not itemize each service individually in the "borrower's" and "seller's" columns.

If more than one individual performs any single service and each person or company charges a fee, their separate fees must be accounted for in this section. You should show the total paid in either the "borrower's" or the "seller's" column and list their individual charges on the line following the word "to." This is true for all services listed on lines 1101 through 1106.

	Borrower's Funds	Seller's Funds
1100. **TITLE CHARGES**		
1101. Settlement or closing fee _____ to		
1102. Abstract or title search _____ to		
1103. Title examination _____ to		

1104. Title insurance binder _____ to		
1105. Document preparation _____ to		
1106. Notary fees _____ to		
1107. Attorney's fees _____ to		
(includes above items numbers;)		
1108. Title Insurance _____ to		
(includes above items numbers;)		
1109. Lender's coverage $		
1110. Owner's coverage $		
1111.		
1112.		
1113.		

Line 1100: Do not enter any information on this line.

Line 1101: Enter the settlement agent's fee.

Line 1102: Enter the fee for the abstract or title search. Remember that if this is part of an aggregate fee charged by a title company or an attorney for a variety of services, you can enter that aggregate fee on line 1108 and provide the line item numbers of the services that were performed for this transaction. This is true for all services listed on lines 1101 through 1106.

Remember, too, that if multiple individuals are paid for the same service, their separate fees must be properly accounted for here.

Line 1103: Enter the title examination fee. If the same person or company performs the abstract or title search and the examination and charges a single fee for both procedures, one fee could be entered on this line. This is only true if that single person or company is not a title company or an attorney; if a title company or attorney performs these or any other services for an aggregate fee, that amount should be entered using lines 1107 and 1108.

Line 1104: Enter the title insurance binder fee; this is sometimes also called a "commitment to insure."

Line 1105: Enter the document preparation fee.

Line 1106: Enter notary fees charged to ensure the authenticity of closing documents.

Line 1107: Enter attorney's fees. If a transaction involves multiple attorneys, one attorney's fees should be entered on line 1107, and the others' fees should be accounted for on line 1111, 1112, or 1113.

Line 1108: Enter total charge for title insurance. If an attorney is also acting as the title agent, note on line 1107 which services are included in the attorney's fee, and note on line 1113 which services are included in the insurance commission.

Lines 1109 and 1110: Enter the separate charges for the lender's and owner's title insurance policies. Do not enter these amounts in the "borrower's" column or the "seller's" column, because the total title insurance charges have already been entered on line 1108.

Lines 1111 through 1113: Enter any title fees or charges that have not been accounted for in lines 1101-1110. For example, if one party must pay a public records office for a certificate of title, that charge would be entered here.

Lines 1200 through 1205 itemize government recording and transfer charges associated with the transaction. This is another fairly self explanatory part of the form; the settlement agent need only list the recording fees on line 1201, the city/county tax/stamps on line 1202 and the state tax/stamps on line 1203. Lines 1204 through 1205 are to be used for any additional charges that are related to government recording and transfer.

	Borrower's Funds	Seller's Funds
1200. **GOVERNMENT RECORDING AND TRANSFER CHARGES**		
1201. Recording fees: Deed $____ ; Mortgage $____ ; Releases $____		
1202. City/county tax/stamps: Deed $____ ; Mortgage $ ____		
1203. State tax/stamps: Deed $____ ; Mortgage $ ____		
1204.		
1205.		

Any other settlement charges that have not already been itemized should be listed on Lines 1300 through 1305. Enter survey costs on Line 1301 and pest or other inspection charges on Line 1302; other inspection charges may be entered here as well, such as hazard inspections (e.g., radon or lead-based paint). Lines 1303 through 1305 are for additional charges not associated with surveys, hazard inspections, or any of the other categories listed in Section L, such as structural inspections or fees for warranty coverage. *Do not* use lines 1303 through 1305 to list the seller's obligatory payoffs, such as liens. These are covered in Section K.

	Borrower's Funds	Seller's Funds
1300. **ADDITIONAL SETTLEMENT CHARGES**		
1301. Survey to		
1302. Pest inspection to		
1303.		
1304.		
1305.		

When all information has been verified and entered in Section L of the form, add up the charges in the "borrower's funds" column and calculate a similar total for the "seller's funds" column. Enter these totals on Line 1400. These totals will also be entered in Sections J and K, on lines 103 and 502, respectively.

	Borrower's Funds	Seller's Funds
1400. **TOTAL SETTLEMENT CHARGES** *(enter on lines 103, Section J and 502, Section K)*		

Borrower's Transaction

Having discussed the "Settlement Charges" section of the HUD-1 form, we will now turn to the part of the form that outlines the buyer's (i.e., the borrower's) costs associated with the transaction. Section J of the HUD-1 form lists the buyer's expenses. Lines 100 through 120 detail the gross amount due from the buyer–that is to say, these lines provide us with a detailed explanation of the buyer's debits. Section J can be left blank on the copy of the HUD-1 form provided to the seller, just as Section K (which details the seller's debits) can be left blank on the copy of the form provided to the buyer. The settlement agent, however, should retain a copy of the form which is fully filled out with information for both principals.

J. SUMMARY OF BORROWER'S TRANSACTION	
100. **GROSS AMOUNT DUE FROM BORROWER:**	
101. Contract sales price	
102. Personal property	
103. Settlement charges to borrower(line 1400)	
104.	
105.	
Adjustments for items paid by seller in advance	

106. City/town taxes_____ to	
107. County taxes _____ to	
108. Assessments _____ to	
109.	
110.	
111.	
112.	
120. **GROSS AMOUNT DUE FROM BORROWER**	

Line 100: Do not enter any information in this line.

Line 101: Enter the property's gross sales price. If the buyer and seller have agreed to separate prices for any personal property being exchanged (such as carpets or appliances), do not include these in the sales price. These separately priced items will be recorded on line 102.

Line 102: Enter the gross sales price of any items of tangible personal property exchanged between the seller and the buyer, such as carpets or appliances. The specifics regarding what counts as personal property vary from state to state, therefore, settlement agents should consult their states' guidelines about what items are correctly considered to be personal property.

Line 103: Enter the total settlement charges to the buyer. We determined this figure in our discussion of Section L; if the settlement agent has already completed Section L, this amount can be found on line 1400.

Lines 104 and 105: Enter any additional amounts that the buyer owes or amounts for which the buyer is reimbursing the seller (such as security deposits). Also, if the buyer is financing construction on the property or is purchasing a manufactured home and has obtained a loan other than a first user loan, the purchase price of the land must be entered on line 104, and the construction costs or price of the manufactured home being placed there must be entered on Line 105. When buyers are financing construction, line 101 is left blank.

Lines 106 through 108: Enter any city taxes, town taxes, county taxes, or assessments that the seller has prepaid and for which the buyer must reimburse the seller.

Lines 109 through 112: Enter any additional prepaid amounts for which the buyer must reimburse the seller.

Line 120: Add the figures from lines 101 through 112, and enter that amount here. This is the buyer's total debit.

Lines 200 through 220 in Section J identify the amounts paid by, or on behalf of, the buyer (that is to say, this section outlines the buyer's credits). Scroll over each line for an explanation of how that line should be completed.

200. **AMOUNTS PAID BY OR IN BEHALF OF BORROWER:**	
201. Deposit of earnest money	
202. Principal amount of new loan(s)	
203. Existing loan(s) taken subject to	
204.	
205.	
206.	
207.	
208.	
209.	
Adjustments for items unpaid by seller	
210. City/town taxes _____ to	
211. County taxes _____ to	
212. Assessments _____ to	
213.	
214.	
215.	
216.	
217.	
218.	
219.	
220. **TOTAL PAID BY/FOR BORROWER**	

Line 200: Do not enter any information on this line.

Line 201: Enter the amount of earnest money or any other money paid against the purchase price before closing.

Line 202: Enter the amount of the new loan(s) made by the lender or first user loan(s), if applicable. Throughout the remainder of the form, the settlement agent should be certain that his or her calculations reflect any known adjustments or charges associated with temporary or permanent financing.

Line 203: Enter the amount of any loan the buyer is assuming, or the amounts of any other liens and encumbrances to which the buyer's title is subject, if applicable.

Lines 204 through 209: Enter any other items that have been paid for by the buyer or paid on the buyer's behalf which have not yet been entered in this part of the form. For example, the settlement agent should use these lines to account for cases in which the seller accepts a note from the buyer for all or part of the purchase price, cases in which the seller accepts other property as trade, and cases in which the seller gives the buyer an allowance to make specific repairs or improvements to the property.

Lines 210 through 212: Enter any accrued city taxes, town taxes, county taxes, or assessments that date from a period prior to closing but which have not yet been paid. Generally, the seller is understood to owe the buyer for these expenses unless they have negotiated another arrangement.

Lines 213 through 219: Enter any additional accrued items dating from a period prior to settlement that have not yet been paid but which will come due to the buyer (such as utilities used but not yet paid for). Again, the seller is generally understood to owe the buyer for these expenses, unless they have negotiated another arrangement.

Line 220: Add the figures from lines 201 through 219, and enter that amount here. This is the buyer's total credit.

Line 300 should be left blank, but lines 301 through 303 are used to calculate the amount of cash due *from* the buyer or the amount of cash due *to* the buyer at closing. On line 301, enter the gross amount due from the buyer, which can be found on line 120. On line 302, enter the buyer's total credit from line 220. Subtract line 302 (the buyer's credit) from line 301 (the gross amount due) to determine the total cash due *from* the buyer (i.e., the borrower) or due *to* the buyer. Enter this amount on line 303. The settlement agent should make certain to avoid confusion by checking the appropriate box on the HUD-1 form to indicate whether the figure on line 303 represents cash due to the buyer or cash due from the buyer.

300. **CASH AT SETTLEMENT FROM/TO BORROWER**	
301. Gross amount due from borrower(line 120)	
302. Less amounts paid by/for borrower(line 220)	
303. **CASH □ FROM □TO BORROWER**	

It may seem odd that cash would be due to a buyer in a real estate transaction. However, one occasionally encounters situations in which the buyer's credit is larger than her or his debit, and in these cases the buyer would *receive* cash at closing. However, in most transactions the amount entered on line 303 will reflect cash *owed by* the buyer.

Seller's Transaction

Now we turn to the third part of the HUD-1 form, which is much like Section J except that now we are concerned with the *seller*, not the buyer. Section K details the seller's expenses associated with the transaction. As we noted before, there is no obligation to share this part of the form with the buyer; Section K can be left blank on the seller's copy of the form, though the settlement agent should retain a copy of the form which is fully filled out with information for both principals.

Lines 400 through 420 list the amounts due to the seller (that is, these lines list the seller's credits). Scroll over each line to see an explanation of how that line should be completed.

K. SUMMARY OF SELLER'S TRANSACTION	
400. **GROSS AMOUNT DUE TO SELLER:**	
401. Contract sales price	
402. Personal property	
403.	
404.	
405.	
Adjustments for items paid by seller in advance	
406. City/town taxes _____ to	
407. County taxes _____ to	
408. Assessments _____ to	
409.	
410.	
411.	
412.	
420. **GROSS AMOUNT DUE TO SELLER**	

Line 400: Do not enter any information on this line.

Line 401: Enter the property's gross sales price. If the buyer and seller have agreed to separate prices for any personal property being exchanged (such as carpets or appliances), do not include these in the sales price. These separately priced items will be recorded on line 402.

Line 402: Enter the gross sales price of any items of tangible personal property exchanged between the seller and the buyer, such as carpets or appliances. The specifics regarding what counts as personal property vary from state to state, therefore settlement agents should consult their states' guidelines about what items are correctly considered to be personal property.

Lines 403 through 405: Enter any additional amounts that the seller is owed. Also, if the buyer is financing construction on the property or is purchasing a manufactured home and has obtained a loan other than a first user loan, the purchase price of the land must be entered on line 404, and the construction costs or price of the manufactured home being placed there must be entered on Line 405. When buyers are financing construction, line 401 is left blank.

Lines 406 through 408: Enter any prepaid city taxes, town taxes, county taxes or assessments that the seller has prepaid and for which the buyer must reimburse the seller.

Lines 409 through 412: Enter any additional prepaid amounts for which the buyer must reimburse the seller.

Line 420: Add the figures from lines 401 through 412, and enter that amount here. This is the seller's total credit.

Lines 500 through 520 identify amounts that the seller must pay and other reductions in the amount due to the seller (that is to say, this section outlines the seller's debits). Scroll over each line to see an explanation of how that line should be completed.

500. **REDUCTIONS IN AMOUNT DUE TO SELLER:**	
501. Excess deposit (see instructions)	
502. Settlement charges to seller (line 1400)	
503. Existing loan(s) taken subject to	
504. Payoff of first mortgage loan	
505. Payoff of second mortgage loan	
506.	
507.	
508.	
509.	
Adjustments for items unpaid by seller	
510. City/town taxes _____ to	

511. County taxes _____ to	
512. Assessments _____ to	
513.	
514.	
515.	
516.	
517.	
518.	
519.	
520. **TOTAL REDUCTION AMOUNT DUE SELLER**	

Line 500: Do not enter any information on this line.

Line 501: This line is only used in particular circumstances. Specifically, it is for use when someone besides the settlement agent (e.g., the seller's broker) holds an amount of earnest money that amount exceeds that his or her commission and the excess amount is to be returned directly to the seller rather than passed through the settlement agent. In these cases, the settlement agent should enter the amount of the excess deposit on this line. The total amount of the deposit, including commissions, should be entered on line 201.

Line 502: Enter the total settlement charges to the seller. We determined this figure in our discussion of Section L; if the settlement agent has already completed Section L, this amount can be found on line 1400.

Line 503: If the buyer is assuming any of the seller's loans or receiving a title which is subject to other liens or encumbrances, the settlement agent should enter that amount here.

Lines 504 and 505: If any first or second mortgage loans are to be paid off as part of the closing process, the settlement agent should enter those amounts here (including the loans' accrued interest).

Lines 506 and 507: On line 506, enter deposits that the buyer has paid to the seller (or to another party who is not the settlement agent) and which were not entered on line 501. Sometimes the seller (or other party who is not the settlement agent) turns over part or all of the deposit to the settlement agent. In these cases, the settlement agent should use line 507 to enter in parentheses on the amount of the deposit that is being distributed as proceeds, and enter on line 506 any amount of the deposit that seller or other party still holds. Also, any time the settlement agent holds the deposit, he or she should make a note on line 507 indicating that the deposit will be distributed as proceeds.

Lines 508 and 509: These lines can be used for a variety of purposes. They might be used to list any liens that the seller must pay off to clear the title. Lines 506 and 507 can be used to list *other* items that the seller is obligated to pay off (i.e., items that are *not* liens). Do not use lines 1301 through 1305 to list the seller's obligatory payoffs. These lines might also be used to detail funds held by the settlement agent for the payment of bills that cannot be prorated at closing due to a lack of information. Any amounts that were entered on lines 204 through 209 (covering general items that have been paid for by the buyer or paid on the buyer's behalf) should be entered here, including seller financing arrangements

Lines 510 through 512: Enter any accrued city taxes, town taxes, county taxes or assessments that date from a period prior to closing but which have not yet been paid. Generally, the seller is understood to owe the buyer for these expenses unless they have negotiated another arrangement.

Lines 513 through 519: Enter any additional accrued items dating from a period prior to settlement that have not yet been paid but which will come due to the buyer (such as utilities used but not yet paid for). Again, the seller is generally understood to owe the buyer for these expenses, unless they have negotiated another arrangement.

Line 520: Add the figures from lines 501 through 519, and enter that amount here. This is the seller's total debit.

Line 600 should be left blank, but lines 601 through 603 are used to calculate the amount of cash due *to* the seller or due *from* the seller at closing. On line 601, enter the total amount due to the seller, which is the total entered earlier on line 420. Then enter the seller's total debit on line 602; this amount is found on line 520. Subtract line 602 (the seller's debit) from Line 601 (the total amount due to the seller) to determine the total cash due *to* the seller or due *from* the seller and enter that amount on line 603. The settlement agent should make certain to avoid confusion by checking the appropriate box on the HUD-1 form to indicate whether the figure on line 303 represents cash due to the buyer or cash due from the buyer.

600. **CASH AT SETTLEMENT TO/FROM SELLER**	
601. Gross amount due to seller (line 420)	
602. Less reductions in amount due seller (line 520)	
603. **CASH** ☐**TO** ☐**FROM SELLER**	

It may seem odd that cash would be due from a seller in a real estate transaction. However, one occasionally encounters situations in which the seller's debits are larger than his or her credits, in which case, the seller would actually need to bring cash to the closing. In most transactions, however, the amount entered on line 603 will reflect cash *owed to* the seller.

Activity: Closing

It is likely that you as a real estate licensee will never be asked to fill out the HUD-1 Settlement Statement. However, if you plan to stay involved in the closing process, you will need to be able to explain costs to the buyers and sellers. The parties may wish to negotiate the terms of the settlement statement, and you may assist with that process. Also, you will probably give buyers and sellers estimates of the costs involved in closing, and knowing how to fill out the HUD-1 Settlement Statement will prepare you for this.

We will now go through a sample closing transaction and give the expenses incurred. Fill in the given information in the correct blanks on the settlement statement. Then, you will be asked to make calculations and provide totals.

Note: The amounts used throughout this example do not necessarily reflect standard rates or rates used in your area.

Buyer B has decided to purchase Seller A's home for $115,000. Buyer B secures a loan for $90,000 from Quality Loans, who charge a loan origination fee of 1 percent and a loan discount fee of 2 percent. Buyer B also pays $400 for appraisal fees and $35 for a credit report, but these were paid outside of the settlement. Buyer B's lender requires that he purchase one year of hazard insurance for $400 and that he deposit the following escrow amounts: for hazard insurance, two months at $30 per month, and for county property taxes, two months at $150 per month.

In this transaction, Seller A is charged $20 for the title search and $20 for the title insurance binder. Seller A also must pay her attorney's fees of $600 for legal representation, document preparation, and notary services. For title charges,

Buyer B pays $600 for title insurance and pays his attorney $250 for legal representation and title examination.

Buyer B is charged a total of $40 for recording fees ($20 for the deed and $20 for the mortgage). Seller A is charged $40 to record two documents to clear the title, $20 to record the release of title, and $150 in state transfer taxes. In this transaction, the buyer is responsible for the survey charges of $100, and the seller pays the $150 termite inspection charge.

Finally, there is the matter of brokers' commissions. In this transaction, only Seller A is represented by a broker, so the commission will not be split. Seller A's broker charges 5 percent of the sale price, so the total commission is $5,750.

More About: Now calculate Buyer B's and Seller A's settlement charges. You can find detailed instructions on filling out the settlement form at http://www.hud.gov/offices/hsg/sfh/res/resappa.cfm.

1. What are the buyer's total settlement charges?

2. What are the seller's total settlement charges?

Answers:

1. $4,050. Remember that expenses that are paid outside of closing do not figure into the total settlement charges.

2. $6,750. Don't forget about the fee for recording two documents to clear the title.

As mentioned previously, the purchase price of the property is $115,000. Buyer B paid $25,000 as a deposit, and the remainder of the purchase price is covered by the $90,000 loan that he obtained. We already calculated the settlement charges, which are $4,050 to Buyer B and $6,750 to Seller A. Seller A also needs to pay off the remaining $45,920.30 from her first mortgage loan.

Seller A prepaid the real estate taxes on this property for the entire year, which totaled $1,200. The date of closing is July 10. For this transaction, prorations are calculated from a 360-day year.

Now figure the total cash going to or from the buyer and to or from the seller. (Lines 303 and 603).

1. Is cash going to or from the buyer?

2. What is the total cash due of the buyer at settlement?

3. Is cash going to or from the seller?

4. What is the total cash due to the seller at settlement?

Answers:

1. From

2. $4,616.67. The formula to figure the amount of days in the period is:

	Months	Days
Amount paid to Dec 31	12	30/month
Closing date July 10	- 7	-10
Prepaid period	5 months	20 days

3. To

4. $62,896.37.

Sales price	$115,000.00
First mortgage	-$45,920.30
Settlement Costs	-$6,750.00
Prepaid taxes	$566.67
Total	$62,896.37

Summary

Settlement statements give a detailed accounting of each principal's expenses associated with a real estate transaction; as a result, these statements also generally reveal the amount that a buyer must bring to the closing. There is no generally accepted format that all settlement statements must follow.

However, all transactions that fall under RESPA regulation are required to use the HUD-1 Settlement Statement form. This means that all transactions involving a federally related loan used to purchase a one- to four-family home must use the HUD-1 Settlement Statement form; this in turn means that nearly all residential purchase transactions will require this form. Therefore, the HUD-1 Settlement Statement is the most commonly used form for settlement statements, and all licensees who deal in residential property should be familiar with it. We should note that even transactions that do not fall under RESPA regulations are permitted to use the HUD-1 form as a settlement statement.

The preliminary part of the HUD-1 Settlement Statement identifies the principals involved in the transaction as well as the property being transferred. This part of the form also specifies what kind of funding will be used in the sale, and designates a settlement agent. The *body* of the HUD-1 form is divided into three major sections:

- Summary of Borrower's Transaction (Section J)
- Summary of Seller's Transaction (Section K)
- Settlement Charges (Section L)

Although the Settlement Charges section (Section L) is the final section of the form, it is often best to complete this section first because the totals from this section are needed for calculations in the other sections of the form.

Sections J and K provide summaries of the borrower's side of the transaction and the seller's side of the transaction, itemizing each party's debits and credits to determine the amount of cash to be exchanged at closing.

Some of the settlement information may not be available until the last minute; there is no legal requirement that the form be fully completed before closing. The buyer may request to receive a copy of the HUD-1 Settlement Statement one day before closing, but even at this late stage, some important expenses or credits may remain unknown. In such cases, the settlement agent should complete the settlement statement to the best of her or his knowledge and ensure that all parties are aware that at least some of the costs given at that point are only estimates.

At closing, the settlement agent should ensure that both the buyer and the seller receive a copy of the settlement statement. Some sections of the form allow for the seller's information to be omitted from the buyer's copy of the statement, and vice versa, thus protecting each party's privacy (see, for example, Section J, which is discussed in detail later in this lesson). However, each principal should receive a copy of the form that has been adequately completed, so that they may use it to draw conclusions about the transaction. In addition, the settlement agent should retain a copy of the settlement form that includes any omitted information for both principals, to provide the fullest possible accounting of the closing transaction.

For escrow closings in which the buyer, the seller or both principals are absent, the settlement statement should be mailed or delivered immediately after closing. In all types of closings, the buyer and the seller should carefully review the settlement statement with their attorneys and brokers to ensure that all of the information it contains is accurate.

There are many details to consider when filling out a HUD-1 Settlement Statement. The settlement agent is responsible for this task; in some states, licensees may act as settlement agents. Regardless of who acts as a settlement agent, that individual must be careful and accurate.

This concludes lesson eight.

Return to your online course player to take the Lesson Quiz.

Lesson 9:
FORECLOSURE

This lesson focuses on the following topics:

- Introduction
- Default
- Foreclosure
- Properties in Distress
- Activity: Fill In the Blanks
- Case Study: Forbearance
- Summary

By the end of this lesson, you should be able to:

- Explain the reasons for default, and define tax liens, insurance and maintenance, delinquency, moratoriums, forbearance, and recasting
- Compare the different procedures that follow a default, identifying the various elements of foreclosure
- Explain what leads to a property being considered in distress, and compare the difference between liquidating and holding a distressed property

Introduction

This lesson is concerned with what happens when the borrower becomes unable to make payments and the lender is forced to take action. In the most extreme of circumstances, lenders must foreclose on a delinquent borrower-that is, take control of the collateral property and sell it at auction to recover losses.

Default

A default is any breach in a contract. Most defaults in mortgage contracts are on the side of the borrower. Not all defaults, however, are failures to make payment on the loan: Defaults can come from nonpayment of taxes, lack of required insurance, or improper use of, or damage to, the property.

A note usually contains an *acceleration clause* to protect the lender in the event of default. This clause states that whenever there is a breach of contract on the part of the borrower, the lender may make the entire amount of the loan due immediately. This protects the lender from having to sue for every late payment as it becomes due. Default occurs when a borrower is delinquent on payments or fails to properly maintain the collateral.

Tax Liens

Real estate loans include a tax clause that states the borrower's obligation to pay property taxes in full when they become due. Most residential mortgage loans use escrow accounts to collect taxes month by month, allowing the lender to closely monitor and ensure the payment of taxes. However, for loans with large down payments, or for commercial real estate loans, the escrow account may be waived, if required at all.

The importance of the escrow method and the tax clause is to protect the lender's position as the primary lien holder on the property. If a borrower failed to make the requisite tax payments, the government could foreclose on the property and sell it to recover back taxes. In such a case, the lender would receive only the sale price of the property, less the taxes owed, which could be significant.

The tax clause allows a lender to treat a borrower who has not paid his or her taxes as in default and, if necessary, foreclose on the property.

Insurance and Maintenance

Since the loan is secured by the lien on the collateral property, the lender will do everything necessary to make sure that the property is taken care of. This includes requiring that the owner have proper hazard insurance and flood insurance, if appropriate. As with taxes, most insurance payments are collected by lenders before they become due; however, with certain loans not having an escrow account, nonpayment or failure to renew insurance can become a problem, and in extreme circumstances, force the lender to foreclose.

For similar reasons, the lender will seek to prevent poor maintenance and disrepair from befalling a property. However, it is difficult for lenders to keep constant watch on every property that serves as collateral for their loans. It is unfortunate, but some frustrated borrowers, when faced with foreclosure, will deliberately damage the collateral. This makes speediness in the foreclosure process, once begun, essential.

Delinquency

A borrower is said to be *delinquent* on her or his payments if he or she fails to pay the principal, interest, taxes, or insurance for a loan on time or at all.

Most lenders would rather work with a borrower in default than foreclose on a property. Lenders are willing to recast the loans of delinquent borrowers or to allow a suspension of payment for a period of time known as a moratorium.

Moratoriums

The word *moratorium* is from a Latin word meaning *delay*. If a borrower is delinquent because of a temporary setback-the loss of a job, illness, a death in the family, and so forth-the lender may consider a moratorium on payments, allowing the buyer to not make principal, interest, or principal and interest payments for a certain period of time.

When the lender may legally foreclose due to default but chooses not to, it is called forbearance. The borrower can work with a lender to develop a payment plan for the missed moratorium payments. Sometimes moratoriums involve recasting, or a change of the loan terms.

Recasting

A lender may recast a loan in place of a payment moratorium or may recast in addition to the moratorium. If there is a moratorium, the borrower will owe more money than what will be covered by the remaining monthly payments:

Moratorium Type	Outstanding Amounts
Interest	Unpaid Principal
Principal	Compounded Interest
Principal and Interest	Unpaid Principal and Compounded Interest

These sums can be repaid through one of three methods. The lender can:

- Increase the monthly payments after the moratorium

- Extend the term of the loan

- Allow for a balloon payment at the end of the current loan term

These methods also may be combined. For example, the lender could increase the monthly payments slightly and extend the term of the loan.

If there is no moratorium period, the lender must recast the loan in such a way as to allow for the borrower's distressed financial situation. For example, lowering the monthly payments and extending the loan term, or providing for a graduated payment structure, perhaps allowing negative amortization.

Foreclosure

Foreclosure is the legal process whereby a lender takes control of a property held by a borrower in default and sells it to recover the lender's losses. Foreclosure usually happens only when the alternatives provided by moratoriums and recasting are not enough to allow the borrower to repay the loan amount. As a general rule, borrowers delinquent for three to four months who have not worked out a repayment plan with the lender are issued a Notice of Default and Intent to Foreclose. It is important to note that the states have varying procedures and foreclosure instruments; therefore, the following information's purpose is to provide general information and procedures.

After the lending institution issues the Notice of Default, it records it in the public registry so that other parties with a lien on the property may be aware of the foreclosure. The lender also must notify each party with a recorded interest in the loan directly. This requires a title search. If a party holding a lien against the property is not notified by the lender, that party may sue later to recover its losses.

At the foreclosure proceedings, all creditors with a claim against the property appear and present evidence of their claim. The court recognizes the claims and their priority and then orders a public sale of the foreclosed property.

Non judicial Foreclosure

Some deeds of trust and mortgage documents contain a power-of-sale clause, which allows the lender to bypass the courts and take possession of and sell a collateral property when the borrower defaults on his or her loan. Additionally, some states allow strict foreclosure, where the lender gives notice of the default, and, if it is not paid in some specified time period, the lender may foreclose on the property, eliminating the borrower's redemption rights (both equitable and statutory). These types of foreclosure are known as non judicial foreclosures because they do not involve a suit and the ruling of the court.

Non judicial foreclosures are beneficial to lenders in several respects. They are simpler, faster, and less costly than judicial foreclosures. In the case of a deed of trust, the lender simply notifies the trustee and instructs her or him to begin the foreclosure. For power-of-sale foreclosures, an auction is held, much like with a judicial foreclosure. For strict foreclosures, there is no auction: The lender takes control of the property and sells it to recover his or her losses.

Although many states that use mortgages rather than deeds of trust do not allow power-of-sale foreclosures, and even fewer states allow non judicial foreclosures, Texas allows both. Some title insurance companies, however, require a property to have been judicially foreclosed before they will issue a policy.

Additionally, in a strict foreclosure, the lender cannot seek a deficiency judgment against the borrower in the event the full amount owed is not recovered from the sale of the property. This is to prevent the lender from selling the property at a price well below the fair market value and then holding the defaulted borrower responsible for the remaining balance of the loan.

Auction

In foreclosures involving an auction, the lender sets a sale date and records a Notice of Sale, which is also sent to the IRS. The sale is public, and anyone may make a bid on the foreclosed property. Typically the lender will bid first, offering the amount of the outstanding loan balance, accrued interest, penalties, and legal fees. The idea is that if anyone else bids higher, the lender will recoup all of her or his losses. If no one bids higher, the lender receives the property and may then sell it for any price he or she desires without having to pay off the other creditors, whose liens are dissolved.

To protect their investment, other creditors may make bids as well. The proceeds of the public sale are paid first to cover the first lien holder's claim, then the second and so on. Therefore, the second lien holder will bid the amount owed the first lien holder plus his or her claim, and the third lien holder will bid that amount plus her or his claim and so on-that is, if the junior lien holders believe that they can recover their claims through a higher successive bid or by selling the property once obtained.

For example, suppose that a foreclosed property is put up for auction. The lender has $80,000 in claims on the property and, therefore, bids $80,000 first. The second has $10,000 in claims, so he bids $90,000. This way, if anyone bids even a dollar more, both the first and second lien holders recover all of their claims. Suppose that there are no further bids. Then the second lien holder pays the $90,000 bid: The lender receives $80,000, and the other $10,000 is in effect *returned* to the second lien holder, but he still has not recovered his $10,000 originally owed to him. At this time he is simply receiving back the money he just spent to win the bid. He is still out $80,000 (received by the lender) and has not yet recovered his original $10,000. So, he needs to sell the property for $90,000 to break even (recover all money owed to him and not to have lost anything).

However, the second lien holder may turn around and sell the property for whatever price he chooses. If he sells it for $100,000, making a $10,000 profit, he does *not* need to give any of that money to other creditors who may have had claims on the property. By not bidding in the auction, these creditors lose their lien on the property. However, they may still recover their lost money through a deficiency judgment against the borrower.

Note: If the property sells for an amount in excess of *all* the claims against it, the borrower receives the surplus.

Deficiency Judgment

Lenders sometimes seek a *deficiency judgment* against a defaulted borrower, guarantor on a loan, or endorsers if a foreclosure sale does not generate enough money to pay off the loan and cover the costs of the foreclosure. Deficiency judgments require the defaulted borrower to pay any remaining balance owed to the lender. Deficiency judgments are usually sought on what is owed after the sale of a foreclosed property, while the property is foreclosed on the basis of defaulted mortgage payments.

Deficiency judgments are limited somewhat by Texas law. It says that an action brought to recover a deficiency must be brought within two years of the foreclosure sale. The person against whom the action is taken may request that the court determine the fair-market value of the property as of the date of foreclosure. If the fair-market value is determined to be higher than the foreclosures sale price, the amount of the claim may be offset.

Some states do not allow deficiency judgments. When deficiency judgments are not allowed, the debt is called *non-recourse financing.* Borrowers who obtain non-recourse financing are not personally liable for the loan. In the event of default, the only way for lenders to collect the remaining balance of a loan is by foreclosure.

In states that do allow deficiency judgments, the foreclosed mortgagor loses not only the property, but also will have to pay additional money to clear his or her debt.

Redemption
Texas does not allow debtors to *redeem* (regain possession of) their property. In states that do, there are two types of redemption: equitable redemption and statutory redemption.

Equitable Redemption
Equitable redemption occurs before the sale of a property. It is derived from common law and allows defaulting debtors to pay the defaulted portion of the debt (as well as costs the lender incurred) in order to reinstate the loan and prevent a foreclosure sale. Other parties with an interest in the real estate also can pay the defaulted portion off, in which case the debtor usually becomes responsible to that party for the redemption cost. The redeemer must pay the entire loan at this time if the debt has been accelerated.

Statutory Redemption
When states allow debtors to redeem a property after a foreclosure sale, debtors are said to have a *statutory redemption* period in which debtors have a specified length of time to recover their property. The court may appoint someone to take control of the property during the statutory redemption period. The purchaser at the foreclosure sale usually has the right to collect rents until the property is redeemed.

Purchaser Receives Deed
If the debtor does not redeem a property during the statutory redemption period, or if the state does not permit a statutory redemption period, then the purchaser at the foreclosure sale receives a deed to the property that is not encumbered by

the debt, but the title transfers *as is*. This type of deed is usually called a *master's* or *sheriff's* deed, because it is typically executed by either a master in chancery or a sheriff.

Deed In Lieu of Foreclosure

A borrower who cannot make the monthly payments for a loan may voluntarily transfer title to the lender to avoid foreclosure. This arrangement has several advantages:

- The borrower's credit is not as damaged, as in the case of a foreclosure.

- The borrower need not worry about a deficiency judgment as long as it is written into the arrangement that the Deed in Lieu of Foreclosure is "in full satisfaction of" the debt.

- The lender does not have to incur the expense of a foreclosure.

A borrower does not, however, just deed the property to the lender when she or he cannot make the monthly payments: Both the borrower and the lender must agree to an arrangement whereby the lender receives title and the borrower receives consideration, such as a release from repayment of the loan. Lenders may be willing to enter into such an agreement to avoid the expense and legal difficulty associated with foreclosure. However, borrowers seeking to declare bankruptcy may be prevented from a deed in lieu of foreclosure if they would otherwise have to include the collateral property in the bankruptcy.

Properties in Distress

A property in distress is one that is in poor condition either physically or financially. The task of managing these properties often falls to a lender who has foreclosed on a property for default. In such a case, the lost loan amount is a sunk cost-it is irrecoverable-and should not affect the owner's decisions. The owner must decide whether to hold the property or sell it.

A physically distressed property may be in poor repair: It may be dilapidated, infested with termites, have a mold problem and so on, or it may have environmental liabilities, such as lead-based paint, asbestos, radon, or other toxic hazards.

A financially distressed property may have low returns or even be running at a loss. It may have several years of taxes in arrears and be completely unmarketable. The owner of such a property is faced with the difficult task of making the property a financially viable asset, either to increase his or her own cash flow or to liquidate it.

Asset managers are a special type of real estate professional. They deal with the purchase, sale, and financing of investment properties. Their goal is to maximize the return of such properties. When a lender receives a distressed property through foreclosure, the task of making the right decisions to minimize losses and, if possible, increase returns often falls to an asset manager.

Liquidating a Distressed Property

In some cases, it will be best to liquidate a property in distress. If operation of the property would result in a loss-that is, total cost would exceed total revenue-selling the property is advisable. It is important to remember that the total cost of retaining the asset should not include any amount the lender lost on the loan, as that is a sunk cost.

A distressed property may be worth no more than the land on which it is situated. Sometimes, however, improvements can make the difference in selling the property as raw land and selling it as an income producer. The owner must compare the expected sale price of the property in its current condition with the expected sale price of the improved property, less the cost of improvement.

The owner also must have an eye to opportunity cost. Even if she could increase her yield by improving the property, if the money that would be used for improvements could turn a greater profit elsewhere, the improvements may not be worth the trouble. In general, the owner should improve the property only if the return of selling it "as is" and investing the improvement money elsewhere is less than the return of making improvements and selling it.

As with any investment decision, the market should be taken into account. If there is small demand for rental property, even minor improvements may be a bad investment. The owner should always take into account the availability of buyers, which is dependent upon the profitability of the investment. If vacancy rates are high, investor demand for rental property will be low, and if inflation is high, demand will be high as well. Improvements should be made only after a market study has been conducted. Sometimes a study will indicate that converting a property from its current or intended use is economically more valuable than improvement.

Even if improvements or conversions can be made to make the property profitable, it may not generate enough net operating income (NOI) to allow a potential buyer to receive financing.

Improving a distressed property may include rehabilitation or refinancing. In the case of a physically distressed property, remediation of a hazard, such as lead-based paint, may be necessary. Even if remediation is necessary before the property can be sold or turned to value, the asset manager is faced with several options. For example, if a particular apartment complex is foreclosed, in part because the tenants recognized an asbestos exposure risk, the cost of reducing the risk to safe residential levels may be more than the cost of converting the complex to hold small offices and reducing the risk to 40-hour workweek levels. This is known as risk-driven remediation.

Holding a Distressed Property

Some distressed properties may be turned to profitable use for their owners through intelligent asset management.

As a general rule, an owner should hold the property if the net present value of all of its future cash flows exceeds the net present value of the owner's best alternative investment opportunity. However, certain conditions may make holding the property undesirable. For example, its current tenants may be upset with past management and desirous to leave, or the owner may want to diversify his or her investment portfolio with other assets.

If the title of a distressed property falls to a lender who has foreclosed the property, she or he may not have the managerial experience necessary to run the property. Such a titleholder may seek to hire a property manager-a licensed real estate professional who specializes in running the day-to-day affairs of the property. Property managers are different from asset managers in that they do not make decisions involving the sale or financing of a property.

Activity: Fill In the Blanks

Below is a word bank of important concepts discussed in this lesson.

Word Bank	
Auction	Foreclosure
Borrower	Lender
Deed in lieu	Moratorium
Default	Physically
Deficiency judgment	Recasting
Delinquent	Redemption
Equitable	Statutory
Financially	Sunk
Forbearance	Tax lien

Fill in the Blanks

1. A defaulted borrower may regain possession of his or her property at any time before it is sold at auction through her or his _____ redemption rights.

2. A lender who has not received the full amount of a defaulted loan may seek a(n) _____ against a borrower to recover the remaining losses.

3. _____ costs, such as an amount lost on a loan, are costs that are unrecoverable and so should not influence a lender's decision to sell or hold a distressed property.

4. A change in the loan terms to allow a borrower to repay unpaid principal amounts or accrued interest is known as _____.

5. A(n) _____ is a period during which the lender allows the borrower to not pay or to only partially repay the principal or interest due.

6. Failure to make principal and interest payments, failure to properly maintain the collateral property and failure to obtain the requisite insurance are all causes of borrower _____ and may result in a borrower losing the property.

7. The _____ receives any amount of the proceeds from the sale of the collateral property at auction that are in excess of all the liens against the property.

8. In some states, a borrower may redeem his or her property after it is sold at auction during the _____ redemption period.

9. To avoid the expense and legal difficulty of foreclosure, a lender may encourage a borrower to execute a(n) _____ of foreclosure and voluntarily transfer title to the property.

10. A lien holder has two chances to recoup his or her losses in the event of foreclosure: First, the lien holder may attempt to purchase the collateral property at _____, and second, the lien holder may seek a deficiency judgment in court.

11. Lenders will include a clause in the mortgage contract requiring that borrowers pay their taxes on time to avoid the possibility of the government foreclosing on a(n) _____ .

12. A property with several years of taxes in arrears would be considered to be _____ distressed.

13. A borrower's right of _____ is her or his right to regain possession of a foreclosed property by repaying the full amount owed, including penalties.

14. The task of managing distressed properties often falls to the _____, who may hire an asset manager to help with the decision to hold or sell the property; or a property manager, if he or she holds it, to help run it.

15. A borrower is said to be _____ if he or she fails to make principal and interest or escrow payments on time or at all.

16. A(n) _____ is a lender's decision not to foreclose on a defaulted borrower, even though the lender may do so legally. Most lenders would rather work with a borrower.

17. A property that is dilapidated, poorly maintained, infested with termites, or out of repair would be considered a (n) _____ distressed property.

18. _____ is the process whereby a lender takes possession of the collateral property of a defaulted borrower and sells it at auction to recover the lost loan amount.

Answers:

1. Equitable
2. Deficiency judgment
3. Sunk
4. Recasting
5. Moratorium
6. Default
7. Borrower
8. Statutory
9. Deed in lieu
10. Auction
11. Tax lien
12. Financially
13. Redemption
14. Lender
15. Delinquent
16. Forbearance
17. Physically
18. Foreclosure

Case Study: Forbearance

Mr. and Mrs. Borrower are in trouble. Mr. Borrower just lost his job at the widget factory, and now they cannot afford to make their monthly mortgage payment. They immediately call their lender and try to work out some forbearance until they can get their finances in order again.

Mr. Borrower was making a gross monthly salary of $1,400, and Mrs. Borrower's job still provides $1,600 gross per month. Their other long-term liabilities include the following:

- Car payment: $250

- Car insurance: $35

- Phone bill: $40

- Cable TV: $25

- Internet: $20

On the phone, they make an appointment with the lender to meet in person and discuss avoiding foreclosure. Their current loan is for $100,000 at 9.75 percent interest for 30 years. The current principal balance is $94,860.71, and the next payment due will be for the 80th month. To decide the best course of action, the lender calculates the family's maximum housing expense, based on a total debt service ratio of 41 percent:

Maximum Housing Expense = (Gross Monthly Income × 41%) − Long-Term Debts
Maximum Housing Expense = ($1,600 × 0.41) − $370
Maximum Housing Expense = $286

This amount is not enough to cover the next month's interest payment of $770.74, but it is well over the amount necessary to cover the principal payment of $88.41. The lender devises the following strategy: He will allow Mr. and Mrs. Borrower to make a payment that covers the principal amount due and partially covers the interest payment. Then, at the end of the loan's term, the extra amount accrued will be due in a lump sum. This arrangement is to last for six months (from the 80th through the 85th months) and would proceed as follows:

Month	Monthly Payment	Principal Payment	Interest Due	Interest Paid	Principal Balance
80	$286.00	$88.41	$771.46	$197.59	$95,346.17
81	$286.00	$89.13	$774.69	$196.87	$95,834.86
82	$286.00	$89.85	$778.66	$196.15	$96,327.52
83	$286.00	$90.58	$782.66	$195.42	$96,824.18
84	$286.00	$91.32	$786.70	$194.68	$97,324.88
85	$286.00	$92.06	$790.76	$193.94	$97,829.64

Note: The Principal balance for a month n is equal to the principal balance for month $n − 1$, plus the interest due that month, minus $286.

At the end of the six-month forbearance period, the principal balance is $97,829.64. The scheduled principal balance (what the balance would have been had there not been a forbearance) for this month is $94,319.36, a difference of $3,510.28. This is the amount that will be due in the balloon payment at the end of the loan term (plus compounded interest on it).

Of course, if after the six-month period, Mr. and Mrs. Borrower are not able to return to making the regular monthly payment on the loan, the lender would have to consider foreclosing on the collateral property. However, by coming to the lender early, as soon as they realized they were in trouble, Mr. and Mrs. Borrower helped avoid greater difficulty than was necessary and found a solution acceptable to both parties.

Summary

Default is a breach in the loan contract. It may have several causes, including delinquency, nonpayment of taxes, or insurance or poor maintenance of the collateral property. If property taxes go unpaid, the collateral property may be foreclosed by the government to recover them; if the property is destroyed without insurance or otherwise damaged, the lender may never be able to recover his or her initial investment. To avoid such circumstances, it may be necessary for the lender to foreclose-that is, to take possession of the collateral and sell it at auction.

However, foreclosure is a last resort. Most lenders would rather work with borrowers to find a way around any difficulties they may be facing. When a lender legally has the power to foreclose but chooses not to, it is called forbearance. A lender's forbearance will generally include a moratorium on payments (a temporary suspension) and sometimes recasting of the loan terms. Only when all manner of forbearance fails will the lender choose to foreclose on the collateral property.

When the lender does decide to foreclose, he or she sends out a Notice of Default and Intent to Foreclose to the borrower, which is also recorded in the public registry. Notice is given to each of the creditors who has a claim on the property. The foreclosure suit is brought to court, and the court orders a public sale or auction.

Sometimes foreclosure occurs without a lawsuit. This is called *nonjudicial foreclosure*. It is usually done through a power-of-sale clause-a clause in the loan document that allows the lender to foreclose without taking the case to court. In addition, some states allow strict foreclosure, where the borrower is required to remedy the delinquency within a certain period after he or she is given notice, and, if the delinquency is not remedied, the borrower loses his or her redemption rights and the lender may foreclose.

Judicial and power-of-sale foreclosures involve an auction. The lender publishes a notice of sale, and, in many cases, the auction is held right outside the county courthouse. From the proceeds of the auction, the creditors are paid in order of the priority of their liens; therefore, this is typically the order in which they bid, starting with the lender. Creditors, if they bid, typically bid the exact amount of their losses, plus the losses of each creditor in a higher lien position. If the property sells for more than is owed all the creditors, the excess goes to the borrower. If it sells for less than is owed the lender, the lender may choose to seek a deficiency judgment against the borrower to recover the difference.

A deficiency judgment is a legal action whereby the lender attempts to recover any losses not recovered in the auction of the collateral property by suing the borrower. Typically, these judgments are disallowed when the lender has bid at auction or used a strict foreclosure process.

Before the foreclosure process is complete, mortgagors in most states have the right to recover or *redeem* their properties by paying off the full amount owed to the lender, including penalties, legal fees, and accrued interest. There is no right of redemption in Texas.

A borrower facing foreclosure may choose instead to execute a deed in lieu of foreclosure, voluntarily giving the lender title to the property, usually with forgiveness of the debt as consideration. This arrangement is beneficial to the lender because it does not involve the legal complications of a judicial foreclosure, and it is beneficial to the borrower because it does not carry the credit stigma of a full blown foreclosure.

A property in distress is one that is in poor condition either physically or financially. A physically distressed property may be in poor repair: It may be dilapidated, infested with termites, have a mold problem, and so on, or it may have environmental liabilities, such as lead-based paint, asbestos, radon, or other toxic hazards. A financially distressed property may have low returns or even be running at a loss. It may have several years of taxes in arrears and be completely unmarketable.

In some cases, it is best to liquidate a property in distress. If operation of the property would result in a loss-that is, total cost would exceed total revenue-selling the property is advisable. Sometimes, however, improvements can make the difference in selling the property as raw land and selling it as an income producer. At other times, the value of the property may warrant a decision to hold it. As a general rule, an owner should hold the property if the net present value of all its future cash flows exceeds the net present value of the owner's best alternative investment opportunity.

This concludes lesson nine.

Return to your online course player to take the Lesson Quiz.

Lesson 10:
CONVENTIONAL LOANS

This lesson focuses on the following topics:

- Introduction
- Conforming Loan Limits
- Private Mortgage Insurance
- Fannie Mae Underwriting Guidelines
- Freddie Mac Underwriting Guidelines
- Activity: Underwriting
- Case Study: Conventional Loan
- Summary

By the end of this lesson, you should be able to:

- Explain what is meant by a conventional loan, and distinguish between conforming and nonconforming loans
- List the current Fannie Mae and Freddie Mac conforming loan limits
- Explain private mortgage insurance (PMI) and state when it is required, when it is advisable, and when it is cancelable
- Detail Fannie Mae underwriting guidelines for loans
- Detail Freddie Mac underwriting guidelines for loans
- Discuss the function of Fannie Mae's Desktop Underwriter and Freddie Mac's Loan Prospector electronic underwriting programs
- List the requirements for a borrower's financial qualifications in a conforming loan, with 100 percent accuracy

Introduction

A conventional loan is any loan that is neither insured by the government (see the lesson on FHA loans) nor guaranteed by the government (see the lesson on VA loans). This lesson will focus on the conventional fixed-rate mortgage, the most basic type of mortgage available. In the next lesson, we will consider alternatives to the fixed-rate mortgage.

Conventional loans are divided into two categories: conforming loans and nonconforming loans. Conventional conforming loans are loans that conform to the guidelines set by Fannie Mae and Freddie Mac and thus can be sold on the secondary market to Fannie Mae and Freddie Mac. Conventional nonconforming loans are loans that do not follow Fannie Mae and Freddie Mac guidelines and thus will not be purchased by Fannie and Freddie on the secondary market (although other secondary market buyers may choose to purchase them).

A loan that is above the conventional loan limit is known as a *jumbo loan*, and faces a somewhat higher interest rate because larger loans imply more lender risk.

Nonconforming loans use application forms of the lender's choosing. Conforming loans use the Uniform Residential Loan Application (Fannie Mae Form 1003 or Freddie Mac Form 65).

Conforming Loan Limits

Fannie Mae and Freddie Mac together set the loan limit amounts, usually once a year. For 2008, these limits are as follows:

2008 Conforming Loan Limits

Property Type	Loan Limit
Single Family	$417,000
Two-Family	$533,850
Three-Family	$645,300
Four-Family	$801,950

For properties in Alaska, Hawaii, Guam, and the U.S. Virgin Islands, the loan limits are 50 percent higher.

Required Net Yield
Fannie Mae and Freddie Mac also publish required net yield (RNY) figures daily. The RNY is the minimum yield at which the secondary lenders are willing to purchase loans from lenders. These RNYs can be accessed at the following Web addresses.

Fannie Mae RNY:
https://www.efanniemae.com/sf/refmaterials/hrny/index.jsp

Freddie Mac RNY:
http://ww3.freddiemac.com/ds1/sell/sffrny.nsf/frmDisplayRNY?OpenForm

Private Mortgage Insurance

Private mortgage insurance (PMI) is insurance paid to a private company by a borrower so that the lender will be insured for the loan amount in case of borrower default. In many cases it is required for the loan to be underwritten; in other cases, it is simply recommended.

The premiums for the insurance may be paid in several ways: as monthly installments, as an up-front payment at closing, or, as a lump sum financed into the loan amount. By federal law, most monthly private mortgage insurance premiums for loans originated on or after July 29, 1999, are automatically canceled when the borrower builds up 22 percent equity in his or her home (based on the original loan balance), or 20 percent equity if the borrower requests cancellation at that time. If the borrower has financed the premium, she or he may be eligible for a refund. So-called high-risk loans, however, may be required to keep the insurance for 15 years, whether or not the borrower has built up 22 percent equity.

The amount of the PMI premiums varies with the size of the borrower's down payment, the kind of loan (for example, fixed-rate vs. adjustable rate mortgage), and the amount of coverage the insurance provides.

For more information, visit the Mortgage Insurance Companies of America Web sites: http://www.mica.com and http://www.privatemi.com.

Fannie Mae Underwriting Guidelines

Desktop Underwriter

Fannie Mae encourages lenders to use its automated electronic underwriting system, Desktop Underwriter (DU). It is designed to reduce the time involved in underwriting, as well as the cost. According to Fannie Mae, some lenders have reported savings of as much as $1,400 in underwriting costs. The system, which can be accessed over the Internet, is available 24 hours a day, seven days a week, to Fannie Mae lenders who subscribe to it.

The system uses preprogrammed information and formulas to conduct a quantitative risk analysis, based on the information the lender provides and three-bureau, merged-file credit reports. It allows the lender to complete a Web version of the Uniform Residential Loan Application, or to fill out a "Quick 1003" using a smaller set of data for a quick recommendation.

DU does not use FICO credit scores in its analysis. Since the technology that produces these scores is owned by Fair Isaac and Co., Fannie Mae cannot use them in compliance with its stated goal of informing applicants why their applications are accepted or rejected. Nevertheless, Fannie Mae encourages lenders to make use of FICO scores in evaluating an applicant's credit.

DU is designed to reduce the subjective element involved in underwriting loans. However, because it does not use FICO scores or consider extenuating circumstances, lenders who use DU still must consider each loan applicant on a case-by-case basis.

Income

Fannie Mae allows a lender to document a non-self-employed applicant's employment with a Verification of Employment (VOE) form, pay stubs from the most recent pay period, and W-2 forms for the previous two years, or a third-party verification. Any employment gaps of more than 60 days must be documented by the lender.

DU will give particular documentation requirements for self-employed borrowers (that is, those who own more than 25 percent of a business). A two-year history of income from self-employment must be established, with the following exception: If the borrower has a one-year history of self-employment and a prior, documented history of non-self-employment doing the same work, her or his income may be considered.

In general, any borrower should have a two-year employment history with the expectation that this income will continue for at least three years. When there is no evidence that income will expire, it is assumed that it will continue. Secondary income also must have a two-year history.

The lender should adjust nontaxable income by adding to the effective income 25 percent of the nontaxable amount or the sum of federal and state taxes that would otherwise be applied to such income, whichever is greater.

Credit

For lenders underwriting conforming loans, Fannie Mae has the following requirements concerning an applicant's credit:

- All credit reports and credit scores are to be no more than 180 days old for new construction and 120 days old for all other loans.

- In general, a period of four years is necessary for a borrower to re-establish bad credit. This requirement is subject to certain exceptions:
  - If the borrower filed a Chapter 13 bankruptcy (a form of bankruptcy in which the debtor reaffirms that he or she will pay all or part of his or her debts), a two-year history may be sufficient.
  - If the borrower was foreclosed on or filed a Chapter 7, 11, or 12 bankruptcy, under extenuating circumstances a two-year history may be sufficient.

- When the credit report indicates that a borrower previously declared bankruptcy, she or he must have four credit references, current within 24 months, no more than two installment or revolving debts, and no past-due payments since the bankruptcy.

- The lender must request a three-bureau merged-file credit report, containing the reports from Equifax, Experian, and TransUnion.

- Mortgage risk analysis must be conducted either with Fannie Mae's Desktop Underwriter or, in the case of manual underwriting, with Fannie Mae's Comprehensive Risk Assessment.

- Any bad credit that is due to extenuating circumstances must be explained in a letter from the borrower and supported with appropriate documentation.

Debt

For lenders underwriting conforming loans, Fannie Mae has the following guidelines concerning an applicant's debt:

- If the credit report indicates any recent inquiries, the lender must establish that no new lines of credit have been opened since the time of the credit report.

- Debts with fewer than 10 months remaining are not included in the total debt service ratio.

- Insubstantial debts, which have less than a two percent effect on the debt service ratio, are not included in that ratio.

- Revolving accounts (such as credit cards) that are paid in full at closing are not included in the total debt service ratio.

Source of Funds

Gifts and Contributions

- Personal gift funds may be accepted from relatives, domestic partners, and fiancé(e)s.

- Personal gift funds may not be used to make the down payment.

- Nonpersonal gift funds are subject to the following limits:

Property Type	Loan-to-Value	Contribution Limit
Primary/Secondary Home	90% < LTV	3%
Primary/Secondary Home	75% < LTV ≤ 90%	6%
Primary/Secondary Home	LTV ≤ 75%	9%
Investment Property	Any LTV	2%

Prepaids

The lender or seller is allowed to pay any or all of the prepaid closing costs for loans with lower than a 95 percent LTV on single-family, owner-occupied, principal residences with no buydown or borrower cash back. The minimum down payment (5 percent) must, however, be paid from the borrower's own funds.

Other Sources

A lender may consider cash reserves from checking or savings accounts and investment instruments such as stocks and bonds. She or he may not, however, consider non personal gift funds or funds that may only be released upon a certain event, such as the applicant's death or retirement. For example, the current cash value of a life insurance policy may be considered a cash reserve, but the amount the policy will pay upon the applicant's death may not be so considered. The Desktop Underwriter will inform the lender how much cash in reserve any particular applicant will need.

Alimony and child support payments also may be considered, if the applicant chooses to reveal such payments and if he or she is purchasing a single-family primary or secondary residence. The lender must obtain documented proof that the payments have been occurring regularly for six to 12 months and will continue for at least three years. Alimony and child support payments should not account for more than 30 percent of the borrower's effective income.

Second Homes

Fannie Mae will buy mortgages for second homes under certain conditions. Only single-family residences located reasonably near the principal residence and suitable for year-round occupancy can qualify. These properties may not be controlled by a party other than the borrower, and their rental income may not be used to qualify for the loan.

Qualifying Ratios

Lenders use two income ratios to qualify applicants: the housing expense ratio and the total debt service ratio. The housing expense ratio is the ratio of the PITI (Principal + Interest + Taxes + Insurance) payment to the borrower's gross income; and the total debt service ratio is the ratio of the PITI payment plus the borrower's long-term debts to gross income. Fannie Mae and Freddie Mac have come to the belief that there is no correlation between the housing expense ratio and the rate of default. Therefore, they have only one qualifying ratio, the total debt service ratio, which is not to exceed 36 percent.

Freddie Mac Underwriting Guidelines

Freddie Mac also has established underwriting guidelines. Many of these are the same or sufficiently similar to Fannie Mae guidelines; therefore, only the important differences will be listed here.

Loan Prospector

Freddie Mac's Loan Prospector (LP) is its equivalent of Fannie Mae's Desktop Underwriter. Lenders enter the same borrower information, and the system determines whether the loan is an "accept," "A-minus caution" or "manual underwrite loan."

Applicant Requirements

Freddie Mac's mortgage underwriting guidelines differ from Fannie Mae's in the following ways:

- Secondary income does not need a two-year history to qualify, provided that the borrower's principal income has such a history.

- There is no minimum income history requirement for self-employed borrowers.

- Freddie Mac requires that all bankruptcy and foreclosures within the past seven years be considered "significant derogatory information" for the applicant. If there are documented extenuating circumstances, a two-year re-establishment of credit is required. If the bankruptcy or foreclosure was due to financial mismanagement, a four-year re-establishment is required.

- The guidelines also require that revolving debts be included in the total debt service ratio, regardless of the balance remaining.

- Lenders and sellers can pay any and all of the closing costs for a 95 percent or less LTV loan where the borrower pays the minimum down payment and does not receive cash back. Unlike seller-financed prepaids with Fannie Mae, the property may be a one- to four-family primary or secondary residence with buydowns or an investment property with no buydowns.

- Retirement accounts may be counted as cash reserves.

- Borrowers seeking loans for investment properties must have at least six months of PITI payments in reserve.

- Only three months of prior child support/alimony payments are necessary, although there must be evidence the income will continue for three years.

Activity: Underwriting

For each of the following items, identify whether it meets or does not meet Fannie Mae underwriting requirements. Circle the answer you think is correct and then check with the answer key.

1. A borrower requires a loan of $360,000 to purchase a single-family home.

    - Meets requirement
    - Does not meet requirement

2. There isn't a way to determine whether a borrower's income will expire within the next three years, although it is expected to.

    - Meets requirement
    - Does not meet requirement

3. A borrower has two consecutive one-year employment histories with different employers.

    - Meets requirement
    - Does not meet requirement

4. A borrower requires gift funds to make his down payment.

    - Meets requirement
    - Does not meet requirement

5. A borrower has a total debt service ratio of 37 percent.

    - Meets requirement
    - Does not meet requirement

For each of the following items, identify whether it should or should not be included in the total debt service ratio for a conforming loan.

6. A borrower's debt has nine months of payments remaining.

    - Should be included
    - Should not be included

7. A borrower has a recently opened a line of credit.

- Should be included
- Should not be included

8. A borrower has a debt with a 3 percent effect on the total debt service ratio.

- Should be included
- Should not be included

9. A borrower plans to pay a revolving account in full by closing.

- Should be included
- Should not be included

Answer Key:

1. Meets requirement
2. Does not meet requirement
3. Meets requirement
4. Does not meet requirement
5. Does not meet requirement
6. Should not be included
7. Should be included
8. Should be included
9. Should not be included

Case Study: Conventional Loan

Borrower A desires to purchase a $200,000 home in Northeast San Antonio. She has saved up enough to put a 20 percent down payment on the house. She comes to Lender B. Lender B wants to approve Borrower A for a conforming conventional loan so that he can sell the loan on the secondary market to Fannie Mae. The lender uses Fannie Mae's Desktop Underwriter to order a three-bureau, merged-file credit report for Borrower A. Borrower A's FICO score is 689, which qualifies her for a 6.124 percent interest rate. Lender B uses this information to fill out Section I of DUs electronic Uniform Residential Loan Application:

I. Type of Mortgage and Terms of Loan

Mortgage Applied for: ___ VA _X_ Conventional ___ Other ___ FHA ___ FmHA			Agency Case No.	Lender Case No. 0016227
Amount $160,000	Interest Rate 6.124%	No. of Months 360	**Amortization Type** _X_ Fixed Rate ___ GPM	___ Other (explain): ___ ARM (type):

The lender fills out Sections II-IV with the specific information of the property being mortgaged and the borrower's personal information. In Section V, the lender adds information about all of the borrower's income that has a documented two-year history:

V. Monthly Income Information

Gross Monthly Income	Borrower	Co-Borrower	Total
Base Empl. Income	$4,600	$	$4,600
Overtime	150		150
Bonuses	50		50
Commissions			
Dividends/Interest			
Net Rental Income			
Other			
Total	$4,800	$0	$4,800

Given the interest rate for which Borrower A qualifies, Lender B is able to calculate a monthly principal and interest payment of $972.07, using a mortgage calculator (he also could have done this by hand, using the methods we've discussed above). From comparable properties he has sold in the past, the lender estimates the hazard insurance and the taxes that will be due on the property:

V. (Cont'd) Combined Housing Expense Information

Monthly Housing Expense	Present	Proposed
Rent	$	XXXXXXXXXX
First Mortgage P&I		$972.07
Other Financing		0
Hazard Insurance		55.00
Real Estate Taxes		211.00
Mortgage Insurance		0

Homeowner Assn.		0
Other		0
Total	$	$1,238.07

The housing expense ratio for borrower A is thus

Combined Housing Expense ÷ Gross Income = $1,238.07 ÷ $4,800 = <u>25.79%</u>

Although Fannie Mae does not use the housing expense ratio, many lenders do, and it is important to be familiar with the means of calculation of these ratios.

Section VI of the application deals with the borrower's assets and liabilities (debts). Borrower A has two open accounts: a checking account at ABC National Bank and a savings account at A&B Savings & Loan. The borrower has brought the previous two months' statements from these institutions as documentation. The lender records the balances in both accounts and adds them to the cash down payment the borrower holds to determine the total amount of Borrower A's liquid assets.

Borrower A's truck is included as a non liquid asset:

VI. Assets

ASSETS Description	Cash or Market Value
Cash deposit toward purchase held by: A	$40,000
List checking and saving accounts below	
Name and address of Bank, S&L, or Credit Union ABC National Bank 123 Broadway, San Antonio, TX	
Acct. no. 555444554	$1,776
Name and address of Bank, S&L, or Credit Union A&B Savings & Loan 828 Pat Booker Rd, Universal City, TX	
Acct. no. 222666226	$7,489
Stock & Bonds (Company name/number & description)	$0
Life insurance net cash value Face amount: $	$0
Subtotal Liquid Assets	$49,265

Real estate owned (enter market value from schedule of real estate owned)	$0
Vested interest in retirement fund	$0
Net worth of business(es) owned (attach financial statement)	$0
Automobiles owned (make and year) 2001 Truck Co. Four-door	$12,335
Other Assets (itemize)	$0
Total Assets a.	$61,600

Borrower A currently has two liabilities: an installment debt in the form of a truck payment to A & Sons Motors and a revolving debt in the form of a credit card from AAA. The credit card has a balance of $356, which would take 36 months to pay off at the minimum monthly payment of $10.

VI. (Cont'd) Liabilities

LIABILITIES	Monthly Payment & Months Left to Pay	Unpaid Balance
Name and address of Company A & Sons Motors 7171 Rolling Hills Rd, San Antonio, TX Acct. no. 88887777887	$ Payment/Months $367.32/24	$8,287.97
Name and address of Company AAA Credit Card Company 112 Rising Sun Ln., Jacksonville, FL Acct. no. 99993333993	$ Payment/Months $10.00/36	$356.00
Alimony/ Child Support/ Separate Maintenance Payments Owed to:	$0	XXXXXXXX
Job Related Expense (child care, union dues, etc.)	$0	XXXXXXXX
Total Monthly Payments	$377.32	XXXXXXXX
XXXXXXXXXXXXXXXXXXXXXXXXX	**Total Liabilities b.**	$ 8643.97

This allows the lender to calculate two important figures: the borrower's net worth (assets minus liabilities) and her total debt service ratio:

Net Worth (a minus l) = \$61,600 − \$8,643.97 = <u>\$52,956.03</u>

Debt Service Ratio = (Housing Expense + Monthly Liabilities) ÷ Gross Income = (\$1,238.07 + \$377.32) ÷ \$4,800 = <u>33.65%</u>

The details of the transaction are spelled out in Section VII of the Uniform Residential Loan Application. Here, the lender estimates the prepaid items and closing costs, which shall be discussed in a later lesson. The amount of cash the borrower must have available for the transaction is stated on line p.

VII. Details of Transaction

Purchase Price	\$200,000
Alterations, improvements, repairs	0
Land (if acquired separately)	0
Refinance (incl. debts to be paid off)	0
e. Estimated prepaid items	1,200
f. Estimated closing costs	3,700
g. PMI, MIP, Funding Fee	0
h. Discount (if Borrower will pay)	0
i. Total costs (add items a through h)	204,900
j. Subordinate Financing	0
k. Borrower's closing costs paid by Seller	0
l. Other Credits (explain)	0
m. Loan amount (exclude PMI, MIP, Funding Fee financed)	160,000
n. PMI, MIP, Funding Fee financed	0
o. Loan amount (add m and n)	160,000
p. Cash Borrower (subtract j, k, l & o from i)	44,900

The borrower's liquid assets (\$49,265) are well in excess of the cash she must have at closing.

The final three sections of the application are VIII Declarations, IX Acknowledgement and Agreement, and X Information for Government Monitoring Purposes. The lender fills these out and receives an "approve/eligible" result from Desktop Underwriter. Because Borrower A has a good credit score (689), her total debt service ratio is below the maximum set by Fannie Mae and Freddie Mac, and she has enough cash on hand to pay the down payment and the costs of closing the transaction, her mortgage is considered a low risk. Lender B underwrites the loan and promptly sells it to Fannie Mae.

Summary

Conventional loans are loans that are neither insured nor guaranteed by the federal government. They are divided into two types: conforming and nonconforming. Conforming loans are those that adhere to the guidelines established by Fannie Mae and Freddie Mac. Nonconforming loans can still be sold on the secondary market, but Fannie Mae and Freddie Mac will not purchase them.

Conforming loan limits are set about once every year. For 2008, the single-family residence limit is $417,000. Conventional loans that exceed the Fannie Mae/Freddie Mac loan limits are called jumbo loans.

Most conventional loans with less than a 20 percent down payment require private mortgage insurance (PMI). This is usually in the form of a monthly premium that the borrower pays to a third-party insurer to cover the lender in the event of default. Federal law requires that PMI premiums be canceled under certain circumstances, such as when the borrower has at least 22 percent equity in the mortgaged property. The amount of the premiums varies with the amount of the borrower's down payment and the amount of coverage afforded by the insurance.

Both Fannie Mae and Freddie Mac have developed electronic underwriting programs, which are called Desktop Underwriter and Loan Prospector, respectively. These programs are designed to decrease the cost and time involved in underwriting and to increase consistency. They do not, however, replace the underwriter, as they do not take into account FICO scores or extenuating circumstances.

Conforming loans have only one qualifying ratio: a total debt service ratio of 36 percent.

This concludes lesson ten.

Return to your online course player to take the Lesson Quiz.

Lesson 11:
ALTERNATIVE FINANCIAL INSTRUMENTS

This lesson focuses on the following topics:

- Introduction
- Adjustable Rate Mortgage
- 80-10-10 Piggyback Loans
- Graduated Payment Mortgages
- Growth Equity Mortgages
- Balloon Mortgages
- Wraparound Mortgages
- Reverse Annuity Mortgages
- Blanket Mortgages
- Open End Mortgages
- Sale-Leaseback
- Permanent Buydowns
- Temporary Buydowns
- Additional Loan Payment Plans
- Summary

By the end of this lesson, you should be able to:

- Define adjustable rate mortgages (ARMs) and compare these to float-to-fixed rate loans.
- Explain the 80-10-10 piggyback loan, and identify the appeal of this loan to a borrower
- Distinguish between graduated payment mortgage (GPM) and growth equity mortgage (GEM), listing the benefits of each.
- Explain a balloon mortgage, and distinguish between a Fannie Mae balloon mortgage and a Freddie Mac balloon mortgage.
- Identify the characteristics of a wraparound mortgage, and compare this to a purchase-money mortgage
- Explain the concepts of reverse annuity mortgages, blanket mortgages, and open-end mortgages, providing examples of each
- Explain the provisions of construction mortgages and the concept of draws

- Explain why a sale-leaseback is beneficial to the purchasing party
- Distinguish between permanent buydown and temporary buydown, listing the two advantages and two disadvantages of temporary buydowns
- Name additional loan payment plans

Introduction

In the previous lesson, we discussed conventional fixed-rate, fixed-payment, fully amortizing mortgages. This lesson is concerned with other types of mortgages-those with variable interest rates (ARMs), with variable payments (GEMs, GPMs), and with incomplete amortization (balloon mortgages). Many of these loans also may be sold on the secondary market, and some can be federally insured or guaranteed (see the lessons on FHA and VA loans).

Adjustable Rate Mortgages

One type of loan gaining popularity with investors is the adjustable rate mortgage (ARM). This loan starts at an interest rate typically lower than the market rate for conventional loans, and the rate is adjusted at set intervals known as adjustment periods. These adjustments are based upon the market fluctuations of some economic indicator external to both the lender and the borrower, such as Treasury securities, called the index.

Each ARM contains a lookback period, which is the number of days before the adjustment period that the last published rate for the index becomes the index rate for that period. For example, if the lookback period for an ARM is 30 days and the index is one-year T-bills, then the index rate for any particular adjustment period is the last published T-bill rate 30 days before the period.

The lender adds a fixed rate called the margin to the index rate at the lookback date to determine the ARM rate for any particular adjustment period. Margins are often given in terms of basis points; 1,000 basis points equals a rate of 1 percent. Therefore, if the margin is 250 basis points above the index, and the index is 6 percent, then the interest rate is 6.25 percent.

ARMs are good for lenders because they help to avoid the interest rate risk inherent in real estate investment. The risk is this: If a lender lends a borrower money at a fixed rate, and the interest rates subsequently go up, the lender loses money in the form of an opportunity cost. That is, if the lender still had the money, he or she could lend it out at a higher rate and make more profit. The ARM avoids this risk because it allows the lender to adjust the rate according to market conditions.

ARMs can have several benefits to the investor who is willing to take the risk. Since the initial interest rates for ARMs are lower than for conventional loans, if the rates remain constant or decrease, the price of the loan can be less over its term. The loan carries a risk as well: Payments can increase to levels well above conventional rates, and if the rates reach the payment cap, negative amortization-an increase in the principal-can occur.

Conforming Arms
Both Fannie Mae and Freddie Mac offer competitive ARM products. Fannie Mae ARMs have the London Interbank Offered Rate (LIBOR), available from Fannie Mae or the Wall Street Journal, as their index.

Float-To-Fixed Rate Loans
Some lenders are now offering loans that are much like ARMs, called float-to-fixed loans. Like an ARM, float-to-fixed rate loans have initial interest rates determined by a margin and an index. After the initial float rate period (one or two years, typically) the loan converts to a fixed-rate loan. These loans allow borrowers to take advantage of the lower earlier rates (as with ARMs) but avoid the risk of later rate increases. Freddie Mac offers a float-to-fixed-to-float loan with beginning and ending periods of floating rates, with a fixed interest rate in between.

Sometimes float-to-fixed rate loans are known as hybrid ARMs. A variant, the fixed-to-float rate hybrid ARM, will be discussed in more depth in connection with VA loans.

Case Study
A customer wants to buy a house that is listed at its appraised value of $90,000. He makes a salary of $39,000 a year, but he is worried that he will not be able to qualify for the 30-year loan he wants because he is currently paying off his new truck and his daughter's college education. Annual taxes on the property are 2.4 percent of the appraised value; insurance is 0.75 percent; and the homeowner's fee is $30 per month. If the current interest rate is 7.35 percent, can he qualify for a loan?

We can enter his data into a conventional loan qualifying worksheet. His gross monthly income is $39,000 annually, or $3,250 a month. We must determine whether or not his total housing expense is less than 28 percent of $3,250 and his total debt service is less than 36 percent of $3,250.

To determine total housing expense, we calculate the PITI payment. Since the loan to value ratio is 100 percent, which in turn is higher than 80 percent, the customer must purchase private mortgage insurance, which at its cheapest now, we find, is 0.5 percent annually. Since principal, interest, taxes, and insurance are all given in percentages, it is best to calculate the amortization payments on a loan relative to one rate, the sum of all the others.

7.35% interest + 2.4% taxes + 0.75% hazard insurance + 0.5% PMI = 11% total rate

More About: With that 11 percent, rate, we can use an amortization schedule-found at http://www.webmath.com/amort.html-to calculate the monthly payment.

Question1
What is the monthly payment required for an 11%, 30-year loan of $90,000?

Answer
 $857.09. A $90,000 loan takes monthly payments of $857.09 to fully amortize over 30 years.

Question 2
What is the customer's total housing expense?

Answer
Adding the $30-per-month homeowner's association fee to the monthly payment, we get $887.09.

Question 3
What is the borrower's housing-expense-to-income ratio?

Answer
Divide the total housing expense, $887.09 by the $3,250 in monthly income, and we get 27.29%. That is just under the qualifying ratio of 28 percent.

Question 4
Does that qualify the borrower for the loan?

Answer
No. The buyer's housing-expense-to-income ratio is under the qualifying limit. But his total debt service ratio also must be calculated. The customer is currently paying $3,000 a year for his daughter's college education and $220 a month for his vehicle. That's $470 a month. His total debts add up to $470 + $887.09 = $1,357.09 a month. The debt service ratio is calculated by dividing total debts by monthly income. Therefore, $1357.09 ÷ $3,250 = 0.4175, or 41.75%.

Question 5
Does the borrower qualify for the loan?

Answer
No. The borrower does not qualify for a conventional loan. His total debt ratio is 41.75 percent, well over the required 36 percent.

But there are more than just conventional loans available. This customer's daughter graduates in three more years, and his truck has only 12 months' worth of payments remaining. The goal would be to get him a loan with low initial payments and increased later payments. There are a few lenders who are willing to offer an adjustable rate mortgage, but these are worrisome because the rate may fluctuate too high for him to pay. He is well over the minimum required total debt service ratio.

The best ARM available has an initial interest rate of 4.35 percent, 3 percentage points below the going rate for 30-year conventional loans. The total rate on the loan will be 8 percent (4.35% interest + 2.4% taxes + 0.75% hazard + 0.5% PMI). At this rate, according to our schedule, the loan will require monthly payments of $660.39 to fully amortize in 30 years at 8 percent. To this we add our $30 homeowner's fee and the $470 truck and college payment to get the total debt service: $1,160.39. This is only 35.7 percent of his $3,250 gross monthly income and would qualify him for the loan.

But in some cases, qualifying isn't enough. We have to consider the worst-case scenario. The margin on this loan is 0.35 percent, and the rate adjusts annually, capped at a 2 percent per interval. The index is U.S. Treasury Bonds, currently paying 4 percent. If the rate increases by the full 2 percent next year, this customer will have paid off his truck, but the effective rate he'll be paying is 10 percent. This requires payments of $789.81, and a total debt service of $789.81 + $30 homeowner's fee + $250 college payment = $1,069.81, only 32.92 percent.

However, suppose that the interest rate went up yet again in the next two years, say only 1 percent per year. Then the interest rate would be 12 percent and the total debt service payments $1,205.75. This would be 1.1 percent in excess of the minimum ratio requirement, and this customer might be at a high risk of default. And this is at an only 1 percent per year increase: The cap is 2 points per year.

While it's unlikely that this worst-case scenario will come to pass, it's still possible. We as real estate licensees must explain the situation to our customers and make a decision as to whether we are willing to take the risk. Remember, it is our risk, too: The default of one of our clients reflects bad judgment on our part.

80-10-10 Piggyback Loans

An 80-10-10 loan, also known as a piggyback loan, is really two mortgages in one. Instead of giving the borrower one fixed-rate loan at the current market rate, the borrower receives two loans, one larger loan for 80 percent of the sale price at the market rate and a smaller loan for 10 percent of the sale price at a higher interest rate. For example, suppose a borrower wanted to purchase a home for $150,000. The lender might offer an 80-10-10 loan in which the borrower pays 10 percent down and receives two loans: one for $120,000 at 7 percent and the other for $15,000 at 9 percent.

The appeal of the 80-10-10 loan is that it does not require the borrower to pay for private mortgage insurance and that, unlike PMI, the interest on the second loan is tax-deductible. However, the 80-10-10 loan has its disadvantages. PMI is cancelable when the borrower's equity reaches 20 percent, whereas the second loan of an 80-10-10 mortgage must be paid as any other loan. Only the individual borrower and those working in her or his interests can decide the best choice. An 80-10-10 loan may seem attractive, with lower payments than a comparable single loan with PMI and greater tax deductions. But if the borrower intends to build equity fast, the PMI loan might save more money in the long run.

Graduated Payment Mortgage

Graduated payment mortgage (GPM) is a blanket term for a family of loans characterized by low initial payments that increase (or "graduate") at set intervals and by set amounts during the term of the loan. Payments usually increase anywhere between 7.5 percent and 12.5 percent annually until reaching a fixed amount that continues for the rest of the term.

GPMs were originally designed to entice first-time homebuyers into the mortgage market. In theory, a young borrower who expects his or her income to increase in the coming years may purchase a house with a GPM whose graduated payments she or he expects to be able to meet in the future as his or her income increases. In practice, however, GPMs have fallen out of favor with many lenders because the paperwork and underwriting considerations are more difficult, and because they carry a higher rate of default.

Nevertheless, some lenders continue to offer GPM plans to interested and qualified borrowers. GPMs are attractive to some lenders because they typically have market interest rates 0.5 percent to 0.75 percent higher than comparable fixed-rate loans. Borrowers who can't qualify for a fixed-rate loan may qualify for a GPM on the basis of the lower initial rates. GPMs can make sense in rapidly appreciating areas, because the increased payments go along with an increase in the value of the property.

Some GPMs negatively amortize because the initial payments are not enough to cover all the interest due. This interest becomes compounded into the principal, causing even more interest to be due at the next payment period. However, not all GPMs have this feature. Some loans may have initial payments that cover all and only the interest, which in turn graduate to amortizing payments in the course of the loan term.

Growth Equity Mortgage

The growth equity mortgage (GEM, sometimes growing or graduated equity mortgage) is similar to the GPM in that it involves an increasing payment schedule. GEMs do not negatively amortize: All of the payment increases go toward principal-that is, equity-from which the mortgage derives its name. Some GEMs have payment increases that are tied to an index. Unlike ARMs, however, it is the rate of the principal payment's increase that is tied to the index rather than the interest rate, which remains constant.

Example: Suppose a borrower takes out a GEM for $80,000 at an interest rate of 7.25 percent that has annual payment increases for 10 years. The payment increases are determined by the mortgage contract to be 80 percent of the change in the per capita income growth index.

The early payments would look like this:

Year	Index Increase	Payment Increase	Monthly Payment	Principal Balance	Fixed Pmt. Balance
0	n/a	n/a	n/a	$80,000.00	$80,000.00
1	n/a	n/a	545.74	79,225.75	79,225.75
2	6.8%	5.44%	575.43	78,064.46	78,393.44
3	6.6%	5.28%	605.81	76,454.41	77,498.74
4	6.9%	5.52%	639.25	74,326.35	76,536.96
5	7.0%	5.60%	675.05	71,614.41	75,503.10
6	6.4%	5.12%	709.61	68,291.13	74,391.74
7	6.2%	4.96%	744.81	64,304.52	73,197.08
8	5.7%	4.56%	778.77	59,621.36	71,912.87
9	6.0%	4.80%	816.15	54,150.11	70,532.40
10	6.3%	5.04%	857.28	47,788.58	69,048.45

The amortization of a fixed-payment loan at the same rate is given on the right of the chart. You can see that the small annual increases in monthly payments (at most 5.6 percent) cause the GEM to amortize at a much faster rate. When the payments level out at year 10, the GEM will take only nine years and three months to be completely paid off, whereas the fixed-payment loan still has 20 years remaining!

Balloon Mortgage

A balloon mortgage is not fully amortizing. It has a short term, usually five or seven years, but payments based on a longer term, as if it were 30 years, for example. At the end of the loan's term, the often-large remaining balance of the mortgage is due as a lump sum. At this time, the borrower can refinance this amount. Some balloon mortgages have a conversion option that allows the borrower to convert the remaining balance to a 25- or 23-year fixed-rate mortgage, based upon the term of the balloon mortgage. The conversion option usually provides for a rate slightly higher than that of fixed-rate mortgages.

The appeal of a balloon mortgage is that it typically has an interest rate that is 0.25 percent to 0.5 percent less than comparable fixed-rate mortgages. Those who plan to sell their homes after five or seven years are in an excellent position to take advantage of this rate reduction. The lower rate gives borrowers increased purchasing power because their housing expense is lower and they qualify for larger loans.

Fannie Mae Balloon Mortgage
Fannie Mae offers a seven-year balloon mortgage with a conversion option to a 23-year mortgage at the end of the balloon mortgage's term (and thus is sometimes referred to as a 7/23 convertible mortgage). The loan is available for single-family principal residences, second homes, Fannie Mae-approved condominiums and investment properties.

Fannie Mae balloons with LTVs greater than 80 percent and less than or equal to 85 percent must have PMI coverage of at least 12 percent; those with LTVs between 85 percent and 90 percent must have at least 25 percent PMI.

Freddie Mac Balloon Mortgages
Freddie Mac offers both five- and seven-year balloon mortgages (referred to as balloon/resets). Freddie Mac allows for the seven-year (but not the five-year) mortgages to be underwritten for borrowers with "A-minus" credit.

Wraparound Mortgage

Wraparound mortgages are not issued by a lender but rather by the seller. Instead of selling the property and receiving a lump sum of cash at closing, the seller deeds the property to the buyer and "lends" him or her the sale price (or the sale price less the borrower's down payment), although the buyer does not actually receive any money. The buyer then repays the loan as she or he would to a lender; in monthly installments, with interest.

This is called a wraparound mortgage, because usually the seller has a mortgage on the property that he or she keeps, paid off with the monthly payments received from the buyer. For this reason, the seller usually charges a higher interest rate than that of the mortgage he or she holds. Nevertheless, this rate can be lower than the current market rate, making it appealing to buyers. Buyers also receive the advantages of no qualifying process and few closing costs. For example, there is no lender's origination fee, appraisal fee, or credit report fee, but there may be legal fees and homeowner's fees.

In a wraparound mortgage, the seller takes on the risk of buyer default. The wraparound mortgage creates a lien on the property, but it is a lien subordinate to the lien created by the seller's mortgage. Thus, if the seller cannot repay her or his lender because of the new buyer's default, the lender's right to recover damages supersedes the seller's. The profit that the seller stands to receive after he makes his mortgage payments is what the seller gets for assuming this risk.

Sometimes the wraparound loan is held by a third-party lender. This party will lend funds to the buyer and use them to pay back the original mortgage of the seller, while pocketing the difference. Often, it is the lender of the first mortgage who issues the wraparound.

Purchase-Money Mortgage

A purchase-money mortgage, like a wraparound mortgage, involves the buyer receiving funds from the seller in the form of a mortgage loan to purchase the property. In a purchase-money mortgage, however, there is no encumbrance from an original mortgage remaining on the property as the seller already has paid off the mortgage.

Reverse Annuity Mortgage

An important concept in all the mortgages discussed so far is equity. A homeowner increases his or her equity by paying down the principal balance of the loan. In a reverse annuity mortgage (RAM), the borrower takes out a loan against the equity that she or he has built up from making years of mortgage payments. Often, this loan is paid to the homeowner in installments.

However, the repayment of the RAM by the homeowner does not occur on a monthly basis, but rather the full amount of the loan is due when the homeowner dies or moves. The idea behind a RAM is that a homeowner will take out the loan to receive a fixed, monthly, tax-free source of income and that, to repay the loan, he or she will sell the property (that is, her or his equity interest in the property).

RAM loans are popular with senior citizens, who may need the added monthly income. The loans typically have a short amortization period (about 10 years) and should be carefully considered by potential borrowers, as it could mean that the borrower would have to sell his or her home at the end of the amortization period and have nowhere to live.

Blanket Mortgage

Blanket mortgages have more than one collateral property that acts as security for the loan. These mortgages typically are used by land developers and commercial investors, but anyone seeking to consolidate mortgage debts may receive such a loan.

Blanket mortgages create a blanket lien on the collateral properties. This means that in the event of default, the lender may foreclose on all of the properties thus encumbered. This can cause problems for those who buy a lot from a developer, because the house may still be encumbered by the developer's blanket mortgage: If the developer defaults, the lender may foreclose on all of the collateral property, including lots that already have been sold.

For this reason, developers often have a release clause included in the mortgage contract. The release clause states that when specific amounts of repayment are reached, as set forth in the contract, individual parcels of land may be released from the mortgage (that is, they become unencumbered). This gives buyers and their lenders more security.

In addition to the release clause, developers often also will include a recognition clause in the blanket mortgage contract. This clause states that a lender who forecloses the developer's mortgage must recognize the rights of the individual homebuyers who have purchased lots from the developer.

Open-End Mortgage

Open-end mortgages are called "open-end" because they allow the mortgagor to borrow additional funds at a later date on top of the original loan amount. This is useful, for example, to a new homebuyer who wishes to buy, for example, furniture or a washer and dryer after the home purchase. Thus the borrower may receive more money without the necessity of refinancing. To pay off the new debts incurred, the monthly payment or the loan term (sometimes both) will be increased, often with a concurrent change in the interest rate. One important type of open-end mortgage is the construction mortgage.

Construction Mortgage
In a construction mortgage, the lender pays funds to a borrower in installments, called draws, as the construction progresses. The sum total of these draws is typically 75 percent of the value of the property when it is completed. At the end of the building's construction, the entire loan amount plus the interest accrued becomes due. This is usually paid for with a long-term mortgage that the borrower has arranged for in advance.

For example, suppose that a borrower is constructing a single-family home whose value, when complete, will be $88,000. The construction loan amount, therefore, will be 75 percent of this or 0.75 × $88,000 = $66,000. Suppose further that the mortgage contract calls for a series of six draws of $11,000 each over six months at a 10 percent annual interest rate. The loan will look like this:

Month	Draw	Interest	Loan Balance
0	$11,000	$0	$11,000.00
1	$11,000	$91.67	$22,091.67
2	$11,000	$184.10	$33,275.77
3	$11,000	$277.30	$44,553.07
4	$11,000	$371.28	$55,924.35
5	$11,000	$466.04	$67,390.39
6	$0	$561.59	$67,951.98

The borrower will want to have a long-term mortgage loan of $67,951.98 at the end of the sixth month when the construction loan balance becomes due. (Notice that the borrower pays almost $2,000 in interest for one six-month period.)

Sale-Leaseback

In a sale-leaseback, the owner of a parcel of real estate sells it and immediately leases it back. This type of arrangement is mostly used by commercial investors who desire to turn their illiquid real estate into cash without losing the use of the asset. In addition, an investor can claim a tax deduction for rent paid on property she or he uses for business. The selling investor often will reserve the right to repurchase the property at the end of the lease period.

The sale-leaseback is beneficial to the purchasing party because (a) the party receives a steady stream of rental income, more or less guaranteed, and (b) the party profits by reselling the property to its original owner at its new market price. If the sellback price were set at the beginning of the lease, the purchase price would be considered a loan for tax purposes, and the selling party would lose many of the tax benefits of the arrangement.

Permanent Buydown

Permanent buydown mortgages have been discussed under the heading of discount points. A borrower pays a percentage of the loan amount, called a discount, thereby lowering the note interest rate. These discounts are either paid as cash at closing or are financed into the loan amount. Fannie Mae will not purchase financed permanent buydown loans, although Freddie Mac will for certain fixed-rate mortgages.

Temporary Buydown

Temporary buydown loans are an alternative to the adjustable rate mortgage or graduated payment mortgage. They provide the borrower with the temporary help he or she needs without any chance of negative amortization and with a predictable payment structure. The disadvantage is that there is a higher loan fee for this type of loan.

Under a buydown plan, the subsidizing party-the borrower, seller, builder, or other party-establishes a buydown fund, which is collected in cash at closing. The required portion of the payment every payment period is paid from the buydown fund. The borrower then makes payments at the bought-down effective rate, which is lower than at the actual lending rate. When the temporary buydown period is over, the lending rate returns to normal.

The lender is collecting a level payment for the entire term of the loan, and any amortization schedule should be calculated as such. To the lender, this is a level payment fixed rate loan. To the borrower, however, this is a stair step or graduated payment loan.

A typical 3-2-1 temporary buydown would be calculated as follows:

Note Rate	Buydwn %	Eff Rate	Pmt @ Note Rate	Pmt @ Eff Rate	Mo Subs	Ann Subs
10	3	7	877.57	665.30	212.27	2547
10	2	8	877.57	733.76	143.81	1726
10	1	9	877.57	804.62	72.95	875
10	-0-	10	877.57	877.57	-0-	-0-
TOTAL						5148

Here, the effective rate is the difference between the note rate and the buydown percentage, and the monthly subsidy required is the difference between the payment that would be collected at the note rate and the payment actually collected at the effective rate. To establish the above buydown at three graduated steps over three years would take a buydown fund of $5,148, the total amount of subsidy required to be paid out over the years.

Advantages of a Temporary Buydown

1. Low initial payments
2. The borrower is most often qualified on the basis of the lower initial payments

Disadvantages of a Temporary Buydown

1. Buydown plans are typically expensive and require a large payment at closing.

2. A buydown is only temporary, and the borrower will have increased monthly payments that may be difficult to afford.

Freddie Mac buys two types of temporary buydown loans: the 2-1 and the 3-2-1 buydowns. The basic 2-1 plan involves a first-year rate reduction of 2 points, lowered to 1 point the second year, and at the fixed note rate for the following years. However, any buydown plan with a greater than 1-point first-year reduction and a second year increase in the interest rate of no more than 1 point falls under the 2-1 heading. The 3-2-1 plan is similar but lasts for three years with a 1-point increase each year up to the note rate.

Fannie Mae's requirements for temporary buydowns are less stringent than Freddie Mac's. They require only that the buydown period not exceed 36 months and that the total annual increase in the interest rate not exceed 1 percent. They allow for increases in the interest rate that are more frequent than annually.

The reduction in the rate is paid for by money held in an escrow account. This account can be established by the borrower, the seller, the builder, or pretty much any party that desires to do so. The seller, for instance, might desire to fund a buydown so that the buyer can qualify for the loan.

Example: suppose a borrower takes out a $100,000 loan at a 9 percent annual rate for 30 years on a 3-2-1 buydown plan.

The payments would look like this:

Year	Rate	Monthly Payment	Mo. Payment from Escrow	Total Payment
1	6%	$599.56	$205.07	$804.63
2	7%	$665.31	$139.32	$804.63
3	8%	$733.77	$70.86	$804.63
4	9%	$804.63	$0	$804.63
5-30	9%	$804.63	$0	$804.63

The cost of establishing the escrow account is the amount of all of the monthly payments from the account or less if the escrow account is interest-bearing. Some lenders will charge points at closing instead of using payments from escrow; however, this can be much more expensive to the borrower. For example, the amount required to establish the escrow account in the example above is $4,983. If the lender charged 6 points (3 + 2 + 1) instead of establishing this account, the buyer would pay $6,000, more than $1,000 more.

Temporary buydowns work with many types of loans. For example, if a hybrid ARM were to have an initial fixed rate for three years, that rate could be reduced with a 2-1 or 3-2-1 buydown.

Additional Loan Payment Plans

There are additional loan payment plans that a real estate licensee should be aware of in order to offer clients the most comprehensive experience possible.

As with any real estate transaction, the real estate licensee should advise both the buyer and seller to seek legal counsel for guidance.

FHA 203k Property Rehabilitation Program
The FHA 203K Property Rehabilitation Program is a government loan designed to preserve the nation's existing housing stock by facilitating renovation and restoration. It features down payments of as little as 3 percent and can involve loan amounts up to 110 percent of the home's after-improved value.

Equity Participation Mortgage
An equity participation mortgage is a mortgage loan in which the lender has a partial equity interest in the property or receives a portion of the income from the property during ownership (if an income-producing property).

Seller Financing
This occurs when the seller of the real estate provides financing for the sale by taking back a secured note in the form of a mortgage, land contract, or deed of trust. Although risky for the seller, this also allows the seller to make the interest income that the lender would normally make. A real estate sales professional should advise both the buyer and seller to seek legal counsel before agreeing to this type of financing arrangement, because terms can be added that can be detrimental to one party or the other.

Summary

The conventional fixed-rate loan is not the only option available to borrowers in today's competitive marketplace, nor is it the only type of loan that secondary market companies are willing to buy. Most loan variations involve changes in the interest rate, as with an adjustable rate mortgage (ARM), or changes in the monthly principal payments, as with a growth equity mortgage (GEM).

ARMs are loans that have an interest rate that varies (adjusts) with a market index. These indexes can be almost any market rate not controlled by lenders and available to the general public, such as one-year U.S. Treasury Securities (T-bills) or the London Interbank Offered Rate (LIBOR). The ARM interest rate is calculated each adjustment period by adding a margin to the index rate at the lookback period. Margins are often expressed in basis points, with 1,000 basis points equal to a rate of 1 percent.

Borrowers are attracted to ARMs because they have lower initial interest rates than conventional loans; lenders are attracted to them because they eliminate the risk of fluctuating interest rates inherent in most real estate investment. Both Fannie Mae and Freddie Mac offer ARM products, including ARM-backed securities. Some lenders offer loans that have adjustable rates in the first few years and convert to fixed-rate loans. These mortgages are known as float-to-fixed-rate mortgages or hybrid ARMs.

Another potentially money-saving option for borrowers is the 80-10-10 (piggy back) mortgage. These mortgages are intended as substitutes for conventional mortgages that require private mortgage insurance (PMI). An 80-10-10 loan is really two loans: one at 80 percent LTV with a competitive market rate and another "piggybacking" loan at 10 percent LTV with a higher interest rate. The increased interest (profit) from the 10 percent LTV loan, to 80-10-10 lenders, is worth the greater risk of a loan without PMI. Borrowers are attracted to these loans because they have lower monthly payments than conventional loans with PMI; however, since the second mortgage is not cancelable, 80-10-10 loans may be more expensive to a borrower over time.

Lenders have the option of varying the amount of the monthly principal payments. This is usually done in one of two formats: the graduated payment mortgage (GPM) and the growth equity mortgage (GEM). GPMs are intended for borrowers who would not be able to make the payments on a traditional mortgage. Early payments are low and increase in steps ("graduate") in the first few years. Often, these loans negatively amortize in the first years. GPMs have a high rate of default and for this reason usually carry a higher interest rate than their fixed-rate counterparts.

GEMs are similar to GPMs but are intended for borrowers who want to pay off their mortgages more quickly. They are essentially mortgages with scheduled prepayment, with payments that increase either by a fixed amount or by some amount determined by a market index. There is no negative amortization.

Balloon mortgages have five- to seven-year terms with payments based on a 30-year fully amortizing loan. At the end of the balloon term, the entire remaining loan balance is due. Some balloon mortgages carry the option of converting the mortgage to a fixed-rate 25- or 23-year loan at the end of their terms.

A wraparound mortgage is any second encumbrance on the property, subordinate to the first mortgage, which makes the payments for that first mortgage. For example, a seller may issue a wraparound mortgage to a buyer that has a higher interest rate than the seller's mortgage, so the seller uses the borrower's payments to make his or her own mortgage payments and pockets the difference.

In a reverse annuity mortgage (RAM), the borrower receives monthly disbursements of the RAM loan over a term of about 10 years, based upon the equity she or he already has in the collateral property. At the end of the loan term, the full amount of the loan plus interest is due. This amount due is usually paid for by selling the property, so this type of loan is usually used by people who do not plan to occupy the property at the end of the term.

Borrowers can reduce the interest rate on many loans through a permanent or temporary buydown. Permanent buydowns reduce the interest rate throughout the term of the loan and are paid for with discount points; temporary buydowns reduce the interest rate for several years and are paid for with escrow accounts established by an interested party in the loan transaction.

This concludes lesson eleven.

Return to your online course player to take the Lesson Quiz.

Lesson 12:
FHA LOANS

This lesson focuses on the following topics:

- Introduction
- Qualifications
- FHA Programs
- Mortgage Insurance Premium
- FHA Underwriting Requirements
- Advantages and Disadvantages
- Practice
- Case study: FHA loan vs. Conventional loan
- Summary

By the end of this lesson, you should be able to:

- Identify who may qualify for FHA loans, listing the benefits and limits
- Outline the qualification process, listing the six CAIVRS applicant categories
- Demonstrate an understanding of the most important FHA programs, especially Section 203(b)
- Explain the mortgage insurance premium (MIP) and list the conditions borrowers must meet to be eligible for a refund on their mortgage insurance
- Explain FHA underwriting requirements, such as down-payment and closing-cost requirements, comparing the advantages and disadvantages of FHA loans
- Complete the FHA qualifying worksheet
- Distinguish between the FHA's mortgage insurance premium (MIP) and PMI, identifying each in a case study

Introduction

The Federal Housing Administration (FHA) is a part of HUD that is charged with increasing homeownership and contributing to building healthy neighborhoods and communities. As part of this mission, the FHA insures private loans made to consumers. Anyone who is a legal resident of the United States may qualify for an FHA loan. Borrowers pay a mortgage insurance premium in exchange for the FHA's insurance and may then take out loans with higher LTVs, lower down payments and longer terms. This is attractive both to first-time homebuyers, who may not have the cash reserves for a down payment, and to lenders, who view the insured loans as less risky.

FHA loans also have several other benefits. For example, FHA-insured loans are not allowed to carry a prepayment penalty (that is, a lender's charge for lost interest on loans that are paid off earlier than expected). In addition, it is easier to qualify for FHA loans in general than for an uninsured mortgage loan. Moreover, FHA programs don't just insure conventional, fixed-rate loans. There are many FHA programs, each involved with insuring a different type of loan.

As of May 2008, limits for FHA insured loans in Texas were as follows:

Type of Property	Basic Limits	High-Cost Area Ceiling
Single-family	$271,050	$332,500
Two-family	$347,000	$425,650
Three-family	$419,000	$514,500
Four-family	$521,250	$639,400

The high-cost area limits vary widely from county to county but are subject to a ceiling that is a percentage of Freddie Mac loan limits. The FHA distinguishes between high-cost and non-high-cost areas because the costs of construction in certain areas would be prohibitive under the lower non-high-cost limits. However, the FHA does not simply want to set all of the limits high and risk insuring large loans in areas where they are not needed.

More About: To determine the FHA loan limits for another state, or an area within a state, use the HUD Web site's FHA mortgage limits finder at https://entp.hud.gov/idapp/html/hicostlook.cfm.

Section 214 of the National Housing Act provides that mortgage limits for Alaska, Guam, Hawaii, and the Virgin Islands may be adjusted up to 150 percent of the new ceilings. The current ceilings in Hawaii are, for example:

One-family	Two-family	Three-family	Four-family
$793,750	$1,016,150	$1,228,300	$1,526,458

Qualifications

As stated previously, the only absolute qualification for an FHA loan is that the borrower be a U.S. citizen or hold a green card. However, HUD keeps a limited denial of participation (LDP) list. This list contains all the borrowers who are suspended, disqualified, or, in some other way, excluded from the FHA programs. A borrower can end up on the list for many reasons, including default on an FHA loan within the past three years or intentional fraud. In addition to this list, lenders are required to check the Government Services Administration's Pro/Non-Pro list (also known as the GSA list).

Lenders can be approved by the FHA to underwrite FHA loans "in house," that is, without being required to submit FHA loan applications to the FHA regional office for approval. These lenders must fill out a HUD 71101 application and pay a one-time, nonrefundable application fee of $1,000. FHA-approved lenders typically save borrowers 10 to 14 days in processing time.

FHA-approved lenders can check a borrower's credit status on the credit alert interactive voice response system (CAIVRS). CAIVRS identifies six applicants, as those with:

- No cases
- A claim (that is, a lender's claim on FHA insurance money)
- A default
- A foreclosure
- A Department of Justice judgment
- Multiple cases

Having a case listed on the CAIVRS, however, is not immediate cause for denial. If it can be shown that a claim or default is not the applicant's fault, as through the person who assumed the loan, a divorced spouse or bankruptcy outside of the applicant's control, consideration may still be given to the application. In order for the lender to make an exception and underwrite the loan, he or she must receive specific permission from the FHA.

Assumption

FHA loans are assumable, but only by others who are creditworthy and qualify for FHA loans. When the loan of one individual or entity is assumed by another, the original borrowing party is released from liability for the repayment of the loan.

FHA Programs

Because the FHA's mission is to increase homeownership and to build healthy communities, it has many programs, all dedicated to this general goal. Some highlights include the following:

Title I
These loans are used for making home improvements up to $25,000. No down payment is required (that is, the LTV may be 100 percent) and the term of the loan may be either 10 or 15 years. 10-year loans have an origination fee of 0.5 percent, and 15-year loans have an origination fee of 1 percent. All improvement loans in excess of $7,500 require a $50 property inspection at six months.

Title XI (Section 202)
Section 202 is a program designed to help housing and services designed for the elderly by advancing interest-free federal capital. If the housing constructed remains available to low-income elderly families for at least 40 years, the advanced capital need not be repaid. The amount of capital advanced is dependent upon the number of units, the number of bedrooms in each unit, and whether the structure has elevators.

More About: For more information, visit the HUD Web site.

Section 203(b)
This is the FHA's main program and the subject of most of this lesson. It insures fixed-interest rate loans for owner-occupied, one- to four-family properties. Terms are available for 10, 15, 25, and 30 years.

Section 203(k)
Non-investors who need a loan in excess of $5,000 to rehabilitate or repair their one- to four-family residences can use a 203(k) loan. The purchaser puts 3 percent down and pays only taxes and insurance for the first six months. If purchasing a property that requires rehabilitation, the borrower can receive one fixed- or adjustable-rate loan that includes the purchase price and the cost of rehabilitation. The funds of the loan are paid into an escrow account from which they are disbursed by the lender upon completion of the rehabilitations.

Section 203(v): Veterans eligible for a VA loan (see next lesson) also may receive an FHA-insured loan under this section to avoid using up their VA entitlement. This loan can be useful for veterans who have already used their VA entitlement or who plan on using it for a different loan.

Section 221(d) (2)
Originally designed for low-income housing, this program was discontinued, effective April 19, 2001.

Section 221(d) (3)
Nonprofit sponsors looking to construct, purchase, or rehabilitate multifamily housing for moderate-income families can insure up to 100 percent of the loan amount under this program. There is no maximum loan amount, and loan terms can be up to 40 years.

Section 221(d) (4)
This is like Section 221(d)(3) but designed for for-profit sponsors. This program will insure only 90 percent of the loan amount.

Section 223(e)
This program insures loans in older, declining urban areas where traditional mortgage finance may be difficult to obtain. Properties must be approved by HUD directly to receive an insured loan under this section. Loan amounts are limited to $18,000 in non-high-cost areas and $21,000 in high-cost areas.

Section 223(f)
Borrowers can get an FHA loan for the purchase, rehabilitation, or refinancing of existing multifamily housing (such as an apartment complex) under this section. Only an individual or a legal entity designed to hold just one asset may receive one of these loans, and only if the property is at least three years old and has no more than 20 percent of its space devoted to commercial services (such as a restaurant on the ground floor).

Section 234(c)
This program insures loans for the purchase of condominium units. It is available only for condominium projects that have been approved by HUD and have at least 51 percent of their units occupied by their owners.

Section 245(a)
Borrowers seeking to purchase a single-family dwelling with an FHA-insured, graduated payment mortgage (see previous lesson) may do so under this section. Graduated payment mortgages of this type are subject to negative amortization because the initial payments are not sufficient to cover the interest due. These loans are attractive to young, first-time borrowers who expect their income to increase and stabilize. The FHA offers five GPM plans, differentiated by the amount of annual increase in payments:

GPM Plan	Annual Increase	Increases For
Plan 1	2.5%	First 5 years
Plan 2	5.0%	First 5 years
Plan 3	7.5%	First 5 years
Plan 4	2.0%	First 10 years
Plan 5	3.0%	First 10 years

Section 251

The FHA also has a program for adjustable rate mortgages with one-year adjustment periods and 30-year terms. The interest rate, which is tied to one-year Treasury bills (T-bills), has a 1 percent annual cap and a 5 percent cap over the life of the loan. FHA-insured ARMs cannot negatively amortize, and they may be bought down.

An FHA ARM has much of the same appeal over a conventional ARM that a fixed-rate FHA loan has over a conventional fixed-rate loan. That is, FHA ARMs have lower down payment requirements, and lenders consider them safer investments. In addition, ARM borrowers can switch over to a fixed-rate loan without refinancing.

Mortgage Insurance Premium

The mortgage insurance premium (MIP) is the FHA's equivalent of private mortgage insurance. Any borrower with less than a 20 percent down payment must purchase the insurance. The borrower pays 1.5 percent of the loan amount upfront at closing and an annual premium depending upon the loan term: 0.5 percent for 30-year loans and 0.25 percent for 15-year loans. The premiums go into an account held by the FHA to repay lost amounts on insured loans in which the borrower defaulted.

The annual premiums can be terminated under certain circumstances. If the borrower prepays the entire balance of the mortgage, the MIP is automatically terminated upon notification to the FHA. Also, if both the lender and the borrower send a written request on a special FHA form to the FHA asking for cancellation of the insurance, and all payments due to the FHA are made, the MIP can be terminated.

The FHA's MIP is not affected by the federal laws that require private mortgage insurance (PMI) to be terminated when the principal balance is reduced by a certain amount, or when a certain point in the loan term has been reached. Thus, some borrowers who receive an FHA-insured loan may be saddled with the MIP for the entire term of the loan.

Certain borrowers may be eligible for a refund on their mortgage insurance. The borrowers must meet all of the following requirements:

- He or she must have acquired the loan after September 1, 1983.
- She or he must have paid an upfront premium at closing.
- He or she must not have defaulted on the loan.
- If the loan was originated before January 1, 2001, it must be terminated before the seventh year.

- If the loan was originated on or after January 1, 2001, it must be terminated before the fifth year.

Refunds are determined by the FHA commissioner and are based on the number of months for which the loan has been insured.

FHA Underwriting Requirements

Minimum Investment

In addition to maximum loan limits and the down payment requirements, the FHA has established certain criteria of minimum investment for all insured loans.

- Borrowers must have a minimum 3 percent cash investment in the property.

- That investment cannot consist of discount points (money paid to buy down the rate of a loan up-front) or prepaid expenses (items paid in advance at closing).

- The difference of the 2.25 percent down payment requirement and the 3 percent investment may consist of some portion of the buyer's allowable closing costs.

- The seller can pay the balance of buyer's closing costs, all prepaid and discount/origination points up to a maximum contribution of 6 percent (3 percent if the loan amount is 90 percent or above).

- No origination fee (usually 1 percent of the loan amount, collected up front to initiate the loan) is required as part of the closing costs.

- Existing credit policies remain intact for those transactions not previously eligible for high LTV (loan-to-value ratio) financing.

Down Payments

Recall that the FHA requires that borrowers make a 3 percent cash investment in the property they are attempting to acquire. Not all of this investment must be in the form of a down payment. Home buyers must put down 1.25 percent of the value of a property if it is equal to or less than $50,000, and 2.25 percent if it is greater than $50,000. The remainder of the cash investment may come from closing costs.

Example 1: If sale price is **$50,000**, then the down payment will be:
$$50,000 \times 0.0125 = \textbf{\$625}$$

Example 2: If sale price is **$115,200**, then the down payment will be:

$$115{,}200 \times 0.0225 = \textbf{\$2,592}$$

For example, suppose a buyer wants to purchase a home with an FHA loan. The sale price is equal to the FHA appraised value of the home, $40,000. Because this value is less than $50,000, the buyer must put down $40,000 × 1.25% = $500. However, this is not enough to meet the 3 percent cash investment requirement. Three percent of $40,000 is $1,200, so the buyer still must pay $700. Since FHA allowable closing costs are $1,146, the buyer may put all $700 toward closing costs. Any costs not covered by the buyer in the 3 percent investment may be paid by the seller. If the 3 percent requirement exceeds the minimum down payment requirement plus the allowable closing costs, the rest must be added to the down payment.

FHA Appraisal

A loan cannot be taken out to buy a property until that property has been inspected by an appraiser approved by the FHA. Appraisal fees are usually about $375 for a house that is about 2,000 square feet.

The FHA has no requirement for the property to sell at or below the appraised value. The sale price can be any price agreed upon by the buyer and seller. However, maximum insurable loan amounts are computed on the FHA appraised value of the property or sale price, whichever is less, and the difference between actual sale price and maximum loan amount must be paid in cash by the borrower as a down payment at closing or the borrower can choose not to buy the home.

The cost of an FHA appraisal is usually a little higher than a conventional appraisal, since the appraiser must be FHA-approved and is also given a checklist of items to inspect for the lender. FHA appraisals are not regular property appraisals, which the purchaser should still have conducted. FHA accepts VA appraisals with some restrictions, provided the appraisal is less than 90 days old.

The FHA requires that a builder's plans meet both state and local building codes in addition to 17 provisions not found in such codes. The property also must be adjacent to a publicly maintained street.

Allowable Closing Costs

The FHA has outlined specific rules regarding the closing costs that may and may not be allocated to the purchaser. Overages must be waived or paid by the seller. For instance, the FHA limits loan origination fees to 1 percent. If a lender charges a 2 percent fee, he must either waive the additional 1 percent or charge it to the seller.

Costs Allowable to the Purchaser

HUD allows the following costs to be charged to the purchaser (although they may also be paid by the seller):

For all loans:

- Appraisal fee
- Credit report
- Compliance inspection fee for FHA appraisal (limited to $75)
- Energy efficient mortgage (EEM) report fee
- Escrow fee (limited to 50 percent of the total amount, and no more than the seller pays)
- Home inspection fee up to $200
- Notary fee
- Origination fee (limited to 1 percent of the loan amount)
- Title insurance

For refinancing:

- Beneficiary statement
- Courier fee
- Reconveyance fee
- Wire transfer fee

The seller may pay for those closing costs that exceed the purchaser's required minimum investment, along with discount points, prepaid items, and the origination fee, up to a maximum of 6 percent of the loan amount. If the seller chooses not to pay these overages at closing, as long as they are under the allowable closing cost limit prescribed by the FHA, they may be financed into the loan amount.

For example, suppose a borrower wants to purchase a $55,000 property that has closing costs totaling $1,000. The borrower must put down 2.25 percent of the purchase price, or $1,237.50. To meet her 3 percent minimum investment requirement, the borrower need pay only $412.50 of the closing costs. Thus, the remaining costs ($1,000 − $412.50 = $587.50) may be financed into the loan.

The loan amount will then be:

Purchase Price − Down Payment + Financed Closing Costs

= \$55,000 − \$1,237.50 + 587.50
= \$54,350

Non-Allowable Costs

Non-allowable closing costs are those that may not be charged to the purchaser but may be charged, for example, to the seller, or be paid with gift funds. They include the following:

- Buydowns

- Document preparation fee

- Flood certification fee

- Processing fee

- Tax service fee

- Underwriting fee

Qualifying Ratios

The current qualifying ratios for FHA-insured loans are a 29 percent housing expense ratio and a 41 percent total debt service ratio.

Direct Endorsement

Some lenders have the authority to approve FHA loans in-house without submitting the file to the FHA regional office for prior approval. This will save 10 to 14 days in processing time.

Note: Check with each lender on this before filling out final purchase contracts so that sufficient days are negotiated in it to close the transaction without being in default.

Additional Facts About FHA Loans

- An individual may hold more than one FHA loan. If the buyer has sold a home on which the FHA loan was assumed within the past year, that loan must be current. If the loan was assumed, it must be current and the buyer must be an owner-occupant OR the loan must be reduced to 75 percent of the maximum loan available to the owner-occupant under 203b, according to a new appraisal.

- Non-realty items should be specified on a separate document, not the contract. If they are put on the contract, the FHA will assign a value to each item and reduce the appraised value of the property accordingly. (If a Non-Realty Items Addendum is part of the contract, do NOT submit it with the loan application. This reduces any confusion by the lender, and the addendum is a legally binding document on its own.)

- Qualifying assumption of FHA loans (nonqualifying before 1986) allow for a release of liability of seller if the buyer assuming the loan is pre-approved by the lender and the transaction has been consummated to the then-applicable FHA standards.

- Escrow of taxes and insurance is required by the FHA.

- Discount points may be charged, payable by either the buyer or seller.

- The FHA requires a larger down payment than a VA loan, which requires none.

- Anyone of legal age and otherwise legally capable of owning property, may obtain an FHA loan. The borrower does not need to be a citizen of the United States (a green card is sufficient).

- Gifts do not have to come from an immediate family member, although no direct business relationship with the borrower can exist.

Advantages and Disadvantages

Advantages of FHA Loans
FHA loans have several advantages over conventional loans. They typically have a lower down payment, and there is never a prepayment penalty charged for making loan payments earlier than they are due. FHA loans can be assumed by other borrowers; however, since 1986, the assumptor has had to go through the same underwriting process-verification of debts and income, etc.-as the original borrower to prove his or her creditworthiness. Sellers can be held liable for an FHA loan if the person to whom they have sold the house assumes the loan without a test of creditworthiness. Another important advantage of FHA loans is that mortgages can be made on a graduated payment schedule, with low monthly payments that increase over time.

Disadvantages of FHA Loans
FHA loans also have several disadvantages when compared with conventional loans. First, processing an FHA loan takes between 15 and 30 days longer than processing a conventional loan. Second, there is a maximum loan amount on FHA loans, and this can be limiting. For example, in 2008, the maximum loan amount in most areas of Texas for a single family home is $271,050. Third, the mortgage insurance premiums must either be paid up-front at closing or be financed. Finally, the FHA loan program does not insure loans to investors, only to homeowners.

Practice

What follows is a breakdown of an FHA loan applicant's monthly income and expenditures and the loan for which he is applying. Determine her or his housing expense to income and total debt service ratios. Assuming that the applicant intends to pay the minimum allowable down payment and borrow the up-front MIP charge, does he or she qualify for the loan?

More About: To determine principal and interest payments, it is best to use a mortgage loan calculator like the one found at
http://www.webmath.com/amort.html

As an example, let's calculate a mortgage loan of $1,000 at 10 percent interest over 15 years.

Example: Using the calculator at the above link, we find that the monthly payment will be $10.75 and are also provided a chart that shows the monthly breakdown of principal vs. interest payments. (http://www.webmath.com/cgi-bin/amort.cgi?amount=1000&years=15&period=12&rate=10&extra=0)

So let's see if the applicant qualifies for the FHA loan using the following information:

Sale price	$82,000
Interest Rate	10%
Terms	15-year loan
Gross Monthly Income	$3,850 combined
Long Term Debts	$75
Child Care	$150
Taxes	$155
Insurance	$30

FHA Qualifying Worksheet
The total loan amount is calculated by subtracting the down payment from the sale price. Since the sale price is in excess of $50,000, the down payment must be at least 2.25 percent of the sale price.

The qualifying loan amount is calculated by adding the MIP to the loan amount. (Remember, with a $100,000 FHA-insured 15-year loan, the borrower would pay a $1,500 MIP at closing ($100,000 × 0.015 = $1,500), plus $20.83 per month ($100,000 × 0.0025 = $250/12 = $20.83). Bearing this in mind, and using the above information, fill in the blanks on the next page.

Sale price $_____ – Down Payment $_____ = Loan Amount $_____

Loan Amount $_____ + MIP (1.5%) $_____ =
Loan Amount for Qualifying $_____

Using what we know (remembering the mortgage calculator at http://www.webmath.com/amort.html and that the annual MIP renewal premium is 0.25 percent for 15 years or less with 10 percent or less down), fill in the following information in the spaces provided. Solution is provided in the end.

Gross Monthly Income = $_____ (A)

Monthly Housing Expenses:	
Principal and Interest (PI)	$_____
Taxes (T)	+_____
Hazard Insurance (I)	+_____
Monthly MIP	+_____
Total Housing Expenses	$_____ (B)

Housing Expense to Income Ratio:

B / A = _____% (should not exceed 29%)

Total Housing Expenses	$_____ (B)
Child Care	+_____
Long Term Debts	+_____
Total Living Expense	$_____ (C)

Total Debt Service Ratio:

C / A = _____% (should not exceed 41%)

Solution
The sale price of the property in question is in excess of $50,000. Therefore, the down payment must be at least 2.25 percent of its amount:
$82,000 × 2.25% = $1,845

The loan amount can be calculated by subtracting the down payment from the sale price:
$82,000 - $1,845 = $80,155

Now, the upfront mortgage premium can be calculated by multiplying the required percentage of down payment, 1.5 percent, by the loan amount.
1.5% × $80,155 = $1,202.33 Mortgage Premium

The total loan amount for qualifying will then be:
$$\$80,155 + \$1,202.33 = \$81,357.33$$

Using a mortgage calculator, monthly principal and interest payments will be:
$874.27 / month

To fill out the required table, we just recopy the tax and insurance figures from the applicant's expense chart. The monthly MIP charge at 0.25 percent per year is ($81,357.33 × 0.0025) / 12 months = $16.95 / month. The total housing expense then is the sum of all dollar amounts in the right column:

Monthly Housing Expenses:	
Principle and Interest (PI)	**$874.27**
Taxes (T)	**+155.00**
Hazard Insurance (I)	**+30.00**
Monthly MIP	**+16.95**
Total Housing Expenses	**$1,076.22** (B)

Remembering that gross monthly income is $3,850 (A), we find the housing expense to income ratio by dividing (B) by (A).

Therefore, the housing expense to income ratio equals $1,076.22 / $3,850 = 0.2795, or **27.95 percent.**

To determine the total debt service (total living expense) we add long term debts and child care to the total housing expense:

Total Housing Expenses	**$1,076.22** (B)
Child Care	**+ 150.00**
Long Term Debts	**+ 75.00**
Total Living Expense	**$1,301.22** (C)

The total debt service ratio is calculated by dividing the total living expense (C) by gross monthly income (A): $1,308.12 / $3,850 = 0.3379, or **33.79 percent.**

Recalling that the total housing expense to income ration should not exceed 29 percent and that the total debt service ratio should not exceed 41 percent, our numbers of 27.95 percent and 33.79 percent indicate that this borrower would be eligible for an FHA loan.

Case Study: FHA Loan vs. Conventional Loan

Borrower A is interested in purchasing a house. She is considering the advantages of an FHA-insured loan over a conventional mortgage. The advantages are many: first is the down payment requirement. The lender from whom Borrower A is receiving the loan requires a down payment of 5 percent for conventional mortgages. For FHA loans, however, the down payment requirement is only 2.25 percent.

The borrower would prefer to put down only 2.5 percent, which she can do only with the FHA loan. This is a big difference: The purchase price of the home is $65,625, so a 2.5 percent down payment is $1,641, and a 5 percent down payment is $3,281. The loan amounts for each type of loan would be

FHA: $65,626 − $1,641 = $63,984

Conventional Loan: $65,625 − $3,281 = $62,344

In addition to the varying loan amounts, the two types of loans have different fees. There are many fees, such as discounts and underwriting fees, which are disallowed by the FHA. A detailed comparison of charges is given below:

Fee Comparison

Type of Fee	FHA	Conventional
Appraisal Fee	$375	$375
Closing Fee	$125	$125
Credit Report Fee	$45	$45
Discount (1 point)	$0	$623
Document Preparation Fee	$0	$300
Flood Certification Fee	$0	$30
Home Inspection Fee	$100	$100
Legal Fees	$200	$285
Mortgage Insurance (upfront premium—1.5%)	$960	$935
Origination Fee (1%)	$640	$623
Processing Fee	$0	$270
Survey Fee	$420	$420
Tax Service Fee	$0	$150
Underwriting Fee	$0	$200
Total	**$2,865**	**$4,481**

A significant difference between the types of financing can be seen in the cash at closing:

FHA: $1,641 Down Payment + $2,865 Closing Costs = $4,506

Conventional: $3,281 Down Payment + $4,481 Closing Costs = $7,762

In some ways the higher down payment of the conventional loan works to Borrower A's advantage by lowering the principal balance and thus the origination fees and charges for mortgage insurance. Another advantage of the conventional loan is that the monthly private mortgage insurance premium is cancelable when her equity reaches 20 percent. This will happen when the borrower has $0.20 \times \$65,625 = \$13,125$ invested in the house. When the principal balance of the loan reaches $13,125 minus Borrower A's down payment of $3,281 (which is $9,844), she can cancel the PMI.

The market interest rate is 7 percent. With a 30-year amortization term, the loan will reach $9,900.30 in the 130th month. The total paid for mortgage insurance at that point will be $3,116.82. On the other hand, if Borrower A secures an FHA-insured loan, the monthly MIP will continue throughout the term of the loan, totaling $6,200.65. In addition to the mortgage insurance savings, the borrower would save $2,287.60 in interest by putting down the larger amount required by the conventional loan (of course, nothing prohibits the borrower from putting 5 percent down on an FHA loan).

In the end, the borrower must decide between saving a greater amount in cash at closing with the FHA loan or saving more over the loan's term in interest and insurance payments. It is important for borrowers to consider the chance of rising income in the future. Future dollars, due to inflation, are worth less than present dollars, and often savings are only nominal. Since Borrower A wishes to save money now and make a lower down payment, she chooses to go with the FHA loan.

Summary

The Federal Housing Administration (FHA), a part of the Department of Housing and Urban Development (HUD), is designed to increase homeownership and contribute to building healthy neighborhoods and communities. As part of this mission, it insures home loans to qualified U.S. citizens and naturalized residents. Lenders view FHA loans as less risky, which allows them to have higher LTVs, lower down payments, and longer terms. The FHA requires that all loans it insures have no prepayment penalties.

The most popular FHA program is Section 203(b). The drawback to this program is the relatively low loan limits it sets. For example, the 2008 limit set on a 203(b) loan for a single-family residence in most areas of Texas is $271,050.

Borrowers must pay the FHA for the insurance it provides. This is in the form of a mortgage insurance premium (MIP), the FHA analog of private mortgage insurance. MIP is required on all FHA-insured loans with less than a 20 percent down payment. A borrower pays 1.5 percent of the loan amount upfront at closing and then an annual premium of 0.5 percent for mortgages with a 30-year term or 0.25 percent for mortgages with a 15-year term. If the loan amount is paid in full within a certain time after its origination, borrowers may sometimes receive a refund for their MIP.

FHA down payment requirements are usually lower than those for conventional loans. Borrowers must have a total 3 percent cash investment in the property, which can be the sum of the down payment and closing costs. For loans of equal to or less than $50,000, the down payment must be at least 1.25 percent of the sale price; for those in excess of $50,000, the down payment must be at least 2.25 percent.

The origination fee paid by the borrower may not exceed 1 percent, although excess may be paid by the seller or waived by the lender. Seller contributions are limited to 6 percent of the loan amount.

The FHA uses two qualifying ratios: a 29 percent housing expense ratio and a 41 percent total debt service ratio.

This concludes lesson twelve.

Return to your online course player to take the Lesson Quiz.

Lesson 13:
VA LOANS

This lesson focuses on the following topics:

- Department of Veterans Affairs
- Underwriting Requirements
- Entitlement
- Eligibility
- Documentation
- Activity: Fill In the Blanks
- Case Study: VA Loan
- Practice
- Summary

By the end of this lesson, you should be able to:

- Explain the purpose and benefits of a VA loan, outlining what a VA loan can be used for
- List the types of loans available to qualified borrowers, and explain each
- Explain the underwriting requirements, and define the role of a VA appraiser
- State the current amount of a veteran's maximum entitlement and calculate remaining entitlement
- Explain the relationship between remaining entitlement and restored entitlement
- State who is eligible for the VA program and describe the documents required to prove one's eligibility
- Identify the necessary documentation for obtaining a VA loan
- Determine whether a veteran meets the VA debt service ratio requirement to receive a guaranteed loan in a practice activity

Department of Veterans Affairs

The Department of Veterans Affairs (VA) is authorized by Congress to guarantee certain loans made by institutional lenders to eligible veterans and reservists. The guarantee on a loan is a maximum amount that the VA will pay to the lender in the event that the holder of a loan defaults. For example, if a borrower's guarantee is $60,000 and he or she defaults, causing the lender to lose $50,000, the VA will reimburse the lender for $50,000. If that same lender were to have lost $70,000, she or he would be able to receive only the amount of the guarantee, or $60,000. All money that the VA pays to reimburse lenders becomes an amount owed to the VA by the veteran borrower of the loan.

VA loans can be beneficial to veteran borrowers. They typically require no down payments and have limits on the amount of closing costs that can be charged to the borrower. There are, however, certain drawbacks to the loans. First, the VA requires veterans to pay a funding fee, which can go as high as 3.3 percent for certain loans. However, this fee is usually offset by the positive aspects of the VA program. Nevertheless, the VA program has the added drawback that only fixed and adjustable rate mortgage loans are available (graduated payment mortgages, for example, will not be guaranteed by the VA). Most VA loans have terms of 30 years. The term is limited to 30 years and 32 days or the remaining economic life of the property as determined by the VA appraisal, whichever is less.

What Can A VA Loan Be Used For?

The use of VA loans is limited by the law. The veteran may use the loan only for the following purposes:

- The purchase or construction of a house intended to be owned and occupied by the veteran

- The refinancing of an extant VA loan to take advantage of lower interest rates

- The refinancing of another mortgage loan on a property owned and occupied by the veteran

- The repair, alteration, or improvement of a property owned and occupied by the veteran

- The simultaneous purchase and improvement of a property intended to be owned and occupied by the veteran

- The purchase of a one-family condominium unit in a complex approved by the VA

- The purchase of a farm residence

- The addition of energy efficient improvements alone or on top of any of the aforementioned purposes

Other purposes are not allowed. These include the purchase of a home for investment or business purposes, of raw land without a simultaneous improvement loan, or of more than one separate residential unit.

Loan Types

In addition to the traditional fixed-rate loan, the VA guarantees two refinancing loans and one type of adjustable rate mortgage: cash-out refinancing and interest rate reduction refinancing loans and hybrid ARMs.

Cash-Out Refinancing

Cash-out refinancing involves a borrower refinancing his or her existing loan and increasing the principal balance in such a way that her or his home equity is reduced. The basic idea is that the borrower is re-borrowing the money that has been repaid.

The VA's limits on the amount of the refinancing are very specific: If the property undergoing the refinancing was purchased less than one year ago, the balance of the new loan may include only the closing (i.e., refinancing) costs and the lesser of either 90 percent of the sale price or the current appraised value of the property (80 percent of the appraised value in Texas).

For example, suppose a borrower takes out a $95,000 VA-guaranteed loan to purchase a $110,000 home. After seven months, she decides to get a cash-out refinancing loan: Her current principal balance is $94,544.75. The current appraisal value of the home is $108,000. Closing costs for the loan will run about $900 total. The maximum principal balance for the refinanced loan will be the lesser of:

(0.9 × Sale Price) + Closing Costs = (0.9 × $110,000) + $900 = $99,900
Appraisal Price + Closing Costs = $108,000 + $900 = $108,900

Of the $99,900 loan, $94,544.75 is put toward the balance of the original loan, and the remaining $5355.25 goes into the borrower's pocket.

If the property undergoing refinancing was purchased more than one year ago, the principal balance of the new loan may not exceed the sum of the closing costs and 90 percent (80 percent in Texas) of the appraised value of the home. There is a further limit that no cash-out loan may be in excess of $417,000 (although if you go above $240,000, you must have built up more equity).

Cash-out refinancing loans require the borrower to have enough VA entitlement to qualify for the loan (entitlement will be discussed in detail later in this lesson); this entitlement cannot include the amount used for obtaining the VA loan that is to be refinanced. These loans, like fixed-rate VA loans, have a maximum term of 30 years and 32 days and are only for owner-occupied homes. The VA funding fee on cash-out loans is 2 percent.

Interest Rate Reduction Refinancing Loan (IRRRL)

An interest rate reduction refinancing loan (IRRRL) is fairly self-explanatory: It is the refinancing of a VA loan such that the interest rate is reduced. However, the VA places certain limits on this refinancing:

- The new loan balance may not exceed the existing loan balance plus refinancing costs and up to $6,000 in energy efficient improvements.

- The veteran may not receive cash from the refinancing.

- The new interest rate must be less than the current interest rate, except for VA ARM loans (see below).

- No more than 2 discount points may be added to the loan.

- No certificate of eligibility is required.

- Unlike with a cash-out loan, the veteran need not have remaining entitlement for an IRRRL: He or she reuses the entitlement for the loan to be refinanced.

- The veteran need not occupy the property against which the IRRRL is a lien.

- The VA funding fee is 0.5 percent of the loan amount and may be financed.

For this sort of refinancing, the borrower should make sure that the interest savings is greater than the costs of refinancing. For example, suppose a borrower has 10 years left on her VA loan with a remaining loan balance of $20,000 at an interest rate of 8.75 percent. She is considering refinancing the loan at a lower rate of 8 percent. The refinancing costs are as follows:

Fee	Cost
Funding Fee (0.5%)	$100
2 Discount Points	$400
Origination Fee (1%)	$200
Other Fees	$200

The total interest that remains to be paid on the current loan will be $10,402. The interest on the refinanced loan is significantly less at $9,119.20. However, with the other costs, the total cost of refinancing comes out to $10,019.20, a savings of only $382.80. It is up to the borrower to decide whether this amount is worth the hassle of refinancing.

Hybrid ARMs

The VA will guarantee a special kind of adjustable rate mortgage known as a hybrid ARM. Hybrid ARMs are so-called because they have aspects of both fixed-rate and adjustable rate mortgages. In the specific case of the VA hybrid, the initial interest rate remains fixed for at least the first three years of the loan term and then may vary with the index.

All VA-guaranteed ARMs, like all FHA-insured ARMs, use the rate of one-year U.S. Treasury securities (T-bills) for an index. The VA, however, does not determine the margin of the ARMs it guarantees. The margin is determined by the market and the individual lender. After the initial fixed-rate period, the adjustment interval may be no more and no less than one year. There is a 1 percent cap on each adjustment and a 5 percent cap over the term of the loan.

For the loan to be approved by the VA, the lender must have the borrower sign a disclosure statement verifying that she or he understands the nature of the loan: that the interest rate may change, how the index rate affects the interest rate, how the borrower may find the index rate, and the frequency of the adjustment intervals. The lender is also required to have the borrower sign a hypothetical monthly payment schedule that shows a "worst-case scenario" for the first five years, in which the interest rate increases by the maximum amount allowable at every adjustment period.

Borrowers only have to qualify at the initial interest rate of the loan. However, temporary buydowns for these mortgages are disallowed by the VA.

Underwriting Requirements

Eligibility for participation in the VA loan program does not guarantee a loan. The VA has certain underwriting standards that lenders must follow in underwriting a guaranteed loan.

Loan Limits
In theory, there is no limit on the amount of a VA loan. However, a veteran is limited to 100 percent of the VA appraised value of the home, plus certain other expenses. Any part of the sale price that is in excess of the home's appraised worth must be paid upfront as a down payment at closing.

The other expenses above the appraised value of a home that may be included in a loan are the cost of any energy efficiency improvements (up to $6,000) and the VA funding fee. The funding fee is a fee charged by the VA for the loan guarantee. It is not the same as the lender's origination fee. Funding fee amounts as of May 2008 are as follows:

Purchase and Construction Loans
If you have a service connected disability that you are compensated for by the VA, the funding fee is waived.

Type of Veteran	Down Payment	First Time Use	Subsequent Use for loans from 1/1/04 to 9/30/2011
Regular Military	None 5% or more (up to 10%) 10% or more	2.15% 1.50% 1.25%	3.3%* 1.50% 1.25%
Reserves/National Guard	None 5% or more (up to 10%) 10% or more	2.4% 1.75% 1.5%	3.3%* 1.75% 1.5%

Cash-out refinancing loans

Type of Veteran	Percentage for First Time Use	Percentage for Subsequent Use
Regular Military	2.15%	3.3%*
Reserves/National Guard	2.4%	3.3%*

- The higher subsequent use fee does not apply to these types of loans if the veteran's only prior use of entitlement was for a manufactured home loan.

Other Types of Loans

Type of Loan	Percentage for Either Type of Veteran Whether First Time or Subsequent Use
Interest Rate Reduction Refinancing Loans	.50%

Manufactured Home Loans	1.00%
Loan Assumptions	.50%

These funding fee percentages expire in September or October of 2011. Energy efficient improvements can include solar heating and cooling systems or any other residential conservation measure.

More About: http://www.homeloans.va.gov/docs/funding_fee_tables.doc

VA Appraisals

For a loan to be approved by the VA, the property to be purchased must be appraised by an approved VA appraiser. A lender requests a VA appraisal by filling out VA Form 26-1805 and submitting it to the nearest Veterans Affairs office. The appraisal process results in a certificate of reasonable value (CRV). VA loans are made on the basis of the value determined by the CRV and no other appraisal; any amount of the sale price in excess of this must be paid by the borrower as a down payment with unborrowed funds. The veteran who buys such a property must also sign a statement acknowledging that he or she is paying a price higher than the reasonable value as determined by the VA. The VA now allows the appraisal's point of contact (POC, usually the lender) to send a request to change the CRV value to the VA appraiser, along with market data in support of the request, within two days of receiving the appraisal.

Closing Costs

The VA strictly limits the fees a borrowing veteran may be charged by the lender. The allowable closing costs are as follows:

- Credit report
- Flood inspection fee (provided the inspection is not done by a VA appraiser or the lender)
- Hazard insurance
- Loan origination fee (up to 1 percent of the total loan amount)
- Recording fees
- Survey
- Title examination
- Title insurance
- VA appraisal fee

- VA compliance inspection fee
- VA funding fee
- Other fees authorized by the VA

These costs are limited to those that the VA considers "reasonable and customary." In addition, fees charged by third parties (such as credit reports or survey fees) cannot be increased by the lender with handling fees or similar charges. Veterans cannot pay fees already paid by other parties in the transaction.

Note: A veteran also may pay prepaid items and reasonable discount points.

Fees Paid By the Lender

All of the following fees must be paid by the lender or seller and may not be allotted to the borrower:

- Attorney's fees
- Brokerage fees
- Document preparation fees
- Escrow fees
- HUD/FHA inspection fees
- Loan application/processing fees
- Notary fees
- Tax service fees

These fees and discount points may be paid by the lender, seller, or any other third party, although seller concessions deemed "excessive," that is, in excess of 4 percent of the total loan amount, are prohibited. Seller concessions include payment of the funding fee, prepaid items, permanent buydowns, and discount points in excess of those determined by the market. Payment of normal discounts and the buyer's closing costs are not considered seller's concessions.

Qualifying Ratios

The VA has no housing expense qualifying ratio; only the total debt service ratio is considered, and it must not exceed 41 percent. The VA sets certain standards for determining whether a veteran meets this requirement.

As with an FHA loan, the lender must call the government's credit alert interactive voice response system (CAIVRS, discussed in the previous lesson) to verify the veteran's creditworthiness. Then the lender should complete the VA Form 26-6393 Loan Analysis according to the VA's underwriting guidelines

Income

VA underwriting guidelines require that the lender adhere to the ECOA. In addition, they recommend that the lender verify a two-year employment history, either with the current employer, or as a continuous two-year history with two or more employers. If a two-year history cannot be verified, the lender should obtain a reasonable explanation why this is so. If the lender submits a loan to the VA for an applicant who has less than a 12-month work history, the lender must include an explanation with the loan submission.

Income that is not likely to continue, or sources of income such as overtime, part-time and second jobs that do not have a two-year history may be used in the lender's calculations to offset debts outstanding for the first two years of the loan period (such as car payments). Income from applicants who work on commission or are self-employed should be considered in much the same way as for a conventional loan.

For military income, the lender should obtain a Leave and Earnings Statement (LES). This statement should contain the same information as a verification of earnings statement. If the LES indicates that the borrower's contract is up within 12 months, the lender should include at least one of the following with the loan submission:

- Documentation showing the applicant has extended his or her contract/enlistment period

- A statement from the applicant that she or he intends to extend his or her contract/enlistment period

- A statement from the applicant's superior officer that the applicant is eligible for an extension or re-enlistment, and that there is no reason she or he would be denied for such

- Verification of an offer of civilian employment to the applicant

- Other exceptionally strong underwriting factors

The LES should indicate income that the applicant receives for his or her military quarters' allowance, subsistence and clothing allowance, and other military allowances, such as overseas pay and combat pay. These types of income are not taxable and can be included in the applicant's effective income calculation only if they can reasonably be expected to continue, due to the nature of the applicant's military duties.

Recently discharged veterans also may be receiving one of two types of separation payments: a special separation benefit (SSB), which is taxable in the year received and may be considered by the lender as a substantial cash reserve, or a voluntary separation incentive (VSI), which is paid and taxed annually and calculated by multiplying the veteran's years of service by two (with a minimum of six years' service). VSI is to be counted in the veteran's effective income. A veteran's disability payments should also be included in her or his effective income.

If the veteran wishes to purchase a multi-unit residence with the VA loan, certain restrictions apply. The applicant must have enough cash reserves to cover six months' mortgage payments and some documentation of his or her experience in acting as a landlord. Rental income from the additional units may be included in the veteran's effective income only if it can reasonably be expected. To account for vacancy, only 75 percent of the property's potential rental income is considered.

If the veteran intends to rent out the property she or he currently occupies when he or she obtains and occupies the new property being purchased with the VA loan, this money may *not* be included in the applicant's effective income, although it may be used to offset the mortgage payments on that property's mortgage. However, income from other properties with an established history may be included in the effective income calculation.

Other forms of income should be considered as they would for a conventional loan. Similarly, the lender should use the IRS's "Employer's Tax Guide" to determine federal income and social security taxes and subtract the appropriate amounts from the veteran's effective income.

Likewise, the borrower's debts should be treated as with a conventional loan. To determine whether the borrower has VA-related debts, the lender should ask whether she or he is now or has in the past received VA disability payments or is the spouse of a veteran killed in service or from service-related injuries. If so, the lender must submit VA Form 26-8937 Verification of VA Benefit-Related Indebtedness. Until the VA completes and returns this form to the lender, he or she may not underwrite the loan.

Credit

The VA sets standards for the consideration of applicants' creditworthiness as well. Credit reports must either be three-file credit reports (that is, Equifax, Experian, and TransUnion) or residential mortgage credit reports (RMCRs).

Entitlement

The VA guarantees only a portion of the total loan amount, based on the size of the loan and the amount of other guarantees the veteran has outstanding. The amount the VA will guarantee is as follows. These figures may change yearly.

Loan Amount	Guarantee Amount
Up to $45,000	50%
Between $45,000 and $144,000	minimum of $22,500 & maximum 40% (up to $36,000)
More than $144,000	25% of the $417,000 Freddie Mac loan limit ($104,250)

The amount of the guarantee is otherwise known as a veteran's entitlement. A lender is typically willing to lend four times a veteran's entitlement, if there is no down payment, or four times the sum of the entitlement and the down payment.

Note: The percentage and dollar amounts of the loan guarantee include the VA funding fee if it is financed in with the loan. No other fees may be financed, unless the veteran is refinancing an extant loan. For the purpose of the examples in this lesson, it is assumed that the funding fee is not financed, unless otherwise stated.

For example, suppose that a veteran wants to purchase a $450,000 home. What size down payment must she have? To solve this problem, first we calculate the amount of the veteran's entitlement, in this case $104,250. We know that

Loan Amount = Sale price − Down Payment = 4 × (Entitlement + Down Payment)
$450,000 − DP = 4 × ($104,250 + DP)
$450,000 − DP = $417,000 + 4DP
$33,000 = 5DP
DP = $6,600

So the veteran must put down $6,600 to receive the loan. Situations like this, however, are unlikely to occur, because the secondary market (Fannie Mae, Freddie Mac, and Ginnie Mae) will only buy VA loans of $417,000 or less. Nevertheless, there is no loan limit on VA loans, and lenders who plan to hold the loan in their own portfolios may make loans of any size to veterans.

Remaining Entitlement

A veteran may hold more than one VA loan. Additional loans are based upon a veteran's remaining entitlement. The remaining entitlement is calculated by subtracting a veteran's used entitlement from the current maximum ($36,000, or $104,250 for certain loans in excess of $144,000).

For example, suppose a veteran purchases a home for $50,000. What is the maximum sale price she can afford for another home on the VA loan program with no down payment? First, we must calculate the veteran's used entitlement. The guarantee for loans between $45,000 and $144,000 is 40 percent of the loan amount up to $36,000: $50,000 × 0.4 = $20,000. So, assuming a lender will lend only four times the veteran's entitlement, the maximum loan amount she can receive is 4 × ($36,000 − $20,000) = $64,000 for a sale price less than $144,000 and 4 × ($104,250 − $20,000) = $337,000 for a price of more than $140,000.

To calculate the remaining entitlement for many veterans, it is necessary to know the amount of the VA guarantees at the time he or she received the first loan. That is, since the guarantee amounts have increased steadily, from $2,000 in the 1930s to $104,250 today, a veteran who used all of her or his entitlement, say, 30 years ago, will nonetheless have remaining entitlement today. Here's an illustration:

Suppose a veteran took out a VA loan for $110,000 in 1985. At the time, the maximum VA guarantee was $27,500, meaning that the veteran used up all of his entitlement. Now suppose the veteran wants to take out another VA loan today, without having paid off the original loan. Even though in 1985 the veteran had *no* entitlement, today he has $36,000 − $27,500 = $8,500 *or* $104,250 − $27,500 = $76,750 in remaining entitlement.

Restored Entitlement

A veteran's remaining entitlement can be "restored" to him or her under certain conditions. First, if the original VA loan amount is repaid in full or the loan is assumed by another eligible veteran, the first veteran may apply to have her or his entitlement restored and to be treated as though he or she had never used the entitlement for the purposes of new loans. The entitlement cannot be restored if the property it was used for has not been sold, except for a one-time exception.

Default

What does it mean for a veteran to have, say, a $36,000 guarantee? Let's consider an example. Suppose a borrower takes out a VA loan of $100,000 at 8 percent interest over 30 years and defaults after 10 years of payments. At that point, the loan balance would be $87,725.52.

If the property is sold at auction to a third party or another creditor, the lender recovers his or her losses and is not owed money by the VA. If, however, the lender's bid is successful, there are two possibilities. First, the VA may elect to purchase the property for the total amount of the unpaid mortgage balance, the accrued interest, the foreclosure costs, and so on. The VA pays this amount regardless of the amount of the guarantee. However, if the VA does not desire to purchase the property, it will pay the lender the difference between the property's appraised value at foreclosure and the remaining loan balance, up to the guarantee amount.

Continuing our example, suppose the appraised value at foreclosure of the property was $74,000. Then the VA would have the option either to pay the loan balance of $87,725.52 plus interest and court costs OR it could pay the lender $87,725.52 − $74,000 = $13,725.52 (which is less than the $36,000 guarantee). The lender would then have to sell the property for at least its appraisal value plus the interest and court costs to recover all of her or his losses.

The VA guarantee makes it less likely that the lender will lose money in foreclosure. However, the lender is required to do what is necessary to avoid foreclosure, such as moratoriums and recasting. The VA may choose itself to make a defaulted loan (a loan with three months of payments still outstanding) current by paying the outstanding amount. In such a case, the VA has a prior claim to the money it advances to the veteran, meaning that if an amount is received from the defaulted veteran in a deficiency judgment, the VA is repaid first.

Eligibility

Qualifications

VA loans, unlike FHA loans, are available only to a select few. The loans are principally for discharged military personnel with wartime service of a specified duration or certain peacetime service, active-duty personnel, and reservists with six years in the reserves or National Guard.

A veteran and his or her spouse (including a common-law spouse) may co-sign a guaranteed loan together. However, an unmarried partner who is a co-borrower with a veteran may not have her or his portion of the loan amount guaranteed by the VA. Several borrowers who are all veterans, whether or not they are related, may purchase a one- to four-family home they intend to occupy as owners, but they are limited by the maximum guarantee amounts.

For example, suppose three veterans who each have full entitlement wish to purchase a three-family home together. The loan they want is $100,000. How much is the VA's guarantee? Even though the veterans have a combined total of 3 × $36,000 = $108,000, the VA will guarantee only $36,000. However, this means each veteran still has $36,000 − ($36,000/3) = $24,000 in entitlement remaining.

Service

To be eligible for the VA loan program, a veteran must have been discharged other than dishonorably. He or she must have served actively for 90 days or have been discharged due to a service-related disability during the following wartime periods:

Wartime	Dates
World War II	September 16, 1940, to July 25, 1947
Korean War	June 27, 1950, to January 31, 1955
Vietnam War	August 5, 1964 to May 7, 1975

Similarly, a veteran who has served 180 days of continuous active duty or been discharged for a service-related disability during the following peacetime periods also is eligible:

Peacetime After	Dates
World War II	July 26, 1947, to June 26, 1950
Korean War	February 1, 1955, to August 4, 1964
Vietnam War	May 8, 1975 to September 7, 1980 (or October 16, 1981, for officers)

U.S. citizens who served with a foreign government allied with the United States. during World War II also may be eligible.

In certain circumstances, those who have served after the post-Vietnam peacetime period and have since been separated from service also may be eligible. To qualify, a veteran must have:

- Completed either 24 months of active-duty service or the entire period for which he or she was ordered or called to active duty (which must be at least 181 days)

- Received a hardship or early-out discharge (USC 1173 and 1171, respectively) after completing 181 days of active-duty service

- Been discharged for a service-related disability, certain medical conditions or an involuntary reduction in military forces

Personnel who served on active duty during the Gulf War (August 2, 1990, to an as-yet undetermined date) also are eligible under the conditions for other peacetime personnel separated from service, except that the 181-day requirement is lowered to 90 days of active-duty service.

All personnel who are currently active and have been so for 181 days (or 90 days during the Gulf War) are eligible.

Those that served six years in either the Selected Reserves or the National Guard are eligible until September 30, 2009.

Spouses of veterans who died in service or from service-related injuries and have not remarried, as well as the spouses of service people missing in action or prisoners of war also are eligible.

Documentation

Certificate of Eligibility

Obtaining a VA loan requires a certificate of eligibility, which only the VA may issue. These certificates must be obtained each time the veteran (a) applies for a loan, (b) applies to have his or her entitlement restored, or (c) applies to refinance her or his VA loan.

A veteran, reservist, or active serviceperson should use VA Form 26-1880 and provide evidence of his or her status.

Assuming VA Loans

Anyone, veteran or nonveteran, may assume a VA loan. There is no limit to the number of VA loans an individual may assume. VA loans originated before March 1, 1988, are fully assumable with no qualifying and no change in terms. VA loans originated after March 1, 1988, are assumable only with a full qualification process on the borrower. There is still no change in the terms of the loan. This provision holds true for the life of the loan. The borrower assuming these loans closed after this date also assumes the obligation of the veteran to the VA.

A 0.5 percent funding fee will be charged on all assumptions of VA loans originated after March 1, 1988. Up to a $500 lender's processing fee also will be charged. The person assuming the loan may be either an owner occupant or an investor.

Activity: Fill In the Blanks

Use the words in the word bank to fill in the blanks.
Answers are given in the end.

Word Bank

Cash-out	Interest rate
Down payment	Reduction
Eligible	Leave and earnings
Energy efficiency	Reasonable value
Entitlement	Remaining
Funding fee	Restored
Guarantee	Seller concessions
Hybrid	T-bills

Fill in the Blanks

1. _____, such as the seller's payment of the veteran borrower's funding fee, are limited to 4 percent by the VA.

2. The _____ is the amount charged by the VA to the borrower for the loan guarantee. This amount is not refundable.

3. The VA appraisal process results in the issuance of a certificate of _____. If the sale price of the house is greater than the amount stated on the certificate, the borrower must pay the difference as a down payment.

4. An interest rate reduction refinancing loan (IRRRL) allows the borrower to finance up to $6,000 in _____ improvements into the principal balance.

5. A(n) _____ refinancing loan allows the borrower to take out the equity he or she has accrued in the home.

6. A veteran whose original VA loan has not been paid in full or assumed can still take out a second VA loan, provided she or he has _____ entitlement.

7. The VA guarantees only one type of adjustable rate mortgage, known as a(n) _____ because it contains elements both of a fixed and an adjustable rate loan.

8. The percentage of the funding fee for an eligible person varies with his or her type of service, prior VA loans and _____.

9. For active military personnel, the lender should obtain a(n) _____ statement to verify employment and income.

10. VA hybrids use the same index as FHA-insured ARMs, one-year U.S. _____. Rate adjustments are limited to 1 point annually and 5 points over the life of the loan.

11. The VA program does not insure or issue loans. It provides a(n) _____ to lenders for a certain specified amount.

12. When a veteran's VA loan is assumed by another eligible borrower or is paid in full, the veteran may apply to have her or his entitlement _____ to receive a new VA loan.

13. A(n) _____ refinancing loan does not require a borrower to have any remaining entitlement and carries only a 0.5 percent funding fee.

14. The VA will guarantee a veteran's loan up to the full amount of that veteran's
_____. The maximum guarantee is raised periodically by Congress.

15. An active serviceperson who has not served in wartime or certain peacetime
periods after war must have served at least 180 days consecutively to be
_____ for the VA-guaranteed loan program.

Answers:
1. Seller concessions
2. Funding fee
3. Reasonable value
4. Energy efficiency
5. cash-out
6. Remaining
7. Hybrid
8. Down payment
9. Leave and earnings
10. T-bills
11. Guarantee
12. Restored
13. Interest rate reduction
14. Entitlement
15. Eligible

Case Study: VA Loan

Suppose a veteran took out a 100 percent VA-guaranteed loan for $90,000 at 8
percent interest for a term of 30 years. Ten years later the veteran wants to sell
his home to a nonveteran for $110,000 (after closing costs and taxes) and
purchase a new residence for $450,000. Can he afford the new home?

The principal balance on his original loan is $78,951.84. If he pays off the full
amount of the loan, he is left with $110,000 − $78,951.84 = $31,048.16. The
maximum entitlement today for a VA loan is $104,250, and lenders will typically
lend only four times the sum of a veteran's down payment and his or her
entitlement. To calculate the required down payment, then, we use the following
formula:

Loan Amount = Sale price − Down Payment = 4 × (Entitlement + Down Payment)
$450,000 − DP = 4 × ($104,250 + DP)
$450,000 − DP = $417,000 + 4DP

$33,000 = 5DP$

$DP = \$6,600$

Therefore, the loan amount would be $\$450,000 - \$6,600 = \$443,400$. But what would be the funding fee? The \$6,600 down payment is 1.5 percent of the sale price, requiring a 3.3 percent funding fee, or $0.033 \times \$443,400 = \$14,632$. This fee, in conjunction with the required down payment (\$21,232), does not exceed the veteran's cash reserves of \$31,048.16 from the sale of his principal residence, so he can afford the new home.

The veteran also could choose another way to structure this deal. He could choose not to pay off the entire original loan amount and take out a second VA mortgage for his new residence. But this would result in two main difficulties: The veteran would have to pay a much higher down payment because he would not have his full entitlement restored, and he would have to qualify at a total debt service ratio that included both mortgage payments. In certain circumstances, although not usually, this might be the best option.

Practice

Use the chart below to determine whether this veteran meets the VA debt service ratio requirement to receive a guaranteed loan. To do this, you will need to use the amortization calculator that was used in the previous lesson, found at http://www.webmath.com/amort.html.

Sale price	$79,900
Taxes	$105
Insurance	$30
Interest rate	10.5%
Term	30 years
Gross monthly income	$3,200 (A)
Long-term debts	$320

Using the worksheet below and the chart on the previous page, determine whether this veteran meets the VA debt service ratio requirement to receive a guaranteed loan.

Monthly Expenses:	
Principle and Interest (PI)	$_____
Taxes (T)	+_____
Hazard Insurance (I)	+_____
Long Term Debts	+_____
Total Expenses	$_____ (B)

Debt-to-income ratio = B / A = _____% (not to be in excess of 41%)

Solution

Using the amortization calculator (http://www.webmath.com/amort.html) we find that the amount and term of the loan results in a monthly payment of $730.88.

Now, using the information given in the first chart we can complete the VA qualifying worksheet.

Monthly Expenses:	
Principle and Interest (PI)	$730.88
Taxes (T)	+105.00
Hazard Insurance (I)	+ 30.00
Long Term Debts	+320.00
Total Expenses	$1,185.88 (B)

You can now calculate the total debt service ratio by dividing the borrower's total expenses (B) by gross monthly income (A):

$1,185.88 / $3,200 = .3705 or 37.05%

This percentage, less than the required 41%, shows that this buyer would be able to qualify for a VA loan.

Summary

The Department of Veterans Affairs (VA) guarantees loans to eligible veterans who have served during wartime or certain peacetime periods, surviving spouses of such veterans, National Guard members, special reservists, and men and women currently in the U.S. armed services. These loans can be used for owner-occupied houses or condominiums, improvements, or refinancing. Typically, there is no required down payment.

The VA guarantees two types of loans: fixed-rate and so-called hybrid adjustable rate mortgages (ARM). A hybrid ARM has a fixed interest rate for a certain determinate period, after which it varies with the index. VA hybrids have an initial three-year fixed-rate period and use one-year T-bills for an index.

All VA loans require a funding fee, which is different from the lender's origination fee. These fees go to pay for the cost of the VA loan guarantee program. The fee is waived for disabled veterans and for the surviving spouses of veterans who were killed in action or who are prisoners of war. For all other veterans, the fee is 2.15 percent with no down payment for the veteran's first VA loan, and 3.3 percent for a second loan; this fee is lowered for those who pay higher down payments. National Guard members and special reservists typically pay a higher fee than veterans of the armed services.

Only the funding fee can be financed into the loan amount. The VA limits the closing costs that can be allocated to the borrower. For example, the lender may charge no more than a 1 percent loan origination fee. The VA also limits seller concessions to 4 percent of the loan amount. However, payment of normal discounts and the buyer's closing costs are not considered concessions.

Veterans qualify only on the basis of the total debt service ratio, which must not exceed 41 percent.

The amount of the loan that the VA will guarantee is the veteran's entitlement. The maximum entitlement amount in 2008 is $36,000 for loans below $144,000 and $104,250 for certain loans in excess of $144,000. A veteran is allowed to hold more than one VA loan. If the full amount of the original loan has not been paid off and the loan has not been assumed by another eligible veteran, the second loan the veteran receives is guaranteed only for the difference between the maximum guarantee and the veteran's used entitlement. If the veteran does pay off the original loan, or it is assumed, she or he can request to have his or her entitlement "restored," that is, returned to the full amount.

To qualify for the VA loan program, a veteran must have served for 90 days of wartime service during or 180 days of continuous active peacetime service shortly after World War II, the Korean War, Vietnam or the Gulf War. There are currently no provisions for veterans who served in Yugoslavia, Afghanistan, or the second war in Iraq. National Guard troops and select reservists must have served for at least six years to be eligible. Any surviving, spouse (not remarried) of a veteran who died in service or from service-related injuries or is a prisoner of war also is eligible.

This concludes lesson thirteen.

Return to your online course player to take the Lesson Quiz.

Lesson 14:
FEDERAL AND STATE LAWS AND REGULATIONS

This lesson focuses on the following topics:

- Equal Credit Opportunity Act
- Truth in Lending Act
- Real Estate Settlement Procedures Act
- Financial Services Modernization Act
- Summary

By the end of this lesson, you should be able to:

- Identify the purpose of the Equal Credit Opportunity Act, and list the restrictions placed on the lender as mandated in the Act
- Explain the Truth in Lending Act, and distinguish between the two principal regulations, Regulation M and Regulation Z
- Explain RESPA and identify the purposes of the various sections
- Explain the enforcement of RESPA against violators of the Act, and state the procedure for filing a complaint
- Distinguish between Titles I–VII of the Financial Services Modernization Act, detailing each with 100 percent accuracy.

Equal Credit Opportunity Act

Title VII of the Consumer Credit Protection Act (CCPA) was passed in 1968 and is known as the Equal Credit Opportunity Act (ECOA). The ECOA protects borrowers seeking credit from unfair and discriminatory practices by lenders. The law is applicable both to lenders and to real estate brokers who arrange financing.

The ECOA provides the following:

1. When someone applies for a loan, the lender may not:

- Discourage the applicant from applying because he or she is of a certain race, nationality, age, marital status, or sex, or because she or he is on welfare

- Require that the applicant disclose her or his race, nationality, sex, or religion, although the lender may ask for voluntary disclosures of all but the applicant's religion
- Ask whether the applicant is widowed or divorced
    - The lender may, however, ask whether the applicant is married or unmarried-and if married, whether he or she is separated. This is true in community property states, including Texas, but not in most states.
- Ask about the applicant's desire to have or raise children
- Ask whether the applicant receives child support or alimony, unless the payments are being used to qualify for the loan.
    - A lender may, however, ask whether the applicant is required to make such payments.

2. When a lender considers a loan, he or she may not:

- Consider the race, nationality, age, marital status, or sex of the applicant
- Consider whether the applicant has a telephone number listed in her or his own name.
    - The lender may, however, consider whether the applicant has a telephone at all
- Consider the racial composition of the area in which the property to be mortgaged is located
- Consider the applicant's age, unless he or she is a minor, or the applicant is over the age of 62 and the lender intends to favor her or him for that reason

3. When evaluating an applicant's income, the lender may not:

- Refuse to consider the applicant's public assistance as though it were any other source of income
- Discount income on the basis of the applicant's sex or marital status
- Refuse to consider or discount income from retirement benefits, annuities and/or pensions
- Refuse to consider alimony or child support, if there is a demonstrable history of payment

4. The lender must:

- Accept or deny an application within 30 days
- Tell an applicant who was denied for a loan the reason for the denial
- Tell an applicant who is offered less favorable terms than she or he applied for the reason for the less favorable terms

The Federal Trade Commission (FTC) and the U.S. Department of Justice are in charge of enforcing the ECOA.

More About: For more information, visit the FTC online at http://www.ftc.gov.

Truth in Lending Act

Overview

Title I of the CCPA of 1968 is known as the Truth in Lending Act (TILA). The Federal Reserve is responsible for enforcing it.

Each of the following loans is covered by the act if the loan is to be repaid in more than four installments or if a finance charge is made:

- Real estate loans

- Loans for personal, family, or household purposes

- Consumer loans for $25,000 or less

The act is designed to help consumers compare the costs of credit from different lenders with one another and with the cost of buying with cash and to protect consumers from unfair and inaccurate credit practices. The act has two principal regulations, referred to as Regulation M and Regulation Z. Regulation M applies to leased property and will, therefore, not be a concern of ours in this course. Regulation Z applies to credit transactions where credit:

- Is extended to consumers

- Is offered on a regular basis (that is, Mr. A offering his friend Mr. B a loan would not fall under Regulation Z, but a car dealership that offered consumer financing on a regular basis would)

- Is either subject to a finance charge, such as an interest rate or financing fees, or is to be paid in four or more installments

- Is to be used for personal, family, or household purposes (that is, not for business, commercial, or agricultural purposes)

- Is a closed-end transaction (that is, any line of credit that is not open-end or revolving)

The regulation requires that certain disclosures be made to all consumers seeking credit. Lenders must disclose:

- The application fee for obtaining the loan

- The address of the property that is to be collateral for the loan

- The total sale price, including the down payment

- The amount financed, which is the sale price plus any other financed fees, less the down payment

- The loan's finance charge, which is the sum of the discounts, fees, and interest payments

- The total amount of the loan payments

- The annual percentage rate (APR), which is the ratio of the finance charge to the total amount of the loan payments

- Any prepayment penalties

- The charge for late payments

- Whether the loan is assumable or not

- If the loan is an adjustable rate mortgage, what the highest possible interest rate is

- If the loan is an ARM, how the periodic interest rate is calculated and how monthly payments are derived from it

Additionally, lenders must provide ARM borrowers with a pamphlet titled "Consumer Handbook on Adjustable Rate Mortgages," or any other literature containing the same information.

Background

The Truth in Lending Act (TILA), 15 USC 1601 *et seq.*, was enacted on May 29, 1968, as Title I of the Consumer Credit Protection Act (Pub. L. 90-321). The TILA, implemented by Regulation Z (12 CFR 226), became effective July 1, 1969. The TILA was first amended in 1970 to prohibit unsolicited credit cards. Additional major amendments to the TILA and Regulation Z were made by the Fair Credit Billing Act of 1974, the Consumer Leasing Act of 1976, the Truth in Lending Simplification and Reform Act of 1980, the Fair Credit and Charge Card Disclosure Act of 1988, the Home Equity Loan Consumer Protection Act of 1988, the Home Ownership and Equity Protection Act of 1994, and the Truth in Lending Act Amendments of 1995. Regulation Z also was amended to implement section 1204 of the Competitive Equality Banking Act of 1987, and in 1988, to include adjustable rate mortgage loan disclosure requirements. All consumer leasing provisions were deleted from Regulation Z in 1981 and transferred to Regulation M (12 CFR 213).

Purpose of the TILA and Regulation Z

The Truth in Lending Act is intended to ensure that credit terms are disclosed in a meaningful way so consumers can compare credit terms more readily and knowledgeably. Before its enactment, consumers were faced with a bewildering array of credit terms and rates. It was difficult to compare loans because they were seldom presented in the same format. Now, all creditors must use the same credit terminology and expressions of rates. In addition to providing a uniform system for disclosures, the act is designed to:

- Protect consumers against inaccurate and unfair credit billing and credit card practices

- Provide consumers with rescission rights

- Provide for rate caps on certain dwelling-secured loans

- Impose limitations on home equity lines of credit and certain closed-end home mortgages

The TILA and Regulation Z do not, however, tell banks how much interest they may charge or whether they must grant a consumer a loan.

Consequences of Noncompliance

Civil Liability

If a creditor fails to comply with any requirements of the TILA, other than with the advertising provisions of chapter 3, it may be held liable to the consumer for:

- Actual damage

- The cost of any legal action together with reasonable attorney's fees in a successful action

If it violates certain requirements of the TILA, the creditor also may be held liable for either of the following:

- In an individual action, twice the amount of the finance charge involved, but not less than $100 or more than $1,000 (effective September 1995, not less than $200 or more than $2,000 for closed-end credit secured by real property or a dwelling)

- In a class action, such amount as the court may allow. The total amount of recovery, however, cannot be more than $500,000 or 1 percent of the creditor's net worth, whichever is less.

Civil actions that may be brought against a creditor also may be maintained against any assignee of the creditor if the violation is apparent on the face of the disclosure statement or other documents assigned, except where the assignment was involuntary.

Criminal Liability
Anyone who willingly and knowingly fails to comply with any requirement of the TILA will be fined not more than $5,000 or imprisoned not more than one year, or both.

Administrative Actions
The TILA authorizes federal regulatory agencies to require financial institutions to make monetary and other adjustments to the consumers' accounts when the true finance charge or APR exceeds the disclosed finance charge or APR by more than a specified accuracy tolerance. That authorization extends to unintentional errors, including isolated violations (e.g., an error that occurred only once or errors, often without a common cause, that occurred infrequently and randomly.)

Under certain circumstances, the TILA requires federal regulatory agencies to order financial institutions to reimburse consumers when understatement of the APR or finance charge involves:

- Patterns or practices of violations (e.g., errors that occurred, often with a common cause, consistently or frequently, reflecting a pattern with a specific type or types of consumer credit)

- Gross negligence

- Willful noncompliance intended to mislead the person to whom the credit was extended

Any proceeding that may be brought by a regulatory agency against a creditor may be maintained against any assignee of the creditor if the violation is apparent on the face of the disclosure statement or other documents assigned, except where the assignment was involuntary.

Joint Notice of Statement of Interagency Enforcement Policy
On July 11, 1980, the federal financial regulatory agencies issued a Joint Notice of Statement of Interagency Enforcement Policy for Truth in Lending (policy guide). The policy guide summarizes and explains the reimbursement provisions of the TILA. It also describes corrective actions the financial regulatory agencies believe appropriate. The policy guide is contained in the appendix of this handbook.

The appendix contains a number of charts that are designed to show how accuracy tolerances apply to finance charges and annual percentage rates for disclosure and reimbursement purposes. Those charts are "Accuracy and Reimbursement Tolerances for Understated Finance Charges," "Accuracy Tolerances for Overstated Finance Charges," "Accuracy Tolerances for Overstated Finance Charges," "Accuracy and Reimbursement Tolerances for Understated APRs," "Accuracy Tolerances for Overstated APRs," and "Finance Charge Tolerances."

The regulatory agencies anticipate that most banks will comply voluntarily with the reimbursement provisions of the TILA. However, if a bank does not act voluntarily to correct violations, the agencies are required by law to use their cease and desist authority to order correction.

Enforcement Policy Applicability to Indirect Paper

Violations identified on disclosures involving third parties are direct-loan violations of law if the bank is the creditor (i.e., if the bank is the entity to which the obligation is initially payable). In such cases, the bank is cited for the violation and may be required to reimburse affected consumers under the enforcement policy.

If a third party is the creditor, a bank's acceptance of the third party's disclosures containing reimbursable violations normally reflects only a need for improved internal controls. However, if affected consumers have not been reimbursed, the OCC will report such third-party violations (consistent with the requirements of the Right to Financial Privacy Act of 1978) to the national headquarters of the regulatory agency supervising the creditor.

Specific Defenses

Defense Against Civil, Criminal, and Administrative Actions

A bank in violation of TILA may avoid liability by:

- Discovering the error before an action is brought against the bank, or before the consumer notifies the bank, in writing, of the error

- Notifying the consumer of the error within 60 days of discovery

- Making the necessary adjustments to the consumer's account, also within 60 days of discovery (The consumer will pay no more than the lesser of the finance charge actually disclosed or the dollar equivalent of the APR actually disclosed.)

The above three actions also may allow the bank to avoid a regulatory order to reimburse the customer.

An error is "discovered" if it is:

- Discussed in a final, written report of examination

- Identified through the bank's own procedures

- An inaccurately disclosed APR or finance charge included in a regulatory agency notification to the bank

When a disclosure error occurs, the bank is not required to redisclose after a loan has been consummated or an account has been opened. If the bank corrects a disclosure error by merely redisclosing required information accurately, without adjusting the consumer's account, the bank may still be subject to civil liability and an order to reimburse from its regulator. The circumstances under which a bank may avoid liability under the TILA do not apply to violations of the Fair Credit Billing Act (Chapter 4 of the TILA).

Additional Defenses against Civil Actions
The bank may avoid liability in a civil action if it shows by a preponderance of evidence that the violation was not intentional and resulted from a bona fide error that occurred despite the maintenance of procedures to avoid the error. A bona fide error may include a clerical, calculation, computer malfunction, programming, or printing error. It does not include an error of legal judgment. Showing that a violation occurred unintentionally could be difficult if the bank is unable to produce evidence that explicitly indicates it has an internal controls program designed to ensure compliance. The bank's demonstrated commitment to compliance and its adoption of policies and procedures to detect errors before disclosures are furnished to consumers could strengthen its defense.

Statute of Limitations
Civil actions may be brought within one year after the violation occurred. After that time, and if allowed by state law, the consumer may still assert the violation as a defense if a bank were to bring an action to collect the consumer's debt.

Criminal actions are not subject to the TILA one-year statute of limitations. Regulatory administrative enforcement actions also are not subject to the one-year statute of limitations. However, enforcement actions under the policy guide involving erroneously disclosed APRs and finance charges are subject to time limitations by the TILA. Those limitations range from the date of the last regulatory examination of the bank, to as far back as 1969, depending on when loans were made, when violations were identified, whether the violations were repeat violations, and other factors.

There is no time limitation on willful violations intended to mislead the consumer. A summary of the various time limitations follows.

- For open-end credit, reimbursement applies to violations not older than two years.

- For closed-end credit, the OCC generally directs reimbursement for loans with violations occurring since the "immediately preceding examination" during which the federal regulator reviewed compliance with the TILA.

- The U.S. Court of Appeals for the Eighth Circuit concluded that the phrase "immediately preceding examination" means the last examination of any kind, whether it included a review for TILA compliance. See First National Bank of Council Bluffs v. OCC, No. 91-2289 (8th Cir. February 19, 1992).

- Unless the ruling is changed by the Supreme Court or Congress, banks in the states covered by the Eighth Circuit (Iowa, Minnesota, North Dakota, South Dakota, Nebraska, Missouri, and Arkansas) are not obliged to follow the OCCs general interpretation. Banks in other areas, however, will continue to be required to comply with the OCC interpretation.

Relationship to State Law

State laws providing rights, responsibilities, or procedures for consumers or banks for consumer credit contracts may be:

- Preempted by federal law

- Appropriate under state law and not preempted by federal law

- Substituted in lieu of TILA and Regulation Z requirements

State law provisions are preempted to the extent that they contradict the requirements in the following chapters of the TILA and the implementing sections of Regulation Z:

- Chapter 1, "General Provisions," which contains definitions and acceptable methods for determining finance charges and annual percentage rates. For example, a state law would be preempted if it required a bank to include in the finance charge any fees that the federal law excludes, such as seller's points.

- Chapter 2, "Credit Transactions," which contains disclosure requirements, rescission rights, and certain credit card provisions. For example, a state law would be preempted if it required a bank to use the terms "nominal annual interest rate" in lieu of "annual percentage rate."

- Chapter 3, "Credit Advertising," which contains consumer credit advertising rules and annual percentage rate oral disclosure requirements. Conversely, state law provisions may be appropriate and are not preempted under federal law if they call for, without contradicting chapters 1, 2, or 3 of the TILA or the implementing sections of Regulation Z, either of the following:

  - Disclosure of information not otherwise required. A state law that requires disclosure of the minimum periodic payment for open-end credit, for example, would not be preempted because it does not contradict federal law.

- Disclosures more detailed than those required. A state law that requires itemization of the amount financed, for example, would not be preempted, unless it contradicts federal law by requiring the itemization to appear with the disclosure of the amount financed in the segregated closed-end credit disclosures.

The relationship between state law and Chapter 4 of the TILA ("Credit Billing") involves two parts. The first part is concerned with sections 161 (correction of billing errors) and 162 (regulation of credit reports) of the act; the second part addresses the remaining sections of Chapter 4.

State law provisions are preempted if they differ from the rights, responsibilities, or procedures contained in sections 161 or 162. An exception is made, however, for state law that allows a consumer to inquire about an account and requires the bank to respond to such inquiry beyond the time limits provided by federal law. Such a state law would not be preempted for the extra time period.

State law provisions are preempted if they result in violations of Sections 163 through 171 of Chapter 4. For example, a state law that allows the card issuer to offset the consumer's credit-card indebtedness against funds held by the card issuer would be preempted, since it would violate 12 CFR 226.12(d).

Conversely, a state law that requires periodic statements to be sent more than 14 days before the end of a free-ride period would not be preempted, since no violation of federal law is involved. A bank, state, or other interested party may ask the Federal Reserve Board to determine whether state law contradicts Chapters 1 through 3 of the TILA or Regulation Z. They also may ask if the state law is different from, or would result in violations of, Chapter 4 of the TILA and the implementing provisions of Regulation Z. If the board determines that a disclosure required by state law (other than a requirement relating to the finance charge, annual percentage rate, or the disclosures required under 226.32) is substantially the same in meaning as a disclosure required under the act or Regulation Z, generally creditors in that state may make the state disclosure in lieu of the federal disclosure.

Format of Regulation Z
The disclosure rules creditors must follow differ depending on whether the creditor is offering open-end credit, such as credit cards or home-equity lines, or closed-end credit, such as car loans or mortgages.

Subpart A (sections 226.1 through 226.4) of the regulation provides general information that applies to open-end and closed-end credit transactions. It sets forth definitions and stipulates which transactions are covered and which are exempt from the regulation. It also contains the rules for determining which fees are finance charges.

Subpart B (sections 226.5 through 226.16) of the regulation contains rules for disclosures for home-equity loans, credit and charge card accounts, and other open-end credit.

Subpart B also covers rules for resolving billing errors, calculating annual percentage rates, credit balances, and advertising open-end credit. Special rules apply to credit card transactions only, such as certain prohibitions on the issuance of credit cards and restrictions on the right to offset a cardholder's indebtedness. Additional special rules apply to home-equity lines of credit, such as certain prohibitions against closing accounts or changing account terms. Subpart C (sections 226.17 through 226.24) includes provisions for closed-end credit. Residential mortgage transactions, demand loans, and installment credit contracts, including direct loans by banks and purchased dealer paper, are included in the closed-end credit category.

Subpart C also contains disclosure rules for regular and variable rate loans, refinancings and assumptions, credit balances, calculating annual percentage rates, and advertising closed-end credit.

Subpart D (sections 226.25 through 226.30), which applies to both open-end and closed-end credit, sets forth the duty of creditors to retain evidence of compliance with the regulation. It also clarifies the relationship between the regulation and state law, and requires creditors to set a cap for variable rate transactions secured by a consumer's dwelling.

Subpart E (sections 226.31 through 226.33) includes disclosure and other requirements for home mortgage transactions having rates or fees above a certain percentage or amount (closed-end credit only) and disclosure requirements for reverse mortgage transactions (open-end and closed-end credit).

The appendices to the regulation set forth model forms and clauses that creditors may use when providing open-end and closed-end disclosures. The appendices also contain detailed rules for calculating the APR for open-end credit (Appendix F) and closed-end credit (Appendixes D and J).

Official staff interpretations of the regulation are published in a commentary that is normally updated annually in March. Good faith compliance with the commentary protects creditors from civil liability under the act. In addition, the commentary includes mandates, which are not necessarily explicit in Regulation Z, on disclosures or other actions required of creditors. It is virtually impossible to comply with Regulation Z without reference to and reliance on the commentary.

Summary of Coverage Considerations

Lenders must carefully consider several factors when deciding whether a loan requires Truth in Lending disclosures or is subject to other Regulation Z requirements. The coverage considerations under Regulation Z appear in the Appendix in a chart designed to help the lender make such decisions. The factors included in the chart are addressed in more detail by Regulation Z and its commentary. For example, broad coverage considerations are included under Section 226.1(c) of the regulation and relevant definitions appear in Section 226.2.

Exempt Transactions

The following transactions are exempt from Regulation Z:

- Credit extended primarily for a business, commercial, or agricultural purpose

- Credit extended to other than a natural person

- Credit in excess of $25 million not secured by real or personal property used as the principal dwelling of the consumer

- Public utility credit

- Credit extended by a broker-dealer registered with the Securities and Exchange Commission (SEC) or the Commodity Futures Trading Commission (CFTC), involving securities or commodities accounts

- Home fuel budget plans

- Certain student loan programs

If a credit card is involved, generally exempt credit (e.g., business or agricultural purpose credit) is still subject to requirements that govern the issuance of credit cards and liability for their unauthorized use. Credit cards must not be issued on an unsolicited basis and, if a credit card is lost or stolen, the cardholder must not be held liable for more than $50 for the unauthorized use of the card.

When determining whether credit is for consumer purposes, the creditor must evaluate all of the following:

- Any statement obtained from the consumer describing the purpose of the proceeds
  - For example, a statement that the proceeds will be used for a vacation trip would indicate a consumer purpose.
  - If the loan has a mixed-purpose (e.g., proceeds will be used to buy a car that will be used for personal and business purposes), the lender must look to the primary purpose of the loan to decide

whether disclosures are necessary. A statement of purpose from the consumer will help the lender make that decision.

- A checked box indicating that the loan is for a business purpose, absent any documentation showing the intended use of the proceeds, could be insufficient evidence that the loan did not have a consumer purpose.

- The consumer's primary occupation and how it relates to the use of the proceeds. The higher the correlation between the consumer's occupation and the property purchased from the loan proceeds, the greater the likelihood that the loan has a business purpose. For example, proceeds used to purchase dental supplies for a dentist would indicate a business purpose.

- Personal management of the assets purchased from proceeds. The lower the degree of the borrower's personal involvement in the management of the investment or enterprise purchased by the loan proceeds, the less likely the loan will have a business purpose. For example, money borrowed to purchase stock in an automobile company by an individual who does not work for that company would indicate a personal investment and a consumer purpose.

- The size of the transaction. The larger the size of the transaction, the more likely the loan will have a business purpose. For example, if the loan is for a $5,000,000 real estate transaction, that might indicate a business purpose.

- The amount of income derived from the property acquired by the loan proceeds relative to the borrower's total income. The less the income derived from the acquired property, the more likely the loan will have a consumer purpose. For example, if the borrower has an annual salary of $100,000 and receives about $500 in annual dividends from the acquired property, that would indicate a consumer purpose.

All five factors must be evaluated before the lender can conclude that disclosures are not necessary. Normally, no one factor, by itself, is sufficient reason to determine the applicability of Regulation Z. In any event, the bank may routinely furnish disclosures to the consumer. Disclosure under such circumstances does not control whether the transaction is covered, but can assure protection to the bank and compliance with the law.

Special Requirements

Proper calculation of the finance charge and APR are of primary importance. The regulation requires that the terms "finance charge" and "annual percentage rate" be disclosed more conspicuously than any other required disclosure. The finance charge and APR, more than any other disclosures, enable consumers to understand the cost of the credit and to comparison shop for credit. A creditor's failure to disclose those values accurately can result in significant monetary damages to the creditor, either from a class action law suit or from a regulatory agency's order to reimburse consumers for violations of law.

If an annual percentage rate or finance charge is disclosed incorrectly, the error is not, in itself, a violation of the regulation if:

- The error resulted from a corresponding error in a calculation tool used in good faith by the bank.

- Upon discovery of the error, the bank promptly discontinues use of that calculation tool for disclosure purposes.

- The bank notifies the Federal Reserve Board in writing of the error in the calculation tool.

When a bank claims a calculation tool was used in good faith, the bank assumes a reasonable degree of responsibility for ensuring that the tool in question provides the accuracy required by the regulation. For example, the bank might verify the results obtained using the tool by comparing those results to the figures obtained by using another calculation tool. The bank might also verify that the tool, if it is designed to operate under the actuarial method, produces figures similar to those provided by the examples in Appendix J to the regulation. The calculation tool should be checked for accuracy before it is first used and periodically thereafter.

Annual Percentage Rate Definition

Credit costs may vary depending on the interest rate, the amount of the loan and other charges, the timing and amounts of advances, and the repayment schedule. The APR, which must be disclosed in nearly all consumer credit transactions, is designed to take into account all relevant factors and to provide a uniform measure for comparing the cost of various credit transactions.

The APR is a measure of the cost of credit, expressed as a nominal yearly rate. It relates the amount and timing of value received by the consumer to the amount and timing of payments made. The disclosure of the APR is central to the uniform credit cost disclosure envisioned by the TILA.

The value of a closed-end credit APR must be disclosed as a single rate only, whether the loan has a single interest rate, a variable interest rate, a discounted variable interest rate, or graduated payments based on separate interest rates (step rates), and it must appear with the segregated disclosures.

Since an APR measures the total cost of credit, including costs such as transaction charges or premiums for credit guarantee insurance, it is not an "interest" rate, as that term is generally used. APR calculations do not rely on definitions of interest in state law and often include charges, such as a commitment fee paid by the consumer, that are not viewed by some state usury statutes as interest. Conversely, an APR might not include a charge, such as a credit report fee in a real property transaction, which some state laws might view as interest for usury purposes. Furthermore, measuring the timing of value received and of payments made, which is essential if APR calculations are to be accurate, must be consistent with parameters under Regulation Z.

The APR is often considered to be the finance charge expressed as a percentage. However, two loans could require the same finance charge and still have different APRs because of differing values of the amount financed or of payment schedules. For example, the APR is 12 percent on a loan with an amount financed of $5,000 and 36 equal monthly payments of $166.07 each. It is 13.26 percent on a loan with an amount financed of $4,500 and 35 equal monthly payments of $152.18 each and final payment of $152.22. In both cases the finance charge is $978.52. The APRs on these example loans are not the same because an APR does not only reflect the finance charge. It also relates the amount and timing of value received by the consumer to the amount and timing of payments made.

The APR is a function of:

- The amount financed, which is not necessarily equivalent to the loan amount. If the consumer must pay at closing a separate 1 percent loan origination fee (prepaid finance charge) on a $100,000 residential mortgage loan, the loan amount is $100,000, but the amount financed would be $100,000 less the $1,000 loan fee, or $99,000.

- The finance charge, which is not necessarily equivalent to the total interest amount.

    o If the consumer must pay a $25 credit report fee for an auto loan, the fee must be included in the finance charge. The finance charge in that case is the sum of the interest on the loan (i.e., interest generated by the application of a percentage rate against the loan amount) plus the $25 credit report fee.

    o If the consumer must pay a $25 credit report fee for a home improvement loan secured by real property, the credit report fee must be excluded from the finance charge. The finance charge in that case would be only the interest on the loan.

    o Interest, which is defined by state or other federal law, is not defined by Regulation Z.

    o The payment schedule, which does not necessarily include only principal and interest (P + I) payments.

If the consumer borrows $2,500 for a vacation trip at 14 percent simple interest per annum and repays that amount with 25 equal monthly payments beginning one month from consummation of the transaction, the monthly P + I payment will be $115.87, if all months are considered equal, and the amount financed would be $2,500. If the consumer's payments are increased by $2 a month to pay a non-financed $50 loan fee during the life of the loan, the amount financed would remain at $2,500 but the payment schedule would be increased to $117.87 a month, the finance charge would increase by $50, and there would be a corresponding increase in the APR. This would be the case whether or state law defines the $50 loan fee as interest.

If the loan above has 55 days to the first payment and the consumer prepays interest at consummation ($24.31 to cover the first 25 days), the amount financed would be $2,500 -$24.31, or $2,475.69. Although the amount financed has been reduced to reflect the consumer's reduced use of available funds at consummation, the time interval during which the consumer has use of the $2,475.69, 55 days to the first payment, has not changed. Since the first payment period exceeds the limitations of the regulation's minor irregularities provisions (see 226.17(c)(4)), it may not be treated as regular. In calculating the APR, the first payment period must not be reduced by 25 days (i.e., the first payment period may not be treated as one month).

Banks may, if permitted by state or other law, precompute interest by applying a rate against a loan balance using a simple interest, add-on, discount or some other method, and may earn interest using a simple interest accrual system, the Rule of 78's (if permitted by law) or some other method. Unless the bank's internal interest earnings and accrual methods involve a simple interest rate based on a 360-day year that is applied over actual days (even that is important only for determining the accuracy of the payment schedule), it is not relevant in calculating an APR, since an APR is not an interest rate (as that term is commonly used under state or other law). Since the APR normally need not rely on the internal accrual systems of a bank, it always may be computed after the loan terms have been agreed upon (as long as it is disclosed before actual consummation of the transaction).

Finance Charge (Open-End and Closed-End Credit)

The finance charge is a measure of the cost of consumer credit represented in dollars and cents. Along with APR disclosures, the disclosure of the finance charge is central to the uniform credit cost disclosure envisioned by the TILA. The finance charge does not include any charge of a type payable in a comparable cash transaction. Examples of charges payable in a comparable cash transaction may include taxes, title, license fees, or registration fees paid in connection with an automobile purchase.

Finance charges include any charges or fees payable directly or indirectly by the consumer and imposed directly or indirectly by the bank either as an incident to or as a condition of an extension of consumer credit. The finance charge on a loan always includes any interest charges and often other charges. Regulation Z includes examples, applicable both to open-end and closed-end credit transactions, of what must, must not, or need not be included in the disclosed finance charge (226.4(b)).

Accuracy Tolerances

Regulation Z provides finance charge tolerances for legal accuracy that should not be confused with those provided in the TILA for reimbursement under regulatory agency orders. As with disclosed APRs, if a disclosed finance charge is legally accurate, it would not be subject to reimbursement.

Under Regulation Z, finance charge disclosures for open-end credit must be accurate. However, since closed-end credit transactions occur in many forms and may have numerous complexities, Regulation Z permits various finance charge accuracy tolerances for closed-end credit.

Tolerances for the finance charge and other disclosures affected by any finance charge are generally $5 if the amount financed is less than or equal to $1,000 and $10 if the amount financed exceeds $1,000. For certain transactions consummated on or after September 30, 1995, those tolerances are superseded.

- Credit secured by real property or a dwelling (closed-end credit only):
    - The disclosed finance charge is considered accurate if it does not vary from the actual finance charge by more than $100.
    - Overstatements are not violations.
- Rescission rights after the three-business-day rescission period (closed-end credit only):
    - The disclosed finance charge is considered accurate if it does not vary from the actual finance charge by more than one-half of 1 percent of the credit extended.
    - The disclosed finance charge is considered accurate if it does not vary from the actual finance charge by more than 1 percent of the credit extended for the initial and subsequent refinancing of residential mortgage transactions when the new loan is made at a different bank.

Note: This excludes high cost mortgage loans subject to 12 CFR 226.32, transactions in which there are new advances and new consolidations.

- Rescission rights in foreclosure:
    - The disclosed finance charge is considered accurate if it does not vary from the actual finance charge by more than $35.
    - Overstatements are not considered violations.

Note: Normally, the finance charge tolerance for a rescindable transaction is either 0.5 percent of the credit transaction or, for certain refinancing, 1 percent of the credit transaction. However, in the event of a foreclosure, the consumer may exercise the right of rescission if the disclosed finance charge is understated by more than $35.

See the "Finance Charge Tolerances" chart in the appendix for help in determining appropriate finance charge tolerances.

Calculating the Finance Charge

One of the more complex tasks under Regulation Z is determining whether a charge associated with an extension of credit must be included in, or excluded from, the disclosed finance charge. The finance charge initially includes any charge that is, or will be, connected with a specific loan. Charges imposed by third parties are finance charges if the bank requires use of the third party. Charges imposed by settlement or closing agents are finance charges if the bank requires the specific service that gave rise to the charge and the charge Comptroller's Handbook–Consumer 17 Truth in Lending is not otherwise excluded. The "Finance Charge Tolerances" chart in the appendix briefly summarizes the rules that must be considered.

Prepaid Finance Charges

A prepaid finance charge is any finance charge paid separately to the bank or to a third party, in cash or by check before or at closing, settlement, or consummation of a transaction, or withheld from the proceeds of the credit at any time.

Prepaid finance charges effectively reduce the amount of funds available for the consumer's use, usually before, or at the time, the transaction is consummated.

Examples of finance charges frequently prepaid by consumers are borrower's points, loan origination fees, real estate construction inspection fees, odd days' interest (interest attributable to part of the first payment period when that period is longer than a regular payment period), mortgage guarantee insurance fees paid to the Federal Housing Administration, private mortgage insurance (PMI) paid to such companies as the Mortgage Guaranty Insurance Company (MGIC), and, in non-real-estate transactions, credit report fees.

Precomputed Finance Charges

A precomputed finance charge includes, for example, interest added to the note amount that is computed by the add-on, discount, or simple interest methods. If reflected in the face amount of the debt instrument as part of the consumer's obligation, finance charges that are not viewed as prepaid finance charges are treated as precomputed finance charges that are earned over the life of the loan.

Finance Charge (Open-End Credit)
Each finance charge imposed must be individually itemized. The aggregate total amount of the finance charge need not be disclosed.

Determining the Balance and Computing the Finance Charge
The examiner must know how to compute the balance to which the periodic rate is applied. Common methods used are the previous balance method, the daily balance method, and the average daily balance method, which are described as follows:

- Previous balance method–The balance on which the periodic finance charge is computed is based on the balance outstanding at the start of the billing cycle. The periodic rate is multiplied by this balance to compute the finance charge.

- Daily balance method-A daily periodic rate is applied to either the balance on each day in the cycle or the sum of the balances on each of the days in the cycle. If a daily periodic rate is multiplied by the balance on each day in the billing cycle, the finance charge is the sum of the products. If the daily periodic rate is multiplied by the sum of all the daily balances, the result is the finance charge.

- Average daily balance method-The average daily balance is the sum of the daily balances (either including or excluding current transactions) divided by the number of days in the billing cycle. A periodic rate is then multiplied by the average daily balance to determine the finance charge. If the periodic rate is a daily one, the product of the rate multiplied by the average balance is multiplied by the number of days in the cycle.

In addition to those common methods, banks have other ways of calculating the balance to which the periodic rate is applied. By reading the bank's explanation, the examiner should be able to calculate the balance to which the periodic rate was applied. In some cases, the examiner may need to obtain additional information from the bank to verify the explanation disclosed. Any inability to understand the disclosed explanation should be discussed with management, who should be reminded of Regulation Z's requirement that disclosures be clear and conspicuous.

When a balance is determined without first deducting all credits and payments made during the billing cycle, that fact and the amount of the credits and payments must be disclosed.

If the bank uses the daily balance method and applies a single daily periodic rate, disclosure of the balance to which the rate was applied may be stated as any of the following:

- A balance for each day in the billing cycle. The daily periodic rate is multiplied by the balance on each day and the sum of the products is the finance charge.

- A balance for each day in the billing cycle on which the balance in the account changes. The finance charge is figured by the same method as discussed previously, but the statement shows the balance only for Comptroller's Handbook–Consumer 19 Truth in Lending those days on which the balance changed.

- The sum of the daily balances during the billing cycle. The balance on which the finance charge is computed is the sum of all the daily balances in the billing cycle. The daily periodic rate is multiplied by that balance to determine the finance charge.

- The average daily balance during the billing cycle. If this is stated, however, the bank must explain somewhere on the periodic statement or in an accompanying document that the finance charge is, or may be, determined by multiplying the average daily balance by the number of days in the billing cycle, rather than by multiplying the product by the daily periodic rate.

If the bank uses the daily balance method, but applies two or more daily periodic rates, the sum of the daily balances may not be used. Acceptable ways of disclosing the balances include:

- A balance for each day in the billing cycle

- A balance for each day in the billing cycle on which the balance in the account changes

- Two or more average daily balances. If the average daily balances are stated, the bank shall indicate on the periodic statement or in an accompanying document that the finance charge is, or may be, determined by multiplying each of the average daily balances by the number of days in the billing cycle (or if the daily rate varies, by multiplying the number of days that the applicable rate was in effect), multiplying each of the results by the applicable daily periodic rate, and adding the products together.

In explaining the method used to find the balance on which the finance charge is computed, the bank need not reveal how it allocates payments or credits. That information may be disclosed as additional information, but all required information must be clear and conspicuous.

Finance Charge Resulting From Two or More Periodic Rates

Some banks use more than one periodic rate in computing the finance charge. For example, one rate may apply to balances up to a certain amount and another rate to balances more than that amount. If two or more periodic rates apply, the bank must disclose all rates and conditions. The range of balances to which each rate applies also must be disclosed. It is not Truth in Lending 20 Comptroller's Handbook–Consumer necessary, however, to break the finance charge into separate components based on the different rates.

Annual Percentage Rate (Open-End Credit)

Accuracy Tolerance

The disclosed annual percentage rate (APR) on an open-end credit account is accurate if it is within one-eighth of 1 percentage point of the APR calculated under Regulation Z.

Determination of APR

The regulation states two basic methods for determining the APR in open-end credit transactions. The first involves multiplying each periodic rate by the number of periods in a year. This method is used for disclosing:

- The corresponding APR in the initial disclosures

- The corresponding APR on periodic statements

- The APR in early disclosures for credit card accounts

- The APR in early disclosures for home-equity plans

- The APR in advertising

- The APR in oral disclosures

The corresponding APR is prospective. In other words, it does not involve any particular finance charge or periodic balance.

The second method is the quotient method, used in computing the APR for periodic statements. The quotient method reflects the annualized equivalent of the rate that was actually applied during a cycle. This rate, also known as the historical rate, will differ from the corresponding APR if the creditor applies minimum, fixed, or transaction charges to the account during the cycle.

If the finance charge is determined by applying one or more periodic rates to a balance, and does not include any of the charges just mentioned, the bank may compute the historical rate using the quotient method. In that method, the bank divides the total finance charge for the cycle by the sum of the average daily balance, adjusted balance, or previous balance method.

If zero, no APR can be determined. The amount of applicable balance is the balance calculation method and may include the balances to which the periodic rates were applied and multiplies the quotient (expressed as a percentage) by the number of cycles in a year.

Alternatively, the bank may use the method for computing the corresponding APR. In that method, the bank multiplies each periodic rate by the number of periods in one year. If the finance charge includes a minimum, fixed, or transaction charge, the bank must use the appropriate variation of the quotient method. When transaction charges are imposed, the bank should refer to Appendix F of this handbook for computational examples.

The regulation also contains a computation rule for small finance charges. If the finance charge includes a minimum, fixed, or transaction charge, and the total finance charge for the cycle does not exceed 50 cents, the bank may multiply each applicable periodic rate by the number of periods in a year to compute the APR.

Optional calculation methods also are provided for accounts involving daily periodic rates. (226.14(d))

Brief Outline for Open-End Credit APR Calculations

Note: Assume monthly billing cycles for each of the calculations below.

APR when finance charge is determined solely by applying one or more periodic rates:

- Monthly periodic rates:
  - Monthly rate X 12 = APR or
  - (Total finance charge ÷ applicable balance1) X 12 = APR

    This calculation may be used when different rates apply to different balances.
- Daily periodic rates:
  - Daily rate X 365 = APR or

    If zero, no APR can be determined. The amount of applicable balance is the balance calculation method and may include the average daily balance, adjusted balance, or previous balance method. Loan fees, points, or similar finance charges that relate to the opening of the account must not be included in the calculation of the APR.
  - (Total finance charge ÷ average daily balance) X 12 = APR or

- o   (Total finance charge ÷ sum of balances) X 365 = APR

APR when finance charge includes a minimum, fixed, or other charge that is not calculated using a periodic rate (and does not include charges related to a specific transaction, like cash advance fees):

- Monthly periodic rates:
  - o   (Total finance charge ÷ amount of applicable balance2) X 12 = APR3

- Daily periodic rates:
  - o   (Total finance charge ÷ amount of applicable balance1) X 365 = APR3

  - o   The following may be used if at least a portion of the finance charge is determined by the application of a daily periodic rate. If not, use the formula above.

    - (Total finance charge ÷ average daily balance) X 12 = APR3 or

    - (Total finance charge ÷ sum of balances) X 365 = APR3

- Monthly and daily periodic rates:
  - o   If the finance charge imposed during the billing cycle does not exceed $.50 for a monthly or longer billing cycles (or pro rata part of $.50 for a billing cycle shorter than monthly), the APR may be calculated by multiplying the monthly rate by 12 or the daily rate by 365.

    The sum of the balances may include the average daily balance, adjusted balance, or previous balance method. Where a portion of the finance charge is determined by application of one or more daily periodic rates, sum of the balances also means the average of daily balances.

    Cannot be less than the highest periodic rate applied, expressed as an APR.

If the total finance charge included a charge related to a specific transaction (such as a cash advance fee), even if the total finance charge also included any other minimum, fixed, or other charge not calculated using a periodic rate, then the monthly and daily APRs are calculated as follows: (total finance charge ÷ the greater of: the transaction amounts that created the transaction fees or the sum of the balances and other amounts on which a finance charge was imposed during the billing cycle4) X number of billing cycles in a year (12) = APR5

Finance Charge (Closed-End Credit)

The aggregate total amount of the finance charge must be disclosed. Each finance charge imposed need not be individually itemized and must not be itemized with the segregated disclosures.

Annual Percentage Rate (Closed-End Credit)

Accuracy Tolerances

The disclosed APR on a closed-end transaction is accurate for:

- Regular transactions (which include any single advance transaction with equal payments and equal payment periods, or an irregular first payment period and/or a first or last irregular payment), if it is within one-eighth of 1 percentage point of the APR calculated under

Regulation Z (226.22(a)(2)).

- Irregular transactions (which include multiple advance transactions and other transactions not considered regular), if it is within one-quarter of 1 percentage point of the APR calculated under Regulation Z (226.22(a)(3)).

Construction Loans

Construction and certain other multiple advance loans pose special problems in computing the finance charge and APR. In many instances, the amount and dates of advances are not predictable with certainty since they depend on the progress of the work. Regulation Z provides that the APR and finance charge for such loans may be estimated for disclosure.

At its option, the bank may rely on the representations of other parties to acquire necessary information (for example, it might look to the consumer for the dates of advances). In addition, if either the amounts or dates of advances are unknown (even if some of them are known), the bank may, at its option, use Appendix D to the regulation to make calculations and disclosures. The finance charge and payment schedule obtained through Appendix D may be used with volume one of the Federal Reserve Board's APR tables or with any other appropriate computation tool to determine the APR. If the bank elects not to use Appendix D, or if Appendix D cannot be applied to a loan (e.g., Appendix D does not apply to a combined construction-permanent loan if the payments for the permanent loan begin during the construction period), the bank must make its estimates under 226.17(c)(2) and calculate the APR using multiple advance formulas.

On loans involving a series of advances under an agreement to extend credit up to a certain amount, a bank may treat all of the advances as a single transaction or disclose each advance as a separate transaction. If advances are disclosed separately, disclosures must be provided before each advance occurs, with the disclosures for the first advance provided before consummation.

In a transaction that finances the construction of a dwelling that may or will be permanently financed by the same bank, the construction-permanent financing phases may be disclosed in one of three ways listed below.

- As a single transaction, with one disclosure combining both phases.

- As two separate transactions, with one disclosure for each phase.

- As more than two transactions, with one disclosure for each advance and one for the permanent financing phase.

If two or more disclosures are furnished, buyer's points or similar amounts imposed on the consumer may be allocated among the transactions in any manner the bank chooses, as long as the charges are not applied more than once. In addition, if the bank chooses to give two sets of disclosures and the consumer is obligated for both construction and permanent phases at the outset, both sets of disclosures must be given to the consumer initially, before consummation of each transaction occurs.

If the creditor requires interest reserves for construction loans, special Appendix D rules apply that can make the disclosure calculations quite complicated. The amount of interest reserves included in the commitment amount must not be treated as a prepaid finance charge.

If the lender uses Appendix D for construction-only loans with required interest reserves, the lender must estimate construction interest using the interest reserve formula in Appendix D. The lender's own interest reserve values must be completely disregarded for disclosure purposes.

If the lender uses Appendix D for combination construction-permanent loans, the calculations can be much more complex. Appendix D is used to estimate the construction interest, which is then measured against the lender's contractual interest reserves.

If the interest reserve portion of the lender's contractual commitment amount exceeds the amount of construction interest estimated under Appendix D, the excess value is considered part of the amount financed if the lender has contracted to disburse those amounts whether they ultimately are needed to pay for accrued construction interest. If the lender will not disburse the excess amount if it is not needed to pay for accrued construction interest, the excess amount must be ignored for disclosure purposes.

Calculating the Annual Percentage Rate

The APR must be determined under one of the following:

- The actuarial method, which is defined by Regulation Z and explained in Appendix J to the regulation.

- The U.S. Rule, which is permitted by Regulation Z and briefly explained in Appendix J to the regulation. The U.S. Rule is an accrual method that seems to have first surfaced officially in an early nineteenth century United States Supreme Court case, *Story* v. *Livingston* (38 U.S. 359). Whichever method is used by the bank, the rate calculated will be accurate if it is able to "amortize" the amount financed while it generates the finance charge under the accrual method selected. Banks also may rely on minor irregularities and accuracy tolerances in the regulation, both of which effectively permit somewhat imprecise, but still legal, APRs to be disclosed.

360-Day and 365-Day Years

Confusion often arises over whether to use the 360-day or 365-day year in computing interest, particularly when the finance charge is computed by applying a daily rate to an unpaid balance. Many single payment loans or loans payable on demand are in this category. There are also loans in this category that call for periodic installment payments.

Regulation Z does not require the use of one method of interest computation in preference to another (although state law may). It does, however, permit banks to disregard the fact that months have different numbers of days when calculating and making disclosures. This means banks may base their disclosures on calculation tools that assume all months have an equal number of days, even if their practice is to take account of the variations in months to collect interest.

Example: A bank may calculate disclosures using a financial calculator based on a 360-day year with 30-day months, when, in fact, it collects interest by applying a factor of 1/365 of the annual interest rate to actual days.

Disclosure violations may occur, however, when a bank applies a daily interest factor based on a 360-day year to the actual number of days between payments. In those situations, the bank must disclose the higher values of the finance charge, the APR, and the payment schedule resulting from this practice.

For example, a 12 percent simple interest rate divided by 360 days results in a daily rate of .033333 percent. If no charges are imposed except interest, and the amount financed is the same as the loan amount, applying the daily rate on a daily basis for a 365-day year on a $10,000 one year, single payment, unsecured loan results in an APR of 12.17 percent (.033333% x 365 = 12.17%), and a finance charge of $1,216.67. There would be a violation if the APR were disclosed as 12 percent or if the finance charge were disclosed as $1,200 (12% x $10,000).

However, if there are no other charges except interest, the application of a 360-day year daily rate over 365 days on a regular loan would not result in an APR in excess of the one eighth of one percentage point APR tolerance unless the nominal interest rate is greater than 9 percent. For irregular loans, with one-quarter of 1 percentage point APR tolerance, the nominal interest rate would have to be greater than 18 percent to exceed the tolerance.

Variable Rate Information

If the terms of the legal obligation allow the bank, after consummation of the transaction, to increase the APR, the bank must furnish the consumer with certain information on variable rates. Graduated payment mortgages and step-rate transactions without a variable rate feature are not considered variable rate transactions. In addition, variable rate disclosures are not applicable to rate increases resulting from delinquency, default, assumption, acceleration, or transfer of the collateral.

Some of the more important transaction-specific variable rate disclosure requirements under 226.18 follow.

- Disclosures for variable rate loans must be given for the full term of the transaction and must be based on the terms in effect at the time of consummation.

- If the variable rate transaction includes either a seller buydown that is reflected in a contract or a consumer buydown, the disclosed APR should be a composite rate based on the lower rate for the buydown period and the rate that is the basis for the variable rate feature for the remainder of the term.

- If the initial rate is not determined by the index or formula used to make later interest rate adjustments, as in a discounted variable rate transaction, the disclosed APR must reflect a composite rate based on the initial rate for as long as it is applied and, for the remainder of the term, the rate that would have been applied using the index or formula at the time of consummation (i.e., the fully indexed rate).

  - If a loan contains a rate or payment cap that would prevent the initial rate or payment, at the time of the adjustment, from changing to the fully indexed rate, the effect of that rate or payment cap needs to be reflected in the disclosures.

  - The index at consummation need not be used if the contract provides a delay in the implementation of changes in an index value (e.g., the contract indicates that future rate changes are based on the index value in effect for some specified period, like 45 days before the change date). Instead, the bank may use any rate from the date of consummation back to the beginning of the specified period (e.g., during the previous 45-day period).

- If the initial interest rate is set according to the index or formula used for later adjustments, but is set at a value as of a date before consummation, disclosures should be based on the initial interest rate, even though the index may have changed by the consummation date.

Variable rate consumer loans secured by the consumer's principal dwelling and having a maturity of more than one year are subject to special adjustable rate mortgage (ARM) disclosures of the regulation under Sections 226.18(f)(2), .19(b) and .20(c).

Payment Schedule
The disclosed payment schedule must reflect all components of the finance charge. It includes all payments scheduled to repay loan principal, interest on the loan, and any other finance charge payable by the consumer after consummation of the transaction.

However, any finance charge paid separately before or at consummation (e.g., odd days' interest) is not part of the payment schedule. It is a prepaid finance charge that must be reflected as a reduction in the value of the amount financed.

At the creditor's option, the payment schedule may include amounts beyond the amount financed and finance charge (e.g., certain insurance premiums or real estate escrow amounts such as taxes added to payments). However, when calculating the APR, the creditor must disregard such amounts.

If the obligation is a renewable balloon payment instrument that unconditionally obligates the bank to renew the short-term loan at the consumer's option or to renew the loan subject to conditions within the consumer's control, the payment schedule must be disclosed using the longer term of the renewal period or periods. The long-term loan must be disclosed with a variable rate feature. If there are no renewal conditions or if the bank guarantees to renew the obligation in a refinancing, the payment schedule must be disclosed using the shorter balloon payment term. The short-term loan must be disclosed as a fixed rate loan, unless it contains a variable rate feature during the initial loan term.

Amount Financed
The amount financed is the net amount of credit extended for the consumer's use. It should not be assumed that the amount financed under the regulation is equivalent to the note amount, proceeds, or principal amount of the loan. The amount financed normally equals the total of payments less the finance charge.

To calculate the amount financed, all amounts and charges connected with the transaction, either paid separately or included in the note amount, must first be identified. Any prepaid, precomputed, or other finance charge must then be determined.

The amount financed must not include any finance charges

If finance charges have been included in the obligation (either prepaid or precomputed), they must be subtracted from the face amount of the obligation when determining the amount financed. The resulting value must be reduced further by an amount equal to any prepaid finance charge paid separately.

The final resulting value is the amount financed.

When calculating the amount financed, finance charges (whether in the note amount or paid separately) should not be subtracted more than once from the total amount of an obligation. Charges not in the note amount and not included in the finance charge (e.g., an appraisal fee paid separately in cash on a real estate loan) are not required to be disclosed under Regulation Z and must not be included in the amount financed.

In a multiple advance construction loan, proceeds placed in a temporary escrow account and awaiting disbursement in draws to the developer are not considered part of the amount financed until actually disbursed. Thus, if the entire commitment amount is disbursed into the lender's escrow account, the lender must not base disclosures on the assumption that all funds were disbursed immediately, even if the lender pays interest on the escrowed funds.

Required Deposit

A required deposit, with certain exceptions, is one which the bank requires the consumer to maintain as a condition of the specific credit transaction. It can include a compensating balance or a deposit balance that secures the loan. The effect of a required deposit is not reflected in the APR. Also, a required deposit is not a finance charge since it is eventually released to the consumer. A deposit that earns at least 5 percent per year need not be considered a required deposit.

Calculating the Amount Financed

A consumer signs a note secured by real property in the amount of $5,435. The note amount includes $5,000 in proceeds disbursed to the consumer, $400 in precomputed interest, $25 paid to a credit reporting agency for a credit report, and a $10 service charge. Additionally, the consumer pays a $50 loan fee separately in cash at consummation. The consumer has no other debt with the bank. The amount financed is $4,975.

The amount financed may be calculated by first subtracting all finance charges included in the note amount ($5,435 − $400 − $10 = $5,025). The $25 credit report fee is not a finance charge because the loan is secured by real property. The $5,025 is further reduced by the amount of prepaid finance charges paid separately, for an amount financed of $5,025 – $50 = $4,975.

The answer is the same whether finance charges included in the obligation are considered prepaid or precomputed finance charges.

The bank may treat the $10 service charge as an addition to the loan amount and not as a prepaid finance charge. If it does, the loan principal would be $5,000. The $5,000 loan principal does not include either the $400 or the $10 pre-computed finance charge in the note. The loan principal is increased by other amounts that are financed which are not part of the finance charge (the $25 credit report fee) and reduced by any prepaid finance charges (the $50 loan fee, *not* the $10 service charge) to arrive at the amount financed of $5,000 + $25 – $50 = $4,975.

Other Calculations
The bank may treat the $10 service charge as a prepaid finance charge. If it does, the loan principal would be $5,010. The $5,010 loan principal does not include the $400 precomputed finance charge. The loan principal is increased by other amounts that are financed which are not part of the finance charge (the $25 credit report fee) and reduced by any prepaid finance charges (the $50 loan fee **and** the $10 service charge withheld from loan proceeds) to arrive at the same amount financed of $5,010 + $25 – $50 – $10 = $4,975.

Refinancings
When an obligation is satisfied and replaced by a new obligation to the original financial institution (or a holder or servicer of the original obligation) and is undertaken by the same consumer, it must be treated as a refinancing for which a complete set of new disclosures must be furnished. A refinancing may involve the consolidation of several existing obligations, disbursement of new money to the consumer, or the rescheduling of payments under an existing obligation. In any form, the new obligation must completely replace the earlier one to be considered a refinancing under the regulation. The finance charge on the new disclosure must include any unearned portion of the old finance charge that is not credited to the existing obligation. (226.20(a))

The following transactions are not considered refinancing even if the existing obligation is satisfied and replaced by a new obligation undertaken by the same consumer:

- A renewal of an obligation with a single payment of principal and interest or with periodic interest payments and a final payment of principal with no change in the original terms.

- An APR reduction with a corresponding change in the payment schedule.

- An agreement involving a court proceeding.

- Changes in credit terms arising from the consumer's default or delinquency.

- The renewal of optional insurance purchased by the consumer and added to an existing transaction, if required disclosures were provided for the initial purchase of the insurance. However, even if it is not accomplished by the cancellation of the old obligation and substitution of a new one, a new transaction subject to new disclosures results if the bank:

- Increases the rate based on a variable rate feature that was not previously disclosed; or

- Adds a variable rate feature to the obligation.

If, at the time a loan is renewed, the rate is increased, the increase is not considered a variable rate feature. It is the cost of renewal, similar to a flat fee, as long as the new rate remains fixed during the remaining life of the loan. If the original debt is not canceled in connection with such a renewal, the regulation does not require new disclosures. Also, changing the index of a variable rate transaction to a comparable index is not considered adding a variable rate feature to the obligation.

Adjustable Rate Mortgages

History and Requirements
National bank adjustable rate mortgage loans (ARMs) may be subject to the OCCs ARM regulation or to special variable rate provisions of the Federal Reserve Board's (FRB's) Regulation Z, or to both. The OCCs ARM regulation was issued originally in March 1981, as 12 CFR 29, and amended significantly on March 7, 1983.

To achieve greater uniformity among the ARM regulations of several financial regulatory agencies, the OCCs regulation was rewritten completely, effective March 11, 1988. The original Part 29 continued to be available until October 1, 1988. The revised regulation was incorporated into 12 CFR 34 which is the OCCs regulation governing real estate lending activities of national banks. The revised OCC ARM regulation modified the definition of an adjustable rate mortgage, reduced the circumstances under which independent indexes are required, and deferred all ARM disclosure requirements to Regulation Z, as amended December 29, 1987. National banks were given until October 1, 1988, to bring existing programs into compliance with the ARM provisions of 12 CFR 34, subpart B, at which time 12 CFR 29 ceased to exist. Subpart B was again modified and simplified effective April 19, 1996.

The OCCs ARM regulation covers any extension of credit made by a national bank with an interest rate subject to adjustment and for the purpose of purchasing or refinancing the purchase of a one-to-four-family dwelling and secured by that dwelling. OCC ARMs may either be open-end or closed-end credit.

Loans subject to the ARM requirements of Regulation Z are closed-end consumer credit transactions secured by the consumer's principal dwelling with a maturity greater than one year and an APR that may increase.

Regulation Z ARMs include purchase-money mortgage loans, as well as closed-end credit extended for other reasons (e.g., for home improvement).

See the Summary of Coverage Rules for ARMs in the appendix for a comparison of ARM coverage requirements between the OCCs ARM regulation and the closed-end ARM requirements of Regulation Z and see the Timing of Truth in Lending Disclosures for ARM Loans in the appendix for an outline of the timing of disclosures for ARMs.

The FRB's changes to Regulation Z, effective on December 18, 1987, require creditors to provide comprehensive information about the variable rate features of closed-end ARMs. National bank and other creditor compliance with the Regulation Z ARM amendments became mandatory on October 1, 1988.

With the regulatory changes that became mandatory October 1, 1988, the only national bank federal disclosure requirements that remained for open-end ARMs were the regular open-end credit disclosures required by Regulation Z. However, in November 1988, the Home Equity Loan Consumer Protection Act became law. That statute required the FRB to amend Regulation Z to include special disclosure requirements for any open-end consumer credit plan secured by the consumer's dwelling. Additional comprehensive disclosure requirements were also included for variable rate plans.

Credit subject to the variable rate disclosure provisions of the Home Equity Loan Consumer Protection Act are open-end consumer credit transactions with variable rates of interest secured by the consumer's dwelling. Such disclosure requirements would apply both to open-end credit consumer ARMs, as defined by the OCC, as well as to any other consumer home equity line of credit (HELC) secured by the consumer's dwelling. Also, the statute applies to both variable and fixed rate HELCs.

OCCs ARM Regulation
The OCCs ARM regulation is intended to encourage national bank participation in the residential mortgage market. It provides a flexible framework within which banks may design adjustable rate mortgages that best meet their needs and those of their borrowers. National banks may make long-term mortgage loans with interest rates that can be adjusted to reflect changes in their cost of funds. At the same time, the regulation protects consumers by requiring national banks,

for certain consumer ARMs, to link interest rates to an independent index. The OCCs ARM regulation permits national banks to design their own adjustable rate mortgage loan programs, subject to certain rules. Banks may offer more than one adjustable rate mortgage loan program as long as the various programs are offered to all borrowers in a manner that does not discriminate on any prohibited basis. Banks may impose limitations that are more restrictive than those provided in the regulation. Also, banks may continue to offer fixed rate mortgages. Balancing the flexibility desired by national banks, the regulation contains certain provisions to protect the interests of borrowers. Those provisions include requiring the use of an independent index for ARMs that are subject both to 12 CFR 34 and 12 CFR 226.19(b). Additionally, ARMs subject to 12 CFR 226.19(b) are required by Regulation Z to have early and comprehensive initial shopping disclosures, as well as notifications of interest rate changes.

Disclosure requirements reflect the belief that the marketplace operates efficiently only if both buyers and sellers are well informed about the transaction. Consumers must be equipped to evaluate a variety of complex mortgage instruments, including adjustable rate mortgages. Initial shopping disclosures serve the dual purpose of educating consumers about the nature of ARMs and equipping them to shop for the appropriate one.

Subsequent notifications aid ARM borrowers in monitoring the paydown of their loans and determining whether changes in installment payment amounts or rates of amortization best serve their needs. Because the regulation relies primarily on disclosure rather than restriction of ARM terms to provide for consumer protection, the OCC views failure to provide timely and substantively complete disclosures as a serious violation of the regulation.

Real Estate Settlement Procedures Act

The Real Estate Settlement Procedures Act of 1974 (12 USC 2601-17) became effective on June 20, 1975. The act requires lenders, mortgage brokers, or servicers of home loans to provide borrowers with pertinent and timely disclosures of the nature and costs of the real estate settlement process. The act also protects borrowers against certain abusive practices, such as kickbacks, and places limitations upon the use of escrow accounts.

An important goal of RESPA is to provide information that will teach consumers to be savvy judges of these services' proper costs, and thus eliminate referral fees and other questionable tacked-on fees that can unnecessarily increase the cost of closing and settlement services. RESPA is enforced by HUD's Office of RESPA and Interstate Land Sales.

HUD promulgated Regulation X (24 CFR 3500), which implements RESPA. The National Affordable Housing Act of 1990 amended RESPA to require detailed disclosures for the transfer, sale, or assignment of mortgage servicing. It also mandates disclosures for mortgage escrow accounts at closing and annually, thereafter, itemizing the charges to be paid by the borrower and from the account by the servicer.

More About: To view the text of Regulation X, please visit the following link: http://www.access.gpo.gov/nara/cfr/waisidx_99/24cfr3500_99.html

RESPA applies to most loans that are secured by a mortgage lien placed on a one- to four-family residential property. These loans include most purchase loans, assumptions and property improvement loans; they also generally include refinancing loans and equity lines of credit. The primary condition for a loan falling under RESPA is that it be what is called a "federally related mortgage loan," defined broadly in RESPA as a loan that is directly or indirectly supported by federal regulation, insurance, guarantees, supplements, or assistance. This term also covers loans that the originating lender intends to sell to a federal program, such as Fannie Mae. This range of loans covers the majority of loans that are secured for home purchases.

Disclosures at Time of Application
When a potential borrower first applies for a mortgage loan, brokers or lenders are required to give the borrower several disclosure documents.

Special Information Booklet
A bank must provide the borrower with a copy of the Special Information Booklet either at the time a written application is submitted, or no later than three business days after the application is received. If the application is denied before the end of the three-business-day period, the bank need not provide the booklet. If the borrower uses a mortgage broker, the broker, rather than the bank, must provide the booklet.

An application includes the submission of a borrower's financial information, either written or computer-generated, for a credit decision on a federally related mortgage loan. It must identify a specific property. The subsequent addition to the submission of an identified property converts it to an application for a federally related mortgage loan.

The booklet need not be given for refinancing transactions, closed-end subordinate lien mortgage loans, and reverse mortgage transactions, or for any other federally related mortgage loan unintended for the purchase of a one-to-four family residential property.

A bank that complies with Regulation Z (12 CFR 226.5b) for open-end home equity plans has conformed with this section.

Part One of the booklet describes the settlement process and the nature of charges, and suggests questions to be asked of lenders, attorneys, and others to clarify their services. It also contains information on the rights and remedies available under RESPA and alerts the borrower to unfair or illegal practices.

Part Two of the booklet contains an itemized explanation of settlement services and costs, and sample forms and worksheets for cost comparisons. The Appendix of the Special Information Booklet contains a listing of government offices from which to obtain consumer information and literature on home purchasing and other related topics.

Good Faith Estimate
A bank must provide, in a clear and concise form, a good faith estimate (GFE) of the amount of, or range of, settlement charges the borrower is likely to pay. The GFE must include all charges that will be listed in Section L of the HUD-1 Settlement Statement. It must be provided no later than three business days after receipt of the written application. If the application is denied before the end of the three-business-day period, the bank is not required to provide the GFE.

The GFE may disclose either an estimate of the dollar amount or a range of dollar amounts for each settlement service. The estimate of the amount or range for each charge must:

- Bear a reasonable relationship to the borrower's ultimate cost for each settlement charge

- Be based upon experience in the locality in which the property involved is located

A bank that complies with Regulation Z (12 CFR 226.5b) for open-end home equity plans is deemed to have met the GFE disclosure requirement of 24 CFR 3500.7. For no cost or no point loans, the GFE must disclose any payments to be made to affiliated or independent settlement service providers. These payments should be shown as POC (Paid Outside of Closing). For dealer loans, the bank must provide the GFE either directly or through the dealer.

For brokered loans, if the mortgage broker is the bank's exclusive agent, either the bank or the broker shall provide the GFE within three business days after the broker receives or prepares the application. When the broker is not the bank's exclusive agent, the bank is not required to provide the GFE if the broker has already done so, but the funding lender must ascertain that the GFE has been delivered.

When the bank requires the use of a particular settlement service provider and the borrower to pay all or a portion of the cost of those services, the bank must include with the GFE:

- A statement that the use of the provider is required and the estimate is based on the charges of the designated provider

- The name, address, and telephone number of the designated provider

- A description of the nature of any relationship between each such provider and the bank. A relationship exists if:

  o The provider is an associate of the bank, as defined in 24 CFR 3500.15(c)(1) (12 USC 2602(8)).

  o The provider has maintained an account with the bank or had an outstanding loan or credit arrangement with the bank within the last 12 months.

  o The bank has repeatedly used or required borrowers to use the provider's services within the last 12 months.

- The statement that, except for a provider that is the bank's chosen attorney, credit reporting agency, or appraiser, if the bank is in a controlled business relationship with the provider, it may not require use of that provider (24 CFR 3500.15).

If the bank maintains a controlled list of required providers (five or more for each discrete service) or relies on a list maintained by others and at the time of application has not decided which provider will be selected, the bank may comply with this section by:

- Providing a written statement that the bank will require a particular provider

- Disclosing in the GFE the range of costs for the required providers and on the HUD settlement statement the name of the specific provider and the actual cost

If the list is less than five providers of service, the names, addresses, telephone numbers, costs, and the business relationship are required.

More About: To view a sample good faith estimate, go to the following link through the HUD Web site: http://www.hud.gov/offices/hsg/sfh/res/resappc.cfm.

Mortgage Servicing Disclosure Document
A bank that receives an application for a federally related mortgage loan is required to disclose to the borrower at the time of application, or within three business days after its submission:

- Whether the servicing of the loan may be assigned, sold, or transferred

- The percentages (rounded to the nearest quartile (25 percent)) of loans made by the bank in each of the last three calendar years for which servicing has been assigned, sold, or transferred or, in the alternative, a statement that the bank has previously assigned, sold, or transferred the servicing of federally related mortgage loans

- The best available estimate of the percentage of loans to be made by the bank that may be assigned, sold, or transferred during the 12-month period beginning on the date of origination

- A summary of the information that will be provided to the borrower if the loan is transferred

- A disclosure of the duty of the bank to:
  - Provide a written acknowledgment of the borrower's qualified written request for information relating to the loan within 20 business days
  - Make corrections, if necessary, or provide a written explanation of why the account is correct, within 60 days of notice
  - Withhold, during the 60-day period, information about any overdue payment to a credit reporting agency

- A written acknowledgment that the applicant has read and understood the disclosure, evidenced by the signature of the applicant

Servicers Must Respond to Borrower's Inquiries

A bank servicer must respond to a borrower's qualified written inquiry and take appropriate action within established time frames after receipt of the inquiry. Generally, the bank must provide written acknowledgment within 20 business days and take certain specified actions within 60 business days of receipt of such inquiry.

During the 60-business-day period following receipt of a qualified written request from a borrower relating to a disputed payment, a bank may not provide information on any overdue payment, or relating to this period or the qualified written request, to any consumer reporting agency.

Disclosures before Settlement

Affiliated Business Arrangement Disclosure

If the bank has either an affiliate relationship or a direct or beneficial ownership interest of more than 1 percent in a provider of settlement services and the lender directly or indirectly refers business to the provider, it is a controlled business arrangement. That arrangement does not violate Section 8 of RESPA and Section 3500.14 of Regulation X, if:

- The bank discloses on a separate piece of paper either at the time of loan application or with the GFEs:
  - The nature of the relationship (explaining the ownership and financial interest) between the provider and the bank

- The estimated charge or range of charges generally made by such provider
- The bank does not require the use of such a provider, with the following exceptions:
  - The bank may require a buyer, borrower, or seller to pay for the services of an attorney, credit reporting agency, or real estate appraiser chosen by the bank to represent its interest.
- The bank receives only a return on ownership or franchise interest or payment otherwise permitted by RESPA in Section 3500.14(g).

HUD-1 Settlement Statement

The HUD-1 Settlement Statement is a standard form that clearly shows all charges imposed on borrowers and sellers in connection with the settlement. RESPA allows the borrower to request to see the HUD-1 Settlement Statement one day before the actual settlement (as discussed below).

The HUD-1 and HUD-1A must be completed by the person conducting the closing (settlement agent) and must conspicuously and clearly itemize all charges related to the transaction. The HUD-1 is used for transactions in which there is a borrower and seller. For transactions in which there is a borrower and no seller (refinancings and subordinate lien loans), the HUD-1 may be completed by using the borrower's side of the settlement statement. Alternatively, the HUD-1A may be used. However, no settlement statement is required for open-end home equity plans subject to the Truth in Lending Act and Regulation Z. Appendix A of 24 CFR 3500 contains the instructions for completing the forms.

Printing and Duplication of the Settlement Statement (24 CFR 3500.9)

Banks have numerous options for layout and format in reproducing the HUD-1 and HUD-1A that do not require prior HUD approval, such as size of pages; tint or color of pages; size and style of type or print; spacing; printing on separate pages, front and back of a single page, or on one continuous page; use of multi-copy tear-out sets; printing on rolls for computer purposes; addition of signature lines; and translation into any language. Other changes not specifically listed in 24 CFR 3500.9 may be made only with the approval of the Secretary of Housing and Urban Development.

One-Day Advance Inspection of the Settlement Statement (24 CFR 3500.10)

Upon request by the borrower, the HUD-1 or HUD-1A must be completed and made available for inspection during the business day immediately preceding the day of settlement, listing those items known at that time by the person conducting the closing.

Delivery

The completed HUD-1 or HUD-1A must be delivered to the borrower, the seller, and the lender at or before settlement. However, the borrower may waive the right of delivery by executing a written waiver at or before settlement. The HUD-1 or HUD-1A shall be mailed or delivered as soon as practicable after settlement if the borrower or borrower's agent does not attend the settlement.

Retention (24 CFR 3500.10(e))

The bank must retain each completed HUD-1 or HUD-1A and related documents for five years after settlement, unless the bank disposes of its interest in the mortgage and does not service it. If the loan is transferred, the bank shall provide a copy of the HUD-1 or HUD-1A to the owner or servicer of the mortgage as part of the transfer. The owner or servicer shall retain the HUD-1 or HUD-1A for the remainder of the five-year period.

Disclosures at Settlement

HUD-1 Settlement Statement

The HUD-1 Settlement Statement shows the actual settlement costs of the loan transaction. Separate forms may be prepared for the borrower and the seller. Where it is not the practice that the borrower and the seller both attend the settlement, the HUD-1 should be mailed or delivered as soon as practicable after settlement.

Initial Escrow Statement

After analyzing each escrow account, the servicer must submit an initial escrow account statement to the borrower at settlement or within 45 calendar days of settlement for escrow accounts that are established as a condition of the loan. The initial escrow account statement must include the monthly mortgage payment; the portion going to escrow; itemized estimated taxes, insurance, premiums, and other charges; the anticipated disbursement dates of those charges; the amount of the cushion; and a trial running balance.

Disclosures after Settlement

Annual Escrow Statement

A servicer shall submit to the borrower an annual statement for each escrow account within 30 days of the completion of the computation year. The servicer must conduct an escrow account analysis before submitting an annual escrow account statement to the borrower.

Annual escrow account statements must contain the account history; projections for the next year; current mortgage payment and portion going to escrow; amount of last year's mortgage payment and the portion going to escrow; total amount paid into the account during the past year; amount paid from the account; balance at the end of the period; explanation of how the surplus, shortage, or deficiency is being handled; and, if applicable, the reasons why the estimated low monthly balance was not reached.

If the new servicer changes the payment or accounting method, it must provide an initial escrow account statement within 60 days of the date of servicing transfer. When a new servicer provides an initial escrow account statement upon the transfer, it shall use the effective date of the transfer of servicing to establish the new escrow account computation year. Pre-rule accounts remain pre-rule accounts upon the transfer of servicing to a new servicer as long as it occurs before the conversion date.

Servicing Transfer Statement

The disclosures related to the transfer of mortgage servicing are required for first mortgage liens of federally related mortgage loans, including all refinancing transactions of such loans. HUD has exempted from the requirements of this section any subordinate lien and has excluded all open-end lines of credit (home equity plans), whether secured by a first or subordinate lien, that are covered under the Truth in Lending Act and Regulation Z. In addition, these requirements shall not apply when the application for credit is denied within three business days after receipt of the application.

When the servicing of a federally related mortgage loan is assigned, sold, or transferred, the transferor servicer (present servicer) must provide a disclosure not less than 15 days before the effective date of the transfer. The same notice from the transferee servicer (new servicer) must be provided not more than 15 days after the effective date of the transfer. Both notices may be combined into one notice delivered to the borrower not less than 15 days before the effective date of the transfer. The disclosure must include:

- The effective date of the transfer of servicing

- The name, address for consumer inquiries, and toll-free or collect-call telephone number of the transferee servicer

- A toll-free or collect-call telephone number for a person employed by the transferor servicer that can be contacted by the borrower to answer servicing questions

- The date on which the transferor servicer will cease accepting payments relating to the loan and the date on which the transferee servicer will begin to accept such payments. (These dates must either be the same or consecutive dates.)

- Any information about the effect of the transfer on the availability of optional insurance and any action the borrower must take to maintain coverage

- A statement that the transfer does not affect any other terms or conditions of the mortgage, except as related directly to servicing

During the 60-day period beginning on the date of transfer, no late fee can be imposed on a borrower who has made the payment to the wrong servicer. The following transfers are not considered an assignment, sale, or transfer of mortgage loan servicing for purposes of this requirement if there is no change in the payee, address to which payment must be delivered, account number, or amount of payment due:

- Transfers between affiliates

- Transfers resulting from mergers or acquisitions of servicers or subservicers

- Transfers between master servicers, when the subservicer remains the same

Applicable RESPA Statutes

Real estate settlement procedures comprise Chapter 27 of Title 12, Banks and Banking, of the U.S. Code. We will go through each section of RESPA, discussing the main points of the act and where you can find them.

More About: To view the Real Estate Settlement Procedures Act in its full form, please visit the following link: http://www.hud.gov/offices/hsg/sfh/res/respa_st.cfm.

Section 2601: Congressional Findings and Purpose

Section 2601 concerns Congress's determination that significant reforms in the real estate settlement process are needed to effect the following changes:

- More effective advance disclosure to buyers and sellers of settlement costs

- Elimination of kickbacks or referral fees which increase costs of some services

- Reduction of amounts buyers must place in escrow accounts

- Reform and modernization of local recordkeeping of land title information

Section 2602: Definitions

<u>Federally Related Mortgage Loan</u>
Any loan (other than temporary financing such as a construction loan) which-

A. Is secured by a first or subordinate lien on residential real property (including individual units of condominiums and cooperatives) designed principally for the occupancy of from one to four families, including any such secured loan, the proceeds of which are used to prepay or pay off an existing loan secured by the same property

B. Satisfies any of the following:

    I.   Is made in whole or in part by any lender the deposits or accounts of which are insured by any agency of the Federal Government, or is made in whole or in part by any lender which is regulated by any agency of the Federal Government

    II.   Is made in whole or in part, or insured, guaranteed, supplemented, or assisted in any way, by the Secretary or any other officer or agency of the Federal Government or under or in connection with a housing or urban development program administered by the Secretary or a housing or related program administered by any other such officer or agency

    III.   Is intended to be sold by the originating lender to the Federal National Mortgage Association, the Government National Mortgage Association, the Federal Home Loan Mortgage Corporation, or a financial institution from which it is to be purchased by the Federal Home Loan Mortgage Corporation

    IV.   Is made in whole or in part by any "creditor," as defined in Section 1602(f) of Title 15, who makes or invests in residential real estate loans aggregating more than $1,000,000 per year, except that for the purpose of this chapter, the term "creditor" does not include any agency or instrumentality of any State

Thing of Value
Any payment, advance, funds, loan, service, or other consideration.

Settlement Services
Any service provided in connection with a real estate settlement including, but not limited to, the following: title searches, title examinations, the provision of title certificates, title insurance, services rendered by an attorney, the preparation of documents, property surveys, the rendering of credit reports or appraisals, pest and fungus inspections, services rendered by a real estate agent or broker, the origination of a federally related mortgage loan (including, but not limited to, the taking of loan applications, loan processing, and the underwriting and funding of loans), and the handling of the processing, and closing or settlement.

Title Company
Any institution which is qualified to issue title insurance, directly or through its agents, and also refers to any duly authorized agent of a title company.

Person
Individuals, corporations, associations, partnerships, and trusts.

Secretary
The Secretary of Housing and Urban Development.

Affiliated Business Arrangement

An arrangement in which:

- A person who is in a position to refer business incident to, or a part of, a real estate settlement service involving a federally related mortgage loan, or an associate of such person, has either an affiliate relationship with or a direct or beneficial ownership interest of more than 1 percent in a provider of settlement services

- Either of such persons directly or indirectly refers such business to that provider or affirmatively influences the selection of that provider

Associate

One who has one or more of the following relationships with a person in a position to refer settlement business:

- A spouse, parent, or child of such person

- A corporation or business entity that controls, is controlled by, or is under common control with such person

- An employer, officer, director, partner, franchisor, or franchisee of such person

- Anyone who has an agreement, arrangement, or understanding, with such person, the purpose or substantial effect of which is to enable the person in a position to refer settlement business to benefit financially from the referrals of such business

Section 2603: Uniform Settlement Statement

This section stipulates that the Secretary must develop and prescribe a standard form for the statement of settlement costs for all transactions involving federally related mortgage loans in the United States. Parts of this form may be deleted in areas with varying legal or administrative requirements. If the borrower is located in an area which customarily provides this statement, then they must be able to inspect it at or before settlement.

Section 2604: Special Information Booklets

The Secretary is required to prepare and distribute booklets in order to help persons borrowing money to finance residential real estate purchases better understand the nature and cost of settlement services. Topics covered include: settlement cost incidents, standard settlement form example, description of escrow accounts used in connection with loans, service provider choices, and unfair practices and charges.

The booklet shall be provided by delivering or placing in the mail no later than three days after the lender receives the application and should include a good faith estimate of charges for specific settlement services.

Section 2605: Servicing of Mortgage Loans and Administration of Escrow Accounts

A servicer is generally the mortgage-holder or a third-party company responsible for servicing a mortgage. This includes collecting payments for principal, interest and escrow. When a mortgage is sold, it is not only the mortgage itself that is transferred, but also the servicing rights of the mortgage. This section discusses what notification is necessary upon transfer of mortgage and servicing rights, in addition to the handling of escrow account monies.

The old/existing servicer must provide written notification to the borrower of the transfer of servicing, assignment, or sale within 15 days prior to the effective date on which the mortgage payment is first due to the new servicer. The new servicer, too, must notify the borrower of the transfer within 15 days after the mortgage payment is first due to the new servicer (the effective date).

If the transfer is preceded by termination of the servicing contract for cause, commencement of bankruptcy proceedings for the servicer, or commencement of FDIC or RTC proceedings for receivership of the servicer, then the notification from both old and new servicers is extended to 30 days after the effective date of transfer.

Both notices from old and new servicers must contain the following pieces of information:

1. The effective date of transfer of the servicing

2. The name, address, and toll-free or collect telephone number of the new servicer

3. A toll-free or collect telephone number for an individual employed by the existing servicer or for the existing servicer department that can be contacted by the borrower to answer inquiries relating to the transfer of servicing.

4. The name and toll-free or collect telephone number for (i) an individual employed by the new servicer or for the new servicer department that can be contacted by the borrower to answer inquiries relating to the transfer of servicing.

5. The date on which the existing (transferor) servicer will cease to accept payments relating to the loan and the date on which the new (transferee) servicer will begin to accept such payments

6. Any information concerning the effect the transfer may have, if any, on the terms , or the continued availability , mortgage life or disability insurance

or any other type of optional insurance and what action, if any, the borrower must take to maintain coverage.

7. A statement that the assignment, sale, or transfer of the servicing of the mortgage loan does not affect any term or condition of the security instruments other than terms directly related to the servicing of such loan.

For 60 days following the effective date of servicing transfer, no one may impose a late fee on the borrower if he or she submits payment before the due date to the original servicer rather than the new servicer, though the new servicer is the one who should be receiving payment.

If the borrower submits a written request for information regarding the loan servicing, the servicer has 20 business days to acknowledge receipt of the request in writing, and 60 business days to resolve the inquiry or complaint by correcting the account or providing a statement of the servicer's position. Also, during this period, the servicer may not provide information regarding any disputed overdue payment to any consumer reporting agency.

Section 2606: Exempted Transactions

Because this chapter refers mainly to residential real estate transactions, it does not apply to credit transactions involving extensions of credit primarily for business, agricultural, or commercial purposes, or to government or government agencies or instrumentalities.

Section 2607: Prohibition against Kickbacks and Unearned Fees

No one may give or accept any fee, kickback, or thing of value for an agreement involving a federally related mortgage loan resulting from a business referral. Also, no one may give or accept a portion, split, or percentage of a charge made or received for the rendering of a real estate settlement service involving a mortgage loan.

This is not to say that attorneys, title companies/agents, or lenders/agents may not receive a fee for services actually performed. Anyone may be paid a bona fide salary, compensation, or other payment for goods or facilities actually furnished or services actually performed.

Payments for cooperative brokerage and referral arrangements between real estate brokers and agents are not prohibited; nor are affiliated business arrangements so long as the appropriate disclosures are made and a written estimate of charges are made by the provider to which the person is referred. In these situations, the person must also NOT be required to use a particular provider of settlement services and the only thing of value they may receive is a return on ownership interest or franchise relationship.

Section 2608: Title Companies; Liability of Seller

No seller of property purchased with a federally related mortgage loan shall require as a condition of sale that the buyer purchase title insurance from a particular company. Any seller who violates this provision is liable to the buyer for three times all charges made for such title insurance.

Section 2609: Limitation on Requirement of Advance Deposits in Escrow Accounts

A lender may not require a borrower to deposit more funds into an escrow account than would be necessary to assure payment of taxes, insurance premiums, or other charges to a property in connection with its settlement.

The appropriate advance deposit is only required to cover the charges for the period:

- Beginning on the last date on which each charge would have been paid according to normal lending practices and local custom

- Ending on the due date of its first full installment payment under the mortgage

- PLUS $1/6^{th}$ the estimated total amount of such taxes, insurance premiums and other charges to be paid during the ensuing 12-month period

A lender is also not allowed to require a borrower to deposit in any such escrow account in any month beginning with the first full installment payment a sum in excess of $1/12^{th}$ the total amount of estimated taxes, insurance premiums, and other charges reasonably anticipated to be paid on dates during the ensuing 12 months in accordance with normal lending practice of the lender and local custom, plus such amount as is necessary to maintain an additional balance in the escrow account not to exceed $1/6^{th}$ the estimated total amount of taxes, insurance premiums and other charges to be paid in the ensuing 12-month period.

However, if the lender determines that there is, or will be, a deficiency, that lender is not prohibited from requiring additional monthly payments into such escrow account to avoid or eliminate such deficiency.

Escrow Account Statements

If the borrower is required to make payments for advance deposits into an escrow account, the servicer must notify the borrower not less than once per year of any shortage of funds in the account.

Regarding initial account statements, the servicer must submit to the borrower at closing or within 45 days after the establishment of the escrow account:

- An itemization of estimated taxes, insurance premiums, and other charges that are reasonably anticipated to be paid from the escrow account during the first 12 months after the account is created
- As well as the anticipated dates of such payments

The servicer may also incorporate this initial statement into the uniform settlement statement according to regulation governing such incorporation.

Servicers are also required to submit a statement to the borrower at least once for a 12-month period, and within 30 days of the conclusion of such period, a statement clearly itemizing:

- The amount of the current monthly payment
- The portion of the monthly payment being placed in the escrow account
- The total amount paid into the account during the period
- The total amount paid out of the escrow account during the period for taxes, insurance premiums, and other charges (which shall be separately identified) and other charges
- The balance in the escrow account at the conclusion of the period

Section 2610: Prohibition of Fees for Preparation of Truth-In-Lending, Uniform Settlement, and Escrow Account Statements
No fees may be imposed by a lender in connection with a federally related mortgage loan for the preparation or submission of any of these statements.

Enforcement of RESPA
Because RESPA sets forth rules for disclosure and prohibits many specific actions by parties involved in real estate settlement services, there are obviously many actions that may be taken against violators of the Act. What follows are enforcement actions, including how long parties have to file suit or complaint for violations of specific actions, as well as what the penalties may be for the violations.

Civil Lawsuits
Individuals have one (1) year to bring a private lawsuit to enforce violations of Section 8 or 9. A person may bring an action for violations of Section 6 within three years. Lawsuits for violations of Section 6, 8, or 9 may be brought in any federal district court in the district in which the property is located or where the violation is alleged to have occurred. HUD, a State Attorney General, or State insurance commissioner may bring an injunctive action to enforce violations of Section 6, 8, or 9 of RESPA within three (3) years.

Loan Servicing Complaints

Section 6 (Section 2605) provides borrowers with important consumer protections relating to the servicing of their loans. Under Section 6 of RESPA, borrowers who have a problem with the servicing of their loan (including escrow account questions), should contact their loan servicer in writing, outlining the nature of their complaint. The servicer must acknowledge the complaint in writing within 20 business days of receipt of the complaint. Within 60 business days the servicer must resolve the complaint by correcting the account or giving a statement of the reasons for its position. Until the complaint is resolved, borrowers should continue to make the servicer's required payment.

A borrower may bring a private law suit, or a group of borrowers may bring a class action suit, within three years, against a servicer who fails to comply with Section 6's provisions. Borrowers may obtain actual damages and costs of the action and attorney's fees, as well as additional damages if there is a pattern of noncompliance. For individuals who have violated this section, additional damages may not exceed $1,000. For class action suits, additional damages may not exceed $1,000 for each member of the class, or the total amount of damages may not exceed the lesser of $500,000 or 1 percent of the net worth of the servicer.

Other Enforcement Actions

Under Section 10 (Section 2609), HUD has authority to impose a civil penalty on loan servicers who do not submit initial or annual escrow account statements to borrowers. This civil penalty is $50 for each failure to submit an escrow statement to a borrower, though they cannot exceed $100,000 total in a 12-month period; a $100 penalty may be imposed for *intentional* disregard to submit the statement. Borrowers should contact HUD's Office of Consumer and Regulatory Affairs to report servicers who fail to provide the required escrow account statements.

For a violation of Section 8 (2607) the violator may not be fined more than $10,000 or imprisoned for more than one year. The violator will be liable for three times the amount of any charge paid for settlement service involved in the violation. Violators of Section 9 (2608) are liable to the buyer for an amount equal to three times all changes made for title insurance, as well.

Filing a RESPA Complaint

Persons who believe a settlement service provider has violated RESPA in an area in which the Department has enforcement authority (primarily sections 6, 8, and 9), may wish to file a complaint. The complaint should outline the violation and identify the violators by name, address, and phone number. Complainants should also provide their own name and phone number for follow up questions from HUD. Requests for confidentiality will be honored. Complaints should be sent to:

Director, Office of RESPA and Interstate Land Sales
U.S. Department of Housing and Urban Development
Room 9154
451 7th Street, SW
Washington, DC 20410

RESPA Activity

The case studies that follow incorporate the information into potential situations and the consequences of possible actions taken by real estate professionals.

The following activities are meant to put your study of this course to good use. Please take your time considering and responding to each activity.

Case Study One

Buyer Z applied for a federal loan for a one-family home through Lender B. To comply with RESPA requirements, Lender B gave Buyer Z HUD's Special Information booklet (containing consumer information about real estate transactions and real estate settlement services) and a Mortgage Servicing Disclosure Statement. What else must Lender B provide to the borrower before closing?

Options

A completed HUD-1 Settlement Statement
A Notice to the Homebuyer Form
A Good Faith Estimate of closing and settlement costs
A copy of IRS Form 1099-S

Correct Answer

A Good Faith Estimate of closing and settlement costs

Case Study One Response

Buyer Z applied for a loan that falls under RESPA regulations. Therefore, within three business days of receiving Buyer Z's loan application, Lender B must send Buyer Z a Good Faith Estimate of the closing and settlement costs, in addition to the HUD Special Information booklet and the Mortgage Servicing Disclosure Statement.

Case Study Two

The U.S. Department of Housing and Urban Development (HUD) and World Savings Bank, FSB, entered into a settlement on July 2, 2003. This settlement was the result of HUD's investigation into World Savings Bank's "For Services Rendered" program. HUD determined that through this program, the bank "solicit[ed] and compensat[ed] real estate agents ("Agents") for assisting prospective borrowers in the completion and submission of mortgage loan applications" through a Web site run by the Bank.

HUD found that the World Savings Bank was thus giving a "thing of value" to real estate licensees in exchange for their referral of business, conduct which violates Section 8 of RESPA. This section of the Act states that "No person shall give and no person shall accept any fee, kickback, or thing of value pursuant to any agreement or understanding, oral or otherwise, that business incident to or a part of a real estate settlement service involving a federally related mortgage loan shall be referred to any person." World Savings Bank contested this judgment but agreed to the settlement, which is not interpreted as an admission of guilt. Using your knowledge of RESPA, what do you think the World Savings Bank was required to do to fulfill the settlement?

Case Study Two Response

Violations of RESPA regulations can lead to serious penalties for both licensees and lending institutions employees. Fines of up to $10,000 can be assessed, as can prison terms of up to a year. Further details about penalties can be found in Section 8 of RESPA.

According to the terms of this particular settlement, World Savings Bank was required to discontinue their "For Services Rendered" program and pay $7,557 to the U.S. Treasury. The settlement allows World Savings Bank to reinstate the program, but if it does so the program must not pay licensees for referring loan applicants; any consideration granted to licensees must be "reasonably related" to goods, services, or facilities that those licensees actually furnish or perform. Any reinstated program must follow all RESPA regulations and other relevant HUD policies.

Case Study Three

After an investigation into the business practices of ARVIDA/JMB Partners (a large builder and realty services company in Florida), HUD alleged that ARVIDA was in violation of RESPA regulations in Section 8(b) and Section 9 that prohibit the "giving or receiving of any portion, split or percentage of any charge made or received for the rendering of a real estate settlement service in connection with a federally related mortgage loan other than for services actually performed."

HUD found that ARVIDA was charging buyers a percentage of the purchase price of their homes as closing costs; in many cases, this entire percentage fee was not actually used to pay closing costs. The remaining portion of the percentage fee was retained by ARVIDA and not specifically accounted for. ARVIDA also imposed an additional $300 charge on buyers who elected not to work with ARVIDA's affiliated title company and instead used independent title agents. ARVIDA denied that these practices violated of RESPA but agreed to enter into a settlement with HUD on September 17, 2001.

Using your knowledge of RESPA regulations, what did ARVIDA/JMB Partners do wrong?

Case Study Three Response

Buyers have the right to use any title company they choose; lending institutions and other realty service providers are not allowed to assess additional fees to penalize individuals who elect not to use title companies affiliated with the service provider. In addition, closing costs must be itemized and properly accounted for, not calculated as a percentage of the sale.

The settlement with HUD required that ARVIDA begin itemizing closing costs, stop imposing extra charges on buyers for using independent title companies and send refund checks to buyers who were charged for using independent title companies within the time period addressed by the settlement. The settlement does allow ARVIDA and its affiliates to continue offering packages of settlement services, as well as discounts and rebates. However, all of ARVIDA's conduct in this regard must follow RESPA regulations and other relevant HUD policies.

Case Study Four

HUD investigated the business practices of Fidelity Financial, Inc., Fidelity National Title Insurance Company, Fidelity National Flood Insurance Company, Fidelity National Tax Service Company, Inc., and their affiliates and employees (FNF). HUD concluded that FNF had violated Section 8(a) of RESPA by "enter[ing] into contracts with lenders (banks, credit unions, and mortgage companies) that contained provisions for free review of existing loan portfolios in exchange for future referrals of business."

Case Study Four Response

RESPA forbids realty service companies from giving things of value in exchange for referrals. HUD determined that a free review of loan portfolios counts as a thing of value.

FNF denied that these practices violated RESPA, but the two parties entered into a settlement on February 28, 2002. This settlement required that FNF abandon this practice, begin charging reasonable fees for all such services, notify existing customers of the change, and pay hefty fines.

Case Study Five

After an investigation into the business practices of TitleVentures.com and its owners, Jerry D. Holmes, Jr., and Jerry D. Holmes, Sr., HUD declared that TitleVentures.com was in violation of Sections 8(a) and 8(b) of RESPA.

One of HUD's findings was that TitleVentures.com had created "preferred attorney" lists. TitleVentures.com referred clients only to attorneys on that list, and attorneys were placed on that list only if they agreed to use TitleVentures.com for any title work generated by the referral, which violates RESPA regulations for referrals. TitleVentures.com and HUD entered into a settlement on July 10, 2003, which required that TitleVentures.com terminate its preferred attorney lists and programs, terminate the operations of 29 title agencies controlled by the company, hold interest in no more than 12 title agencies for three years after the date of the settlement, operate all title agencies in accordance with guidelines established in the settlement and pay a fine of $7,750.

If TitleVentures.com wanted to continue to refer its clients to attorneys, how could this be done in compliance with RESPA regulations?

Case Study Five Response
RESPA does not allow companies to give or accept payment or any other "thing of value" in exchange for referrals. TitleVentures.com could refer clients to attorneys as long as there was no pre-established compensation arrangement between the title company and the attorneys, such as their previous agreement that the attorneys would reciprocate for referrals by giving title work back to TitleVentures.com. In addition, TitleVentures.com could not require that their clients use one of the recommended attorneys.

Case Study Six
According to HUD's investigation, Coldwell Banker United, Realtors®, was found to have violated RESPA regulations. HUD asserted that Coldwell was accepting "virtual tours" for free or below cost from various title companies ("virtual tours" are a service which allows a person to use the Internet to find photographs and information about properties for sale, as well as interior and exterior views of those properties). HUD deemed such virtual tours to be "things of value." Coldwell denied that this practice violated RESPA, but the two parties entered into a settlement on July 22, 2003. The settlement required that Coldwell pay reasonable fees for virtual tours and not accept any tour for free. Coldwell was also required to pay $5,200 in fines and to notify all of its real estate licensees about the settlement agreement.

Why does RESPA prohibit real estate professionals from accepting virtual tours for free from title companies?

Case Study Six Response
Real estate professionals are not allowed to accept payment or any other "thing of value" from a title company, lending institution, or other business in exchange for referring clients. Although in this situation there was no direct arrangement between the real estate firm and the title companies, accepting things of value could create an implied relationship. RESPA regulations require that appropriate compensation be paid for services and goods received.

Financial Services Modernization Act

The Financial Services Modernization Act is also known as the Gramm-Leach-Bliley Act. This lesson will provide a summary of the provisions of the act.

TITLE I-Facilitating Affiliation among Banks, Securities Firms, and Insurance Companies

- Repeals the restrictions on banks affiliating with securities firms contained in Sections 20 and 32 of the Glass-Steagall Act

- Creates a new "financial holding company" under Section 4 of the Bank Holding Company Act. Such holding company can engage in a statutorily provided list of financial activities, including insurance and securities underwriting and agency activities, merchant banking, and insurance company portfolio investment activities. Activities that are "complementary" to financial activities also are authorized. The nonfinancial activities of firms predominantly engaged in financial activities (at least 85 percent financial) are grandfathered for at least 10 years, with a possibility for a five-year extension.

- The Federal Reserve may not permit a company to form a financial holding company if any of its insured depository institution subsidiaries are not well-capitalized and well-managed, or did not receive at least a satisfactory rating in their most recent CRA exam.

- If any insured depository institution or insured depository institution affiliate of a financial holding company received less than a satisfactory rating in its most recent CRA exam, then the appropriate federal banking agency may not approve any additional new activities or acquisitions under the authorities granted under the act.

- Provides for state regulation of insurance, subject to a standard that no state may discriminate against people affiliated with a bank

- Provides that bank holding companies organized as mutual holding companies will be regulated on terms comparable to other bank holding companies

- Lifts some restrictions governing non-bank banks

- Provides for a study of the use of subordinated debt to protect the financial system and deposit funds from "too big to fail" institutions and a study on the effect of financial modernization on the accessibility of small business and farm loans

- Streamlines bank holding company supervision by clarifying the regulatory roles of the Federal Reserve as the umbrella holding company supervisor, and the state and other federal financial regulators, which "functionally" regulate various affiliates

- Provides for federal bank regulators to prescribe prudential safeguards for bank organizations engaging in new financial activities

- Prohibits FDIC assistance to affiliates and subsidiaries of banks and thrifts

- Allows a national bank to engage in new financial activities in a financial subsidiary, except for insurance underwriting, merchant banking, insurance company portfolio investments, real estate development, and real estate investment, so long as the aggregate assets of all financial subsidiaries do not exceed 45 percent of the parent bank's assets or $50 billion, whichever is less. To take advantage of the new activities through a financial subsidiary, the national bank must be well-capitalized and well–managed. In addition, the top 100 banks are required to have an issue of outstanding subordinated debt. Merchant banking activities may be approved as a permissible activity beginning five years after the date of enactment of the act.

- Ensures that appropriate antitrust review is conducted for new financial combinations allowed under the act.

- Provides for national treatment for foreign banks wanting to engage in the new financial activities authorized under the act.

- Allows national banks to underwrite municipal revenue bonds

TITLE II-Functional Regulation
- Amends the federal securities laws to incorporate functional regulation of bank securities activities.

- The broad exemptions banks have from broker-dealer regulation would be replaced by more limited exemptions designed to permit banks to continue their current activities and to develop new products.

- Provides for limited exemptions from broker-dealer registration for transactions in the following areas: trust, safekeeping, custodian, shareholder and employee benefit plans, sweep accounts, private placements (under certain conditions), and third party networking arrangements to offer brokerage services to bank customers, among others

- Allows banks to continue to be active participants in the derivatives business for all credit and equity swaps (other than equity swaps to retail customers)

- Provides for a "jump ball" rulemaking and resolution process between the SEC and the Federal Reserve regarding new hybrid products

- Amends the Investment Company Act to address potential conflicts of interest in the mutual fund business and amendments to the Investment Advisers Act to require banks that advise mutual funds to register as investment advisers

TITLE III-Insurance
- Provides for the functional regulation of insurance activities

- Establishes which insurance products banks and bank subsidiaries may provide as principal

- Prohibits national banks not currently engaged in underwriting or sale of title insurance from commencing that activity. However, sales activities by banks are permitted in states that specifically authorize such sales for state banks, but only on the same conditions. National bank subsidiaries are permitted to sell all types of insurance including title insurance. Affiliates may underwrite or sell all types of insurance including title insurance.

- State insurance and federal regulators may seek an expedited judicial review of disputes with equalized deference

- The federal banking agencies are directed to establish consumer protections governing bank insurance sales.

- Pre-empts state laws interfering with affiliations

- Provides for interagency consultation and confidential sharing of information between the Federal Reserve Board and state insurance regulators

- Allows mutual insurance companies to redomesticate

- Allows multi-state insurance agency licensing

TITLE IV-Unitary Savings and Loan Holding Companies

- De novo unitary thrift holding company applications received by the Office of Thrift Supervision after May 4, 1999, shall not be approved.

- Existing unitary thrift holding companies may be sold only to financial companies.

TITLE V-Privacy

- Requires clear disclosure by all financial institutions of their privacy policy regarding the sharing of nonpublic personal information with both affiliates and third parties

- Requires a notice to consumers and an opportunity to "opt out" of sharing of nonpublic personal information with nonaffiliated third parties subject to certain limited exceptions

- Addresses a potential imbalance between the treatment of large financial services conglomerates and small banks by including an exception, subject to strict controls, for joint marketing arrangements between financial institutions

- Clarifies that the disclosure of a financial institution's privacy policy is required to take place at the time of establishing a customer relationship with a consumer and not less than annually during the continuation of such relationship

- Provides for a separate rather than joint rulemaking to carry out the purposes of the subtitle; the relevant agencies are directed, however, to consult and coordinate with one another for purposes of assuring to the maximum extent possible that the regulations that each prescribes are consistent and comparable with those prescribed by the other agencies

- Allows the functional regulators sufficient flexibility to prescribe necessary exceptions and clarifications to the prohibitions and requirements of Section 502.

- Clarifies that the remedies described in section 505 are the exclusive remedies for violations of the subtitle

- Clarifies that nothing in this title is intended to modify, limit, or supersede the operation of the Fair Credit Reporting Act

- Extends the time period for completion of a study on financial institutions' information-sharing practices from six to eighteen months from date of enactment.

- Requires that rules for the disclosure of institutions' privacy policies must be issued by regulators within six months of the date of enactment. The rules will become effective six months after they are required to be prescribed unless the regulators specify a later date

- Assigns authority for enforcing the subtitle's provisions to the Federal Trade Commission and the federal banking agencies, the National Credit Union Administration, the Securities and Exchange Commission, according to their respective jurisdictions, and provides for enforcement of the subtitle by the states

TITLE VI-Federal Home Loan Bank System Modernization
- Banks with less than $500 million in assets may use long-term advances for loans to small businesses, small farms, and small agri-businesses

- A new, permanent capital structure for the Federal Home Loan Banks is established. Two classes of stock are authorized, redeemable on six months and five years notice. Federal Home Loan Banks must meet a 5 percent leverage minimum tied to total capital and a risk-based requirement tied to permanent capital.

- Equalizes the stock purchase requirements for banks and thrifts

- Voluntary membership for federal savings associations takes effect six months after enactment

- The current annual $300 million funding formula for the REFCORP obligations of the Federal Home Loan Banks is changed to 20 percent of annual net earnings.

- Governance of the Federal Home Loan Banks is decentralized from the Federal Housing Finance Board to the individual Federal Home Loan Banks. Changes include the election of chairperson and vice chairperson of each Federal Home Loan Bank by its directors rather than the Finance Board, and a statutory limit on Federal Home Loan Bank directors' compensation.

TITLE VII-Other Provisions

Requires ATM operators who impose a fee for use of an ATM by a noncustomer to post a notice on the machine that a fee will be charged and on the screen that a fee will be charged and the amount of the fee. This notice must be posted before the consumer is irrevocably committed to completing the transaction. A paper notice issued from the machine may be used in lieu of a posting on the screen. No surcharge may be imposed unless the notices are made and the consumer elects to proceed with the transaction.

Provision is made for those older machines that are unable to provide the notices required. Requires a notice when ATM cards are issued that surcharges may be imposed by other parties when transactions are initiated from ATMs not operated by the card issuer. Exempts ATM operators from liability if properly placed notices on the machines are subsequently removed, damaged, or altered by anyone other than the ATM operator.

- Clarifies that nothing in the act repeals any provision of the CR
- Requires full public disclosure of all CRA agreements

Requires each bank and each nonbank party to a CRA agreement to make a public report each year on how the money and other resources involved in the agreement were used

- Grants regulatory relief regarding the frequency of CRA exams to small banks and savings and loans (those with no more than $250 million in assets). Small institutions having received an outstanding rating at their most recent CRA exam shall not receive a routine CRA exam more often than once each five years. Small institutions having received a satisfactory rating at their most recent CRA exam shall not receive a routine CRA exam more often than once each four years.

- Directs the Federal Reserve Board to conduct a study of the default rates, delinquency rates, and profitability of CRA loans

- Directs the Treasury, in consultation with the bank regulators, to study the extent to which adequate services are being provided as intended by the CR

- Requires a GAO study of possible revisions to S corporation rules that may be helpful to small banks.

- Requires federal banking regulators to use plain language in their rules published after January 1, 2000.

- Allows federal savings associations converting to national or state bank charters to retain the term "federal" in their names

- Allows one or more thrifts to own a banker's bank

- Provides for technical assistance to micro enterprises (meaning businesses with fewer than five employees that lack access to conventional loans, equity, or other banking services). The Small Business Administration will administer this program.

- Requires annual independent audits of the financial statements of each Federal Reserve Bank and the Board of Governors of the Federal Reserve System.

- Authorizes information sharing among the Federal Reserve Board and federal or state authorities.

- Requires a GAO study analyzing the conflict of interest faced by the Board of Governors of the Federal Reserve System between its role as a primary regulator of the banking industry and its role as a vendor of services to the banking and financial services industry.

- Requires the federal banking agencies to conduct a study of banking regulations regarding the delivery of financial services, and recommendations on adapting those rules to online banking and lending activities

- Protects FDIC resources by restricting claims for the return of assets transferred from a holding company to an insolvent subsidiary bank

- Provides relief to out-of-state banks generally by allowing them to charge interest rates in certain host states that are no higher than rates in their home states.

- Allows foreign banks generally to establish and operate federal branches or agencies with the approval of the Federal Reserve Board and the appropriate banking regulator if the branch has been in operation since September 29, 1994, or the applicable period under appropriate state law

- Expresses the sense of the Congress that individuals offering financial advice and products should offer such services and products in a nondiscriminatory, non-gender-specific manner

- Permits the chairman of the Federal Reserve Board and the chairman of the Securities and Exchange Commission to substitute designees to serve on the Emergency Oil and Gas Guarantee Loan Guarantee Board and the Emergency Steel Loan Guarantee Board

- Repeals Section 11(m) of the Federal Reserve Act, removing the stock collateral restriction on the amount of a loan made by a state bank member of the Federal Reserve System

- Allows the FDIC to reverse an accounting entry designating about $1 billion of SAIF dollars to a SAIF special reserve, which would not otherwise be available to the FDIC unless the SAIF designated reserve ratio declines by about 50 percent and would be expected to remain at that level for more than one year

- Allows directors serving on the boards of public utility companies to also serve on the boards of banks

Summary

The Equal Credit Opportunity Act (ECOA) protects borrowers from unfair and discriminatory lending practices. It applies both to lenders and to real estate brokers who arrange financing. It prohibits lenders from discriminating on the basis of race, nationality, sex, religion, marital or family status, or receipt of public assistance. It requires lenders to accept or deny each application within 30 days and to tell an applicant who was denied a loan or who is offered less favorable terms than he or she applied for the reasons why. The Federal Trade Commission (FTC) and the U.S. Department of Justice are in charge of enforcing the ECOA.

The Truth in Lending Act (TILA) is designed to help consumers compare the costs of credit from different lenders with one another and with the cost of buying with cash. It is designed to protect consumers from unfair and inaccurate credit practices. It requires certain disclosures to consumers seeking credit, including the application fee for obtaining the loan, the annual percentage rate (APR), any prepayment penalties, the charge for late payments, and (if the loan is an ARM) the highest possible interest rate of the loan. Additionally, lenders must provide ARM borrowers with a pamphlet titled "Consumer Handbook on Adjustable Rate Mortgages," or any other literature containing the same information. The Federal Reserve is responsible for enforcing the act.

The Real Estate Settlement Procedures Act (RESPA) stipulates certain procedures and disclosures that must occur during closing in most federally related loans. It requires that within three days after receiving a loan application, lenders must provide applicants with a booklet titled "Settlement Costs and You," published by HUD; a truth-in-lending statement indicating the total credit costs and APR of the loan; and a good-faith estimate of settlement costs. RESPA also requires that any time the closing agent refers a borrower to a firm with which the lender is affiliated; the lender must inform the borrower of the connection through an Affiliate Business Arrangement (AfBA) Disclosure stating the relationship and that the buyer need not use affiliated firms. HUD is responsible for enforcing the act.

The Financial Services Modernization Act of 1999 repealed the Glass-Steagall Act, opening up competition among banks, securities companies, and insurance companies.

This concludes lesson fourteen.

Return to your online course player to take the Lesson Quiz.

Lesson 15:
CONVENTIONAL LOANS

This lesson focuses on the following topics:

- Computerized Loan Origination (CLO)
- Automated Underwriting Systems
- Automatic Underwriting On the Internet
- Investment in Real Estate
- Summary

By the end of this lesson, you should be able to:

- Explain Computerized Loan Origination (CLO), identifying the new "final" rule of the CLO as issued by HUD
- Explain automated underwriting systems, distinguishing between Freddie Mac's Loan Prospector and Fannie Mae's Desktop Underwriter
- Explain the development of automatic underwriting on the Internet
- Discuss the concept of true value in investment in real estate

Computerized Loan Origination (CLO)

A method of transmitting loan application information from a computer terminal, which may be located in a mortgage loan originator's office or in a real estate agent's office, to a major lender's mainframe computer is called computerized loan origination. The lender's underwriter analyzes the information submitted and can give an approval in a few days, subject to certain verifications. This is now called "manual" underwriting as contrasted to "automated" or analysis by a computer.

On June 7, 1996, HUD issued a "final" rule, part of which addressed CLO. Most of the rule's provisions became effective on January 14, 1997. The former rule allowed a CLO provider to charge any fee deemed fair so long as the borrower agreed in writing. The new rule restricts the CLO provider's charge, limiting it to a "reasonably related value of the services provided." Further, a listing of only one lender (formerly permitted) with only basic information on products would be considered "no or nominal compensable services."

Automated Underwriting Systems

HUD has encouraged the use of computerized loan analysis. It believes properly designed computer programs can minimize the vagaries of human judgment in loan qualification and act in a less biased manner. It expedites the loan process and usually saves the borrower money. In 1995, both Freddie Mac and Fannie Mae, subject to HUD oversight, implemented the use of computers for loan processing.

Both Freddie Mac and Fannie Mae offer automated underwriting systems that can process a loan in a few days at about half the cost. Loan approvals can be given in a few minutes (subject to verifications on qualified borrowers). Subsequent improvements of both systems have simplified the procedures and show a further cost reduction.

In the summer of 1999, both systems were made available on the Internet. Once a broker is connected on a Web site, the information from an application is put into a computer, an underwriting decision is obtained, and a specific seller/servicer is identified to act as sponsor for the loan transaction. The Internet system has been approved by the major credit repositories for the transmission of credit reports. Thus, mortgage originators can receive credit data and an automated underwriting decision in a single process.

Freddie Mac's Loan Prospector

After some experimentation, Freddie Mac released its Loan Prospector program nationally on February 14, 1995. The program uses artificial intelligence to underwrite loans and assess creditworthiness. Freddie Mac made clear at the time that usage would be limited to its approved seller/servicers who are required to verify the data submitted.

The lender (who is the seller/servicer) must verify the applicant's employment, income, and assets. This information is put into Freddie Mac's automated computer system, which can produce an answer in a few minutes' time. Initial reports indicate that nearly half of all applicants can be automatically approved, which means they are "accepted." This means the loan can be purchased by Freddie Mac.

If the loan-to-value ratio is greater than 80 percent, then the application is forwarded to a private mortgage insurer chosen by the lender. All major mortgage insurers are represented on the Freddie Mac system.

Those applications not classified as "accepted" are labeled by the computer as either "refer" or "caution." Both categories are returned to the lender's underwriting department. "Refer" is given reasons why the loan has been referred to the lender for further information.

For applications classified as "caution," the referral indicates there are some serious reasons why the loan cannot be purchased. Loan Prospector does tell the lender where to focus additional underwriting.

Fannie Mae's Desktop Underwriter

In late April 1995, Fannie Mae released two programs to its seller/servicers. The basic program, called Desktop Underwriter, uses artificial intelligence and the Fannie Mae information from its seller/servicer guide to analyze loan applications. A second program, called Desktop Originator, is designed to allow an agent or a mortgage broker to take an application in a potential borrower's home with a laptop computer, relaying the information to the lender (seller/servicer).

Information on the loan and the applicant must come from the same form as used by Freddie Mac: the Uniform Residential Loan Application. The lender must verify the information and then submit it to Fannie Mae through its Desktop Underwriter. A response can be provided within 60 seconds on "approved" applicants. The lender is responsible for notifying the originator, who notifies the applicant.

In October 1997, Fannie Mae announced that it has completed the integration of two additional risk assessment systems to its Desktop Underwriter program. These are for jumbo loans and sub-prime loans. Fannie Mae now has a pilot program that allows lenders to obtain a loan purchase decision from GE Capital Mortgage Services on jumbo and nonstandard "A" credit (top-rated creditworthy applicants) mortgages by submitting an application to Desktop Underwriter. In addition, for sub-prime loans, it has completed integration of its Desktop Underwriter with Standard & Poor's LEVELS risk-management tool. The program is a loan-level econometric model of the rating agency's criteria for determining loan loss estimates and credit enhancement requirements for mortgage-backed securities.

In 1998 Fannie Mae added a third appraisal alternative with its newest version of Desktop Underwriter 4.0 to the two already accepted. Fannie Mae continues to improve the services offered and introduced Version 7 in May of 2008. The new version is designed to reduce the time of loan decisions to four minutes and to speed up the appraisal portion of the underwriting process.

Fannie Mae encourages lenders to use their automated electronic underwriting system, Desktop Underwriter (DU). It is designed to reduce the time involved in underwriting, as well as the cost. According to Fannie Mae, some lenders have reported savings of as much as $1,400 in underwriting costs.

The system uses a large basis of preprogrammed information and formulas to conduct a quantitative risk analysis, based upon the information the lender provides and three-bureau, merged-file credit reports. It allows the lender to complete a Web version of the Uniform Residential Loan Application, or to fill out a "Quick 1003," using a smaller set of data for a quick recommendation.

DU does not use FICO credit scores in its analysis. Since the technology that produces these scores is owned by Fair Isaac and Co., Fannie Mae cannot use them in compliance with its stated goal of informing applicants why their applications are accepted or rejected. Nevertheless, Fannie Mae encourages lenders to make use of FICO scores in evaluating an applicant's credit.

DU is designed to reduce the subjective element involved in underwriting loans. However, because it does not use FICO scores or consider extenuating circumstances, lenders who use DU still must consider loan applicants on a case-by-case basis.

Automatic Underwriting On the Internet

In June 1999, Fannie Mae made its automated underwriting system available on the Internet. Its Desktop Underwriter system is open to its seller/servicers and mortgage brokers can now access its Desktop Originator through Web sites. In July, Freddie Mac announced the release of its latest version of Loan Prospector on the Internet, allowing direct access to automatic underwriting by mortgage brokers and correspondents.

Once connected to a Web site, brokers will be able to input specific loan applications, obtain an underwriting decision, and identify a specific wholesale seller/servicer, with whom the broker has a relationship, to act as a sponsor for the loan transaction. The wholesaler would then handle the loan in a traditional manner.

Freddie Mac reports that its Loan Prospector system has been approved by all three major credit repositories for the transmission of credit reports via the Internet. This will allow mortgage originators to receive credit data and an automated underwriting decision in a single process. Paperwork involved has been further reduced for loans that meet the "accept" criteria. For these loans, borrowers will be required to submit only one W-2 form, one pay stub and one month's bank statement. Through mid- 2008, more than 40 million loans have been assessed by Loan Prospector.

Investment in Real Estate

Growth in stock market values has been a dominant factor in the economy of the 1990s. It has exceeded growth in housing values in most of the country. But to compare the values simply on a dollar basis overlooks the basic service performed by housing. Shelter is an obvious necessity of life and must be considered in any comparison of value. It is just more difficult to assess than dollar value.

In the commercial market for real estate, value has returned to a sound basis. In the 1980s, a psychological boom dominated the industry, perhaps encouraged by the impractical prices paid by the Japanese and others for real estate. In the 1990s, investors looked for a return on the dollar invested rather than a capital gain through speculative growth in property value. It is a far more practical approach.

Summary

Computerized loan origination is a method of transmitting loan application information from a computer in a real-estate agent or loan originator's office to a major lender. The lender's underwriter analyzes the information and can usually give an approval in a few days. This is called "manual" underwriting.

Automated underwriting systems use artificial intelligence to analyze loan applications. HUD has encouraged automated underwriting, because decisions made by computer are faster and less expensive, and also eliminate any potential bias. In 1995, both Freddie Mac and Fannie Mae implemented the use of computers for loan processing. Freddie Mac's underwriter is called Loan Prospector, and Fannie Mae's is called Desktop Underwriter. Both are now available on the Internet.

This concludes lesson fifteen.

Return to your online course player to take the Lesson Quiz.

Lesson 16:
1031 EXCHANGES

This lesson focuses on the following topics:

- Introduction
- Like Kind Property
- Capital Gains
- Simultaneous Exchanges
- Delayed Exchanges
- Qualified Intermediaries
- Three-Party Trades
- Reverse Exchanges
- Installment Sales
- Activity: Exchanging Numbers
- Case Study: Delayed Exchange
- Summary

By the end of this lesson, you should be able to:

- Define capital gains and discuss the consequences of taxes on real property and how taxes may affect decisions, especially for investment or business property
- Explain the purpose of Internal Revenue Code (IRC) Section 1031
- Define like kind and discuss what property qualifies for a like-kind exchange
- Distinguish between realized and recognized gain and explain how it is important to the tax laws
- Calculate an investor's adjusted basis in a property, and identify the relationship to boot
- Explain how boot is calculated
- Describe the different ways of doing 1031 exchanges, such as a simultaneous exchange and a delayed exchange
- Identify the role of the qualified intermediary (QI) as a safe harbor in the delayed exchange
- Explain the delayed (Starker) exchange format—the 45/180-day time limits and the rules for replacement property identification

- Explain the reverse exchange format, detailing the exchange accommodation titleholder (EAT), title parking, and describing allowable arrangements between the exchanger and the EAT
- Explain how an investor can leverage saved capital from tax-deferred exchanges, citing examples
- Explain the tax benefits of installment sales

Introduction

Real estate taxes can be expensive and should be included in the analysis of any purchase. This is especially true in the purchase and sale of investment property, where investors pay taxes on the capital gains they realize from the sale of their properties (although at a much lower rate than income tax rates). To alleviate the tax liability even further, Congress has passed Internal Revenue Code (IRC) Section 1031. Based upon the "continuity of investment" principle, the code allows an investor or business to sell investments and reinvest the proceeds in investments of like kind, deferring all capital gains taxes until the sale of the acquired investments. This process can go on indefinitely—that is, an acquired property can be relinquished to acquire a new property, which is then relinquished, and so on. For the purposes of the law, all business and investment real estate is treated as like kind property and thus may be "exchanged" under Section 1031.

Like Kind Property

IRC Section 1031 states that the words like kind "have reference to the nature or character of the property and not to its grade or quality." The nature or character of real estate is broadly construed by the law: Just as aircraft are of like kind to aircraft and gold coins are of like kind to gold coins, investment property is of like kind to investment property, whether it is improved or used in different ways (a strip mall vs. an apartment complex, for instance).

However, the law has certain requirements. In order for an exchange to qualify for tax deferral, the following must apply:

- Both the relinquished property and the replacement property must be in the United States.

- The relinquished property must be held by the exchanger for business or investment purposes, although the party acquiring it need not.

- The exchanger must intend to hold the replacement property for business or investment purposes, regardless of its prior use.

- The exchange must be conducted within the time limits established by the IRC and the Internal Revenue Service (IRS).

- The parties in the exchange may not be related (for example, mother and son, uncle and niece, or brother-in-law and brother-in-law).

- If either property is a vacation property, the exchanger may not use or have used it more than 14 days out of the year or 10 percent of the time that it is or was rented.

Capital Gains

A capital gain is the amount of money in excess of the original amount (the basis) invested in a property that an investor receives from the sale of a property.

Basis

The basis that a taxpayer has in a property is the figure used to calculate gain or loss in a transaction. It is essentially the cost to the taxpayer of obtaining and maintaining the property. If a taxpayer buys a property for $50,000 and makes $10,000 in capital improvements, his basis is $60,000, less depreciation. Supposing no depreciation, if that same taxpayer sells the property for $100,000, he or she has realized $40,000 in gain.

Since a taxpayer's basis is the figure used for calculating her or his gain or loss when a property is sold, it is never adjusted for appreciation. That is, if a taxpayer has a basis of $60,000 in a property that appreciates to $100,000 in value, his or her basis is still $60,000.

A taxpayer pays taxes on recognized gain. In a 1031 exchange, all gain (except for boot, discussed below) is deferred: That is, it is not recognized and the taxpayer does not pay taxes on it at the moment. However, when the replacement property is sold or when the replacement for the replacement is sold, the realized gain over all of the previous transactions is recognized and taxed.

The basis the taxpayer has in the replacement property is just the basis she or he had in the original property, if no boot is given or received. Thus, if a taxpayer exchanges a property in which he or she has a $60,000 basis, but which is valued at $100,000, for another property valued at $100,000, his or her basis in the new property is the original basis of $60,000.

Boot

Boot is anything of value an investor receives in an exchange other than the property. If the exchanger receives a distribution of a portion of the cash proceeds (known as cash boot) or if his or her debt amount is effectively reduced (known as mortgage boot), then she or he will have to report and pay taxes on the boot as capital gain.

For example, if a taxpayer exchanges a property in which she has $30,000 in equity for a property in which the previous owner had $20,000 in equity and she receives a $10,000 cash boot to balance the equity, she must recognize a $10,000 gain for tax purposes that calendar year. Likewise, if a taxpayer exchanges a property with $40,000 in loans still outstanding for one with $10,000 in loans, his or her total debt has effectively been reduced by a $30,000 mortgage boot, which is recognizable and taxable.

Boot also affects the basis a taxpayer has in the replacement property. Since the basis is the cost for the taxpayer to obtain and maintain the property, any boot given is added to the basis in the replacement property, and any boot received is subtracted from the basis.

Suppose an investor owns a property that cost her $25,000. In the next several years, she makes $12,000 in capital improvements to the property, and it depreciates $4,000. When the investor decides to exchange the property, it is valued at $75,000. She exchanges it for a property valued at $56,000 with $10,000 in loans still outstanding, and the other party pays cash boot for the difference. After the exchange, she makes $5,000 in improvements to the new property and pays off the loan. She sells the property for $82,000. How much in capital gains should she report?

The investor's basis in the relinquished property is the cost plus capital improvements, less depreciation, or:

$$\$25,000 + \$12,000 - \$4,000 = \$33,000$$

In the exchange, the other party gives cash boot for the difference of the equities in the two properties or:

$$\$75,000 - \$56,000 + \$10,000 = \$29,000$$

The investor receives this boot and conveys a $10,000 mortgage boot to the other party. The net boot received by the investor is thus:

$$\$29,000 - \$10,000 = \$19,000$$

She must report this amount as capital gains for the calendar year of the exchange. The new basis in the replacement property is then the old basis less the net boot received:

$$\$33,000 - \$19,000 = \$14,000$$

To this is added the $5,000 in capital improvements made to the replacement property, for a final basis of $19,000. The investor's gain when she sells the replacement property is the difference in her basis and the sale price of the property:

$$\$82,000 - \$19,000 = \$63,000$$

All this gain is recognized by the IRS in the year of the sale.

Simultaneous Exchanges

In a simultaneous exchange, the sale of the relinquished property and the purchase of the replacement property occur on the same day.

This type of exchange no longer has any inherent advantage for tax planning and, therefore, is used far less frequently than before. Some investors still try to accomplish simultaneous exchanges, primarily to avoid or reduce the payment of multiple closing fees or exchange fees to a facilitator. There is significant danger and legal exposure in this attempt, since many unforeseen events can cause the closing to be delayed on one of the properties, leaving the investor with a failed exchange and the obligation of taxes that would otherwise have been deferred.

Even if a simultaneous closing is anticipated, documenting the transaction as a delayed or deferred exchange is recommended to avoid difficulty, should closing of the replacement property be delayed for some reason.

Delayed Exchanges

The most common type of 1031 exchange is the delayed exchange, also known as the Starker exchange, after the famous court case that allowed it. In the delayed exchange, first the exchanger closes the sale of the relinquished property then identifies a replacement property or properties and, finally, purchases the replacement(s) with the proceeds from the earlier sale.

Delayed exchanges must occur within a time frame set by the IRS. The replacement property must be identified by the exchanger within 45 days of closing the first relinquished property. These identifications must be made in writing, signed by the exchanger, and delivered to a non disqualified party in the exchange (for disqualified parties, see the section on the qualified intermediary, below). Identifications can be revoked and new identifications made before the 45-day cutoff, but after that cutoff only identified properties may count as replacement properties for the purposes of tax deferral. Properties purchased before the cutoff are considered to be identified.

The exchanger can identify more than one property. In fact, the IRS provides specific guidelines on how properties can be identified. Each exchanger must choose one of the following rules for property identification:

The 3-Property Rule
The exchanger may identify up to three replacement properties, regardless of their fair-market value.

The 200% Rule
The exchanger may identify any number of properties, provided the sum of their fair market values is less than or equal to 200 percent of that of the relinquished property or properties.

The 95% Rule
The exchanger may identify any number of properties, provided he or she receives 95 percent of their fair-market value when the exchange is complete. (Remember that the exchanger need not acquire all of the identified properties).

The second time limit on 1031 exchanges is that the last replacement property must close no later than 180 days after the closing of the first relinquished property. If the federal tax due date falls before the 180th day, the tax due date becomes the new deadline for completion of the exchange, unless the exchanger files for an extension with the IRS.

Leverage
The principal benefit to the 1031 exchange, aside from tax savings, is the investor's ability to leverage the proceeds of a sale to acquire new property. Consider an example. Suppose that an investor holds a property whose market value is $500,000. When she purchased the property originally, she paid $375,000 for it, and it has since depreciated $75,000. So her adjusted basis in the property is:

$$\$375,000 - \$75,000 = \$300,000$$

And her total capital gains are:

$$\$500,000 - \$300,000 = \$200,000$$

Now, investors pay taxes both on their capital gains and on their recaptured depreciation. The amount of depreciation recovered is equal to the original purchase price of the property less the adjusted basis at the time of sale, if the property is sold for more than its original purchase price. If it sells for less, the recaptured depreciation is the final sale price less the adjusted basis at the time of sale. Properties sold at a loss (that is, for less than their adjusted bases) recover no depreciation. In this case, the investor's recaptured depreciation is:

$$\$375,000 - \$300,000 = \$75,000$$

However, an investor's gains are not taxed twice, once as recaptured depreciation and once again as capital gains. So an investor who realized $200,000 in capital gains, $75,000 of which was recaptured depreciation, would pay capital gains for only $200,000 − $75,000 = $125,000.

At the time of this writing, federal capital gains taxes are 15 percent, and taxes on recaptured depreciation are 25 percent. Investors in some states also must pay state capital gains taxes, which vary from state to state. (Texas has no capital gains tax.) Suppose that the investor has $150,000 in mortgage loans still outstanding at the sale of her property, which she intends to pay off with the proceeds of the sale. Let the state capital gains tax rate be 9 percent. The amount of money, therefore, that she has to leverage after the sale will be:

Sale price − Loans − Federal and State Capital Gains Taxes − Recaptured Depreciation
= $500,000 − $150,000 − (($125,000 × 0.15) + ($125,000 × 0.09)) − ($75,000 × 0.25)
= $500,000 − $150,000 − $30,000 − $18,750
= $301,250

In a 1031 exchange, however, the investor may defer both capital gains and recaptured depreciation taxes. Thus, the amount of money she has to leverage is

$$\$500,000 - \$150,000 = \$350,000$$

The difference is significant-$55,000-yet it is even more than it seems. Lenders are typically willing to lend 75 percent of the purchase price on a qualified real estate investment. In essence, this means a borrower can buy four times the amount of money he or she has to invest. If our investor does not defer her taxes, the maximum sale price of a property she can buy is $301,250 × 4 = $1,180,000. However, if she uses the 1031 exchange laws, she can purchase an investment worth $350,000 × 4 = $1,400,000 or $1.4 million—$195,000 more!

Qualified Intermediaries

Most exchanges occur with the help of a qualified intermediary (QI). The QI is a principal in the exchange who does not seek to acquire or relinquish property, other than to facilitate an exchange between the other principals. A QI is not required for any exchange that does not involve the selling of the exchanger's property (as in the rare two-party exchange, where two investors "swap" properties), but it is, however, required in all other exchanges.

The QI enters a transaction out of personal interest; the law requires that she or he not be a representative of the exchanging party. That is, the QI cannot be the exchanger's salesperson or broker, lawyer, accountant, or escrow officer (in the tax law, these are referred to as "disqualified parties"). He or she should not be related to the exchanger, either; the qualified intermediary seeks to profit himself, not the other principals in the exchange.

A good QI works closely with the other parties in the exchange. She or he should be an expert in the exchange process and be able to explain that process, advise the several parties involved and provide instructions to the escrow officer.

A qualified intermediary is the only IRS safe harbor for the delayed exchange. This means that exchanges involving a QI will not be scrutinized by the IRS, unless there is some further cause for such scrutiny.

Three-Party Trades

Certain exchanges, as mentioned above, do not require a qualified intermediary. One of these, the earliest form of exchange, was the two-party trade. In such a trade, neither property is sold: One investor deeds his property to another investor who in turn deeds his property to the first investor. Then, if there is a disparity in equity, the investor who "gains" will pay nondeferrable cash boot to the other party.

It is often difficult to conduct a two-party trade because it requires the two parties to want each other's property. There is enough case law, however, to justify a three-party exchange. These exchanges can be of three types, known as the Alderson exchange, the Baird exchange, and direct deeding, and as with a two-party trade, they do not require the use of a qualified intermediary.

The Alderson Exchange
In the 1963 Ninth Circuit court case Alderson v. Commissioner, the selling party, Alderson, had contracted with a buyer to sell their property. After contracting, Alderson found a property owned by a third party for which he desired to exchange the property under contract. The buyer then purchased the latter property with the money he would have used to buy Alderson's property, and exchanged it for Alderson's property. The court held that this was a valid means of exchanging, and thus no gain or loss was to be recognized in the transaction under Section 1031 of the Internal Revenue Code. Exchanges of this type are now known as Alderson, ABC, or reverse Missouri Waltz exchanges.

Alderson exchanges are conducted without the use of a qualified intermediary. For this reason, they have certain drawbacks. For instance, the buyer assumes liability for the property he or she purchases to exchange, without having interest in the property. If the original Seller's Disclosure failed to disclose, for example, certain hazardous waste information and the buyer does not recognize this before exchanging the property, she or he could be held liable for nondisclosure. Furthermore, if the selling party loses the ability to transfer title to the property being relinquished, the buyer is stuck with a property that he or she does not necessarily want. The Alderson exchange requires much faith on the part of both parties, and thus, may be less preferable than a delayed exchange through a qualified intermediary.

The Baird Exchange

Another format of the three-party exchange is known as the Baird exchange, after the case J.H. Baird Publishing Co. v. Commissioner. In the Baird exchange, the seller and buyer simultaneously exchange properties, and the seller sells the property he or she has received to a third party for cash. These exchanges are also known as ACB or Missouri Waltz exchanges.

The benefit to a buyer under the Baird format is that she or he does not have to pay capital gains taxes on the property he or she relinquishes. The seller, however, has to pay those taxes when she or he sells that property to the third party. This can be beneficial to the seller, in certain circumstances. For instance, if the properties exchanged were of roughly the same value, and the seller's adjusted basis in the property he or she exchanged was less than her or his adjusted basis in the property he or she received and sold, then the seller would pay less in capital gains taxes (that is, because the seller made less money technically, although not actually).

Baird exchanges suffer from similar drawbacks to those of Alderson exchanges. They, too, are conducted without the aid of a qualified intermediary. If a third party is not found, the seller in the Baird exchange may be stuck with a property he or she does not want. If the seller's adjusted basis in the property he or she receives is less than his or her adjusted basis in the one he or she relinquishes, the seller may wind up paying more capital gains taxes than if he or she had just sold the relinquished property. In such instances, the buyer will typically offer cash compensation for the seller's added taxes.

The Four-Party Exchange

The four-party exchange is a variation of the Baird exchange that occurs when the would-be seller of the exchange does not want to gain title to and sell the property of the buyer. A third party, known as an accommodator, buys the seller's property, exchanges it with the buyer for the buyer's property, and sells the buyer's property to a fourth party. This way, the seller in the exchange does not have to worry about the salability or condition of the buyer's property. Because of the use of an accommodator, this type of exchange is sometimes known as an accommodation exchange.

Direct Deeding

The third and final kind of three-party exchange is called direct deeding. In direct deeding, Party A transfers the title of his or her property to Party B, receiving no property or money from Party B. Party B then pays a third party, Party C, some cash amount. Party C then transfers title of her or his property to Party A. This is known as non sequential deeding, in contrast to the sequential deeding of a two-party transfer through a qualified intermediary. Because no party pays or deeds to another party who pays or deeds to him or her, this is sometimes known as a pot exchange.

Direct deeding has been in use only since 1990, when the IRS first allowed it in the place of sequential deeding. In sequential deeding, the deed is transferred to a qualified intermediary, who then transfers the deed to the receiving party, and this process is repeated for the second exchanged property. This leads to a total of four title transfers, compared with the two transfers of a direct deeding trade. Thus, the parties in a direct deeding exchange pay fewer title transfer fees and taxes. Moreover, this type of exchange eliminates the need for a qualified intermediary and, thus, the risk that an intermediary undertakes in the exchange. It is up to the parties involved to decide whether these benefits outweigh the benefits of having the security and expertise of a qualified intermediary.

Reverse Exchanges

Title Parking

A reverse 1031 exchange is like a delayed exchange, except that the replacement property is acquired before the exchanger relinquishes any property. It is, in essence, the delayed exchange in reverse. The reverse exchange is difficult to complete because the IRS requires that the exchanger not have title to both the replacement property and the property to be relinquished, if taxes are to be deferred.

The primary issue to contend with was the problem of "constructive ownership." Technically, the parking entity had to pass the "burdens and benefits of ownership test" to prove that he or she truly owned the property, rather than just possessed bare legal title. The fear was that if the taxpayer were to retain all of the burdens and benefits of ownership, while mere legal title was parked, the taxpayer would be treated as the owner of the replacement property, and the point of parking would be defeated. The test, established in Grodt & McKay Realty v. Commissioner, deemed that a taxpayer will be considered to have taken on the burdens and benefits of ownership if and only if he or she:

- Possesses legal title
- Has an equity interest in the property
- Is vested with the right of possession

- Receives profits from the operation or sale of the property
- Pays property taxes
- Bears the risk of damage or loss to the property

As you can well imagine, ensuring that the parking entity had undertaken the benefits and burdens of ownership and finding an entity that would be willing to do so could be rather difficult. On top of that, the reverse exchange had not, at that point, been validated by the IRS. The need for guidelines and procedures to perform a valid, tax-free reverse exchange led the IRS to release Revenue Procedure 2000-37 on September 15, 2000, which provides a safe harbor for investors.

The procedure outlined in 2000-37 involves a new entity, called an exchange accommodation titleholder (EAT, or sometimes just AT) and an agreement, the qualified exchange accommodation agreement (QEAA).

The Exchange Accommodation Titleholder

The exchange accommodation titleholder (EAT) operates in the reverse exchange in a manner similar to the qualified intermediary's role in the delayed exchange. That is, the EAT's job is to purchase and hold title to a property the exchanger desires with the intent of facilitating a property exchange between the buyer and another party. Like the qualified intermediary, the EAT must be a qualified party (not a representative such as an accountant or broker). Unlike a qualified intermediary, however, the EAT is, for all intents and purposes, the buyer. He or she determines the conditions for closing the sale with the exchanger and takes on the benefits and burdens of ownership, save the following (as set forth in Revenue Procedure 2000-37):

- The EAT need not have an equity investment in the property.
- The EAT need not guarantee loans undertaken in the transaction (that is, the exchanger may guarantee the loans).
- The EAT need not take on liability for damages, loss, costs, or other expenses involved with holding the property.
- The EAT need not profit from a sale of the property and transfer of title to the exchanger.

The Qualified Exchange Accommodation Agreement

Revenue Procedure 2000-37 requires the exchanger to sign a contract with the EAT, called a qualified exchange accommodation arrangement (QEAA). The procedure sets forth the following conditions for a safe harbor reverse Starker exchange:

- The EAT must have what are termed qualified indicia of ownership. These include such things as holding legal title or other applicable principals of ownership, such as a contract for deed. Further, the EAT must be subject to federal income tax. Indicia of ownership must be maintained at all times until the property is transferred as described in section 4.02(5) of the revenue procedure.

- The taxpayer must have bona fide intent that the property held by the EAT be either the replacement or the relinquished property in an exchange that is intended to qualify for un recognition of gain (in whole or in part) under Section 1031.

- The taxpayer and the EAT must enter into the QEAA no later than five days after the transfer of qualified indicia of ownership to the EAT. The QEAA must state that the EAT is holding title for the benefit of the taxpayer in order to complete an IRC Section 1031 under this Revenue Procedure and that the taxpayer and EAT agree to report the acquisition, holding, and disposition of the property. In addition, the agreement must state that both parties will be treated as the beneficial owner for tax purposes and report it as such on its tax returns.

- In the event that the replacement property is held by the EAT, the taxpayer must identify within 45 days the property to be relinquished. If EAT holds the relinquished property, the taxpayer must identify the replacement property within 45 days. This must be done in accordance with the multiple property identification rules in Section 1031.

- The EAT must transfer the property it holds within 180 days of the date of acquisition to either the taxpayer (in the event EAT held the replacement property) or the buyer (in the event the EAT held the relinquished property).

- The combined period of time during which the relinquished property and the replacement property are held cannot exceed 180 days.

Permissible Agreements

The following agreements are permissible arrangements between the EAT and the taxpayer, many of which provide significant elbow room for both parties and allow the EAT to remain relatively uninvolved in the management and ownership of the property.

- The EAT may act as both the qualified intermediary and the EAT, provided that he or she satisfies the qualified intermediary safe harbor provisions.

- The taxpayer may guarantee all or part of the obligations of the EAT including debt and incurred expenses.

- The taxpayer may lend or advance funds to the EAT.

- The EAT may lease the property to the taxpayer, either with a rent or rent free.

- The EAT may enter into a management agreement with the taxpayer.

- The taxpayer may act as contractor and/or supervisor with respect to the property.

- The EAT and the taxpayer may enter into agreements using puts and calls at fixed or formula prices for subsequent dispositions.

Installment Sales

The tax laws also allow sellers to defer portions of capital gains taxes on installment sales. For tax purposes, installment sales are any sales that involve payment in installments extending into another tax year. This can result in a taxpayer paying fewer taxes when:

- The taxpayer remains in the same tax bracket. This is because, as time goes on, inflation causes money to lose value. The taxpayer may pay the same amount, but that amount is worth less than if she or he had paid it in the year of sale.

- The taxpayer moves into a lower tax bracket.

However, if the taxpayer moves into a higher tax bracket, he or she will have to pay more taxes on the installment method. Thus, the IRS allows taxpayers to opt out of the installment method and pay all of their capital gains taxes upfront or, at any time, to pay the remaining capital gains taxes.

To calculate the taxes due during each payment period, the taxpayer must first calculate her or his gross profit percentage. This is the percentage that the gross profit is of the sale price. To find gross profit, use the following formulas:

Gross Profit = Sale Price − Adjusted Basis − Recaptured Depreciation

For example, suppose an investor purchases a property for $50,000, which depreciates to $40,000 when he sells it for $65,000. The investor's gross profit is then:

$65,000 − $40,000 − $10,000 = $15,000

The gross profit percentage is $15,000 ÷ $65,000 = 23.08%

Once the investor determines his profit percentage, he can determine how much of each payment counts as taxable gains. This is done with the following formula:

Taxable Gain = Gross Profit Percentage × (Payment Amount − Interest)

Thus, in our example above, if the seller receives a payment of $800, $200 of which is interest, his taxable gain on the payment is

$$0.2308 \times (\$800 - \$200) = \$138.48$$

So, if the seller pays a 28 percent tax on capital gains, he will pay 0.28 × $138.48 = $38.77.

Activity: Exchanging Numbers

1. In 1996, Investor X paid market value for Property A based upon a cap rate analysis. If X's desired cap rate was 8 percent and the net operating income (NOI) of Property A was $24,000, how much was the sale price?

2. In order to purchase the property, X needed to finance 75 percent of it. What was the size of the loan she obtained?

3. It is now 2006, and X has held Property A for exactly 10 years. Assuming a straight-line depreciation of 2.564 percent annually, how much value has the property lost through depreciation?

4. If the present value of all capital improvements that the investor made to the property (after they, too, have been depreciated) is $28,750, what is her adjusted basis?

5. Property A's original NOI was $24,000. If this income increased at a rate of 12.6 percent annually, what is the property's current NOI?

6. Investor X wants to use a delayed exchange to sell Property A and purchase Property B. If current demand has determined an 8 percent cap rate and Property A has an NOI of $30,240, what is its market value?

7. Suppose Investor X sells Property A for its market value of $378,000. Her adjusted basis in the property was $251,830. How much does the investor realize in capital gains?

8. The original purchase price of Property A was $300,000, its final selling price was $378,000 and Investor X's adjusted basis is $251,830. How much is the investor's recaptured depreciation?

9. Given realizations of $126,170 in capital gains and $48,170 in recaptured depreciation, and 15 percent and 25 percent taxes respectively, what amount of taxes is deferred in the exchange (provided all taxes are indeed deferred)?

10. Investor X can receive a loan of up to four times the capital she has to invest. If she sells Property A for $378,000 and has a $104,678.50 mortgage balance, what is the maximum sale price she can afford?

11. If the investor wants to purchase a property for the maximum she can afford, $1,093,286, and she desires an 8 percent capitalization rate, what annual NOI would the property have to have?

12. Investor X used the proceeds from the sale of Property A to pay off her outstanding mortgage balance of $104,678.50. Does she receive mortgage boot in the exchange?

Answers

1. Value = NOI ÷ Cap Rate = $24,000 ÷ 0.08 = $300,000

2. 0.75 × Sale Price = 0.75 × $300,000 = $225,000

3. Depreciation = Rate × Time × Original Value = 0.02564 × 10 × $300,000 = $76,920

4. Adjusted Basis = Purchase Price + Capital Improvements − Depreciation = $300,000 + $28,750 − $76,920 = $251,830

5. Current NOI = Original NOI × Rate × Time = $24,000 × 0.126 × 10 = $30,240

6. Value = NOI ÷ Cap Rate = $30,240 ÷ 0.08 = $378,000

7. Capital Gain = Sale price − Adjusted Basis = $378,000 − $251,830 = $126,170

8. If the final selling price is greater than the original purchase price, Recaptured Depreciation = Purchase Price − Adjusted Basis = $300,000 − $251,830 = $48,170

9. Taxes Deferred = (Capital Gain × 0.15) + (Recaptured depreciation × 0.25) = ($78,000 × 0.15) + ($48,170 × 0.25) = $11,700 + $12,042.50 = $23,742.50

10. Maximum Sale Price = 4 × (Capital from Sale − Mortgage Balance) = 4 × ($378,000 − $104,678.50) = 4 × $273,321.50 = $1,093.286

11. NOI = Value × Cap Rate = $1,093,286 × 0.08 = $87,462.88

12. Mortgage boot is defined as a net decrease in one's total mortgage debt. Since the investor takes on a greater mortgage debt (three-quarters of $1,093,286) than that she paid off, no boot is received in the exchange, and thus all taxes are deferred

Case Study: Delayed Exchange

An investor holds a parcel of real estate worth $280,000, which he desires to exchange for several other properties to diversify his holdings. He has a few replacement properties in mind, but he does not want to go through the risky business of conducting a simultaneous exchange. He contacts a firm that acts as the qualified intermediary in like kind exchanges because the transaction he plans to conduct involves the sale of the relinquished property and because a qualified intermediary is the only safe harbor recognized by the IRS for a delayed exchange.

He closes the sale of his property on June 29. In the sales contract, he included a Like Kind Property Exchange Addendum, (1) to establish his intent to conduct a like kind exchange under IRC Section 1031, (2) to state that there is no expense or liability that the buyer will incur and (3) to permit the assignment of the contract to the QI. The investor provides this contract to the QI, who prepares the Exchange and Escrow Account Agreement, the Assignment of Contract, and the Notification of Assignment. The QI then contacts the settlement attorney and gives her specific instructions regarding the closing process. The property sells for its fair-market value of $280,000, and closing costs run the investor about $20,000. This leaves him with $260,000 in equity to invest in replacement properties. These funds are deposited in the escrow account that the QI has set up for the exchange.

The investor must identify all of the properties he plans to use in the exchange before the end of the 45-day identification period. He wants to purchase several single-family rental properties across town. The properties he is currently considering are the following:

- A two-story house at 917 Maple Lane-Asking price: $88,000

- A large house with an above-ground pool at 6010 Sunny Terrace-Asking price: $160,000

- A fixer-upper at 1205 Main St-Asking price: $75,000

- A beautiful townhouse at 1314 W 35th St-Asking price: $156,000

- A condo on 9th Street-Asking price: $95,000

The investor, obviously, can't use the 3-Property Rule for identification, because he is considering five properties. He also can't use the 200% Rule, because the total fair-market value of all the properties is $574,000, which is 205% of the fair-market value of the relinquished property. Thus, he is constrained by the 95% rule and must receive at least 95% of the fair-market value of the five properties by the end of the 180-day period.

When the investor identifies these properties, he does so in writing, using their legal descriptions, and gives the identification to the QI. The investor makes his identifications on July 18, leaving him 160 days to purchase the properties.

Conceivably, the investor can receive loans to purchase each of the replacement properties. Assuming a 75 percent LTV, he has $160,000 × 4 = $640,000 to spend. The fair-market value of all of the properties, however, is only $574,000. He estimates that he will pay about $7,000 in closing costs for each property, for a total of 5 × $7,000 = $35,000. He also plans to make about $15,000 in capital improvements to the house on Main Street. He can count this toward the exchange value of the property as an Improvement Exchange. The total available to him being $640,000, and his total investment being $624,000, this still gives him room to take out loans with a slightly lower LTV or to make capital improvements to the other properties.

Summary

To allow investors to exchange their current holdings for other assets without incurring significant tax liabilities from capital gains and recaptured depreciation taxes, IRC Section 1031 provides specific guidelines for tax-deferred like kind exchanges. Under the law, two properties are of like kind if they have the same nature or character. Thus all real estate is considered to be of like kind, although 1031 exchanges are limited to property held for business or investment and are exclusive of noncommercial residential property.

In a sale, capital gains are the amount an investor receives in excess of his or her adjusted basis in the property. The basis is, in essence, the amount of money an investor has put into a property (its purchase price plus the cost of any improvements) less depreciation. An investor's basis in a replacement property is just her or his basis in the just relinquished property. When an exchanger receives something of value other than property in the exchange, this is known as boot. If it is money, it is called cash boot; if it is a reduction in a loan amount, it is called mortgage boot. Any actual gain an investor receives is realized gain, although only recognized gain is taxed. The 1031 exchange laws allow an investor to defer recognition of all non boot capital gains and recaptured depreciation until the sale of the replacement property.

The most common type of 1031 exchange is the delayed exchange. Here, the investor sells the relinquished property before he or she purchases a replacement (as opposed to at the same time or afterward). The law provides strict conditions on how a delayed exchange may be accomplished. The exchanger must identify all of the replacement properties no later than 45 days after the sale of the relinquished property and may delay purchasing all the properties for which she or he is exchanging no later than 180 days. The law also limits the identification of replacements and provides three rules that the exchanger may use.

The tax benefit of the 1031 exchange is linked to its most important benefit: greater leverage. By deferring recognition of gain, investors have more capital and thus can receive larger loans. Based upon a typical 75 percent LTV, investors have four times the amount of deferred taxes to invest in a replacement property or properties.

Most exchanges are conducted with the aid of a qualified intermediary (QI). QIs are non disqualified parties through which the titles to both the replacement and relinquished properties pass. They are recognized by the IRS as the only safe harbor in the delayed exchange, meaning that exchanges conducted with the aid of a QI will not be scrutinized by the IRS unless there is some further cause for such scrutiny. QIs are not required in any exchange that does not involve the selling of the exchanger's property, which include two-party trades, Alderson exchanges, Baird exchanges and direct deeding.

Another popular, although slightly more difficult, exchange is the reverse exchange. This occurs when the exchanger acquires the replacement property before he or she relinquishes any property. This can be difficult because the exchanger is not allowed to hold title to both properties. For this reason, most of these exchanges are conducted under the safe harbor of Revenue Procedure 2000-37. This procedure requires the use of an exchange accommodation titleholder (EAT, or sometimes just AT), who has a certain contract, called a qualified exchange accommodation agreement (QEAA), with the exchanger. In short, the EAT holds title to either the relinquished or replacement property during the exchange, allowing the exchanger to use it in accordance with the QEAA. A list of allowable arrangements between the exchanger and the EAT is set forth in Revenue Procedure 2000-37.

This concludes lesson sixteen.

Return to your online course player to take the Lesson Quiz.

Lesson 17:
CONTRACTS

This lesson focuses on the following topics:

- Introduction
- Types of Contracts
- Implied Contracts
- Express Contracts
- Bilateral Contracts
- Unilateral Contracts
- Executed Contracts
- Executory Contracts
- Valid Contracts
- Void Contracts
- Voidable Contracts
- Unenforceable Contracts
- Legally Valid Contracts Overview
- Mutual Assent
- Legally Competent Parties
- Consideration
- Lawful Objective
- Adherence to Statute of Frauds
- Contract Performance Overview
- Performance of a Contract
- Non-Performance of a Contract
- Contracts Overview
- Legal Forms
- Sales Contracts
- Listing Agreements
- Option Agreements
- Contract-For-Deed Agreements
- Leases
- Insight into Contracts, Purchase Agreements, and Sales Agreements
- The Statute of Limitations
- The Uniform Commercial Code
- Promulgated Contract Forms

- Contracts for Deed
- Activity
- Contracts, Purchase Agreements, and Sales Agreements Field Applications
- Summary

By the end of this lesson, you should be able to:

- Identify the differences among the various types of contracts
- Know the three elements of a contract
- Identify the five components of a legally enforceable contract
- Discern between valid, void, voidable, and unenforceable contracts
- Explain the different types of contract performance
- Apply the laws, doctrines, and statutes that govern real estate contracts, including the Uniform Commercial Code and the Statute of Limitations
- Distinguish the differences among the different types of real estate contracts
- Recall the important elements of leases and listing agreements
- Recognize and complete the forms promulgated by TREC
- Explain the key differences between contracts for deed and other real estate contracts
- List and describe government clauses required in certain contracts
- Apply the knowledge gained from this course to complete a contracts activity

Introduction

Real estate professionals expend a great deal of effort on listings. Obtaining, showing and selling listings occupy much of any licensee's working time. Because these listings are so important to a successful licensee, it would be unfortunate if a transaction fell through because of a misunderstanding or uncertainty surrounding an agreement to buy or sell a listing.

To avoid these problems, licensees should make an effort to understand contracts, which are the legally binding agreements that prevent such misunderstandings and uncertainties in real estate transactions. Clear, mutually acceptable agreements are an essential component of the legal transference of ownership, and contracts are the instruments by which such agreements are legalized in real estate transactions.

Parties who are entering into an agreement regarding ownership or other kinds of interest in real estate need a contract because it establishes the terms of the agreement in clear and comprehensible language. It allows the parties to understand their role in their agreement and to know what is expected of them. If either party disputes the agreement, the parties should be able to use the contract to resolve any confusion. A well defined and comprehensive contract establishes the facts of the agreement in mutually accepted terms, and it can often prevent the parties from having to go to court to resolve their conflicts.

Both parties are liable for carrying out the terms of the contract—that is, they are obligated to perform (or refrain from performing) any actions required by a legally valid contract which they have signed or otherwise accepted. Because contracts create obligations that can be legally enforced, it is extremely important both parties understand and accept *all* of the stipulations in any contractual agreement. This requires they understand the different types of contracts that exist (so they know what options they have); they should also be able to recognize the basic components of a legally valid contract, so they can tell whether a given contract will have the legal effects it should.

Because contracts serve many purposes, they take many forms. This lesson will focus on those that are most commonly involved in real estate transactions, though the lesson will also provide a more general discussion of the various types of contracts that exist. For example, legally valid contracts can be written or oral. Another perhaps surprising fact about contracts is that (depending upon the intent of the agreement) a contract can require action on the part of all the contracting parties or it can impose obligations on only one of the contracting parties.

Because of the variety of contracts and the important differences between them, it is prudent for the contracting parties to consult with knowledgeable professionals who can help guide them through the process of choosing and accepting a contract. This lesson will examine these issues and other related topics as we consider the following types of contracts.

Types of Contracts

This first lesson discusses the general types of contracts available along with their purposes and differences. Contracts take on specific forms in order to carry out specific purposes and can be as simple or as complicated as a situation may require. Contracts do not always have to be written and signed. A strictly oral or implied contract can be just as legally binding as a written contract.

Contracts can require the action of all the parties involved or merely the action of one party along with just the acceptance of the one party's action from the other parties. The real estate industry relies heavily on certain types of contracts which facilitate the tasks at hand. It is wise to acquire the consultation of a professional who can guide all parties involved through the process of choosing, writing, and accepting a contract catering to their needs.

Note: Oral contracts are established when the offeror states the offer and the offeree accepts the offer. In an oral contract, there are no formal or written documents spelling out the terms and conditions of their agreement. Instead, each party relies on the word of the other. Oftentimes, oral contracts are called verbal contracts in everyday speech. The term "verbal" simply means "in words." This would make all contracts verbal contracts, regardless of whether they are written or spoken. For legal purposes it is best to use the term "oral contract" (meaning a *spoken* agreement) when we want to identify a contract that is not recorded in writing.

Implied Contracts

Implied contracts are inferred from the actions of various parties, but are not necessarily written or spoken. Even though these contracts are established by the parties' conduct rather than a written document or an explicit discussion, they can have all of the legally binding power of more explicit contracts.

For implied contracts to be legally enforceable there must be an exchange of promises. One party offers money, services, property rights, etc., in exchange for something else of value. Implied contracts have an offer and acceptance which are simply understood and not explicitly spoken or written.

Examples of Implied Contracts

- When individuals visit their doctor for an examination, they generally expect to pay for the exam at the end of the visit. It is the general social conventions surrounding medical practices combined with an individual's acceptance of the doctor's services which create an implied contract between doctor and patient. The patient owes the doctor compensation for services rendered.
- When an individual dines at a restaurant, orders food, and eats it, she or he creates an implied contract with the restaurant. The individual is expected to compensate the restaurant for the meal.
- When an individual takes a taxi cab to one's destination, this creates an implied contract with the cab driver. The passenger must compensate the cab driver for the transportation provided.

Note: Social conventions play a large role in creating implied contracts. To avoid errors, oversights, and misunderstandings from an individual not familiar with a specific service, many individuals take steps to spell out the terms of implied contracts. Taxi cab drivers post rates on the windows of their taxi cab. Restaurants post prices on their menus. This makes it clear services are for sale, not a gift.

Real estate licensees should not let any aspect of their services be defined by an implied contract. Implied contracts do not help avoid errors, oversights, and misunderstandings of an agreement with individuals outside the real estate industry. Implied contracts are likely to be a source of confusion. For example: A licensee can show prospective clients many properties and not be their real estate agent.

Express Contracts

Express contracts are oral and written contracts in which the parties explicitly state, or "express," their intentions and their expectations regarding the contract. They stand in contrast to implied contracts where the existence of a contract (and the nature of its terms) is inferred from the parties' conduct.

If one party deviates from the agreed-upon terms of an express contract, the injured party can seek damages and legal recourse. Express contracts essentially serve as a reference in the event of errors, oversights, and misunderstandings. An express contract best serves as a reference when it is written.

Example of Express Contracts

- A lease agreement is an express contract in which both the lessee (tenant) and the lessor (landlord) sign the agreement. If the lessee fails to uphold the terms in the lease, then the lessee is subject to the conditions set forth in the lease agreement concerning such violation. Most written leases explicitly state the penalties (such as late fees or eviction), for violations (such as non-payment of rent), which provide prospective tenants and landlords an opportunity to see and consider all terms before accepting a lease.

Bilateral Contracts

This is an agreement in which both parties give consideration and promise to perform the actions specified in a contract. This kind of contract creates reciprocal obligations, in which each party is mutually obliged to the other.

Examples of Bilateral Contracts

- In a bilateral contract, Party A must promise to do something for Party B and Party B must promise to do something for Party A. This contract obligates both parties to fulfill certain terms. To satisfy or complete a bilateral contract, all parties involved must carry out their promises.

- In a real estate transaction, the buyer (Party A) promises to pay the seller (Party B) the agreed-upon price and the seller (Party B) promises to transfer the property title to the buyer (Party A). There are thus specific things both of them must do before the contract can be considered complete. If the buyer pays the seller, but the seller does not transfer the title, then the contract is not complete and the buyer can seek legal recourse against the seller for failing to honor the obligations imposed by the contract.

Unilateral Contracts

This is a contract made between two or more parties in which only one of those parties makes a promise or otherwise accepts an obligation. In short, this is a contract in which only one of the contracting parties is bound to act.

Examples of Unilateral Contracts

- In a unilateral contract, Party A makes a commitment and Party B accepts this commitment. This contract is completed or fulfilled when Party A has carried out the commitment. There is nothing Party B *must* do to execute such a contract. Party A does not have to agree to the contract openly or explicitly. Instead, Party A agrees to the contract by carrying out the action specified in the contract.

- A broker promises to pay a $1,000 bonus to any salesperson who brings in 10 new listings, not knowing who will bring or will not bring 10 new listings. This does not obligate a salesperson to anything. The broker unilaterally agrees to give $1,000 to any salesperson who satisfies the set performance standards. No salesperson in the office has to agree to anything but may collect on the promise if he or she chooses.

Executed Contracts

This is a pre-existing contract in which all terms have been fulfilled by all parties. There are many kinds of contracts, but all contracts become an executed contract once all parties have completed their contractual obligations.

When a contract is fulfilled, then it is executed, or ceases to exist. It has no further legal power to bind any of the parties and is not considered to have any meaningful legal existence.

Example of Executed Contracts
A buyer pays a seller the agreed price for an agreed property and the seller has transferred the title to the buyer. If there are no further stipulations in their particular contract, then they have an executed contract.

Executory Contracts

This is a contract which is not completely executed or performed. The terms are not fully carried out or are in the process of being carried out by one or more parties in the agreement. Usually, executory contracts are created when one party fulfills his or her end of the agreement, but the other party has not yet fulfilled her or his part of the agreement.

Example of Executory Contracts
A broker promises to pay the top salesperson $5,000 at the end of the year. The broker does not pay anyone this bonus at the year's end. The broker and the top salesperson have an executory contract, where the salesperson has fulfilled one end of the contract, but the broker has not fulfilled his or her promise.

Valid Contracts

Valid contracts are legal agreements meeting all the essential, basic requirements of the law. They accurately reflect the contracting parties' intentions making them legally binding and legally enforceable for all parties involved.

The five components of a valid contract are:

- Mutual assent
- Legally competent parties
- Consideration
- Lawful objective
- Adherence to a statute of frauds

Void Contracts

This is a contract failing to meet the legal requirements defining a valid contract. A void contract is not legally enforceable against any of the contracting parties. It is a contract in name only. All contracts have the potential to become void contracts, because all contracts can be invalidated if they involve minors, mentally incompetent individuals, misrepresentation, fraud, or illegal actions.

Example of Void Contracts
If Party A and Party B enter into a contract, but the fulfillment of the contract involves an illegal activity, the contract is void, that is either the parties to the contract or terms of the contract have rendered it void. The contract was not valid in the first place.

Voidable Contracts

This is a valid contract structured so it can be terminated or rescinded by either party. Voidable contracts specifically permit one or both parties to opt out of an agreement under specific reasons, often having to do with non-performance of some or all terms of the contract.

Example of Voidable Contracts
A seller agrees to deliver a valid title clear of any financial obligations to the buyer. Their contract specifically states the buyer can opt out of the agreement with no legal consequences if such conditions are not met. The buyer discovers a lien has been placed on the title. The voidable contract now permits the buyer to invalidate the contract and walk away without facing legal repercussions, because the seller failed to produce the kind of title required in the contract.

Unenforceable Contracts

This is a *valid* contract which cannot be enforced legally due to a technicality or it contradicts a state's legislation.

The most common reasons a valid contract becomes unenforceable are:

Statute of Frauds
A state law establishing the features of a valid contract. The law generally requires certain types of contracts to be set out in writing and written contracts be signed by all the parties bound by the contract.

Statute of Limitations

A state's statute of limitations is a law establishing a time limit for civil suits, setting a maximum period of time to elapse between the dates an injury occurs or the basis for a legal claim is discovered and the date a civil lawsuit is filed. There are also federal statutes setting maximum time limits regarding federal crimes and suits filed in federal courts. All claims must be filed prior to the statutory deadline or the legal right to press a claim is barred.

Doctrine of Laches

The doctrine of laches is a principle that courts use to bar dated claims. Under this doctrine, unreasonable delay or negligence in asserting or defending one's rights can create a legal bar to equitable relief if a delay or negligence has importantly influenced the conduct of the person responsible for the violation.

Note: Licensees should acquaint themselves with the specific requirements set out in their state's statutes, because there are frequently subtle differences between one state's statutes compared to another state's statutes.

Examples of Unenforceable Contracts

- The statute of limitations for collecting a returned check is three years. If Party A does not file suit or take action to collect Party B's debt within three years (that is, within the amount of time allotted by the statute of limitations), then the contract in the form of a personal check between Party A and Party B becomes unenforceable. This is not because the contract fails to meet any of the legal requirements for validity, but the time period in which the contract must be enforced has expired.

- Person A has a legitimate claim against her old firm for sexual harassment. She waits many years to file her claim, but is still within the statute of limitations. During those many years she waited, the alleged harasser has passed away and all witnesses have moved. Person A does not have a reasonable explanation for her delay in filing the claim. The courts deny her claim under the doctrine of laches, as she has no explanation for the delay in filing her claim. A trial cannot be held without the accused harasser, evidence, or witnesses. In this case, Person A receives no legal relief on a valid claim still within the statute of limitations due to her negligence in filing her claim within a reasonable time period.

Legally Valid Contracts Overview

A legally valid contract is an agreement meeting all essential, basic requirements of the law reflecting the contracting parties' intentions, making it legally binding and legally enforcing for all parties. If a contract is not legally valid, other facts in or about the contract are unimportant because it ceases to legally exist.

Mutual Assent

A major requirement for a legally valid contract is mutual assent. This requires all the contracting parties to agree to *all* of the contract's provisions and conditions. Parties can indicate their agreement to a contract's provisions and conditions via actions and/or words.

Mutual assent requires:

- An offer and an acceptance
    - A counteroffer to the original offer can exist
    - Acceptance of the original offer is not required
- The absence of fraud, misrepresentation, or duress
- The absence of mistakes

Example of Mutual Assent

A buyer offers to purchase a seller's property for a mutually agreed upon price of $50,000. Both the seller and buyer agree to this price. The seller transfers the title to buyer, and the buyer places a down payment on the property. The seller and buyer show mutual agreement to their real estate contract through their actions.

Offer and Acceptance

When making an offer it is important to remember:

- The offeror is the person extending the contract.
- The offeree is the person accepting the contract.

An offer remains open until it:

- Is accepted
- Is rejected
- Is retracted prior to acceptance

Example: The offeror can revoke the offer at any time whether the offeree technically accepted the offer or not.

- Is countered
- Expires

There are three types of acceptance:

- Express acceptance
    - Is a candid and unqualified outward manifestation of an agreement
    - Is such as: "Yes, I agree to your offer."
- Implied acceptance
    - Is when the parties bound by the contract *act* in a manner implying acceptance of the offer
    - Is expressed when all parties involved act out the contract's obligations instead of openly stating an agreement or acceptance
- Conditional acceptance
    - Requires a specific condition to be satisfied or an event to take place before acceptance of the contract
    - Can be viewed as a counteroffer
    - Is such as: "I will buy this shirt if you give me a 20% discount."

Example of Offer and Acceptance
A seller advertises that a property is selling for $250,000. A buyer contacts the seller by phone and verbally accepts the terms of his offer of $250,000 for the title to the property. The seller accepts the money and gives the buyer the title to the property. The buyer accepts the title to the property and gives the seller $250,000. The contract is signed, the money is deposited into the seller's account, and the title is transferred into the buyer's name.

Question 1
What is the offer in this example?

Answer
The seller offering the property for $250,000 represents the offer.

Question 2
What is the acceptance in this example?

Answer
The buyer expressly accepts the offer when he calls him on the phone.

Question 3
You would consider this to be what type of contract?

a. Bilateral contract

b. Unilateral contract

c. Voidable contract

Answer

A unilateral contract is made between two or more parties in which only one of those parties makes a promise or otherwise accepts an obligation. In short, this is a contract in which only one of the contracting parties is bound to act. Therefore, this is not a unilateral contract.

A voidable contract is a valid contract structured so it can be terminated or rescinded by either party. Voidable contracts specifically permit one or both parties to opt out of an agreement under specific reasons often having to do with non-performance such as a prenuptial agreement. Therefore, this is not a voidable contract.

A bilateral contract is when both parties give consideration and promise to perform the actions specified in a contract. This kind of contract creates reciprocal obligations, in which each party is mutually obliged to the other. Given the three options, this is a bilateral contract. It can also be considered an express contract.

Counteroffers

Counteroffers are attempts to find mutually acceptable contract terms. The counteroffer is a modification of the terms the offeree does not agree to and are presented to the offeror as a modified contract. An offer is considered to be rejected if the offeree makes changes to the offer. A new offer (the counteroffer) is now on the table.

Example of Counteroffers

The seller advertises a property is selling for $250,000. A buyer contacts the seller and offers him a counteroffer of $225,000 for the property. The seller tells the buyer he is considering the offer. The buyer states to the seller the offer will be revoked in two weeks. The seller has two weeks to make a decision.

The seller has the following options:

- To accept the offer by
    - Express acceptance
    - Implied acceptance
    - Conditional acceptance
- To reject the offer by
    - Allowing the offer to expire
    - Verbally rejecting the offer

The buyer can:

- Wait until the offer is accepted
- Wait until the offer is rejected
- Retract the offer prior to acceptance
- Wait until the offer is countered
- Wait until the offer expires

Fraud and Misrepresentation

Contracts involving fraud, misrepresentation, or duress create a situation in which the parties involved are unable to make a free, fully informed decision about the agreement.

Fraud is intentional misrepresentation or concealment of significant facts. Fraud includes false statements, false promises, and intentional failure to disclose important information resulting in losses for other parties.

Misrepresentation means to give a false or misleading representation of; usually with intent to deceive or be unfair.

Note: Innocent misrepresentation is not fraud. Innocent misrepresentation occurs when an individual provides incorrect information, but does not intentionally deceive another person. For example, suppose a buyer visits a seller's home and notices a hiking trail behind the property. The seller speaks highly of the trail and the benefits it adds to the location. The buyer loves the prospect of living near a trail and makes an offer on the house, which the seller accepts. The city closes the trail to the public two weeks before the buyer moves into the home. The seller genuinely did not know about the city's plans to close the trail and had no intention of misrepresenting the trail as a benefit of his property. The seller did not intentionally withhold information with the intention of deceiving the buyer.

Example of Fraud and Misrepresentation

Suppose a buyer tells a licensee to look for a home in a safe neighborhood in which the buyer can raise a family. The licensee shows the buyer a wonderful three-bedroom home. The buyer specifically asks if crimes have recently been committed in the area. The licensee states there have been no crimes committed in the area. The licensee knows five cars in the area were stolen within the last three months. The licensee purposefully withholds information which will affect the buyer's decisions about a specific property. The licensee is now committing fraud.

Duress

Duress is compulsion by threat; specifically: unlawful constraint.

When a contract is not freely accepted it is made under duress. The contract is not legally binding and may be revoked. However, it is not enough for the offeree simply to say a contract was made under duress in order to invalidate a contract; duress needs to be legally proven.

Example of Duress
A tenant blackmails a landlord into reducing the rent. A new contract, or lease, is made under duress. This new contract is not legally enforceable if the landlord can legally prove the contract was made under duress for reason of blackmail.

Mistakes
Mistakes regarding the terms or conditions of a contract occur when there is an unintentional ambiguity or an oversight affecting the entire agreement. A contract containing mistakes is not a contract. Ambiguity or an oversight can turn one contract into a completely different contract.

Example of Mistakes
A seller advertises a beachfront property is for sale. A buyer contacts the seller to view the property. The seller explains he or she is not available to show the property, but to look over the exterior of the property if she or he chooses to do so. After viewing the property, the buyer makes an offer on the property. Upon further discussions with the buyer, the seller realizes the buyer misinterpreted the directions and viewed the wrong property. The buyer made a mistake, and his offer cannot rightly be viewed as a contract with the seller.

Legally Competent Parties

The notion of "legal competency" implies two things:

- Individuals involved are of 18 years of age or older or have parental consent

- Individuals without impaired mental capacity

Majority laws protect minors from entering into agreements they do not have the experience or knowledge to understand fully. A contract in which one or more of the contracting parties is a minor is considered void or voidable. If the contract is considered void, it ceases to have legal existence. If the contract is considered voidable, the minor can withdraw from the contract at any time and the majority party is still bound to the contract until such time.

Mental competency laws protect individuals of unsound mind from agreeing to terms they do not fully understand. Individuals who have been declared mentally incompetent by a judge or are under the influence of drugs or chemicals and incapable of comprehending contracts (but who have not officially been declared incompetent by a judge) cannot legally enter into a contract.

If an individual wishes to enter into a contract with someone of unsound mind, he or she must involve a third party who is "legally competent" and has power of attorney to represent the mentally incompetent individual in legal matters.

Power of Attorney

There are two terms you need to know for this section:

Principal

This is the individual giving another person the power of attorney to act on her or his behalf.

Attorney-in-fact

This is the person to whom the power of attorney is granted.

There are four basic types of power of attorney:

- **Limited power of attorney**:

    o Grants limited rights to the attorney-in-fact

    o Is revoked if principal becomes mentally disabled

    o For example, the principal gives an attorney-in-fact (for example, a friend) check-writing powers while on an extended vacation

- **Ordinary power of attorney:**

    o Grants broad powers to the attorney-in-fact over personal finances

    o Is revoked if principal becomes mentally disabled

- **Durable power of attorney**

    o Grants the broadest powers of all to the attorney-in-fact

    o Remains effective if principal becomes incapacitated

- **Springing power of attorney:**

    o Becomes effective when the principal becomes mentally disabled or otherwise incapacitated

    o Allows the principal to provide his or her own definition of "incapacitated"

- Here are two examples:
    - The principal wants to limit the term "incapacitated" to a judgment, rendered by the court, stating the principal is senile.
    - The principal defines "incapacitated" as lapsing into a coma for more than a specified number of days.

The power of attorney gives the attorney-in-fact power over the principal's affairs for various purposes, such as:

- To buy or sell real estate on the principal's behalf
- To manage the principal's properties
- To conduct the principal's banking transactions
- To invest the principal's money
- To make legal claims and conduct litigation
- To give gifts on the principal's behalf

Consideration

All contracts must have consideration exchange, which means:

- No one may obtain anything of value without providing some form of compensation (in a contract, you cannot get something for nothing).
- Examples of compensation include:
    - Money
    - Property
    - Giving up a right or valid claim
    - Making a promise to do or not to do something
    - Services
- If there is no consideration, then the contract is not legally binding.
- All contracts are created out of self-interest and all parties acknowledge the self-interested character of the contract, and agree something valuable is changing hands because of the contract.

Lawful Objective

Thus far, we have discussed legally competent parties and mutual assent as features of a legally valid contract. The third feature of a legally valid contract is that it must have a lawful objective. This requirement means that a contract cannot explicitly or implicitly call for any illegal activities. When a contract has a lawful objective, it considers all the relevant laws and statutes to ensure that the contract is not suggesting or requiring actions that are against the law. Lawful objective in a contract includes:

- Considering all relevant laws and statutes

- Confirming there are no illegal action(s) being required of any parties involved

- Becoming void if it implicitly or explicitly requires illegal conduct

- Being held accountable for attempting to fulfill a contract devoid of lawful objective

Adherence to Statute of Frauds

The statute of frauds is a state law establishing the features of a valid contract. It generally requires certain types of contracts to be set out in writing and written contracts to be signed by all the parties bound by the contract. The statute of frauds can vary slightly from one state to another. A statute of frauds is designed to prevent dishonorable conduct. The statute of frauds generally does not void a valid contract failing to adhere to a statute of frauds, but makes this voidable. This contract remains valid until one party opts to void it.

Note: The term "statute of frauds," is derived from "An Act for Prevention of Frauds and Perjuries." This was an act ratified by the English Parliament in 1677, over 300 years ago.

A majority of states' statute of frauds require contracts to be in writing if:

- It involves the sale or transfer of real estate.

- It concerns debts or specific duties.

- The terms extend for a period of more than one year.

- The terms extend beyond the lifetime of the promissor.

- It involves the sale of goods valued at $500 or more under the Uniform Commercial Code.

Note: The Uniform Commercial Code (UCC) is a body of statutory laws aiming to regulate important categories within contracts and to standardize business transactions. Every state, except Louisiana, has a Uniform Commercial Code.

More About: You can view the Uniform Commercial Code (UCC) online:http://www.law.cornell.edu/ucc/ucc.table.html.

Real Estate Applications of the Statute

Most real estate contracts are in writing. The statute of frauds applies to most of real estate contracts including, but not limited to:

- Trust deeds

- Mortgages

- Leases for periods of longer than one year

- Rights to rights-of-way through property and any and all encumbrances incurred or suffered by the owners, or by operation of law

Note: The statute of frauds does not apply to lease agreements of a year or less.

Parol Evidence Rule

Parol literally means "word of mouth." Parol evidence, then, are the terms and conditions the parties discuss before the final contract is written. This discussion provides evidence of what the parties expect from the contract. However, the parol evidence rule holds that when important details of an agreement discussed between two or more parties fail to make it into the written contract, the written, signed contract is given authority over any parol evidence.

This rule can be invoked when a court is deciding whether to admit parol evidence during a contract dispute. Once a court reviews the contract in question, the details of the case are used to decide whether the parol evidence rule should apply.

Contract Performance Overview

This section will discuss what must happen to fulfill the terms of a contract after it has been made and accepted. The result will be either the performance or non-performance of a contract. We will discuss the performance of a contract first.

When there is a contract, there must be an offer, acceptance, and performance. We will cover the two types of agreements that affect performance: forbearance agreements and performance agreements. We will also cover performance of a contract by novation and assignment.

Performance of a Contract

A contract aims to create a specific state of affairs desired by both of the contracting parties. The obligations a contract imposes on the contracting parties are the actions required to make this desired state of affairs a reality. Thus, once an offer has been made and accepted, the terms of the contract need to be carried out in order to complete (or "execute") the contract. This means what is legally called "performance" needs to occur–the contracting parties need to successfully complete their contractual obligations and duties. The terms of a contract have not been met until performance occurs, i.e., until the parties fully carry out their responsibilities.

Example: Once Seller A accepts Buyer B's offer and they sign a real estate purchase contract, Seller A performs his or her contractual duties by transferring the title to Buyer B, and Buyer B performs his or her contractual duties by paying the purchase price to Seller A.

Time Is of the Essence
All contracts should contain language emphasizing all promises are to be completed in a timely fashion. They may include the specific statement "Time is of the essence." This phrase essentially means the specified times and dates in the contract are mandatory, and failure to meet these deadlines may result in being held liable for compensatory damages.

Typically, contracts also contain a section similar to the following paragraph:

The Seller and the Purchaser will make full settlement in accordance with the terms of this Contract ("Settlement") on, or with mutual consent, before, _____ ("Settlement Date") except as otherwise provided in the Contract.

This section establishes a fixed date, which serves as a set point for making judgments about what counts as timely performance. Writing a date into the contract helps to make "timely" a more objective notion.

Emphasizing timely performance helps to ensure all parties perform according to the terms of the contract within the allotted period of time. If one party fails to meet the deadline, she or he is subject to whatever penalties are established for breaching the contract. He or she may also face various kinds of legal liability, depending on the nature of the contract and the events resulting from breaching it.

Forbearance Agreements
Forbearance agreements require one or more of the contracting parties to refrain from actions a party is otherwise legally entitled to perform.

For example, if a borrower cannot repay a loan within the agreed-upon time period, then the borrower can ask the lender for a forbearance agreement. In this case, if the lender granted a forbearance agreement, the lender would effectively be promising not to take action against the borrower for non-payment during the period covered by their agreement. The lender has the legal right to pursue this debt, but the lender waives this right when she or he makes a forbearance agreement with the borrower.

Performance Agreements

Performance agreements require the contracting parties either to perform certain actions or to uphold certain contractual promises. Performance agreements exist in addition to the contract itself. They do not require the performance of contractual duties, but do require the parties to carry out actions facilitating the successful completion of their contractual duties.

For example, imagine a tenant enters into a lease agreement. Within this lease agreement, the tenant is responsible for damages made to the apartment during her tenancy. The tenant also enters into a performance agreement which prohibits pets living in the apartment. The purpose of this performance agreement is to reduce the likelihood of damages to the apartment and facilitates the landlord's goal of keeping tenants from doing any significant damage to the apartment.

Assignment

Sometimes, one or more of the parties involved in a contract want to withdraw from it without actually terminating the contract. In cases like these, the contracting parties have the option of transferring their rights and duties to a third party. This transferal is known as "assignment." When these duties and rights are transferred (or assigned) to another party, the party who originally assumed the contractual obligations usually remains secondarily liable for the terms in the contract, unless the original party is expressly released from those duties. This means, if the individual to whom the rights and obligations are transferred fails to fulfill those obligations, then the other parties to the contract can demand performance from the original party.

For example, a buyer agrees to purchase a home already under an existing loan, often referred to as an agreement to "take on payments." The person who originally took out the loan transfers the loan responsibilities to the new buyer. However, the person who initially took on the loan remains as a party to the agreement in case the new buyer defaults on the loan.

Novation

Novation is an alternative to assignment. Novation is the act of substituting one contract with a new contract. Sometimes the contract as a whole is not substituted; sometimes a certain obligation in the contract is substituted with a new obligation, or one party in the contract is substituted with a new party. Legally, it is understood to be the exchange of one contract for another.

A new contract under these circumstances is generally understood to be subject to the same promises and obligations as the original contract.

Promissory Estoppel

Estoppel
Refers to a legal limit on enforcing a claim or right at odds with what was previously said or done.

Promissory Estoppels
Connected to the basic concept of estoppel; aims to stop a party from altering or rescinding a promise.

Promissory estoppel is used to force all parties to continue to be held legally liable to their contractual obligations made without consideration exchange. This legal doctrine is used to force all parties to honor a contract which does not satisfy an otherwise important condition of a legally valid contract.

In general, it is used to keep parties from defaulting on reasonable contracts if it results in a serious injustice to the other party. If courts judge the person making the promise could reasonably have expected the other contracting party to rely on the promise, and the party did rely on the promise, then courts often force the promise-maker to perform rather than let the other party suffer significant damages simply for taking the promise-maker at his or her word.

Non-Performance of a Contract

A "breach of contract" occurs when there is a violation of the terms of a legally binding agreement. When a breach of contract occurs, the non-breaching party may be able to seek recourse via an array of legal options, including rescinding the contract, suing for damages or suing for performance of the contract. Contracts can be breached in different ways and to varying extents. Breach of contract is violation; an act of commission.

The injured party also retains the option of discharging the contract. When a contract is discharged, the terms and conditions of the contract are either cancelled or satisfied. Most contracts contain a section discussing when a discharge is allowed and the full consequences of a breach of contract.

Discharging a Contract
There are several situations in which one or more of the contracting parties can usually discharge a contract:

Partial Performance

Occurs when one or more of the contracting parties perform only a portion of the agreed-upon contractual duties. The party who suffers damages by the other party's failure to perform can seek legal restitution or discharge the contract.

Substantial Performance

Created when a party performs the majority of the contract's requirements but does not perform according to the contract's stipulations. The injured party has usually performed enough of contract's obligations to gain legal enforcement of the other party to complete the contract.

Non-Performance Due To Legal Issues

Requires one or all parties involved to act illegally. Any party called upon to perform illegal acts is not required to meet the terms of the contract and can discharge the contract.

Mutual Agreement

Occurs when all parties mutually agree to cancel the contract.

Operation of Law

Occurs when a contract is not legally valid or becomes unenforceable due to a statute of frauds, a statute of limitations or other legal regulations. Enforcing such contracts is a violation of the law.

Breach of Contract

A breach of contract occurs when the terms or conditions of a contract are violated. When one of the contracting parties violates the contract's terms, he or she assumes the consequences of breaching, which are generally set out in the contract itself. In these cases, the party who has honored her or his contractual obligations has the right to seek compensation for any damages suffered as a result of the other party's breach.

Consequences of a Breached Contract

When there is a breach of contract, the non-breaching party or the party who fulfills (or wants to fulfill) his or her part of the contract has four options:

- **To Forfeit**
  - There is no longer any contractual relationship.
  - This means the seller is entitled to keep the earnest money and all other payments collected from the prospective buyer.

- **To Rescind**
  - This means the non-breaching party can cancel the contract entirely.

- o It also means the seller must return all payments received from the buyer.

- **To Sue For Specific Performance**
  - o "Specific performance" is a court order requiring all parties to carry out the promises stipulated in a contract.
  - o This is a court enforcement of the original contract.

- **To Sue For Compensatory Damages**
  - o This means the party who fulfilled the promises of the contract can take the party who failed to fulfill the promises of the contract to court in order to recover any damages suffered due to the breach of contract.
  - o This does not force the parties to abide by the original contract, but it does require the party who breached the contract to compensate the party who did not.

Something subtly similar to breach of contract is "default." When a party fails to *comply* with any of the conditions in a contract that party is said to have "defaulted" on the contract.

Example: Default can be failure to make timely debt payments or to comply with other non-monetary conditions of an agreement.

A default is failure to comply; an act of omission. Default and breach of contract are NOT the same.

Contingencies

Contingencies are stipulations or conditions which must be satisfied before the contract can be performed. Most real estate contracts should include at least two contingencies:

Financing Contingency
Makes the purchase contract conditional upon the buyer's ability to obtain financing.

Inspection Contingency
Makes the purchase contract conditional upon the outcome of the home inspection report or appraisal report.

If contingencies are not met, the contract can be discharged.

Example: If a buyer agrees to pay $150,000 for a house, but the appraisal report concludes it is only worth $120,000, the buyer can back out of the agreement. In this case, the contract should be discharged, and the buyer should receive his or her deposit back.

However, if the prospective buyer backs out of the contract for reasons not stipulated or allowed for in the contract, she or he has breached the contract and thereby forfeits his or her deposit.

Example: If the prospective buyer has signed the purchase contract, but decides at the last minute she or he does not want the property because he or she has found a better property, that buyer will lose her or his deposit unless he or she honors the original contract.

Contracts Overview

Real estate professionals need to be familiar with the different contracts governing their industry. Whether they are listing a property, selling a property, or closing a sale, contracts are involved and licensees need to be able to understand and evaluate them. These skills help to ensure real estate professionals provide their clients with comprehensive service; having a good grasp of contracts and the roles they play helps licensees to foresee and to correct oversights and mistakes affecting transactions—thereby protecting themselves against legal liability.

This lesson discusses the most common legal forms used within the real estate industry.

Note: Licensees are only authorized to fill out standardized contract forms created by their real estate commission or created by an attorney. They are not authorized to create contract forms or to provide any other kind of legal advice to their clients. This is practicing law without a license and the unauthorized practice of law is not only imprudent (because it makes a licensee vulnerable to serious legal liability), it is illegal. If a licensee thinks a special contract form should be created, or believes his or her clients need legal guidance, the licensee should refer those clients to a licensed attorney.

Legal Forms

To help licensees develop a useful understanding of real estate contracts, this lesson will discuss sales contracts, listing agreements, option agreements, contracts-for-deed, and leases.

- Sales Contracts, including:
    - Legal property description

- o Earnest money contract
- o Escrow account
- o Purchase-and-sale agreement addendum
- o Lead-based paint addendum
- o Terminating a sales contract
- Listing Agreements, including:
  - o Exclusive right-to-sell listing
  - o Exclusive agency listing
  - o Open listing
  - o Net listing
  - o How to terminate a listing agreement
- Option Agreements
- Contract-for-deed agreements
- Leases, including:
  - o Leasehold estates
  - o Estate for years
  - o Periodic estate
  - o Estate at will
  - o Tenancy at sufferance

When creating a contract with other parties, it is important to:

- Make sure you fully understand and accept all written terms and conditions for which you are to be held legally responsible
- Make sure you fully understand the penalties for failing to abide by all terms written in the contract
- Discuss any questions or doubts you have about the agreement before it is put into writing and especially *before* you sign it

Written and signed contracts in the process of being carried out are to be used as a reference if any confusion arises throughout its execution. If a contract is going to cover all the bases and avoid any confusion or misunderstandings, then it needs:

- To be well organized
- To be well thought out
- To use clear and concise language

- To avoid any legal jargon and complicated phrasing
- And last but not least, have all five requirements of a legally valid contract!

Contract Components

Most contracts generally have two sections:

- The duties and obligations section:
    - Listing the expectations, terms, and deadlines of the agreement
    - Establishing the requirements for contract fulfillment
- The representations and warranties section:
    - Containing statements ensuring any goods and services described in the contract will be provided or performed according to the terms of the contract
    - Establishing a guarantee

Sales Contracts

Sales contracts, also called "purchase contracts," are the most important documents in real estate transactions. They establish the details of an agreement between a buyer and a seller along with their rights and obligations. They are the prospective buyer's written offer to a property owner to purchase a specific piece of real estate.

Sales contracts include:

- The price the buyer agrees to pay
- The amount of earnest money the buyer will pay
- Mortgage details and any financing conditions the prospective buyer wishes to stipulate
- The deposit the buyer agrees to put down
- When and where the closing of the transaction will take place
- Inclusions and exclusions (that is, an itemization of personal property like appliances which may or may not be included in the selling price)
- An appraisal section and a termite and pest inspection section
- Warranties
- Acceptance procedures and deadlines
- Property disclosures

Sales contracts establish a relationship between the buyer and the seller. This relationship requires a little give and take of all the parties, usually involving the seller transferring the property title to the buyer and the buyer paying the negotiated price to the seller.

Sales contracts protect both the buyer and seller by creating a legal framework which strongly encourages both parties to uphold their end of the bargain. Valid sales contracts must have all five requirements of a legally valid contract plus an additional, sixth condition:

- Sales contracts must contain a legal description of the property being conveyed.

Legal Property Description

A legal property description makes it clear to all parties exactly what property is being bought or sold. It can be used by the courts to clarify any disputes about the property.

Note: A property's street address provides identification, but not enough. It is insufficient because "123 Main Street" might be the address of any given property in any given town which happens to have a street called "Main Street." If we spell out the address further, as "123 Main Street, Anytown, Anystate," this does not tell us the size of the property or the specific boundaries of the property. Not all properties even have a street address. This requires a legal description, and we need a way of describing property that can apply to all real estate.

A legal property description must include:

- **Metes and Bounds:** Metes and bounds is a legal land description method identifying a lot's exact dimensions and location in reference to a fixed and permanent monument.
    - **Metes:** Refers to the distance measurements used in the description
    - **Bounds:** Refers to the directions of the boundaries enclose the parcel of real estate.
- **The Rectangular Survey System:** The rectangular survey method, also known as a government survey or U.S. public lands survey, uses a more refined version of the longitude and latitude system of mapping. This method uses a surveyed grid of meridians, baselines, townships, and ranges to describe a particular piece of land.
- **Recorded Plats:** Also known as the "lot-block-tract system," the "recorded survey" or the "recorded map" method. It uses the metes and bounds method of land description to locate the borders of each parcel, and once

the surveyor establishes the property's perimeter, he or she records the dimensions on a plat (map) for easy reference. This map is filed with the proper local authority, such as the county clerk or the county records office.

Given this general overview, the important thing for the reader to remember is a sales contract must contain a legal property description uniquely identifying the property involved in the transaction.

Earnest Money Contract

Earnest money contracts are used to show a serious and able intent by the buyer to purchase a property while the actual sales contract is being put together. This is done in order to reserve a property the buyer is interested in purchasing. Once a purchase contract is signed, the buyer then begins to fulfill the earnest money contract as a step towards completing the sales contract.

What is earnest money?

- Earnest money is money a potential buyer pays as a deposit along with the offer in order to show serious intent.

Deciding what constitutes a reasonable amount of earnest money is made by mutual agreement between the buyer and the seller. A seller may stipulate a deposit, or earnest money, is nonrefundable in an effort to ensure a buyer is serious when she or he puts down a deposit. The amount of the earnest money can depend on the buyer's level of interest in the property. Earnest money also provides the seller with some compensation if the deal ultimately falls through, in order to cover any expenses incurred by the seller or broker.

As you know, earnest money is not one of the five requirements of a legally valid contract. It also does not serve as consideration in a sales contract. It can be used to meet the terms of the sales contract, such as serving as a down payment.

Now, earnest money cannot be deposited until the offer is accepted and the seller notifies the buyer of the acceptance. There is usually a license law limiting the amount of time in which a licensee may make a deposit, or deposit earnest money, after the contract is executed. Two to three working days is generally the maximum time span. Licensees handling earnest money should be familiar with this section of their license laws.

Most states require that earnest money contracts:

- Be in writing
- Be signed by the parties bound by the contract

- Contain evidence of intent to convey ownership interest
- Identify the seller and the buyer
- Identify the property being transferred in the transaction

Usually, a title insurance company holds the earnest money, or "holds the check," until the offer is accepted. When a broker is involved, license laws generally require these funds be deposited into an escrow account.

Escrow Account

Placing money into an escrow account is placing earnest money into the custody of a third party until a contract is executed. Escrow accounts ensure the funds are available to be dealt with honorably, either to meet the terms of an agreement or to compensate the parties involved for their time and effort if there is a default.

Purchase and Sales Agreement Addendum

Addendums are additions to a completed contract. They are attached as requirements and/or supplementary information to the contract and also must be accepted by all parties involved.

Addendums contain items, such as:

- Additional agreements
- Disclosures
- Contingencies

For example, an addendum might state if certain components of a home inspection, property appraisal, or loan application do not work out the way one party expects, then either party has the right to withdraw from the contract without penalty.

Other common addenda include:

- Third party financing condition addenda
- Loan assumption addenda
- Lead-based paint addenda
- Seller financing addenda

Some states' license laws require the use of standardized contracts and addenda. Each state's real estate commission has their own addenda forms and standardized contracts, which are prepared by an attorney.

Lead-Based Paint Addendum

The lead-based paint addendum is the most common addendum, used with properties built before 1978. It establishes the seller's knowledge of the use of lead-based paint on the property and ensures the seller has provided the buyer with any and all documents pertaining to the use of lead-based paint on the property. It often includes contingencies allowing the buyer to withdraw from the contract if an inspection shows there are any undisclosed lead-based paint hazards on the property.

Terminating a Sales Contract

Sometimes individuals enter into a contract and later decide to withdraw from the contract. A sales contract is terminated under the same conditions as any contract. There are also specific cases where a contract is simply cancelled.

Example: If the buyer is uncertain as to whether he or she is going to obtain adequate financing, then the buyer must explain this to the seller when making an offer on a property. A financing addendum should be included in the sales contract, which allows the buyer to withdraw from the contract if she or he is unable to get a loan.

A sales contract can be discharged when:

- There is a breach of contract, giving the four choices discussed earlier.
- There is non-performance due to illegal terms or other specific terms.
- The parties involved mutually agree to its termination.
- It is rendered unenforceable due to operations of the law, such as:
    - When the statute of limitations has expired

Listing Agreements

A listing agreement is basically an employment contract made between a seller or owner and a licensee. It is not a sales contract or lease agreement, even if the marketed property is sold or rented. It includes marketing the property and obtaining and submitting offers to lease or buy the property.

Again, most states require a listing agreement be in writing if it is to be enforceable in court, and they provide standardized forms for listing agreements which comply with state regulations and multiple listing service standards.

Note: In addition, the National Association of REALTORS© (the largest real estate trade organization) develops its own forms for REALTORS© (i.e., licensees who are members) to use. Even though many brokerages and services develop their own listing agreement forms, these forms share many of the same features, which are discussed later in this section.

Listing agreements create a relationship, called an "agency relationship," authorizing a licensee to represent the principal (the seller or owner) and the principal's property to third parties (buyers or tenants).

It places a licensee in a position of trust or fiduciary duty, or an "allegiance." In this case, the licensee owes the principal the duties of loyalty, confidentiality, obedience, full disclosure, care, diligence, and accountability for all funds entrusted to him or her.

The licensee generally agrees to provide all of the real estate services the seller requires until the property is actually sold or rented. A licensee might allow other people (such as salespeople) to help carry out her or his contractual duties provided they do so under his or her supervision.

The licensee is usually given the legal status of "special agent" for the principal. This means the licensee is under contract for one specific act or business transaction (i.e., finding a buyer or tenant). Each state's license law discusses the specific requirements and duties of special agents. These laws can also define which parties (e.g., salespeople) may act on an agent's behalf and under what circumstances. Real estate professionals should always consult their states' laws for the specific details affecting their work.

Four common types of listing agreements are:

- Exclusive right-to-sell agreements
- Exclusive agency listing agreements
- Open listing agreements
- Net listing agreements

Exclusive Right-To-Sell Listing Agreement
In an exclusive right-to-sell listing agreement, a licensee is exclusively granted the right to offer the property for sale. It even requires the seller to pay the licensee a commission on the selling price of the property regardless of who sells the property. Many brokerage firms limit their listing agreements to this type of contract.

Exclusive Agency Listing Agreement
In an exclusive agency listing agreement, one licensee is exclusively authorized to be the principal's agent. Unlike the exclusive-right-to-sell listing, the seller retains the right to sell the property. This means if the principal finds a buyer, then the principal does not pay the listing agent a commission. For the licensee

to be entitled to a commission, the licensee must sell the property. In other words, the licensee's efforts resulted in the sale, or the licensee produced the ultimate buyer of the property.

Open Listing Agreement
Open listing agreements allow property owners to employ one or more licensees to market their property. The property owner still retains the right to sell the property without paying a commission to any licensee marketing the property. The licensee who procures the sale is entitled to receive the commission. Open listing agreements are most commonly used by builders and developers who work with many licensees in the marketing of new homes and lots.

Net Listing Agreement
Net listing agreements allow licensees to keep the amount of the selling price, which is more than what the seller is asking for the property, minus the closing costs. This agreement is rarely used because it creates a conflict of interests between the licensee's interests and the property owner's interests.

Example: If the property owner is not aware the property is worth quite a bit more than the asking price, a licensee who is aware of the actual property value stands to benefit a great deal from a net listing agreement. That is, if the licensee withheld this information from the property owner.

Licensees are required by their fiduciary duty to provide a property owner with all and accurate information required to protect the property owner's interests. Because net listing agreements present such an opportunity for dishonesty, they are illegal in some states. Licensees should always consult their state laws before entering into net listing agreements.

Multiple Listing Service
Aside from the listing agreements discussed above, some states have a multiple listing service option in which brokers agree to share their listings with other brokers by pooling the information in a database in exchange for a share of the commission earned by a transaction. The most common form of such an arrangement is brokers being members of a board of REALTORS© or real estate agents with all members agreeing to be bound by rules governing that organization.

As part of agreeing to be a member, such entities usually have their own listing agreement form with a stipulation clause giving the listing broker both the authority and an obligation to share the listing with other brokers by submitting the property information into the MLS database, unless the seller specifically requests that the property not be listed in MLS. (There is usually an option for this in the agreement.) And, as part of being advertised in the MLS system, the seller's broker advertises a fee or commission that will be paid to the "cooperating" broker in a sales transaction.

The *cooperating broker* is the other broker or salesperson that shows the listed property to a buyer who subsequently purchases the property, entitling the cooperating broker to the fee or commission as the "procuring cause." The amount offered to a cooperating broker is at the sole discretion of the listing broker. If the cooperating broker or salesperson represents the buyer, the listing agent must receive authorization from the seller in order to share a part of the commission, although this is usually covered in the original listing agreement.

A multiple listing service offers advantages to the owner/seller, brokers, and buyers. The owner/seller receives greater exposure of her or his property through the MLS system and the property is, in turn, shown by a larger number of brokers and salespeople to a larger audience of buyers. As a result, the increased exposure of the property gives the broker more opportunity to sell the property, earning the commission. The buyer also benefits by having the opportunity to select more properties from which to purchase.

MLS systems have set rules established by the member brokers as to how soon a broker must enter the property listing into the system, thereby keeping the broker from attempting to "hide" the listing so other member brokers don't have a chance to help show it. Other rules are also set by each system to allow for fairness amongst members.

Terminating a Listing Agreement

Listing agreements may be terminated:

- If the property is not sold within the specified time period stated in the original contract (i.e., expired contract)
- By unilateral revocation by the owner or licensee for just cause
- For example:
    - A seller refuses to cooperate with licensee in order to show the property
    - The seller wants to terminate the agreement due to lack of activity

If there is any type of falling out between the seller and the listing licensee, it is usually prudent to terminate the listing agreement rather than exacerbate hard feelings and/or risk ending up in litigation.

More specific reasons for terminating a listing agreement include:

- The fulfillment of the listing agreement (i.e., the property sells)
- The property owner declares bankruptcy.

- A bankruptcy court has the right to block the sale of a property and assign a trustee over the bankrupt property to assist with obtaining court approval to proceed with selling a property. This automatically stays any further action by law.

- The property being destroyed or damaged beyond repair

- The death or incapacity of the property owner

- The death or incapacity of the licensee

- A mutual agreement between the licensee and the property owner–usually required to be documented in writing

- A change in the permissible use of the property, such as a zoning change

- For example:

  - A property previously zoned for commercial use is located in an area no longer permitting commercial operations.

  - A licensee originally retained to sell a property as commercial can no longer legally execute such a contract.

Option Agreements

An option agreement is also referred to as:

- A "lease purchase"

- A "lease option"

- A "lease-option-to-buy"

This kind of agreement combines the components of a basic lease contract with an option-to-purchase contract.

In an option agreement, the optionee (a buyer or tenant) pays the optioner (a seller or landlord) an option fee (a nonrefundable deposit) which is ultimately applied to the purchase price of the property. The option fee in effect "buys" the optionee the choice to buy or not to buy the property at the end of the lease agreement.

Once the option fee is paid, the corresponding monthly payments are usually applied towards the purchase price of the property or considered as a down payment on the property. The optionee retains the option of purchasing the property (according to the terms of the option agreement contract) during the term of the lease. Once the lease expires, the option expires.

A legally enforceable option agreement must define the following elements:

The Option Fee
This is the deposit the optionee must make in order to have the option to purchase the property during the lease term. The option fee is nonrefundable and is applied to the purchase price of the property only if the optionee decides to purchase the property.

The Option Term
This is the amount of time the optionee has to exercise his or her right to purchase the property; the contract should specify the final date by which the optionee must either exercise the option or lose the option.

The Methods For Exercising The Option
This part of the contract should describe the steps the optionee must take in order to exercise the option to purchase. Most option agreements require the optionee to send the optioner a written intent to purchase the property.

The Payment Agreement
Often, rent payments (monthly payments) are credited towards the purchase of the property. The option agreement should clearly address the guidelines for these types of situations.

Contract-For-Deed Agreements

A contract-for-deed agreement is also known as:

- A "land contract"
- An "installment contract"
- A "contract of sale"

A contract-for-deed agreement is a conditional agreement regarding the sale of real estate which requires the buyer to uphold certain promises *after* taking possession of the property.

Example: A contract-for-deed agreement might allow a buyer to defer a portion of the purchase price, still taking possession of the property but paying out the remaining balance over time, in installments. Effectively, this makes the buyer a long-term renter who actually receives legal title after paying a certain amount of money to the seller.

What sets apart a contract-for-deed agreement from a regular sales agreement is the seller retains the legal title of the property while the buyer takes possession of the property and holds the "equitable title" to the property. Even though there is an exchange of payment, there is not a transfer of the property title until all conditions of the contract are satisfied.

In a contract-for-deed agreement the seller must provide the buyer with:

- Copies of a current survey
- A tax certificate
- An insurance policy
- Property condition disclosures
- Information regarding utilities, liens, and financing terms

Leases

A lease is an agreement between a tenant (lessee) and a landlord (lessor) allowing the tenant to occupy the landlord's property and for specified payments to be paid at a specified rate for a specific period of time. A comprehensive lease agreement defines the tenant's rights and obligations as well as the landlord's rights and obligations, the time period covered by the contract and the amount of money the tenant must pay to the landlord for use of the property.

Reversionary Right
This means possession of the property *reverts* to the landlord after the lease term has expired. The landlord's interest in the property is specifically known as a "leased fee estate plus reversionary right."

Land ownership is described by two basic terms:

Freehold Estate
The property owner has actual ownership and possession of the land (or real estate) but said ownership and possession will not last for a legally specified period of time.

Leasehold Estate
The tenant has possession of the property (but does not own it), and her or his estate in the property lasts for a limited period of time.

Leasehold Estates
A leasehold estate is a type of property interest allowing tenants to occupy and use a property they do not own. Leasehold estates are established when a tenant has possession of a property and has the legal right to use the property, but he or she does not have actual ownership interest (i.e., the tenant does not hold legal title and cannot legally sell the property). Instead, the tenant has a

special kind of "possessory estate" in the property for the duration of his or her lease, as long as she or he honors the terms and conditions of the lease contract.

There are four general types of leasehold estates:

- Estate for years
- Periodic estate
- Estate at will
- Tenancy at sufferance

We will now discuss the details of these various leasehold estates.

Estate for Years

Estate for years, or "tenancy for years," is a leasehold estate with a specific starting date and a specific ending date. The exact span of time is decided by the landlord, agreed to by the tenant, and ranges from days to years. The tenant in this agreement occupies and uses the property as long as the terms of the lease agreement are honored. The agreement can be discharged under the conditions previously discussed.

Once an estate for years expires, no special action is required by either the landlord or the tenant to terminate it. Instead, it is implicitly understood the contract is terminated. If the tenant wishes to continue to occupy and use the property, the lease must be renewed. Renewal requires the landlord and tenant to come together and expressly agree either to renew the existing lease or to create a new one.

Periodic Estate

A periodic estate, or a "periodic tenancy," defines tenancy as automatically continuing for consecutive periods of time. They are most commonly referred to as month-to-month leases. This kind of lease is generally understood to be automatically renewed at the end of each lease period, until the landlord or tenant takes special action (such as submitting a written request) to terminate the lease agreement.

Example: In a month-to-month lease, both the tenant and the landlord generally have the option of terminating the lease agreement at the end of any given month. However, if neither party expressly terminates the lease, then it is usually understood the lease is renewed for another month.

Estate at Will

An estate at will, or a "tenancy at will," is created by a lease agreement which permits either the tenant or the landlord to terminate the lease agreement at any given time. Usually, the terminating party is required to give written notice and ample warning to all parties involved. The distinguishing feature of an estate at will is its lack of a specific tenancy period. Apart from this, the landlord and the tenant involved in an estate at will agreement have all or most of the rights and obligations they would have under any other type of leasehold estate.

Tenancy at Sufferance
A tenancy at sufferance is not a lease agreement. It is created when a tenant continues to occupy the property beyond the period specified in a previously existing lease agreement without the consent of the landlord. This does not mean the tenant is remaining on the property after the landlord has expressly asked him or her to leave. It does mean, however, the tenant is still understood to be violating the law.

In a tenancy at sufferance, the landlord and the tenant have chosen to ignore the fact their formal lease agreement is expired. Everyone goes on as before, but there is no formal lease contract governing their relationship or defining the tenant's estate in the leased property. When this occurs, the tenant is referred to as a "holdover tenant."

When a tenant remains in possession of a property beyond the expired lease agreement, the landlord has a right to evict the tenant. If the tenant continues to pay the landlord rent after the formal lease has expired, and the landlord accepts, then the tenancy at sufferance can become a periodic estate.

Insight into Contracts, Purchase Agreements, and Sales Agreements

This section presents you with comprehensive questions and dilemmas which will require you to apply the information you have learned in this lesson.

Question 1
Why should licensees follow the requirement imposed by most states' statute of frauds and put all real estate contracts in writing?

Answer
Putting real estate contracts in writing helps to prevent misunderstandings and provides each party with a clear description of her or his role in completing the contract. If the parties have a detailed contract, they will often not need to go to court to settle disputes because they know the terms of their contract will be upheld in a court of law. Parties cannot dispute an accepted contract which defines its terms clearly.

It is also helpful to have a written contract because fixing the terms and conditions of the contract in this way means none of the contracting parties can change the terms of the agreement without the other parties' consent.

Question 2
Suppose an individual wants to lease a property. She knows she will need the property for at least a year, but is not sure whether she will need it for longer than that, and would like not to have to go to the trouble of renewing her lease at the end of the first year. In this case, what type of leasehold estate does the tenant want?

Answer
This tenant wants a periodic estate. This kind of leasehold estate allows the tenant to have a fixed lease period–it is not like an estate at will, in which there is not specified lease term. However, the lease agreement creates a periodic estate; allowing the lease to automatically renew at the end of the lease period, unless the landlord or the tenant takes special action to terminate it. Therefore, someone who would like to have their lease automatically renew after the term is up–and, thus avoid the effort of renewing it herself–should ask for a lease agreement creating a periodic estate.

Question 3
What is the difference between an express contract and an implied contract?

Answer
The primary difference between an express contract and an implied contract can be deduced from their names. An express contract is an agreement in which the terms are clearly stated (*expressed*). The parties to an express contract understand the terms and obligations of the agreement and have openly accepted them. An implied contract, on the other hand, is an agreement in which the terms are not openly stated, but are instead inferred from the parties' actions. Therefore, an express contract can be distinguished from an implied contract by determining whether the contract's terms and conditions are actually stated outright or are merely implied.

Question 4
What is the difference between a *void* contract and a *voidable* contract?

Answer
A *void* contract is a contract that, for various reasons, has no legal validity. For example, an agreement that does not meet the minimum requirements of a contract would have no legal effect or impact. A contract that is not legally valid cannot be enforced against any of the contracting parties. A *voidable* contract, on the other hand, contains the essential components of a valid, enforceable

contract, but also contains provisions that allow the contract to be terminated or rescinded by either party.

Question 5
Why might a principal grant power of attorney to another party?

Answer
Individuals (known as "principals") give another person the power of attorney when they grant that person the power to act on their behalf (either in general or in some limited realm of their affairs). People grant limited power of attorney for a variety of reasons–for example, some individuals might grant other people power of attorney over their financial affairs because they feel they do not have the expertise needed to make necessary decisions. More sweeping power of attorney is often granted when a person loses (or anticipates losing) the mental or physical competence needed to oversee his or her own affairs.

Question 6
What are the differences between a leasehold estate and a freehold estate?

Answer
There are two basic terms used to describe land ownership, "freehold estate" and "leasehold estate." In a freehold estate, the property owner has actual ownership and possession of the land (or real estate), and her or his ownership lasts for an *unspecified* period of time. In a leasehold estate, the tenant has possession of the property (but does not own it), and his or her estate in the property lasts for a *limited period* of time.

Question 7
What is the purpose of the statute of frauds?

Answer
In most states, the basic function of the statute of frauds is establishing the features of a valid contract. For example, a state's statute of frauds will generally require certain types of contracts to be set out in writing and written contracts to be signed by all the parties bound by the contract. Licensees should acquaint themselves with the specific requirements set out in their states' statutes because there are frequently subtle differences between one state's statute of frauds and those of another state.

The Statute of Limitations

Each state has a statute of limitations, which places a limit on the amount of time that an individual has to take legal action against another individual in order to recover any losses and/or damages. In Texas, the statute of limitations is four years for written contracts and two years for oral contracts.

The Uniform Commercial Code

The Uniform Commercial Code (UCC) strives to standardize commercial and business transactions throughout the country. Currently, all states, except for Louisiana, have adopted the UCC; each state has its own version of the Code. In Texas, real estate professionals should refer to Section 9 of the Texas Business and Commerce Code. This section relates to using personal property to secure a loan or credit purchase.

Section 9 requires that real estate sales transactions use a *security agreement*, which is a document that contains a description of the loan collateral. The security agreement essentially establishes the lender's right to confiscate the collateral if the borrower defaults on the loan. Section 9 also requires that a *financing statement*, which is the final contract documenting the negotiation process between the lender and borrower, be filed at the county clerk's office. The financing statement also contains a notice of the security agreement. Once the financing statement has been recorded, it serves as notice to subsequent buyers and mortgagees of the security interest in that property.

Promulgated Contract Forms

The Texas Real Estate License Act established the Texas Real Estate Broker-Lawyer Committee; this Committee is in charge of drafting and revising standard contract forms that are used by real estate professionals. By having the Committee create and modify contract forms, all real estate professionals will be able to use the same forms for the same type of real estate transactions. Once the Committee has created a contract form, the Texas Real Estate Commission (TREC) decides whether they will mandate those forms for their salespeople and brokers. TREC can promulgate contract forms, , and temporary residential lease forms. If TREC decides to mandate that a certain form be used for a specific transaction, real estate professionals *must* use that particular form.

However, there are four exceptions when a real estate licensee does NOT have to use a form mandated by TREC:

1. Transactions where the licensee acts as the principal, and not an agent
2. Transactions where the government requires that a different form be used for a particular real estate transaction
3. Transactions where the seller has created and supplied the contract forms
4. Transactions where there are no standard contract forms mandated by TREC, and the licensee uses a form prepared by an attorney approved by the Texas Real Estate Broker-Lawyer Committee.

Contract Forms Promulgated by TREC

The following is a list of contracts that real estate licensees in Texas must use in their real estate transactions:

1. One to Four Family–Resale, All Cash, Assumption, Third-Party Conventional, or Owner Financed
2. One to Four Family FHA Insured
3. VA Guaranteed Loans
4. Unimproved Residential Property
5. New Home, Incomplete Construction
6. New Home, Completed Construction
7. Farm and Ranch
8. Condominium (Cash, Assumption, Conventional)
9. Condominium (FHA and VA)

Anyone can obtain these forms from TREC; however, only licensed and/or certified salespeople and brokers should complete these forms because they are trained and experienced with handling contract forms. TREC has established specific guidelines that oversee the preparation of contracts by real estate licensees. Section 16 of the Texas Real Estate Licensing Act (TRELA) covers a licensee's ability to prepare legal documents. Essentially, Section 16 states that a licensee should not create legal documents that define a principal's legal rights; real estate licensees should use the appropriate TREC approved forms for the appropriate contract situations. When filling out the TREC contract forms, licensees should only include information that they know is factual and truthful. The licensee should only include the information that is mandated by the form; if the licensee needs to add more information, and there is a contract addendum, lease or form promulgated by TREC for that information, the licensee must use that form.

Contracts for Deed

Texas currently does not have a promulgated contract for deed; therefore, real estate licensees should suggest that both parties obtain the services of an attorney to create or review a contract for deed. Parties should always ensure that terms of the contract are clearly established and that they understand those terms. Having an attorney review the contract prior to its signing prevents each party from being responsible for any obligations and damages of which he or she is unaware.

Defaulting on a Contract for Deed

When the buyer defaults on a payment, the seller has the right to forfeit the contract, which allows her or him to keep all payments received and evict the buyer. In Texas, the seller must give the buyer a specific statutory notice before forfeiture or cancellation if the subject property is going to be the buyer's residence.

The notice period depends on how much the buyer has paid towards the purchase price.

- If the buyer has paid less than 10% of the purchase price, the notice period must be 15 days.

- If the buyer has paid 10% of the purchase price, the notice period must be 30 days.

- If the buyer has paid 20% or more of the purchase price, the notice period must be 60 days.

Repossession

In some installment contracts, there are clauses that allow the seller to recover possession of the property, in the case that the buyer defaults. These clauses disallow the buyer from recording the title without the seller's consent. If the buyer records the sales contract with the public recorder, he or she shows that she or he has an interest in the property; this places a cloud on the seller's title. When this happens, this makes the process of repossession difficult for the seller because another party has shown ownership interest in the property. Most states outlaw these types of clauses; however, it is not illegal in Texas.

Federal Clauses

The government requires that specific clauses be added to contracts in two particular instances.

1. Before a buyer receives an FHA Appraised Value or a VA Certificate of Reasonable Value on the property, an *amendatory language clause* must be added to the sales contract. This clause ensures that the buyer can terminate the contract without suffering a loss if the agreed purchase price exceeds the appraised value. The amendatory language clause can be found in the TREC form for FHA insured or VA guaranteed financing; it must be used verbatim, which means the clause must be stated as it is found on the form.

2. When there is an earnest money contract, the Federal Trade Commission (FTC) requires that all new home builders and sellers must include *insulation disclosures* with the contract. Insulation disclosures should describe the type, thickness, and R-value of the insulation used in the

home. The insulation disclosure may be found in the TREC promulgated New Home Insulation Addendum.

Activity

In this exercise, you will use terms from a word bank to fill in blanks in sentences. The word bank contains a list of terms referring to various types of contracts we have studied in this lesson. These terms will fill in the blanks of the sentences you will see on the following pages. Choose the term from the word bank to fill in the appropriate blanks. Answer key is provided in the end.

Word Bank

Implied contract
Express contract
Bilateral contract
Unilateral contract
Void contract
Voidable contracts

Fill in the Blank

1. A(n) _____ is an agreement which may be terminated or rescinded by either party.

2. A(n) _____ is an agreement that has no legal effect or impact because it does not meet the minimum requirements of a contract.

3. A contract in which two parties are involved, but only one party is bound to act, is called a(n) _____.

4. An oral or written contract in which both parties explicitly state their conditions and promises is called a(n) _____.

5. When the terms and conditions of a contract are inferred from the parties' conduct, this contract is called a(n) _____.

6. An agreement in which both parties are bound by mutual or reciprocal obligations is called a(n) _____.

Answer Key

1. Voidable contract
2. Void contract
3. Unilateral contract
4. Express contract
5. Implied contract
6. Bilateral contract

Contracts, Purchase Agreements, and Sales Agreements Field Applications

Please consider the following case studies. After reading the situations, decide how one could resolve the dilemma or complication. Please make sure your response caters not only to the individual in the given situation but to the community as well.

Case Study One
Patient A visits Doctor B for an annual examination. During the exam, Doctor B checks over Patient A's heart rate, cholesterol level, and physical condition. At the end of the exam, Doctor B tells Patient A he is in great condition. As Patient A leaves the examination room, the receptionist hands Patient A a bill for $200. Patient A looks over the bill and tells the receptionist he is not responsible for the bill because he never agreed to receive the doctor's services. In fact, Patient A says Doctor B never explained what he would be charged–he claims, therefore, he does not have to pay for Doctor B's services. The receptionist explains to Patient A all clients must pay for the doctor's services, whether they received shots, exams, or medicine. Who is correct in this situation?

Case Study One Response
Patient A is incorrect in this case, because there does not have to be a verbal exchange in order to create a binding contract.

Many of our daily interactions create or rely upon *implied contracts*. No words or written documents must be exchanged for an implied contract to be created. The terms and conditions of this kind of contract are inferred from the parties' conduct.

All legally binding contracts involve the exchange of consideration, i.e., the exchange of something valuable, such as money or a promise, which is given to show acceptance or acknowledgement of a contract. In this case, Doctor B provided Patient A with his services, which have a known market value. Although Patient A did not gain from this interaction materially (e.g., the doctor did not pay him or give him anything tangible), he still gained the satisfaction of knowing he was in good health.

Case Study Two

Seven years have gone by since Client C failed to pay proper commission to Broker B. Finally, Broker B decides to file a lawsuit against Client C to collect the unpaid balance. However, when Broker B attempts to file this claim, he is told the statute of limitations for collecting debts in that state is six years. The clerk explains to Broker B he now has an unenforceable contract and cannot force Client C to pay. Broker B replies the contract contains all the components of a legally enforceable contract, and Client C should, therefore, be forced to pay the debt. Is Broker B correct?

Case Study Two Response

Broker B is mistaken. His contract may well be legally valid, which is to say it meets the following conditions:

- The contract was made between legally competent parties.

- The contract was mutually agreeable to all contracting parties.

- The contract has a lawful objective.

- The contract involves some sort of consideration (i.e., something of value given to show acceptance or acknowledgement of a contract, such as funds or a promise).

- The contract must comply with the requirements imposed by the statute of frauds.

However, the validity of Broker B's contract is not at issue here. Even if the contract was valid when it was made, the problem at present is the statute of limitations for enforcing the contract has expired. This means the contract is now *unenforceable*–i.e., Client C cannot be forced to pay Broker B's commission– because enforcing the contract would violate the state's statute of limitations. In this case, Broker B has no enforceable claim against Client C because the statute of limitations bars him from seeking compensation.

Case Study Three

Principal A has granted her son power of attorney because she wants him to be able to take over her affairs if some event renders her incapable of making her own decisions. After talking to her lawyers, Principal A decides to grant her son a springing power of attorney; she signs all the legal paperwork needed to create this agreement, as does her son. One week later, the son walks into Principal A's bank asking the bank transfer $20,000 to his account so he can place a down payment on a house for Principal A.

The bank clerk explains to the son he does yet not have a functional power of attorney and he must wait for Principal A to become mentally or physically impaired before he can exercise his springing power of attorney. The son tells the bank having the power of attorney allows him to make executive decisions for Principal A, regardless of whether she could make those same decisions herself. Who is correct?

Case Study Three Response
The bank clerk is correct in this case.

A springing power of attorney allows the person who receives this power (the attorney-in-fact) to take over control of the principal's affairs only when the principal becomes incapable of making decisions–that is, it *springs* into effect at this time. When establishing a springing power of attorney, the principal will usually specify an event or a type of event which, if it occurs, will mark the beginning of the power of attorney and empower the attorney-in-fact to act on the principal's behalf. For example, a principal might indicate he or she wants the attorney-in-fact to take over if the principal suffers a stroke or becomes paralyzed. Until this event occurs, however, the attorney-in-fact does not have any power to make decisions for the principal.

Case Study Four
Homebuilder A calls Tile Supplier B, and asks for an estimate of the cost of tiles for a building project. Homebuilder A tells Tile Supplier B he can only afford to pay $5,000 for tiles. Tile Supplier B tells Homebuilder A his company can provide the kind and number of tiles Homebuilder A needs for $5,000. Homebuilder A agrees to this price and Tile Supplier B says he will deliver the order in two weeks. Two weeks later, as Homebuilder A is nearing completion of his home, Tile Supplier B delivers the tile order to Homebuilder A. However, Tile Supplier B explains to Homebuilder A he will have to charge an extra $5,000, due to unexpected import tax increases. Tile Supplier B says Homebuilder A is responsible for any additional costs. Homebuilder A refuses to pay the extra $5,000. Tile Supplier B replies unless A pays, he will take A to court to recover his losses. Who would probably win this case in court?

Case Study Four Response
It is very unlikely Tile Supplier B could win this case in court.

There was a spoken understanding between A and B about the cost of the tile, but they did not exchange any consideration, which means their agreement lacks one of the important features of a legally valid contract. Promissory estoppel is a legal doctrine that can be used to force a party to keep a contractual promise without the exchange of consideration–that is, the doctrine can be used to force a party to honor a contract which does not satisfy one of the important conditions of a valid contract.

In general, this doctrine is used to keep people from defaulting on otherwise-reasonable contracts when their doing so would result in serious injustice to the other contracting party. If courts judge the person making the promise could reasonably have expected the other contracting party to rely on the promise, and that party did rely on the promise, then courts will often force the promise-maker to perform rather than let the other party suffer significant damages simply for taking the promise-maker at his or her word.

In this case, it is clear A would suffer a significant and totally unanticipated detriment if B is permitted to force A to pay this additional charge. Homebuilder A has already started his project, working under the assumption Tile Supplier B would deliver tiles at the quoted price of $5,000. Homebuilder A explicitly stated he could not afford to pay more than $5,000, and would, thus, suffer a significant loss if he had to pay Tile Supplier B $10,000.

In a court of law, Tile Supplier B would be held accountable for his original quote of $5,000; he cannot rescind his original quote without renegotiating his agreement with Homebuilder A. Tile Supplier B offered Homebuilder A a quote of $5,000, which A accepted. For Tile Supplier B to collect $10,000 from Homebuilder A, he would have to make a new offer of $10,000 to Homebuilder A, and Homebuilder A would have to accept this new offer.

Case Study Five

Buyer B owes Seller A a total of $2,000, which must be paid before they can proceed with their sales contract. A and B created a payment agreement under which Buyer B was to pay Seller A five payments of $400 each. Buyer B made two payments to Seller A, but has defaulted on the last three payments. Because Buyer B is not honoring the terms of their agreement, Seller A now has four options: he can rescind the contract, he can forfeit the contract, he can sue for specific performance, or he can sue for compensatory damages. In this case, Seller A decides to rescind the contract. Buyer B contacts Seller A and explains to A that since A rescinded the contract, A needs to return the $800 B has given him. Seller A explains to Buyer B he does not owe B anything since B defaulted on the contract. Who is correct?

Case Study Five Response

Buyer B is correct here. In this case, Seller A must return all payments to Buyer B. When a seller rescinds a contract, she or he is required to return any payments he or she has received from the buyer. When a seller opts to rescind a contract, this means he or she cancels or voids the contract; the situation is then as if the agreement never existed. If Seller A wanted to keep the payments, he should have forfeited the contract. This would have allowed him to keep any earnest money, payments, or deposits he might have received.

Case Study Six

After viewing Seller A's property, Buyer B makes an offer on the property. Seller A tells Buyer B he will consider the offer and will let Buyer B know in two weeks. However, two weeks pass by without Seller A contacting Buyer B; Buyer B assumes Seller A has rejected his offer, so he makes an offer on another property. Three days later, Seller A contacts Buyer B to accept the offer. Buyer B tells Seller A since he did not contact him within two weeks, he assumed Seller A declined the offer. Seller A tells Buyer B the offer was never officially rejected, because he never expressly informed Buyer B he was rejecting his offer. Seller A claims Buyer B must honor his offer on Seller A's property, but Buyer B thinks Seller A is mistaken. Who is correct?

Case Study Six Response

Buyer B is correct here. There are two ways an offer can be rejected: it can be rejected outright or the offer can be allowed to expire, in which case it is understood to have been implicitly rejected. When an offer is made, the seller is generally given a specific amount of time to accept the offer expressly and officially. Once the time period is up, the offer is understood to have been rejected. In this case, Seller A specifically stated he would let Buyer B know about the status of his offer within two weeks, which means Buyer B can assume the offer has been rejected (by expiration) after two weeks. He is not bound to his offer.

However, after Buyer B made the offer on A's property, even though he had heard nothing regarding the status of the offer, it would have been in everyone's best interest for him to retract his original offer before making an offer on another property. Buyer B has the right to retract his offer if he has not heard of its express acceptance, as was true in this case.

Case Study Seven

Tenant A is an independent contractor for a consulting company, a job which requires him to relocate frequently. Tenant A approaches Landlord B and explains he is looking for a small apartment to rent, but he does not know how long he will be able to stay in that particular city. Tenant A asks Landlord B if he can create a lease under an estate for years. However, Landlord B suggests they create a lease under a periodic estate. Is one type of lease agreement more beneficial to Tenant A than another, or would they both be equally useful?

Case Study Seven Response

A lease agreement creating a periodic estate would probably be most beneficial for Tenant A. A periodic estate (also known as a "periodic tenancy") is created by a lease agreement that defines tenancy as automatically continuing for consecutive periods of time. Most of us are familiar with month-to-month leases, which are an example of the kind of agreement that creates a periodic estate. This kind of lease is generally understood to be automatically renewed at the end of each lease period, until the landlord or tenant takes special action (such as submitting a written request) to terminate the lease agreement. For example, in a month-to-month lease, both the tenant and the landlord generally have the option of terminating the lease agreement at the end of any particular month. However, if neither party expressly terminates the lease, then it is usually understood the lease is renewed for another month.

This arrangement fits better with Tenant A's unpredictable schedule than does a lease agreement creating an estate for years. An estate for years lease need not actually extend for years–it can be for days, weeks, or months, too. However, regardless of the period of tenancy established in the lease, it is still the case that the period is fixed. Because Tenant A is unsure how long he will be in the area, a fixed period of any kind might prove to be either too long or too short to meet his needs. A lease creating a periodic estate gives Tenant A greater flexibility; it also means Tenant A will not have to meet with his landlord to renew or otherwise renegotiate his lease. He can simply stay until he needs to leave, and all he needs to do when he wants to leave is to make sure he provides his landlord with proper notice he is terminating their lease agreement.

Case Study Eight

Buyer B takes a tour of Seller A's property and decides to make an offer on it. Seller A tells Buyer B he will consider the offer and make a decision in three weeks. In order to show he is making a serious offer in good faith, Buyer B gives Seller A $3,000 as earnest money. He signs an earnest money contract, which stipulates if he withdraws from the contract, his earnest money is not refundable. However, one week later, Buyer B finds another property he likes better, and retracts his offer on Seller A's property. Buyer B asks Seller A to return the earnest money since Seller A never accepted his offer. Seller A explains to Buyer B the earnest money is non-refundable and he is entitled to keep it. Who is correct?

Case Study Eight Response

In this case, Seller A is entitled to keep the earnest money.

Earnest money is generally used to show the buyer is making a serious offer in good faith. It is also often used as a kind of "marker" to reserve the property while the final contracts are being drawn up or the offer is being considered. Usually, earnest money is kept in an escrow account or is held by a title insurance company to ensure there are funds available to compensate for any losses a seller or broker might suffer if the buyer withdraws from the contract.

In this case, Seller A has a signed agreement with Buyer B stipulating earnest money is non-refundable. It is true Seller A had not yet expressly accepted Buyer B's offer, but it is also true Buyer B had no reason to think A had rejected his offer. In addition, the fact he had deposited earnest money with A indicates A was giving his offer serious consideration. If B wanted to reclaim his earnest money, the simplest way of doing this would have been to wait for three weeks–

the time period within which A said he would make a decision regarding B's offer. At that point, B could reasonably infer A had rejected his offer, and it would have been A, not B, who had withdrawn from the contract, in which case the stipulations making B's earnest money non-refundable would not apply.

Case Study Nine

Minor A signed a contract with Homeowner B, agreeing to mow Homeowner B's lawn for the entire summer. In return, Homeowner B agrees to pay Minor A a flat rate of $200 for the whole summer. However, one month later, Minor A tells Homeowner B he no longer wants to mow Homeowner B's lawn. Homeowner B tells Minor A he signed a legal contract and he is bound by the terms of contract. Homeowner B says if Minor A does not complete the contract, he will take him to court to force performance. Minor A tells Homeowner B since he is not yet 18, he is not legally capable of entering into contracts and the fact he is a minor makes their contract legally void. Who is correct?

Case Study Nine Response

Minor A is correct.

A void contract is a "contract" that has no legal effect–but because it has no legal power, it is a contract only in name. The contracting parties may have *intended* to create a contract, and the agreement they created may even superficially resemble a contract. However, for a variety of reasons, a contract may fail to meet the legal requirements that define a valid contract. When this happens, the contract's stipulations and conditions cannot be legally enforced. A void contract cannot impose any obligations, establish any legal rights or otherwise perform any of the functions of a legally valid contract.

For these reasons, if Homeowner B were to take Minor A to court in an effort to have the contract legally enforced, Homeowner B would lose. Minor A is not legally capable of entering into contracts. Therefore, Minor A cannot be bound by the terms of his contract with Homeowner B. However, Minor A can hold Homeowner B accountable for any labor wages he accrued during the summer, and Homeowner B will most likely have to compensate Minor A for the amount of work he did during the summer despite the fact A did not fulfill the entirety of their agreement.

Case Study Ten

Salesperson A shows Buyer B an oceanfront property. Buyer B asks Salesperson A if the beach in front of the property is part of the lot she would be purchasing if she bought the home. Salesperson A tells Buyer B it is, even though he knows it is not. Relying on Salesperson A's claims, Buyer B places an offer on the property. Three days later, the offer is accepted, and three weeks later, Buyer B moves into the property. However, soon thereafter, Buyer B discovers the area in front of the beach does not belong to her–instead it is city property. Buyer B files a lawsuit against Salesperson A, claiming fraud. Is she likely to win?

Case Study Ten Response
Presuming she can show Salesperson A knowingly gave her false information, Buyer B is likely to win this case.

Fraud occurs when an individual purposefully deceives another individual to gain something of value. Usually fraud consists of a failure to disclose vital information, making a false promise, or telling a lie. In this case, Salesperson A knowingly told Buyer B the property she was considering included the beach area. Since Salesperson A intentionally deceived Buyer B, he is liable for any damages and losses Buyer B suffered as a result of deception.

It is also worth noting fraud can invalidate an otherwise-legal contract. So if, for example, Salesperson A and the person selling the beachfront home conspired to deceive Buyer B, her contract with this buyer would almost surely be legally invalidated and she would not be bound by any of its terms.

Summary

Agreement is an essential component in the legal transference of ownership. In real estate, contracts are the instruments by which agreements are reached for the conveyance of property. Whether a salesperson is promising to sell a property within a specified period of time, a prospective buyer is placing an offer on a house, or a seller is considering an offer on property, some type of contract is involved.

Before entering into a legally binding agreement, real estate professionals must fully understand the contracts that govern their industry. If a real estate professional makes a mistake while preparing a contract, he or she will be held liable for that mistake. Therefore, it is vital that real estate professionals are able to protect themselves against errors, oversights, and misunderstandings.

In this lesson, we learned about the types of general contracts as well as the different kinds of real estate contracts. We began by providing you with an overview of the various types of contracts: bilateral, unilateral, implied, express, executed, executory, valid, void, voidable, and unenforceable. Once introduced to the different types of contracts, we learned about what makes a contract legally enforceable, this being the five components that make a contract valid: mutual assent, legally competent parties, consideration, lawful objective, and adherence to a statute of frauds.

This lesson introduced you to two of the three factors that create a contract: offers and acceptances. When there is an offer and acceptance, the parties can either perform their respective parts of the contract or breach the contract by not fulfilling their obligations. Then we discussed the third component of a legally binding and enforceable contract-performance. There are four basic types of contracts in real estate: sales contracts, option agreements, contract for deeds and leases; these types of contracts being those that deal in the governance of the real estate industry which, as a real estate professional, you should be familiar with.

This concludes lesson seventeen.

Return to your online course player to take the Lesson Quiz.

Lesson 18:
REAL ESTATE PRACTICE

This lesson focuses on the following topics:

- Introduction
- Critical Thinking Questions
- Case Studies
- Summary

By the end of this lesson, you should be able to:

- Demonstrate the ability to apply what you have learned in this course to situations that you will likely encounter in your career, through analyses of case studies, real world situations, critical thinking questions, and other activities.

This final lesson is chock-full of case studies, real world situations, critical thinking questions, and activities designed so that you can be prepared to deal with the situations that you are likely to encounter in your career.

Real Estate Practice

This module has covered many specifics over a relatively short period of time. To ensure that you get a comprehensive understanding of the material, we will integrate the information provided in this module through a series of comprehension activities, questions, and case studies.

Activity

In this activity, we present information about a hypothetical borrower. You will use your knowledge of real estate finance to answer questions and make calculations.

Borrower B has a three-year employment history with A&J Publishing, where she currently makes $45,000 per year. In the past year, she also made $9,500 by doing extra work on the side for other publishing companies on a contract basis, but she has been doing contract work for only 14 months.

Question 1

Would the secondary income ($9,500) be included for the purposes of obtaining a loan?

Answer

To conform to Fannie Mae and FHA guidelines, the borrower generally should have a two-year history for all employment, including secondary employment (Freddie Mac does not have this guideline, as long as the borrower has a two-year history for his or her primary income). However, there are always extenuating circumstances and exceptions. In this situation, if the evidence is strong that the income will continue, and, because the secondary income is from the same type of work as the borrower's primary income, the chances are good that Fannie Mae and the FHA would accept the borrower's secondary income. Because of this, the lender decides to add Borrower B's secondary income to her primary income.

Question 2

What is Borrower B's total annual income?

Answer

$45,000 + $9,500 = $54,500.

The lender sends off for credit reports and scores from all three credit reporting companies, and the average of the three scores is 680. For a fixed-interest loan, the lender determines the interest rate based upon FICO scores; for a score of 680, the lender is willing to offer an interest rate of 6.124 percent on a fixed-rate loan, and slightly less for an adjustable rate mortgage.

Question 3

Borrower B wants to purchase a home that is listed for $90,000. The lender estimates taxes at 2.5 percent of the sale price per year. What will the monthly tax payment be on a $90,000 property?

Answer

($90,000 × 0.025) ÷ 12 months = $187.50

Question 4

In the particular area where the property is, hazard insurance runs $1,500 a year. What is the total monthly taxes plus insurance payment for this property?

Answer

The monthly insurance payment is $125 ($1,500 ÷ 12 months = $125), and the total monthly taxes + insurance payment is $312.50 ($187.50 + $125).

Question 5

What is the maximum monthly principal + interest payment that Borrower B can afford? Using a housing expense ratio of 33 percent, calculate the maximum monthly payment.

Answer

Ratio = (Principal + Interest + Taxes + Insurance) ÷ Gross Monthly Income, so 33% = (P + I + $312.50) ÷ $4,541.67. The maximum monthly principal + interest payment that Borrower B can afford is $1,186.25.

Question 6

Borrower B wants to purchase a house that is listed for $90,000. The amount of her down payment depends upon which type of loan she chooses, so assume that she will need a loan for $90,000. Can she afford this loan? Assume an interest rate of 6.124 percent and a term of 30 years. You can use the online mortgage calculator found at http://ray.met.fsu.edu/~bret/amortize.html.

Answer

Entering all known amounts into the mortgage calculator gives us an estimated monthly principal + interest payment of $546.79. This amount is less than Borrower B's maximum monthly payment of $1,186.25, so yes, the borrower could afford a loan of at least $90,000.

The lender has determined that, based upon the housing expense ratio, Borrower B could afford to purchase the property. The lender has also decided that Borrower B's FICO score is high enough for her to be considered creditworthy. However, the lender's final qualification is that Borrower B's total debt service ratio be less than 36 percent.

Question 7

Borrower B's long-term debts include a credit card with a minimum monthly payment of $30, telephone and utility bills of approximately $200 every month and car insurance of $75 per month. She also has a car payment of $312, but she will make her last payment on the car in two months. What is the amount of Borrower B's total monthly liabilities?

Answer

Borrower B's monthly liabilities are a total of $305. Her car payment is not calculated into the total. Because it will be paid off within six months, it is not considered a long-term debt.

Use the following formula to solve for Borrower B's debt service ratio:

(PITI + all long-term debts) ÷ gross monthly income = total debt service ratio
PITI = Principal + Interest + Taxes + Insurance
PITI = $546.79 + $312.50

PITI = $859.29

Debt service ratio = (PITI + long-term debts) ÷ gross monthly income
Debt service ratio = ($859.29 + $305) ÷ $4,541.67
Debt service ratio = 0.256
Debt service ratio = 25.6%

Question 8
If the lender requires that a borrower's debt service ratio be no higher than 36 percent, does Borrower B qualify?

Answer
Yes, 25.6 percent is lower than the lender's maximum debt service ratio of 36 percent, so Borrower B qualifies.

Now that Borrower B has qualified for a loan, she needs to decide which type of loan best suits her needs. She expects that her income will remain stable, neither growing by more than small annual raises nor decreasing. She is drawn to the idea of an adjustable rate mortgage because of the initial low interest rate, but she's nervous about the idea that a fluctuating market could have her paying higher interest rates in the long run. She is usually a low-risk investor.

Question 9
Which type of mortgage would Borrower B probably go with in this situation?

Answer
Borrower B did qualify for the fixed-rate mortgage, and she has no compelling reason to choose a graduated payment or growth equity mortgage. Although she was drawn to the adjustable rate mortgage because of the initial low interest rate, she is nervous about the possibility of ending up with higher rates. Because of this, she would probably choose a fixed-rate mortgage.

Borrower B has qualified for a fixed-interest mortgage at 6.124 percent interest. However, Borrower B has saved only $3,000 toward a down payment. The lender points out that FHA-insured loans require only a total of a 3 percent cash investment; Borrower B will have to put down 2.25 percent as a down payment, and the remainder will be applied to the closing costs. Borrower B decides that this is the best option for her.

Question 10
What will Borrower B's down payment be?

Answer
The property is listed at $90,000, and 3 percent of that is $2,700. The borrower must put down 2.25% of the total 3% required investment: 2.25% of $90,000 is

$2025. The additional $675 can be applied towards allowable closing costs. Additional closing costs can be paid off then or added to the principal. This brings the current principal amount to $87,975

Finally, FHA requires any borrower with less than a 20 percent down payment to purchase mortgage insurance. The borrower pays 1.5 percent of the loan amount up-front at closing and an annual premium depending on the loan term: 0.5 percent for 30-year loans and 0.25 percent for 15-year loans. The premiums go into an account held by the FHA to repay lost amounts on insured loans on which borrowers defaulted.

Question 11
How much mortgage insurance premium will the borrower have to pay upfront at closing?

Answer
1.5 percent of $87,975, or $1,319.63. However, this may be wrapped into the mortgage.

Question 12
How much will the borrower's annual premium be?

Answer
For the 30-year, fixed-interest mortgage, Borrower B will pay 0.5 percent per year as a premium. This comes to $439.88.

Critical Thinking Questions

Question 1
When a borrower prepays his or her loan, the lender receives the loan amount back quicker than anticipated. Why then would a lender want to add prepayment or lock-in clauses to a note?

- Lenders deal in long-term financing. They carefully balance incoming payments with outgoing payments so that they never have too much or too little money tied up in investments. When borrowers prepay their loans, the lenders' schedules of payments need to be recalculated; these problems are compounded by the large number of loans lenders deal with at once. Prepayment penalties and lock-in clauses provide a structure for lenders to calculate reliable payment schedules.

- A lender makes money from interest cash flows. Interest is paid on the principal balance of the loan that is still outstanding. If a borrower prepays the loan, the principal is reduced and the lender receives less money from interest. Therefore, some lenders will add a prepayment clause stating that only a certain amount of the principal may be paid each year, prepayment penalties to recover losses from interest or a lock-in clause that disallows prepayment entirely.

Question 2
Are deeds of trust more useful than mortgages to lenders who are in lien-theory states as opposed to title-theory states?

- No. In a lien-theory state, both mortgage documents and deeds of trust are interpreted merely as liens on the property, while the borrower retains its title. A deed of trust allows a trustee to hold title on behalf of the borrower, but it does not give the lender better protection in the case of foreclosure. Deeds of trust have the same drawbacks and benefits in a lien-theory state as they do in a title-theory state.

- Yes. In a lien-theory state, the mortgage document is interpreted as a lien on the collateral property, while the borrower retains its title. A deed of trust vests a third party (the trustee) with title to the property, effectively giving title to the lender. This, of course, is not necessary in a title-theory state where the mortgage document itself is interpreted as giving title to the lender and allowing the borrower only certain equitable rights.

Question 3
Why do so many of the purchasers of real estate loans on the secondary market require credit reports from more than one bureau?

- Each credit reporting bureau has its own version of the proprietary credit scoring software. Even though the credit information of each bureau is substantially the same, the interpretation of this information-the credit score-differs greatly between the different bureaus. The purpose of requiring the reports of several bureaus is to make more objective the subjective process of credit scoring by comparing the scores of several bureaus.

- The software used by the several credit reporting companies is substantially the same; however, the information collected by each bureau may differ greatly. This can result in reports that present widely divergent views on a borrower's creditworthiness and significantly different credit scores. The purpose of requiring the reports of several bureaus is to ensure that all the relevant credit information of a borrower has been collected.

Question 4

Which law is most relevant to Fannie Mae and Freddie Mac's decision not to use FICO scores in underwriting loans?

- The Fair Credit Reporting Act (FCRA). This act contains a clause that says that credit scoring may not be used in qualifying borrowers for real estate loans. It limits the use of credit scores to revolving credit and certain installment debts, such as automobiles. It also allows the use of a credit score for refinancing existing real estate loans but not for originating loans that are used to purchase or construct real property.

- The Equal Credit Opportunity Act (ECOA). This act contains a clause that says that lenders are required to tell borrowers who have been rejected for a loan the reason for which they were rejected. Since the software that produces credit scores is proprietary, lenders (such as Fannie Mae and Freddie Mac) do not have access to the exact reason for which any particular score was low or high. While the law does not prohibit using credit scores, this practice fits well with Fannie Mae and Freddie Mac's stated goal of keeping loan applicants well-informed.

Question 5

Which would be a better predictor of borrower default; the housing expense ratio or the debt service ratio?

- The housing expense ratio is less likely to predict future default because of its wide variability. A borrower's housing expense, even on fixed-payment loans, changes dramatically each year: as the principal balance shrinks, the premiums for mortgage insurance decrease, and as the property appreciates or depreciates, the annual taxes on it fluctuate significantly. The total debt service ratio, on the other hand, by encompassing more of a borrower's obligations, is less likely to change and thus is a better indicator of a borrower's future financial status.

- The purpose of the income qualifying ratios is to predict future default rates as a function of a borrower's debt obligations. The housing expense ratio does not account for a borrower's total liabilities and thus is a less useful predictor. For example, two borrowers may have the same income and need a loan of the same amount; their housing expense ratio would be the same, but one borrower could have substantially more debt than the other and is, therefore, much more likely to default.

Question 6

If the original purchase price of a property is equal to its final selling price, what is the total tax rate (capital gains and recaptured depreciation) on the sale? Suppose that the capital gains tax is 15 percent and the recaptured depreciation tax is 25 percent.

- 25 percent. The recaptured depreciation is equal to the original purchase price minus the adjusted basis; the capital gain is equal to the final selling price minus the adjusted basis. If the purchase and selling prices are the same, recaptured depreciation equals capital gain-that is, the investor receives no gain except for the recaptured depreciation, and this is taxed at a rate of 25 percent.

- 40 percent. The recaptured depreciation is equal to the original purchase price minus the adjusted basis; the capital gain is equal to the final selling price minus the adjusted basis. If the purchase and selling prices are the same, recaptured depreciation equals capital gain, and they are taxed at rates of 25 percent and 15 percent respectively, with a total tax rate of 40 percent.

Question 7
In addition to not wanting to have his or her money tied up in the event of a legal difficulty, why else might a buyer want to put as little money as possible down in the earnest money deposit?

- The earnest money contract is not a contract for sale until the seller ratifies it. Buyers will seek the best deal on a house and may not always offer enough for the seller or may require terms to which the seller is unwilling to agree. For this reason, buyers may want to make several offers at once. This increases the likelihood that an offer favorable to the buyer will be accepted. However, buyers need to keep as much money as possible to make these offers, especially because if more than one is accepted, the buyer will lose the earnest money deposit for the property he or she does not choose to purchase.

- Putting down a large sum of money in the earnest money deposit strongly reduces a buyer's bargaining ability. The seller knows that the buyer will not back out of the deal and risk losing the deposit, which allows the seller to push the terms in his or her favor. For this reason, a buyer will choose to put down as little money as possible to preserve her or his bargaining position, but at least enough to make the seller believe he or she is serious.

Question 8
Why might a deed involve a consideration amount such as "for $10 and other good and valuable consideration" rather than, say, nothing at all?

- The phrase "for $10 and other good and valuable consideration," like the grantor's testament in the acknowledgment clause, is completely customary. It helps the parties, if it becomes necessary, to prove that the document including the consideration is a deed, because it has the customary form of one. However, this can never be conclusive proof, as deeds do not require consideration.

- All valid contracts require some sort of consideration. Consideration is what distinguishes a contract from a gift. By including it in the sales contract, the buyer and seller are guaranteed the legal protection afforded to contracts (for example, regarding their enforceability).

Question 9

What could be an advantage of an escrow closing as opposed to a face-to-face closing?

- Escrow closings are conducted by a disinterested third party. This eliminates many of the difficulties of a direct face-to-face closing. For example, in a face-to-face closing, the buyer (or buyer's agent) gives his check to the seller (or seller's agent) and the seller gives the deed to the buyer. In an escrow closing, however, these items are both given to the escrow agent, who ensures that the title is acceptable and that the borrower's check has cleared before transferring the title or the money.

- Escrow closings are more affordable: escrow agents are government officials whose job it is to facilitate real estate and other large financial transactions. Since their salaries are paid with tax dollars, they are relatively cheap. For this reason, most buyers and sellers use an escrow closing rather than incurring the expense of hiring an attorney or a private closing agent.

Question 10

Are rents an accrued or a prepaid item? How should they be prorated?

- Rents are accrued items, and the buyer should receive the daily rate for the rent to, or through, the day of closing, as stipulated in the sales contract.

- Rents are prepaid items, and the seller should receive the daily rate for the rent to, or through, the day of closing, as stipulated in the sales contract.

Answers:

1. Most of a lender's income is indeed from interest cash flows. It is in the borrower's interest to prepay a loan and thereby pay less interest over its term; likewise, it is in the lender's interest to limit prepayment if possible and to receive the maximum amount of interest payments. This is done through the use of prepayment clauses and penalties and lock-in clauses. It is also the reason why borrower-friendly institutions such as the FHA disallow such clauses and penalties in loans they insure.

2. Whether or not the lender uses a mortgage or a deed of trust as security for the loan amount, in a lien-theory state the lender can have, at most, a lien against the property, never the title. Some lien-theory states allow the lender to take possession of the property in foreclosure even before he or she has received the title through the proper legal procedures. These lenders must nevertheless respect the borrower's rights of redemption.

3. The different credit bureaus each have different information on a borrower. They collect credit information independently and may not always collect the same information. One extreme case is credit inquiries. If a creditor inquires with one bureau about a consumer's credit, that bureau will have a record of the inquiry, whereas the other bureaus might not. By requiring the reports of several bureaus, buyers on the secondary market can ensure that they have all the available credit information for a borrower.

4. The ECOA's purpose is to protect borrowers who are seeking credit from unfair and discriminatory practices by lenders. In this vein, it requires that lenders disclose the reason for which a borrower was denied for a loan. This law is not interpreted to mean that lenders are not allowed to use credit scoring in underwriting loans. Its spirit, however, is clear, and for the same reason, Fannie Mae and Freddie Mac do not require these scores to qualify borrowers. The FCRA has no provision limiting the use of credit scores in real estate lending.

5. The reason the debt service ratio is a better predictor of future default is that it takes into consideration the No. 1 factor that can lead to default; a borrower's total obligations (debt) being too high. Monthly housing payments for conventional loans are fairly constant: The principal and interest payments do not change from month to month or year to year, mortgage insurance premiums decrease gradually over time, and real estate taxes do not usually fluctuate significantly.

6. Income from the sale of a property is taxed on the basis of what type of income it is. Funds up to, and including, the full amount of accrued depreciation on a property are taxed as recaptured depreciation; proceeds after that are taxed as capital gains. So if the taxable gains are equal to the recaptured depreciation, all of the gain is taxed as recaptured depreciation, at the higher rate of 25 percent. However, it is not also taxed as capital gains.

7. There are several reasons a buyer might refrain from putting a large sum of money down in the earnest money deposit. One main reason is the possibility of legal difficulty: A buyer does not want to have significant cash resources tied up for a long period of time. Buyers may also want to make several offers at once, requiring them to have available funds to go around.

Finally, a buyer may want to keep his or her funds to collect interest before the down payment is paid at closing. A large earnest money deposit does not reduce the buyer's bargaining position.

8. All valid contracts do indeed require consideration. In a contract, two willing parties exchange something of value with each other. It is not necessary that the items exchanged be of equal value-allowing the use of the phrase "for $10 and other good and valuable consideration." This makes it easier to prepare deeds and keeps the particular sale price out of the local title transfer records.

9. Escrow closings eliminate several of the disadvantages of the face-to-face closing by requiring the escrow agent to validate the good condition of the title and the purchaser's funds. Escrow closings have an additional advantage over face-to-face closings in that the closing can be conducted without either the seller or the buyer being present. Escrow agents are not government officials-they are lawyers, title or trust companies, or companies specializing in escrow transactions. Sometimes escrow closings can be more expensive than face-to-face closings, because they require the added cost of hiring a third party for the transaction; at other times escrow closings may be just as cheap as a face-to-face closing.

10. Rents are accrued items. The buyer purchases an income-producing property and expects to receive the rent during her or his ownership. Rent is paid at the beginning of the month for a tenant's stay through that month. Thus when the seller receives the rent at the beginning of the month, it becomes a loss for the buyer-in effect, an expense paid, and, therefore, an accrued item. For this reason, rent is divided at closing between the buyer and the seller. A prepaid item is an expense that the seller has paid before closing for which the buyer will owe him or her.

Case Studies

Case Study One: Wraparound Mortgage
Seller S is looking to sell her house. She has had difficulty finding a buyer but finally locates Buyer B, who is very interested. Buyer B visits several lenders at various lending institutions-commercial banks, savings and loans, and credit unions-but just doesn't have the credit necessary to obtain a loan.

Seller S talks with Buyer B about the following option: She could lend him the money herself to buy the property at 1 point above the rate on her existing mortgage. S originally paid $30,000 for the home at 7.35 percent and is now selling the home for $44,000 after only 10 years, 20 years before the expiration of her mortgage's term.

S sees a potential to turn the sale into a cash flow. She is currently paying $204.65 a month in principal and interest payments. For a loan of $44,000 at 8.25 percent, B would be paying $330.56 a month. That's a monthly cash flow of $125.91. However, this money comes at a risk. If B defaults on the loan, S still has the obligation to repay her original mortgage. Ideally, she would just sell the house, but as she has had such a difficult time finding a borrower to begin with, there is the worry that she may not be able to sell it in time to not default on her original mortgage. If her lender has to foreclose to recover his losses, S will lose money overall.

Additionally, S cannot use the projected cash flows from B to qualify for a mortgage on a new home, as they do not have an established two-year history. However, as she believes B is unlikely to default and does not need the cash flow to qualify, she decides to go ahead with the loan.

Buyer B is willing to take advantage of this offer for several reasons. First, since he has not been able to qualify with any lender, he doesn't have many other options. Second, he saves money in closing costs—no lender's origination fees, application fees, or other costs associated with the lender. Third, and most importantly, the interest rate offered by S is less than the current market rate. Even though B is paying 1 point above S's interest rate, since S locked in that rate 10 years ago, B is able to avoid the greater than 1 point increase in market rates that has since occurred. Such rates on wraparound mortgages that are between the original rate and the current market rate are known as *blended rates*.

Of course, wraparound mortgages aren't always available. If Seller S's original note had contained a due-on-sale clause, she could not have sold her property to Buyer B and still kept her mortgage.

Case Study Two: Foreclosure

Lender A has not received a mortgage payment from Borrower B in four months. After the first missed payment, Lender A sent the borrower a letter informing him of his delinquency. Borrower B did not respond to the letter or the lender's subsequent phone calls. Because the loan was FHA-insured, after two months, the lender contacted the local FHA office.

The FHA investigated the situation. Under such circumstances, the FHA's goal is to do what is necessary to help the borrower avoid foreclosure. This can be accomplished through compromises with the lender or an interest-free loan from the FHA to make the loan current. An FHA loan counselor talks with Borrower B and learns that he was recently laid off and feels as though he cannot afford to make the monthly payment. The loan counselor informs him of his several alternatives and persuades him to speak with the lender.

With the lender, Borrower B tries to work out a payment plan. The loan counselor has advised B to bring an itemized list of his monthly expenses to the meeting. This way they will be better able to decide what might be the best approach to resolve the borrower's delinquency to avoid foreclosure. Borrower B's expenses are as follows:

Expense	Cost
Groceries	$250
Medicine	$50
Car Payment	$200
Car Insurance	$30
Phone	$20
Miscellaneous	$75
TOTAL	**$625**

The borrower's loan is for $30,000 at 9 percent interest for 30 years, and the monthly payment is $241.39. Although Borrower B's unemployment benefits have been canceled, he still receives enough in welfare to cover his monthly expenses, although not enough to also cover the monthly mortgage payments. Which of these expenses do you think the borrower could eliminate to help make the loan payments?

Groceries
It is unlikely that anyone could eliminate their grocery expenditures and still get by. People need food to live. However, this does not mean that a grocery bill could not be reduced, which would be an option in this situation.

Medicine
The health and well-being of oneself and one's family should not be sacrificed if at all possible. Since there are other, less important expenses the borrower might eliminate, he should not consider eliminating his medical expenses.

Car payment
Although a car is an important part of anyone's life, it is not essential when compared to one's shelter. The worry with selling a car, however, might be that the borrower owes more on the car than it is worth. Under such circumstances, the borrower would not be able to pay off the entire car loan and would have to continue making car payments for a time. The blue book value of the car and the borrower's total liability should be taken into account when a plan is made to avoid foreclosure.

Car insurance
Since the car payment may be eliminated by selling the car, the car insurance may also be eliminated. Of course, if the car cannot be sold, the insurance should not be eliminated; even to save a borrower from foreclosure, a lender should never recommend that a borrower break the law.

Phone

Unlike the house payment, food, medicine, and utilities, a telephone is not essential. Furthermore, unlike a car payment, it is not often so costly that it would affect a borrower's ability to make his or her house payments. However, in certain circumstances, a borrower may wish to consider eliminating her or his phone if it is the difference between owning and not owning the house, or the borrower could eliminate "extras" such as voice mail and call waiting and avoid making long-distance calls.

Miscellaneous

There are some expenses not included on the list that would be essential expenses of the household, such as clothing and shoes. However, every household has several expenses that are hardly necessary. These can include cable television, the Internet, music, and movies, dining out, and so on. Anyone in enough financial difficulty to be in danger of losing his or her home should be willing to make the lifestyle changes necessary to continue making monthly loan payments.

The lender begins by encouraging Borrower B to sell his car so that he can make his mortgage payments. However, B feels that having a car will be necessary for him to find a new job.

The lender realizes that Borrower B will not be able to make his payments if he refuses to sell his car. Usually, the lender would want B to attempt to sell the house to pay off the loan amount. In this case, however, B has waited too long to come to the lender, and the lender does not want to incur the further expense (through lost interest) of waiting for the house to be sold.

The market in the property's neighborhood is not particularly good at the moment, and there are several other houses up for sale that have remained unsold for some time.

With this in consideration, the lender suggests a deed in lieu of foreclosure. The borrower, however, does not share the lender's pessimistic view of the house's salability and wants to try the market himself. They agree that the lender will allow a moratorium on payments for two months but that after that point, if the house is unsold, the lender will have to foreclose.

When two months have gone by, the house remains unsold. The lender fills out FHA Form 2068 Notice of Default and sends it both to the FHA and Borrower B. At this point, the FHA has the right to make the loan current by lending, interest-free, the amount owed the lender in PITI payments, penalties and legal fees. This is what is known as a partial claim: The FHA pays the amount out of its MIP funds, thereby creating a lien on the property. The FHA requires, however, that the following conditions be met:

- First, that the borrower is between 4 and 12 months delinquent on the loan payments
- Second, that the borrower be able to begin making monthly mortgage payments in full

Since B has yet to find a new job, the second of these conditions is not fulfilled, and the FHA will not advance him the funds. The case is taken to court for a judicial foreclosure, and a sales date is named by the lender.

The auction is held in front of the courthouse. It is important at this point for the lender to know the exact amount of debt owed. He calculates it as follows:

Expense	Cost
Principal Balance	$26,325.85
Accrued Interest (5 months)	$1,002.14
Penalties	$500
Attorney's Fees	$550
Other Legal Fees	$200
TOTAL	**$28,577.99**

In an FHA foreclosure case, the lender will usually bid the amount of the debt. If there is a higher bidder, the lender will recover all of her or his losses and that will be the end of the matter. If, on the other hand, there is no higher bidder, the lender will take control of the property and have two choices: Either the lender may sell the property on the open market to recover his or her losses or the lender will deed the property to the FHA for the mortgage insurance. This will cover the lost principal amount, accrued interest, penalties, and attorney's fees up to a certain amount.

The maximum amount of attorney's fees that the FHA will pay in a mortgage insurance claim varies from state to state. For Texas, the rates are as follows:

**HUD Schedule of Standard Attorney's Fees
(not hourly rate), Effective 09/1/2005**

Nonjudicial foreclosure: $600
Chapter 7 bankruptcy clearance: $650
Chapter 11, 12, and 13 bankruptcy clearance: $ 1,000
Possessory action: $325
Deed-in-lieu: $400

In this case, since the lender believes the property is not salable at the price of the debt, the lender will file the insurance claim with the FHA. It is then the FHA's job to sell the property to recover its mortgage insurance losses.

Case Study Three: Appraisal (Cost Approach)

Appraiser A is hired to appraise a residential property for a lender, who intends to issue a conventional loan based on the appraised value of the property. The appraiser intends to use the cost approach method to value the property.

To begin, the appraiser determines the total square footage of the property by measuring its exterior dimensions. She makes a sketch of the perimeter and calculates the following totals:

Garage: 144 square feet
Downstairs living area: 1,296 square feet
Upstairs living area: 1,296 square feet
Total living area: 2,592 square feet

To determine the cost of reconstructing the property, the appraiser uses a construction cost manual. These manuals are published quarterly by private companies and detail the cost per square foot of different types of construction, including foundation work, frames, roofing, plumbing, and so on. The manuals also contain regional multipliers, which adjust for the variance in construction costs from region to region. The manual tells the appraiser that this particular type of residential property runs nationally at a cost of $73.04 per square foot of living area and $48.44 per square foot of garage/carport area. The multiplier for the region is 0.88, so the reconstruction value of the house is

> Living Area × Cost Per Square Foot = Living Area National Cost
> 2,592 × $73.04 = $189,319.68

> Garage Area × Cost Per Square Foot = Garage Area National Cost
> 144 × $48.44 = $6,975.36

> Living Area Cost + Garage Area Cost = Total National Cost
> $189,319.68 + $6,975.36 = $196,295.04

> Total National Cost × Regional Multiplier = Actual Cost
> $196,295.04 × 0.88 = $172,739.64

Having determined the actual cost of reconstructing the property, the appraiser must then determine the cost of purchasing the land. This, quite obviously, cannot be done using the cost approach; the appraiser must compare the sale prices of comparable parcels recently sold in the area. In this case she has three parcels to compare:

Parcel 1: 24,058 square feet for $71,211.68 in 2003
Parcel 2: 19,944 square feet for $63,980.80 in 2003

Parcel 3 126,602 square feet for $335,495.30 in 2004

Parcels 1, 2, and 3 sold for $2.96, $3.20, and $2.65 per square foot respectively. The appraiser adjusts each square footage rate for the size and location of the parcels and determines a likely price of $3.05 for the subject parcel. The subject parcel sits on a lot 108 feet × 142 feet, which is 15,336 square feet. By her estimate, it would cost $46,774.80 to buy a comparable parcel at the current price level.

The appraiser's final task is to determine the depreciation of the property. She has two options for determining this value: First, she can examine the property thoroughly, noting its physical wear and tear, its functional problems, its design flaws and so on, deducting value for each one separately to arrive at a total depreciation figure. This requires a keen eye and has as a central problem that not all defects are observable. The condition of the plumbing or electrical systems, for instance, cannot easily be determined.

The second method of depreciation is known as the straight-line method, and it is the principal method used in depreciating commercial property for tax purposes. This method starts by determining an effective age for the property. For tax purposes, the effective age is always the actual age of the property. In reality, however, this is not always so: Some properties are better or worse kept than comparables and, therefore, have greater or less depreciation. Once the effective age of the property is determined, the appraiser estimates its economic life—the number of years of its entire physical life for which it will be salable. The total depreciation is determined with the following formula:

Total Depreciation = (Effective Age ÷ Economic Life) × Replacement Cost

The subject property's actual age is 16 years, and the appraiser believes this to be its effective age as well, for it seems no better or worse kept than the other comparable properties in the vicinity. She estimates its total economic life to be 41 years. Therefore, its total depreciation is

(16 ÷ 41) × $172,739.64 = $67,410.59

From this figure, the appraiser can estimate the property's value:

Current Value = Reconstruction Cost + Land Value − Depreciation
Current Value = $172,739.64 + $46,774.80 − $67,410.59
Current Value = $152,103.85

This she rounds to $152,100 in her final estimate. If the lender is offering a 90 percent LTV loan, the loan amount will be $152,100 × 0.9 = $136,890.

Case Study Four: Investment Financing

Mortgage Broker B is trying to secure a loan for an investor to purchase a small office building. She needs two things: first, to show the lender what the property is worth (its net present value or NPV) and that it is a solid investment (it has a high internal rate of return or IRR). To do this, Broker B will create a pro forma financial statement and use a discounted cash flow analysis.

For the purpose of illustration, once again we will limit our pro forma to a five-year projection, although it is customary to use 10-year projections. The office building in consideration has four offices: two 1,100-square-foot offices and two 1,500-square-foot ones. The rent for the smaller offices is $5.15 per square foot and for the larger offices, $5 per square foot. There are currently no vacancies in the building, but Tenant A's lease is up in two years, and Tenant C's lease is up in five.

The investor expects to find a new tenant for Office A within six months and for Office C within a year. However, the investor also expects that she will need an 18-month, 25 percent discount to attract new tenants. The gross income for the building, factoring in a 5 percent rent increase for new tenants, looks like this:

	Year 1	Year 2	Year 3	Year 4	Year 5
Monthly Rent:					
Office A	$5,665	$5,948	$5,948	$5,948	$5,948
Office B	$5,665	$5,665	$5,665	$5,665	$5,665
Office C	$7,500	$7,500	$7,500	$7,500	$7,500
Office D	$7,500	$7,500	$7,500	$7,500	$7,500
Total × 12	$315,960	$319,356	$319,356	$319,356	$319,356
Vacancy	$0	-$35,688	$0	$0	-$90,000
Concessions	$0	-$8,922	-$17,844	$0	$0
Gross Annual Income:					
	$315,960	$274,746	$301,512	$319,356	$229,356

After calculating the gross income, we must calculate the operating expenses to determine the Net Operating Income (NOI). Broker B estimates that the first year's maximum monthly expenses will be $1.75 per square foot:

Maximum Monthly Expenses = Total Square Footage × Rate = 5,200 × $1.75 = $9,100

Broker B expects these expenses to increase by 2 percent annually. She estimates that 78 percent of the total monthly expenses will be fixed and 22 percent will be variable:

	Year 1	Year 2	Year 3	Year 4	Year 5
Monthly Expenses:					
Maximum	$9,100	$9,282	$9,468	$9,657	$9,850

Fixed	$7,098	$7,240	$7,385	$7,532	$7,683
Vacancy %	0%	21.15%	0%	0%	28.85%
Variable	$2002	$1,610	$2,083	$2,125	$1,542
Net Annual Operating Expenses:					
	$109,200	$106,200	$113,616	$115,884	$110,160

The pre-tax cash flow for any particular year is the NOI minus non-operating expenses, such as the annual mortgage payment and the broker's commission. The purchase price for the property is $1,875,000. The investor is seeking a 75 percent LTV loan, or $1,406,250. At the lender's interest rate of 9.733 percent, the annual mortgage payment for a 30-year loan will be $136,879. The broker's commission is 1 percent of the gross income:

	Year 1	Year 2	Year 3	Year 4	Year 5
NOI	$206,760	$168,546	$187,896	$203,472	$119,196
Mortgage	$136,879	$136,879	$136,879	$136,879	$136,879
Commission	$3,160	$2,747	$3,015	$3,194	$2,294
Pre-Tax Cash Flow:					
	$66,721	$28,920	$48,002	$63,339	-$19,977

To determine the after-tax cash flow, we must take the original NOI and subtract the tax-deductible expenses, the mortgage interest and the broker's commission to determine the taxable income (for simplicity's sake, depreciation has been left out, but remember that it, too, is tax-deductible and that it is taxed when recaptured at sale). Then, we multiply the taxable income by the tax rate (here, 20 percent), and subtract this from the pre-tax cash flow:

	Year 1	Year 2	Year 3	Year 4	Year 5
Deductions:					
Interest	$126,563	$125,634	$124,622	$123,518	$122,316
Commission	$3,160	$2,747	$3,015	$3,194	$2,294
Taxable Income	$77,037	$40,165	$60,259	$76,760	$0
Taxes@20%	$15,407	$8,033	$12,052	$15,352	$0
After-Tax Cash Flow:					
	$51,314	$20,877	$35,950	$47,987	-$19,977

The projected NOI for Year 6 is $200,000. Broker B expects investors in that year to seek a cap rate of 8% and thus the property to sell for $200,000 ÷ 0.08 = $2,500,000. Our use of this number to calculate the NPV of the property, however, is idealized for the sake of example, as it does not take into account the costs of selling the property-marketing, broker's commission, closing, capital gains taxes, and so on. We calculate the investment's NPV, using a discount rate of 7 percent, as follows:

Year	ATCF	$(1 + Discount)^{year}$	NPV
0	-$1,875,000	1.000000	-$1,875,000
1	$51,314	1.070000	$47,957
2	$20,877	1.144900	$18,235
3	$35,950	1.225043	$29,346
4	$47,987	1.310796	$36,609
5	$2,480,023	1.402552	$1,768,221
			Total: $25,368

Notice that the after-tax cash flow (ATCF) in Year 5 is equal to the ATCF from our pro forma, -$19,977, plus Broker B's estimated selling price for that year. This NPV is calculated on the basis of a five-year holding period; in most real-world situations it would be calculated for 10 years. While the cash flows from future years would increase the total NPV, the future value of the final selling price will decrease through the years, thereby decreasing the total NPV.

We can also calculate the internal rate of return (IRR) of this investment using the pre-tax or after-tax cash flows. It is probably best, for comparing investments, to use the pre-tax cash flow because, for instance, interest rates are given pre-tax. Since the IRR calculation cannot be done with a mathematical formula, Broker B uses MS Excel. The program returns an IRR of 8 percent.

It is up to the lender to decide whether these numbers—the NPV and IRR—are enough to warrant her investment. The lender's cash flows come from interest on the mortgage loan and are not dependent upon the rates of return of the property. However, the loan required is a sizable investment, and the lender must ensure that if she receives the property in distress through default, she will be able to recover her investment.

Case Study Five: Refinancing

Suppose an investor owns a single-family residence that she rents out for extra income. She purchased the property with a loan for $80,000 at 8 percent for 30 years. After 15 years, she wonders if she should refinance the property at a lower rate of 7 percent.

The investor's balance at the end of 15 years will be $61,425.25, and her monthly payment will be $587.01. She uses an amortization schedule to figure out what her new monthly payments will be, given her current balance. She figures that the new payments will be $552.11 per month, a savings of $34.90 each month. This may not seem like a lot, but it adds up. Overall, the investor will save:

$$\$34.90 \times 12 \text{ months} \times 15 \text{ years} = \$6,282$$

The savings may look more appealing now, but the investor still must weigh the cost of refinancing against the savings. She estimates the following charges:

Fee	Charge
Application Fee	$25
Appraisal Fee	$250
Attorney's Fee	$100
Credit Report	$50
Document Preparation Fee	$100
Home Inspection Fee	$200
Loan Origination Fee (1.5%)	$921
TOTAL	$1,646

The $1,646 that the investor pays to refinance lessens her overall savings. It also may become a burden to her in the short run, in that she must pay all of the fees up-front and wait to recoup the charges. Suppose the investor rents the house out for $730 per month. It will take her 10 months until she begins to see the savings:

Month	Rent	Loan Pmt	Profit	Charges	Total
1	$730.00	$552.11	$177.89	-$1,646.00	-$1,468.11
2	$730.00	$552.11	$177.89	-$1,468.11	-$1,290.22
3	$730.00	$552.11	$177.89	-$1,290.22	-$1,112.33
4	$730.00	$552.11	$177.89	-$1,112.33	-$934.44
5	$730.00	$552.11	$177.89	-$934.44	-$756.55
6	$730.00	$552.11	$177.89	-$756.55	-$578.66
7	$730.00	$552.11	$177.89	-$578.66	-$400.77
8	$730.00	$552.11	$177.89	-$400.77	-$222.88
9	$730.00	$552.11	$177.89	-$222.88	-$44.99
10	$730.00	$552.11	$177.89	-$44.99	$132.90

If the investor can afford refinancing and can afford not to make a profit on the refinanced property for 10 months, it might be a good idea. In the end, she would save $6,282 − $1,646 = $4,636.

Case Study Six: 80-10-10 mortgage vs. Conventional mortgage with PMI

A borrower is considering the option of an 80-10-10 piggyback mortgage instead of a conventional mortgage with PMI. If she is seeking to borrow 90 percent of the sale price of a $100,000 property, how long will she have to keep the house for the piggyback loan to become unprofitable? Assume the following:

- 80-10-10 first loan: $80,000 at 8 percent for 30 years

- 80-10-10 second loan: $10,000 at 11 percent for 30 years

- Conventional loan: $90,000 at 8 percent for 30 years

- PMI: 0.75 percent annually until principal balance reaches 20 percent

The 80-10-10 loan will carry a total monthly payment of $682.24 (an 80 percent LTV payment of $587.01 and a 10 percent LTV payment of $95.23). The conventional loan, however, carries a steeper payment of $716.64 ($660.39 + $56.25 PMI). This means that the borrower would save $34.40 per month until the PMI was canceled after month 111. After that, the conventional loan payment would drop to $660.39 and the borrower would lose $21.85 per month, comparatively. This can be illustrated with the following graph:

Money Saved with an 80-10-10 Mortgage

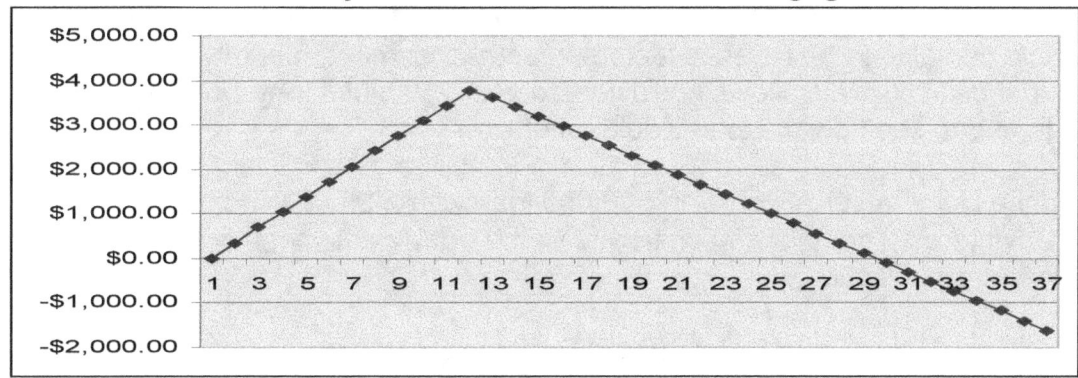

The x-axis (horizontal) is given in *tens of months* (that is, 1 = 10 months, 2 = 20 months and so on). After the payment in the 286th month, the borrower begins to lose money when compared to the fixed-rate loan whose PMI has been canceled.

If the borrower plans to keep the loan after the 24th year, she should obtain a conventional loan with PMI. However, if she is likely to sell the house and repay the loan before that, the piggyback loan may be more profitable. To avoid more cash losses, the borrower must make sure that the loan does not have a prepayment penalty.

Case Study Seven: FHA 245(A)
Graduated Payment Mortgage

Homebuyer A wants to purchase a house with a graduated payment mortgage (GPM). She needs an $80,000 loan and doesn't currently have the income to qualify for a conventional fixed-rate mortgage. Since she expects her income to increase in the coming years, a GPM is an excellent alternative to conventional financing. Additionally, the Federal Housing Administration (FHA) offers several GPMs in the Section 245(a) plan.

Homebuyer A is interested to know what her payment schedule would be like for an FHA GPM. There are several ways for her to find this information. First, she could go to the Department of Housing and Urban Development's (HUD) Web site and use the GPM calculator:

HUD GPM Calculator:
http://www.hud.gov/offices/hsg/sfh/gpm/gpm_calc.cfm

At this Web site, anyone may download a free MS DOS program to calculate payments for a graduated payment loan. Some computers, however, may have difficulty running the program. For this reason, prospective borrowers also may wish to look up the GPM payment factors published with the GPM Calculator.

The payment factors on this Web site are per $1,000 of the loan amount. Therefore, if a loan was for $20,256 and the monthly mortgage payment factor was 8.1791, then the monthly payment would be 8.1791 × 20.256 = $165.68. The site contains three types of factors: monthly payment, monthly MIP, and principal balance. This allows borrowers to see how much they would pay each month and to see how the loan would amortize.

Suppose Homebuyer A wants an $80,000 loan with a 30-year term at 10.25 percent interest The following chart shows the borrower's monthly payments and the loan's amortization.

FHA Graduated Payment Mortgage

Year	Pymt Factor	MIP Factor	Mo. Pymt	Prin. Bal
1	8.1791	0.4175	$687.73	$80,364.85
2	8.3863	0.4190	$704.42	$80,563.11
3	8.5932	0.4196	$721.02	$80,571.74
4	8.8080	0.4192	$738.18	$80,365.10
5	9.0282	0.4175	$755.66	$79,914.64
6	9.0282	0.4145	$755.42	$79,188.62
7	9.0282	0.4106	$755.10	$78,384.58
8	9.0282	0.4062	$754.75	$77,494.16
9	9.0282	0.4013	$754.36	$76,508.04
10	9.0282	0.3959	$753.93	$75,415.97

Notice that the monthly payment in the chart above is calculated with the formula

Monthly Payment = 80 × (Payment Factor + MIP Factor)

Thus, it includes the principal, interest, and mortgage insurance premium but not the taxes or hazard insurance. Suppose the sale price of the property is $83,000 and the lender estimates real estate taxes at 2.5 percent of the sale price annually. This ends up being a monthly rate of $172.92. If hazard insurance is $900 annually ($75 a month), then the total monthly payment for the first year will be $935.65.

Considering just the FHA's total housing expense ratio of 29 percent, Homebuyer A would need a gross monthly income of at least $3,226.38 to qualify for the graduated payment loan. This is more than $200 less per month than the income the borrower would need to qualify for a fixed-payment loan.

However, the GPM has certain disadvantages. For instance, despite the borrower's $3,000 down payment, she only has $2,428.26 (about 3 percent) in equity after the first three years. Furthermore, the total cost of the loan is significantly more than that of a fixed-payment conventional loan. This is because the interest rate is a half point above the market rate, and in the early years the loan collects compound interest. Additionally, the loan payments increase by a fair amount annually, which may prove to be trouble if the borrower does not receive the expected increase in income.

Case Study Eight: VA Hybrid Arm

Serviceperson A is looking for a loan. She has been on active duty for more than 181 consecutive days and will continue her service in the Army for the next several years. She has obtained a Certificate of Eligibility from the Department of Veterans Affairs and hopes to qualify for a VA loan with Lender B.

Serviceperson A wants to purchase a $46,000 property. Since she may leave in the next five to seven years, she was hoping to take advantage of the early low interest rates of a VA hybrid ARM. The interest rate is 9.25 percent and the hybrid ARM rate 50 basis points below it, or 8.75 percent.

A expects to put 5 percent of the purchase price down and finance the VA funding fee of 1.5 percent. Thus the total loan amount will be:

$46,000 × 0.95 (portion not put down) × 1.015 (funding fee) = $44,355.50

At the interest rate of 8.75 percent the monthly payment for the first three years of fixed payments will be $348.94. The lender estimates that annual taxes will be 2.75 percent of the sale price or:

0.0275 × $46,000 = $1,265

In addition, he estimates a hazard insurance payment of $1,000, leaving a total PITI payment of:

$348.94 Principal and Interest + ($1,265/12) Taxes + ($1,000/12) Insurance = $537.69

Since Serviceperson A is relatively young, she has no long-term obligations. She also has very little credit, but the lender believes this risk to be offset by the 40 percent VA guarantee. A's net effective annual salary (after deductions) is $15,950, giving her a total debt service ratio of:

$$\$537.69 \div (\$15{,}950/12) = 40\%$$

This is below the VA qualifying ratio of 41 percent. When Lender B completes the VA Loan Analysis worksheet, he sends the loan to be approved by the Department of Veterans Affairs.

Case Study Nine: Closing

A buyer is in the process of purchasing a house. Closing day is March 12. To the offices of the escrow agent she must bring the following:

- Documents proving that she has obtained a loan

- A cashier's check for the loan amount

- The (nonfinanced) cash due at closing

The loan amount is equal to the sale price minus the down payment plus the sum of all the financed fees. The sale price, as set forth in the sales contract, is $120,000. The buyer has agreed to put 5 percent of that down, or $6,000. In addition, the lender is allowing her to finance the following fees:

Fee	Charge
Origination Fee (1%)	$1,140
Underwriting Fee	$250
Appraisal Fee	$375
Survey Fee	$425
TOTAL	**$2,190**

This leaves a total loan amount of:

$$\$120{,}000 - \$6{,}000 + \$2{,}190 = \$116{,}190$$

Note that the origination fee is 1 percent of the amount loaned for the sale price and not 1 percent of the total loan amount. The rest of the money the borrower must bring is the non financed cash due at closing. This consists of the following:

- The required amount for establishing an escrow account

- The lender's discount points

- The down payment, less the earnest money deposit

- Any non financed fees

- The sum of all the prepaid items, less the sum of all the accrued items

The amount required to establish the escrow account is calculated based on the first 12 months of payments. First, we determine a monthly escrow payment by dividing the borrower's total tax and insurance liabilities by 12. The borrower has the following liabilities: July taxes, $500; October hazard insurance, $400; December taxes, $700; and February taxes, $860. The monthly escrow payment, based upon these figures, would then be:

$$(\$500 + \$400 + \$700 + \$860) \div 12 = \$205$$

Month	Escrow Payment	Liabilities	Escrow Balance
March	$0	$0	$0
April	$205	$0	$205
May	$205	$0	$410
June	$205	$0	$615
July	$205	$500	$320
August	$205	$0	$525
September	$205	$0	$730
October	$205	$400	$535
November	$205	$0	$740
December	$205	$700	$245
January	$205	$0	$450
February	$205	$860	-$205
March	$205	$0	$0

Thus the lender will require an initial escrow payment of $205 to cover the February deficiency.

Additionally, the borrower will have to bring the discount she is paying for her loan rate and her down payment. She is paying 1½ discount points, or 1.5 percent of the loan amount:

$$0.015 \times \$116,190 = \$1,742.85$$

She should also bring the $6,000 down payment, less her earnest money deposit of 1 percent of the sale price, or $1,200:

$$\$6,000 - \$1,200 = \$4,800$$

Of course, the buyer must bring the non financed fees as well. These include

Fee	Cost
Attorney's Fee	$300
Closing Fee	$175
Credit Report Fee	$45
Document Preparation Fee	$250
Home Inspection Fee	$125

Processing Fee	$250
Recording Fee	$50
Tax Service Fee	$150
Termite Inspection Fee	$65
TOTAL	**$1,410**

Finally, the buyer needs to bring the difference of the prepaid and accrued items. As you will remember, a prepaid item is an expense that the seller has paid before closing for which the buyer owes in proportion to his or her share; and an accrued item is an expense that the buyer will pay after closing for which the seller owes in proportion to her or his share.

In this case there is only one prepaid item, the annual hazard insurance payment, and two accrued items, the two property tax payments. In the state the borrower is in, prorated items are calculated on a calendar year to (rather than through) the day of closing.

For each expense, we must calculate a daily rate. The hazard insurance payment is $400 on October 1. The daily rate is:

$$\$400 \div 365 \text{ days} = \$1.10/\text{day}$$

This payment is made in advance of the time of coverage and covers October through October. Therefore, the borrower will owe for the period including March 12 through September 30, or 172 days. This works out to be:

$$\$1.10/\text{day} \times 172 \text{ days} = \$189.20$$

This is the money that the buyer owes the seller. However, the buyer receives a credit for all of her accrued items. The daily rates for the two tax payments, T1 and T2, are:

$$T1 = \$500 \div 365 \text{ days} = \$1.37$$

$$T2 = \$700 \div 365 \text{ days} = \$1.92$$

For the first tax payment, $500 on July 1, the seller owes for 292 days; and for the second, on December 1, 104 days:

$$T1 = \$1.37/\text{day} \times 292 \text{ days} = \$400.04$$

$$T2 = \$1.92/\text{day} \times 104 \text{ days} = \$199.68$$

Thus, the total amount of money the borrower must bring to closing is

The loan amount	$116,190.00
Plus the escrow fee	$205.00
Plus the discount	$1,742.85
Plus the down payment	$4,800.00
Plus the fees	$1,410.00
Plus prepaid insurance	$189.20
Minus accrued taxes	-$599.72
TOTAL	**$123,937.33**

Case Study Ten: Reverse Exchange

An investor owns a property worth $150,000, which he would like to exchange under Section 1031. He has not yet found a buyer for his property, but he has already found a replacement property, which he worries will be bought by another investor if he does not act quickly. He decides to conduct a Reverse Exchange under the IRS safe harbor of Revenue Procedure 2000-37.

The investor decides to purchase the replacement property by parking its title with an exchange accommodation titleholder (EAT). The property he is looking to buy is listed for $520,000. The investor advances $130,000 to the EAT, which then takes out a 75 percent LTV loan that the investor guarantees. The EAT purchases the replacement property.

The investor and the EAT immediately sign a qualified exchange accommodation agreement (QEAA) stating that the EAT is holding the property for a like kind exchange under Revenue Procedure 2000-37 and that, for tax purposes, the EAT is to be treated as the beneficial owner of the property. The investor then exchanges the relinquished property with the EAT for the replacement property, gaining title and all the benefits of ownership.

When the EAT receives the relinquished property, he or she leases it to the investor rent-free. The investor has 180 days, less the time the EAT held the replacement property, to find a buyer for the relinquished property, because the combined time of the EAT's holding both properties cannot exceed 180 days.

When the investor finds a buyer for the relinquished property, the EAT enters into a contract of sale with the buyer for the listing price of $150,000. At closing, the EAT deeds the property to the buyer and receives the proceeds from the sale, paying out the closing costs and other fees. It then repays the investor the $130,000 advance for the purchase of the replacement property.

At the end of the year, both the EAT and the investor report the exchange to the IRS on form 8824.

This concludes lesson eighteen.

Return to your online course player to take the Final Exam.